THE INSIDER/OUTSIDER PROBLEM
IN THE STUDY OF RELIGION

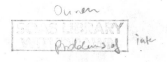

Controversies in the Study of Religion

Series Editor: Russell T. McCutcheon

This anthology series brings together related scholarly essays which are of particular importance for studying a variety of methodological and theoretical issues in the academic study of religion. Each anthology is organized around original introductory essays written by the volume editor. The series' emphasis is on writers involved in theoretical controversies and debates that address traditional as well as current problems and issues in the field, issues to which students should be introduced. Each volume investigates a common problem in the study of religion from a variety of theoretical viewpoints, thereby providing a collection of extended discussions between a group of scholars grappling with a common topic.

THE INSIDER/OUTSIDER PROBLEM IN THE STUDY OF RELIGION

A Reader

Edited by

RUSSELL T. McCUTCHEON

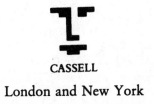

CASSELL

London and New York

Cassell
Wellington House, 125 Strand, London WC2R 0BB
370 Lexington Avenue, New York, NY 10017-6550

First published 1999

British Library Cataloguing in Publication Data
A catalogue record for this book is available from the British Library.
ISBN 0 304 70177 7 (Hardback)
0 304 70178 5 (Paperback)

Library of Congress Cataloguing-in-Publication Data
The insider/outsider problem in the study of religion: a reader /
edited by Russell T. McCutcheon.
    p.   cm. – (Controversies in the study of religion)
    A collection of previously published essays.
    Includes bibliography references and index.
    ISBN 0-304-70177-7 (hardcover). – ISBN 0-304-70178-5 (pbk.)
    1. Religion–Study and teaching.   I. McCutcheon, Russell T.,
1961–   . II. Series.
BL41.I46   1998
200'. 7'2–dc21   98-4479
                                                                 CIP

Typeset by BookEns Ltd, Royston, Herts.
Printed and bound in Great Britain by
Redwood Books, Trowbridge, Wiltshire.

CONTENTS

❧❧❧

Contents

PREFACE

❧❧

The idea for this series entitled *Controversies in the Study of Religion* goes back to conversations I had with Donald Wiebe at his office in Trinity College, University of Toronto, around 1990. One of the problems with the way in which the study of religion is taught in both the undergraduate and graduate setting is that instructors often present their data as self-evident; they fail to identify for their students the complex and contested theoretical, definitional, and methodological issues that have shaped the field over the past 100 years. What we decided was that the field needed a series of in-class anthologies that put into instructors' and students' hands influential essays discussing these ongoing debates and controversies. In this way, not only would students confront the so-called data of the field (the assorted myths, rituals, traditions, and institutions they learn about), but they would also examine the often hidden background issues, assumptions, and problematics so necessary to any scholarly field. In a word, they would develop critical thinking skills. This series attempts to fill just this need.

Although several volumes are currently in various phases of preparation, *Controversies in the Study of Religion* opens with this volume on the insider/outsider problem, one of the most important issues confronting scholars who study human behavior, institutions, and belief systems. Despite the fact that I have my own particular interest in how this debate is settled, this anthology is meant as an inclusive introduction to the larger issues and various stands currently available to the scholar of religion. Therefore, I have attempted to provide useful, fair, and accurate introductions to the issues and, in my selection of essays, to reprint creative avenues into discussing issues of theory and method in classrooms. That my selections hardly exhaust the sources that can be consulted on the insider/outsider problem will be evident from the many references and detailed endnotes that accompany each essay. Because of this wealth of material I have decided not to provide lists of suggested readings; each essay's references are suggestion enough. Also, despite my own personal commitment to gender inclusive language, as well as my thoughts concerning the antequated nature of such terms as "primitive" or "archaic religion," I have not tampered with, or "corrected," the language of the authors represented here. Apart from making its own individual contribution to the issue at hand, each essay in this collection is also an example of scholarship at one particular moment in history, suggesting that the essays can profitably be read on any number of levels.

Where some of the essays may already be, or soon might be, considered classics, others arise from books or journals possibly not known very well to some in the field—all of which, however, deserve to be known. For readers who may need some additional information to understand portions of some essays, I have added the occasional editor's footnote to explain a concept or a foreign language phrase. Finally, although the anthology will no doubt be used in a number of different, creative ways by instructors (e.g., as the sole resource for a class, augmented by readings in their own class readers, or as a complement to various theme-based course books), I would recommend that the collection is most useful if the essays—or at least the parts—be read in order for the insider/outsider problem builds as the anthology progresses.

For their assistance in conceptualizing both the series and this volume, I must thank Willi Braun, Gavin Flood, Rosalind Hackett, Darlene Juschka, Jack Llewellyn, Tim Murphy, William Paden, and Donald Wiebe. In addition, Jeff Ruff deserves my heartfelt thanks not only for discussing and proofing the introductions but also for optically scanning and initially formatting many of the essays. Although the series was initially conceived at the University of Toronto, I am grateful for the support of the Departments of Religious Studies at both the University of Tennessee and the Southwest Missouri State University where this particular volume took shape. Finally, I must thank Janet Joyce at Cassell for her foresight and enthusiasm for this project.

Russell T. McCutcheon
Springfield, Missouri

For Don –
teacher and friend

As we say in German, *können* is not *kennen*, we might say in English *to can*, that is to be cunning, is not *to ken*, that is to know; and it would then become clear at once that the most eloquent speaker and the most gifted poet, with all their command of words and skillful mastery of expression, would have but little to say if asked what language really is! The same applies to religion.

F. Max Müller, *Lectures on the Science of Religion*, 1893

If we do not persist in the quest for intelligibility, there can be no human sciences, let alone any place for the study of religion within them.

Jonathan Z. Smith, *Imagining Religion*, 1982

General Introduction

❧❧

Can You Climb Out of Your Own Skin?

Atticus stood up and walked to the end of the porch. When he completed his examination of the wisteria vine he strolled back to me.

"First of all," he said, "if you can learn a simple trick, Scout, you'll get along a lot better with all kinds of folks. You never really understand a person until you consider things from his point of view—"

"Sir?"

"—until you climb into his skin and walk around in it." (Lee 1982: 29–30)

So wrote Harper Lee in her Pulitzer prize-winning novel, *To Kill a Mockingbird*. Originally published in 1962, it is the story of a small town lawyer, Atticus Finch, who defends Tom Robinson, a black man unjustly accused of attacking a white woman. Set in the Southern United States of the 1930s, the novel not only portrays the highly charged and highly polarized race relations that constitute the daily experiences of many people, both then and now, but also allows the reader to join Atticus in the middle of the swirling controversy. Although a white man, his commitment to the cause of justice places Atticus in the position to defend Robinson, a man who, in the public's eye, is presumed guilty from the outset of the trial. Throughout the novel, Atticus Finch moves across a number of boundaries—social, economic, and racial—negotiating his various crossings in ways that many of his contemporaries either cannot see or choose not to notice.

And so it makes sense that, after listening to his young daughter's complaints about her day in school, Atticus offers what seems to be simple, home-spun advice: "You never really understand a person until you consider things from his point of view ... until you climb into his skin and walk around in it."

What we have in Atticus's few words is the making of one of the most important issues in the study of human behavior and institutions, a problem which, in the academic study of religion, is generally termed the insider/

1

outsider problem. In a nutshell the problem is whether, and to what extent, someone can study, understand, or explain the beliefs, words, or actions of another. In other words, to what degree, if any, are the motives and meanings of human behaviors and beliefs accessible to the researcher who may not necessarily share these beliefs and who does not necessarily participate in these practices? Do students of culture have virtually unimpeded access to the intentions and meanings of the people, societies, or institutions they study or, to take the contrary view, are all human observers cut off from ever being able to see past their own biases, contexts, and presuppositions?

Simply put, *must we*, or *can we*, take Atticus's advice and climb out of our own skin? Can we ever walk a mile in the shoes of another? It is a problem that must be faced by all scholars of the human condition: psychologists, sociologists, anthropologists, historians, political scientists, among others, must confront not only the question of *how* to study the intentions and actions of human beings and groups but *whether* such a study can take place at all. The first involves a question of *method* (what tools must we use to access the meanings and motives of our subjects); the second requires us to defend the *theory* of human cognition, behavior, and organization upon which our methods are based. Is the person we study, often termed simply as "the other," an open book, an enigma, or simply a neutral screen onto which the observer projects his or her own desires and fears? Depending on which of these three theoretical options we choose, our study will proceed in dramatically different ways, relying on different tools and methods, reaching significantly different ends.

Getting Inside by Studying Human Experiences (empathetic)

Clearly, Atticus believes that the gap between insiders and outsiders—a gap representing, for example, differences in class, gender, race, or religion—*can be*, and in fact *ought to be*, overcome, that one can leave one's own skin behind and climb into another's, if only for a moment. In fact, one could go so far as to say that many works of fiction generally presume from the outset that the reader can get into the skins and minds of their characters and vicariously re-experience their emotions and intentions. Although it is not the only narrative technique available to a writer, the common privilege enjoyed by the invisible, all-knowing narrator allows the reader to peer into the thoughts and wishes, fears and pleasures, of a character in a way not available to us in our usual social relationships.

There is a long tradition in scholarship that sees the researcher as having a similar—though not as extensive—privilege. Based on the assumption that certain tendencies, capacities, or, in a word, experiences, are shared by all human beings, one group of scholars maintains that the gap between the subject under study and the scholar who happens to be doing the studying can be overcome, whether those gaps are in time (as in when one studies an ancient civilization through the science of archeology) or social space (as in when one studies contemporary groups different from one's own with the tools of sociology or anthropology). Despite their apparent agreement with Atticus, such scholars would, however, disagree with just how easy it is to overcome the gap; for, contrary to Atticus's advice, it is not a "simple trick."

This first option owes much to a split between what German scholars in the nineteenth century termed *Geisteswissenschaften* and *Naturwissenschaften*— the former signifies the science (*wissenschaft*) of studying the spirit (*Geist*) while the second signifies the science of studying nature. The difference between the two, or so it was argued, was that unlike the sciences that study the various aspects of the natural world (for example, geology, astronomy, chemistry, physics, or even anatomy), the study of human subjects involved the researcher in studying questions of the meanings and intentions of these actors. In other words, it was held that human beings are far more complicated than insects, plants, rock formations, and even animals precisely because *we* have desires, hopes, fears, expectations, and reasons for doing what we do and saying what we say—reasons which may not be all that apparent from an initial study of those of our behavior that can be observed by an outsider. In a word, we have a *spirit*. Unlike the study of tornadoes and glaciers, for instance, the study of humans must take into account that human beings are conscious, free, moral agents. Unlike migrating birds whose behaviors can be predicted based on certain discernable regularities in the weather and the position of the sun in relation to the earth, humans are creative and therefore their behavior and beliefs are unpredictable. Accordingly, human behavior and belief systems cannot be reduced to the study of mere regularities, simple patterns, and constant laws, as if all human beings in situation W will do X, will say Y, and think Z.

The challenge, then, is to develop tools that will allow researchers to enter into the experiences and meanings of another, to access the private moments of human perception, thereby enabling one to bridge the gulf between subject and object. When applied to the study of religion, the field known as *phenomenology* is in large part devoted to developing techniques for non-critical, empathetic descriptions of human behavior as the basis for making a creative leap across the divide. Such empathy allows the researcher to develop what one might term a deep understanding of the actors' intentions and meanings—literally sharing their feelings and emotions. Understandably, once they have been accurately described and felt, the art of translating and interpreting the actor's experiences, behaviors, and claims (the art of *hermeneutics*), and restating them in terms of the language and experiences of the observer, will be necessary.

The Challenge of Building Theories from the Outside

Yet there is also an equally long tradition in European scholarship that would judge the desires of the other to be opaque to the researcher—sometimes even to the subjects themselves—thereby necessitating the development of special tools for the study of their motives and fears. This alternative tradition would not warrant the split between the sciences of the natural world and those of the spirit and would, instead, assert that as members of the natural world, human beings are just as prone to lawlike, predictable behavior as are molecules, rain clouds, and animals. Unlike characters in a novel, whose emotions and desires are transparent to the reader, the thoughts and desires of human subjects are not all that apparent. This group would maintain that the privilege routinely afforded the reader by the very structure of many fictional narratives (be it a film or a novel) is nowhere to be found in real life. One case in point would be the development of psychoanalysis where analysts employ a number of techniques to determine what they believe to be the subconscious roots of their patient's trauma, roots that are often intertwined with the patient's early development as an independent being. In particular, Sigmund Freud's (1856–1939) theory was that because of the dynamic and anti-social nature of one's basic need for gratification (which Freud called the pleasure principle), these egotistical desires are by definition repressed and banished to the realm of the subconscious. Therefore, to study what Freud took to be the elementary but repressed and disguised aspects of human nature requires, from the outset, tools that bypass the conscious, waking, and rational capacities of human subjects who continually disguise, or often fail to recognize, their own basic desires and needs.

Whereas the first option outlined above emphasizes the scholarly outsider's ability to get inside and re-experience the subject's own experiences and states of mind, this option sees such a move as virtually impossible and instead concentrates on developing scholarly theories capable of explaining and predicting the complex patterns of human behavior. Where the first addresses issues of meaning and interpretation—based on the assumption that humans have spirits that set them apart from animals and objects—this approach is based on studying only that which can be observed empirically; its goal is to determine the causes and regularities of human actions and beliefs. That the theories these scholars develop often disagree with the explanations insiders themselves supply for why they have done or said something is to be expected because this group of scholars would argue that insiders do not necessarily have access to the same information as does the observer. The first group of scholars would see this potential conflict as evidence that empirically based theories that treat human behavior as a series of actions and reactions do not take the free creativity of the insider seriously enough.

Understandings and Explanations

When discussing these first two options, an important point to identify is the differing emphases that can be placed on both the word "understand" and the word "explain." Much like Atticus Finch, the first group of scholars outlined above endeavor to understand the *meaning* of people's beliefs and actions, an activity which involves nuanced and accurate description of what the belief or action means to the insider followed by a creative interpretation which enables the researcher to find meaning in beliefs, symbols, and behaviors that may arise from a dramatically different world than their own. The German word *Verstehen*, associated with the work of those who practice the human sciences in the tradition of *Geisteswissenshcaften*, communicates the full scope of what such researchers mean by "understand": it is nothing less than a re-experience of the experiences of another. Such a view of the human sciences owes much to the German scholar Wilhelm Dilthey (1833–1911). Dilthey maintained that *Verstehen* entailed "re-living" the lived experiences of other people, our research subjects. In this way, Dilthey is often described as the father of the modern hermeneutical method. Derived from the name of the Greek messenger-god Hermes (upon whom successful communication with enemies and strangers depended), the art of hermeneutics is simply the art of correctly interpreting the meaningful claims and actions of other people, especially when their meaning is not altogether clear or certain.

Those scholars whose practice of the human sciences has been influenced by the alternative tradition identified above, namely *Naturwissenschaften*, would question this preoccupation with determining insider meanings. For them, human beliefs and actions are not studied as distinct sorts of productions, ones which entail meaning and moral value. Rather, as already suggested, they are treated as but one more instance of the complex workings of the natural world, a world which operates according to observable regularities that can be described and recorded. Based upon this assumption, the effort to study human behavior aims at developing not understandings but causal analysis, or, in a word, explanations (e.g., What caused this to happen?). Based on certain generalized regularities in their observations, generalizations which they might label as laws, such researchers attempt to determine the economic, political, psychological, etc., causes of behavior X or belief Y such that when factor W is present one might predict that behavior X or belief Y will follow. As such, these scholars look for general trends in the comparative data of human behavior that can be used to generate a prediction about a future state of affairs, a prediction which could either confirm or falsify their explanatory theory of human behavior.

However, given that all such theorizing is based on *inductive logic* (the method by which general conclusions about the world are drawn from repeated observations of particular cases), no such theory can ever attain unquestioned

disregard reductionist approach

status for, as in the case of the claim that "All swans are white" or "When released from a height the chalk will drop to the floor," one is never completely certain whether the next observation will confirm or falsify the theoretical claim, regardless of how well supported the theory has been up to this point in time. The clear dangers of placing too much confidence in inductively based conclusions should be more than apparent to us: we all have had experiences where our routine predictions concerning how the world works—predictions based on what seems like countless successful, unproblematic past experiences—have been easily shattered. Think no further of the last time you saw someone walk straight into a patio door which they thought to be open!

It should be clear, then, that there is a significant difference in assumptions between those who aim to understand the meaning of others' actions and beliefs and those who seek to explain the very existence or presence of these actions and beliefs. Where the former engage in the art of interpreting meanings the latter *predictions* seek to explain observable regularities and predict future outcomes. That reliving experiences constitutes the focus of the first group should make perfect sense; that public, empirical, and therefore observable actions, claims, and statements hold the attention of the second group should be equally sensible. That each group has severe criticisms of the other should be more than apparent.

Methodological Agnosticism: Do Not Pretend that Conclusions are Certain *(agnostic)*

Where the focus on only studying private experiences seems to validate the claims of the insider all too quickly, and where the emphasis on developing explanatory theories can all too easily dismiss insider's claims, there is an option which some describe as a mediating position. Aiming to avoid both validating *or* dismissing, this third option attempts to remain neutral when it comes to questions of truth and value; instead, it emphasizes issues of accurate description and comparison at the expense of drawing value judgments. Simply put, this third option attempts to bracket out, or avoid asking, all questions concerning the truth of someone's claims. Termed *methodological agnosticism*, this option is grounded in epistemology (from the Greek *episteme*, meaning, knowledge), or the study of the conditions necessary for there to be knowledge in the first place. If the researcher does not necessarily participate in the world of the insider, a world in which it might make perfect sense to ascribe intentions and motivations to what the researcher may hold to be inanimate objects, then by what means can the researcher label the insider's claims as right or wrong, as healthy or unhealthy, as accurate or delusional? If the researchers' goal is not to evaluate (either positively *or* negatively) but simply to describe the diversity, similarity and utter complexity of human behaviors and beliefs, then they may opt for this mediating stance.

Around 1869, the term "agnosticism" was coined by the early evolutionary biologist and essayist Thomas H. Huxley (1825–1895) to denote what we might simply refer to as a profession of ignorance: "It came into my head," Huxley later wrote, "as suggestively antithetical to the 'gnostic' of Church history, who professed to know so much about the very things of which I was ignorant" (Huxley 1900 vol. 1: 462). Whereas "gnostic" is derived from the Greek *gnosis*, meaning to know a spiritual mystery, "agnostic" simply designates a lack of such knowledge. The term "gnostic" has long been applied to a particular religion, the Gnostics, which existed alongside Judaism and early Christianity during the first few centuries of the common era. This group claimed special knowledge derived from secret revelations.

Contrary to claiming any such special knowledge that transcended the knowledge gained through the reasoned use of our senses, Huxley proposed that agnosticism entailed the recognition that there are limits to what human beings can know and that it was idle speculation to try to settle matters which were beyond these limits (such as what happens after death). In his words, agnosticism

> is not a creed, but a method, the essence of which lies in the rigorous application of a single principle. That principle is of great antiquity; it is as old as Socrates; as old as the writer who said, "Try all things, hold fast by that which is good"; it is the foundation of the Reformation, which simply illustrated the axiom that every man should be able to give a reason for the faith that is in him; it is the great principle of Descartes; it is the fundamental axiom of modern science. Positively, the principle may be expressed: In matters of the intellect, follow your reason as far as it will take you, without regard to any other consideration. And negatively: In matters of the intellect do not pretend that conclusions are certain which are not demonstrated or demonstrable. That I take to be the agnostic faith. (1901: 246)

It should be clear, then, that although the term arises with Huxley in the mid-nineteenth century, we can understand a number of figures in the history of European philosophy as having presumed this, or a closely related, stand when it comes to matters of knowledge.

To be agnostic does not mean one is a disbeliever (as is meant by the term atheism), but, instead, it means that one is in the position of not having sufficient information from which to make a decision on matters of truth. Admitting not to have the knowledge, then, necessitates a different sort of scholarship from that of those who claim to possess the privileged knowledge of either the empathetic *or* the explanatory observer. For example, given that to date there has been no empirical evidence sufficient to prove or disprove beliefs in the existence of an all-powerful, purposeful being who created, controls, and continues to direct the universe, some researchers have concluded that the only productive manner in which to study those who make such a claim is to avoid arbitrating and evaluating and simply to begin describing, cataloguing, and comparing the various claims in favor or against the existence of such a deity. One who claims that a god either does or does not direct the world may be right; but then again, they may be wrong. In light of no publicly testable and debatable evidence one way or the other, there is little to be gained from trying to prove or dismiss such claims.

Somewhat similar to the manner in which Huxley defines agnosticism as a *method of analysis*, by methodological agnosticism one means that the researcher selects a number of tools, or methods of research, that purposely avoid asking questions of truth where there exist no means of acquiring empirical evidence to determine that truth. Of course to be methodologically agnostic hardly means that one is personally agnostic. While this may of course be the case, it may equally be that as a committed insider or committed outsider one recognizes the limited nature of the assumptions which constitute one's stand on such issues as whether there is meaning to life, whether anything happens after physical death, and whether there is a god. In both the cases of believers and non-believers, one may acknowledge that faith commitments are fundamentally important, commitments which may very well defy rational explanations and the rules of evidence we usually accept when making claims about the world around us. As such, to gain entrance into a public debate with people who hold different (possibly competing or contradictory) sets of commitments, one might opt for this neutral stance. Such a position is essential to the phenomenological method discussed above, a method of nuanced, neutral description which aims to take claims at face value and develop a complex comparative scheme whereby, for example, all symbolisms of snakes in worldwide mythologies are collected and cataloged. In this case the researcher has little interest in whether such myths are true or false. Instead, they are motivated by what they see to be the intriguing similarities or astounding differences of these narratives.

Reflexivity and the Relativity of Insides and Outsides

Apart from these three positions (empathetic, explanatory, agnostic), there is yet a fourth approach to the insider/outsider problem. It agrees in part with the first option outlined above: it is indeed important to study inner states and experiences of free, creative human beings. However, it also agrees in part with the second: there is a significant gap between researcher and subject. Finally, it differs significantly from the third in that the researcher and subject alike are both seen to be enmeshed in the human situation, making this much sought-after neutrality a mere illusion. The conclusion in this case is that the experiences that we as scholars are able to study *are none other than our own.*

According to this option, all scholarship has an autobiographical aspect which is often overlooked or sometimes outright ignored and disguised. However, because it is presumed that all human beings share similar experiential states, researchers can bridge the gap between insider and outsider through generalizing their own personal experiences—insomuch as researchers are themselves human beings embedded within the same complex worlds as their subjects—to those experiences of other human beings. Where the first option bridges the gulf between insiders and outsiders by determining the insider's experiences through nuanced interpretive tools, this option bridges the gulf by means of projecting the researcher's own experiences onto the other. It is a position best understood as the reflexive stance.

This emphasis on reflexivity is largely dependent on a recent development known as postmodernism, a diffuse scholarly tradition that arises from such fields as literary criticism, art, and philosophy. Although one would be hard-pressed to offer one definitive definition of postmodernism, we can at least suggest that it is a way of looking at the world which emphasizes playfulness and differences over rules and sameness; it stresses the metaphoric and slippery nature of language over the modernist, objective, factual understandings of how communication proceeds; it addresses the manner in which meaning is not something possessed by a word, an action, or an object as much as it is the product of a series of relations which comprise the word or the object.

According to postmodernists, any one word in this present sentence—for example, the word "word"—has meaning precisely because of the words which appear on either side of it, and they themselves have meaning insomuch as words appear either side of them, and so on, and so on. If we take this to the logical end—if there is one—sentences, paragraphs, chapters, whole texts, libraries, let alone all the books you have already read and the experiences and actions of all other authors and all other readers all come together in a complex system to produce the thing we call meaning. It is a system of inter-relations that we often overlook, to our own detriment, or so the postmodernist might inform us. For to overlook this game of meaning-making which we are all playing is to mistake metaphors for stable facts, to misperceive active processes for stable entities, to misread verbs for nouns and re-presentations as mere presentations. These were all the mistakes of modernism, according to postmodernists. And so, when the French postmodernist philosopher Jacques Derrida says, "there is no outside the text," what he seems to imply is that readers and writers, observers and subjects, outsiders and insiders, are all equally immersed in the same pool of meaning-making, making it all up as they go along. We are all in the text; there is no way out and there is no position of luxurious all-knowing or neutral narration.

The reflexive stance is a position which addresses the manner in which all observations are inextricably entwined with the self-referential statements of the observer. For example, the sentence, "There are no facts" can itself be

9

taken as a straightforward, factual statement—or can it? Or, a better instance would be the widely known example, "Rule number one, there are no rules." What does it mean to say something like this? Does it contradict itself? And if not, by just what authority can such a rule be exempt from itself? For scholars who adopt the reflexive option, studying others explicitly involves a high degree of reflexivity, a turning back onto the researcher of his or her own questions and answers. Claims that the researcher is able to make objective or neutral claims about the world at large are therefore highly suspect to the reflexive scholar for she or he would maintain that the world at large is just what it is for you or I *precisely because* you and I are what, who, and where we are. For instance, our choice of question shapes the answer we will receive; interviewing just the men of a society will tell us just as much about a researcher's presuppositions and biases regarding who counts in a society as it tells us about the society under question. Reflexive scholars, therefore, are more interested in questions of point of view and the stance of the observer than they are with issues of neutrality, objectivity, and fact. They are like artists who paint themselves, their subjects, and sometimes even their audience into their own canvases, allowing the observer to see the artist painting the picture of the artist painting the picture of the viewer watching the artist paint a picture; all of this challenges the viewer to see themselves actively viewing, even making, the picture a picture.

Where does it stop, you might ask. For the reflexive scholar, it never does. Like those word puzzles where you circle the letters that form a word, whether the letters run backwards, forwards, on an angle, horizontal or vertical, human experience goes on and on in all directions and is constantly in the process of constructing new meaning and reality. Your job as a scholar is simply to jump into the middle of the puzzle, in the middle of life, and start circling words, making metaphors and meaning. For, like life or language, the meaning game was up and running before you arrived on the scene at birth (after all, none of us invented the languages we speak) and will continue to be played long after you depart from the stage. We simply popped up in the middle of it.

Plan of the Book

This volume is an introduction to the manner in which scholars studying religion have negotiated the controversy over insiders and outsiders. Each part opens with a brief introduction that outlines some of the key features to the readings and excerpts which develop a coherent position in answer to the problem. In these introductions readers will find what we might label a road map that will assist them in reading the pieces and identifying some of the central issues and assumptions important for understanding the issues in question. Each of these parts then closes with one or two readings that highlight some of the shortcomings to this particular way of addressing the insider/outsider problem. In this way, the reader can follow an argument while it builds and then acquire some of the tools necessary for critically engaging it.

Part I provides a theoretical background to the issue, offering a selection of classic readings from such fields of study as linguistics and anthropology where much of the terminology and techniques relevant to this issue were first developed. In particular, we will meet there the terms "emic" and "etic" which are often used to refer to the positions of insiders and outsiders, respectively. Part II traces the development of studying private religious experiences empathetically as the means for overcoming the gulf between insiders and outsiders. Part III moves to the emphasis on ascertaining the observable and predictable regularities in human behavior which allow the observer to study human behavior objectively. Part IV differs from both of these positions by offering the option known as "methodological agnosticism" which, it is maintained, enables the observer to remain neutral when it comes to ascertaining the truth or falsity of the beliefs under study, making the observer neither an insider nor an outsider. Part V applies the notion of reflexivity to the study of human behavior and highlights the degree to which scholarship on religion is surprisingly autobiographical. Finally, the last part offers essays on recent events in the news that challenge students to push themselves in understanding human behaviors.

This volume is designed to allow instructors and students to trace several coherent, competing approaches to one uniform problem in the study of religion. By extension, the reader will become familiar with a number of related issues in the field as well as a number of writers, both past and present, who have made significant contributions. By its very nature, this problem is equally applicable to virtually all other sciences of the human condition, and so, despite the high degree of specificity of the readings, the collection should be of relevance to students outside the study of religion.

Although there will be no one way of using this collection of readings, their order and presentation lends itself to a format in which each reading or position as a whole is explored descriptively and then investigated through in-class debates or seminars where students are challenged either to develop and apply in greater detail the position in question, or to delineate a line of reasoning capable of criticizing its assumptions and findings.

References

Huxley, Thomas 1900. *Life and Letters of T. H. Huxley*. 2nd ed. 3 vols. Leonard Huxley (ed.). London: Macmillan.

——1901. *Science and the Christian Tradition: Essays*. New York: D. Appleton.

Lee, Harper 1982 (1960). *To Kill a Mockingbird*. New York: Warner Books.

Part I

THEORETICAL BACKGROUND: INSIDES, OUTSIDES, AND
THE SCHOLAR OF RELIGION

INTRODUCTION

ରେଷ୍ଟ

The Study of Religion as a Cross-Disciplinary Exercise

Because much of the original work on the insider/outsider problem has been done in fields outside the academic study of religion, it is only fitting to open this anthology with essays that arise from fields outside the study of religion. The academic study of religion has developed into a cross-disciplinary field that draws on the work of a variety of scholars: any book on the subject will more than likely build on the work carried out by anthropologists, scholars of antiquity, economists, historians, literary critics, philosophers, psychologists, sociologists, to name only a few. The various stands that scholars of religion take to address the insider/outsider problem owe much to work carried out in these fields. The four pieces in this part represent the work of Horace Miner, an anthropologist, Kenneth L. Pike, a linguist, Alasdair McIntyre, a philosopher, and Clifford Geertz, also an anthropologist.

However, prior to introducing these four readings, we need to discuss two concepts of basic importance to the insider/outsider problem, concepts originally used in the study of language but quickly adopted by anthropologists.

Emic and Etic Defined

Emic and etic are technical terms that Kenneth Pike (1967) originally derived from the suffixes of the words "phonemic" and "phonetic"; the former refers to any unit of significant sound in a particular language and the latter refers to the system of cross-culturally useful notations that represent these vocal sounds. Although both words are derived from the same Latin root (*phōnēma*, meaning "sound"), phon*emic* designates the complex sounds themselves while phon*etic* specifies the signs and systems scholars devise to represent the manner in which the basic phonemic units of a language are to be pronounced and compared. For example, according to the International Phonetic Alphabet, reprinted in the front of most dictionaries, the character that represents the sound made by the first consonant in the word, *zip*, is *z*, whereas the related but slightly different sound produced by the *s* in the word *vision* is designated by the character 3, both of which are not to be confused with the sound made by the letter *s* in the word *sip* (designated by *s*) or the sound of the *sh* in a word like *ship* (designated by ʃ). Even though the same letter may be used in spelling certain words (such as the *s* in *sip* and *vision*), in practice the letter is pronounced in many different ways. The characters of the Phonetic Alphabet provide a way to specify and symbolize these differences. Moreover, knowing how the *d* sounds in a word like *dog*, combined with our knowledge of the specific sound of the *s* in *vision*, allows us to combine the two sounds to represent what the *j* sounds like in the word *jam* (its Phonetic Alphabet character therefore is the combined *d*3).

The point of all this is that while the phoneme represents the various units of sound that combine to produce a spoken word in a particular language (and any one language will have a specific, sometimes unique, set of phonemes upon which it is based), the phonetic representation of these sound units is based on an outsider's attempt to transcribe and compare these sounds in relation to a system of written characters that can be used in the study of all languages. Accordingly, phonetic analysis has an explicit comparative aspect to it.

That spoken sounds in just one language, let alone many languages, are a complicated affair is evident. To the proficient users of any language this may or may not be an interesting issue; after all, they are involved in using, articulating, developing a language for certain practical purposes. To these users the varied ways of producing the *s* sound might all just appear to be self-evident. But to a non-user of this language, the ways in which these subtle distinctions are produced by speakers is intriguing. How is it that one word comes out of our mouth and is not confused with another? And how can we compare sounds produced in two different languages? Speakers simply seem to know that they must shape their mouths and tongues differently to vary the sounds they produce. For example, think of the many sounds designated by the letter *o*, whether alone or in combination with other letters: goat, got, wagon, boil, boot, book, poor, pour, brow, and sour. Scholars who study phonetics will examine the mechanics of speaking these various words: if and how the tongue touches the teeth when the sound is produced (e.g., a lingual-dental such as *th*); how the lips are used (e.g., a labio-dental, with the teeth touching one lip, such as the sound of an *f*; a bilabial, produced with the two lips, such as the sounds of the *p* or *b*); or whether the tongue and the soft palate (the rear roof of the mouth) is being employed to produce a sound in the back of the mouth (such as in lingual-velars like *k* or *g*). Phonetics scholars, then, develop a comparative basis which is itself outside the language systems they are studying (after all, no language users write in the Phonetic Alphabet) to study not simply one language but *the phenomenon of human language itself.*

The Emic and Etic Viewpoint Applied

Therefore, we can now understand what Pike meant when he specified that while the "etic viewpoint studies behavior as from outside of a particular system," the "emic viewpoint results from studying behavior as from inside the system" (1967: 37) Roughly, then, emic is to the inside as etic is to the outside. An important clarification, however, is that the emic perspective is not simply to be equated with the insider's own viewpoint; for, in the case of language, language users are extremely proficient at speaking their language, at making this or that sound distinct from other sounds, but they are often hardly interested in *studying it*. By even attempting to *reproduce*, rather than simply *produce*, a sound faithfully, the linguist has already acknowledged that she or he is a student of the language under study and is not to be confused with a speaker of the language. Even if the linguist is a native speaker of the language, there is a difference between simply using a language, on the one hand, and discussing, systematizing, and comparing those uses, on the other. It would seem, then, that even insiders can become outsiders.

The emic perspective, then, is the outsider's attempt to produce as faithfully as possible—in a word, to describe—the informant's own descriptions or production of sounds, behavior, beliefs, etc. The etic perspective is the observer's subsequent attempt to take the descriptive information they have already gathered and to organize, systematize, compare—in a word, redescribe—that information in terms of a system of their own making—the International Phonetic Alphabet for example. This theoretical system proposed by the student is therefore the basis for comparison and analysis when she or he studies other languages, cultures, societies, religions, etc. For example, one might ask, "Does this language have sounds that can be represented by the ʒ?" Or, "Does this society have an aspect which can be analyzed in terms of the economic category of class, and then compared to other societies which also have classes?" If, for instance, one were interested in determining the history of a spoken language, entailing the identification of the family of which it is a member (e.g., "Does Italian share anything in common with French, and how are they both related to German, Latin, or Sanskrit?"), such etic, comparative study would be crucial. If, however, one wished simply to learn the language for oneself, or only to describe customs as accurately as possible, there may be no such need to develop the comparative basis afforded by the etic perspective.

Which Perspective is Authoritative?

What is of particular interest is the degree to which a researcher emphasizes either of these two perspectives. Which viewpoint is to be authorized? Is etic scholarship to be judged by the informant? (For example, one might dispute that the *s* can be represented in terms of so many different Phonetic Alphabet characters, for an *s* is simply an *s*.) Is the informant to be judged by the comparative conclusions reached by the observer? (For example, a researcher might conclude that language X is simplistic when compared to language Y.) Does scholarship operate apart from the concerns of insiders or is it intimately connected to their lives? Is the goal of scholarship on human behavior, beliefs, and institutions to have the people whom we are studying agree with our conclusions and generalizations? Or, is it instead the goal of developing logical, scientific theories on why it is that humans do this or that in the first place, regardless of what they think? To whom do scholars of human behavior answer?

The Canadian scholar of the study of religion, Wilfred Cantwell Smith, is widely known for authorizing the religious insider when it comes to judging the quality of scholarship. Cantwell Smith stated quite unequivocally that no statement made by the scholar of religion is valid unless the religious believer could accept it as correct. If this rule were to be accepted, then insiders become the final authority in determining what is and what is not a correct statement about their religion. Perhaps such a rule has some value in ensuring that the scholarly description of the insider's behavior and claims is accurate but does such a rule apply when the researcher is attempting to determine just why it is that one insider acts this way and another acts that way? Or what of the case where the researcher finds an intriguing gap between the insider's claims and their behavior? Could not the insider be acting for reasons of which they are not completely aware? Should not the study of human behavior be clearly based on criteria outside those of the actors themselves?

These are precisely the concerns of a well-known anthropologist, Marvin Harris (1979). He has argued that the goal of scholarship on human behaviors is not to determine what the insider might mean by their beliefs or actions but, instead, to discern explanations for why it is that they do or think what they do. Accordingly, Harris critiques Pike for authorizing the emic at the expense of the etic. According to Harris, Pike maintains that although scholarship necessarily starts with etic categories and theories it should attempt to shake off the inevitably insufficient outsider categories in favor of the proper insider understandings. Instead of attempting to determine (and thereby authorize) the insider's beliefs, Harris is interested in studying the material (e.g., political or economic) causes behind human behaviors and beliefs. Therefore, he critiques the "emic bias" in Pike's work for, in Harris's opinion, such a bias prevents comparative, analytic study where no insider claims are privileged. According to Harris, our goal as scholars is not simply to report and repeat what our informants tell us, for that makes us simply passive documenters of indigenous claims. Instead, and contrary to such scholars as Pike and Cantwell Smith, Harris argues that although research on human institutions and beliefs begins with descriptive information, the overall goal is to develop a generalized theory of one's own making and testing that can be used to elucidate all sorts of human behaviors. After all, in developing a theory of religion in general, no one religious viewpoint could come to dominate for we are not attempting to develop a Christian theory of religion, a Hindu theory of religion, or a Buddhist theory of religion. Instead, we are seeking criteria from outside each of these particular systems so as to compare and then explain them all together. Simply put, for Harris etic or analytic scholarship is not constrained by the way in which the people we study say they act or think. Instead, it is constrained by the rules that comprise rational, comparative, scientific analysis.

Our High Places of Safety?

Although this initial survey of the thoughts of Pike and Harris will not settle the issue, it does bring into sharp relief that there is something at stake in addressing and settling the insider/outsider problem. Simply put, the future of the human sciences are at stake for, depending on how one settles the insider/outsider problem, scholars of human behavior could either be seen as observers capable of making novel claims about the causes of human action or as participants making autobiographical claims of no necessary analytic consequence.

To begin our study, this part opens with what has become a classic (and fun) essay for illustrating some of the perils of the insider/outsider problem. Although Miner's study of the body rituals of the intriguing Nacirema people was first published in the US in 1956, this ethnography (or a descriptive account of people's customs and behaviors) is still one of the most effective means for placing readers in the midst of the difficulties of making claims about "other" people, their motives, feelings, and the value of their cultures. Whereas for some readers, Miner is being descriptively accurate in his remarks on these "exotic" people, to others his tone is consistently condescending and judgmental, while to yet others he is engaged in a complex form of satire, especially the ironic way in which the famous anthropologist Bronislaw Malinowski is quoted at its close regarding the "high places of safety in the developed civilization" from which the scholar works. A careful reading of his essay will therefore demonstrate the complex ways in which apparently neutral description often carries with it both interpretation and evaluation, as well as suggest the difficulties of distinguishing a stable "us" from a "them." The moral of this story? The apparently simple task of talking about other people is not as simple as it may at first appear.

Can Sceptic and Believer Understand Each Other?

"In any discussion between sceptics and believers," writes Alasdair MacIntyre in the opening line to his essay, "it is presupposed that, even for us to disagree, it is necessary to understand each other." This often overlooked assumption is precisely what MacIntyre examines in his well-known essay. He is interested not in whether the sceptic and the believer can agree on this or that matter, but whether they can establish a shared basis upon which they would later base such agreements or disagreements. In other words, can they even understand each other?

For anyone either to agree or to disagree with another person, they must first understand just what the person is talking about and what they are claiming. For two people even to be engaged in a conversation of any kind presupposes at least one crucial thing: that they are both talking about the same thing (and in the same language). If they are not, they soon end up talking past one another and, even if they continue to speak, their conversation comes to a bitter end. For instance, if two people were conversing on the role played by religion in human affairs, they would not get very far if for one of them "religion" constituted the revelation of a loving deity and for the other religion was merely a psychological delusion—they are clearly not talking about the same thing. For either to arrive at an understanding of other's position, they must already have understood and appreciated the assumptions and vocabularies of their dialogue partner. This common starting point makes their conversation possible—two people speaking different languages or defining their terms in different ways can hardly converse with one another. For conversation to take place, then, the partners need a degree of commensurability; they need a common measure, a common basis, upon which to build.

What happens, then, when the conversation partners are in fact speaking radically different languages or when their speech involves radically different sets of assumptions and vocabularies? Is understanding possible in this case? This is MacIntyre's question: Can the sceptic understand the believer (or *vice versa*)? For, as MacIntyre portrays them, these two people start with sets of assumptions so different that they are in fact incommensurable—there exists no shared or common system of measure that unites their discourses. It is not so much that the sceptic and the believer are, as the old saying goes, "like apples and oranges," for both of these are fruits, both inevitably share some important aspects and, therefore, they are commensurable. Insomuch as one believes a loving deity exists (believer) and the other does not (sceptic), the sets of assumptions that ground their conversation are, to MacIntyre, incommensurable. Simply put, a gulf lies between them and because of this they cannot hope to understand each other. The closest they can come is that each understands the claims of the other *but in a completely different way from the other's own self-understanding*. For example, whereas some believers understand their references to "God loves me" to refer to a powerful but caring being that exists apart from, and nurtures, the world, the sceptic who had read even only a little Freud would have little choice but to understand such "God-talk" as the result of the believer's own deeply felt insecurities.

The implications for the insider/outsider problem in the study of religion should be clear: according to MacIntyre, outsiders cannot hope to understand insiders (and *vice versa*). To phrase it another way, to truly *understand* an insider one must *become* an insider; to understand is to be. Although his essay is specifically about Christian insiders, it is nonetheless applicable to all believers: according to him, the "sceptic and believer do not share a common grasp of the relevant concepts."

In a later essay we will again return to MacIntyre's provocative argument. Donald Wiebe, a Canadian scholar specializing in the relations (or lack of) between the study of religion and theology, tackles MacIntyre's thesis and suggests that there is much at stake in the way in which the latter understands scholarly research to come about. In other words, Wiebe argues that MacIntyre's understanding of what is involved in *coming to an understanding* requires attention if we are to overcome the great divide the latter sees between insider and outsider.

Or is it All Just a Question of Degree?

But is this divide between insider and outsider as great as MacIntyre presumes? Instead of being limited only to either the insider's or the outsider's viewpoint, we might ask whether there is a mediating position in this debate. The anthropologist Clifford Geertz might provide just such a position. Geertz argues that, instead of seeing the insider and outsider positions as polar opposites, involving an either/or from the researcher, perhaps it is all a question of degree. Using a terminology capable of suggesting the relative, more-or-less nature of one's viewpoint (that of experience-near and experience-distant perspectives), Geertz suggests that we have misunderstood the work of studying other people if we think our only options are either an "ethnography of witchcraft as written by a witch" or "an ethnography of witchcraft as written by a geometer." The challenge—or, as Geertz puts it, the trick—is to take the experience-near concepts of our informants and to place them "in illuminating connection with experience-distant concepts theorists have fashioned to capture the general features of social life." Where an informant might talk of "fear," the psychologist might talk of "phobia"—but just what are the relations between these two concepts? Surely fear does not exhaust the notion of phobia, demonstrating that the usefulness of such scholarly categories as "phobia" is, at least in part, to be judged by the degree to which they can be used to distinguish and compare, on one level, the similarities and differences in the reports and behaviors of the people we study. Therefore, where the scholar strives to compare, interpret, and explain what they think the insider is experiencing, the informant is most often involved simply in experiencing it.

⌈To demonstrate just what is involved with moving from experience-near to experience-distant concepts, Geertz investigates the differing conceptions of "self" or "person" (both of which are experience-distant concepts) that he has studied in three different societies (Java [now Indonesia], Bali, Morocco). Unlike Pike, Geertz does not prioritize the insider's (or experience-near) concepts and experiences. Unlike Harris, Geertz does not aim to provide an explanation of their experiences and behaviors. Unlike MacIntyre, Geertz does not presume that the starting points of insiders and outsiders are incommensurable. Instead, by means of admittedly comparative, experience-distant categories, he aims simply to interpret and understand what it is that someone might mean when they say or do this or that. ⌋

Although this opening part ends with Geertz's intermediate position, this should not suggest that this position wins the day. It will be left to readers, as they work their way through the following parts, to make their own decisions as to the relative merits of the various positions scholars take to solve the insider/outsider problem.

References

Harris, Marvin 1979. *Cultural Materialism: The Struggle for a Science of Culture*. New York: Random House.

Pike, Kenneth 1967. *Language in Relation to a Unified Theory of the Structure of Human Behavior*. 2nd edition. The Hague: Mouton.

1

HORACE MINER, *Body Ritual Among the Nacirema*

≈≈

The anthropologist has become so familiar with the diversity of ways in which different peoples behave in similar situations that he is not apt to be surprised by even the most exotic customs. In fact, if all of the logically possible combinations of behavior have not been found somewhere in the world, he is apt to suspect that they must be present in some yet undescribed tribe. This point has, in fact, been expressed with respect to clan organization by Murdock (1949: 71).[1] In this light, the magical beliefs and practices of the Nacirema present such unusual aspects that it seems desirable to describe them as an example of the extremes to which human behavior can go.

Professor Linton first brought the ritual of the Nacirema to the attention of anthropologists twenty years ago (1936: 326),[2] but the culture of this people is still very poorly understood. They are a North American group living in the territory between the Canadian Cree, the Yaqui and Tarahumare of Mexico, and the Carib and Arawak of the Antilles. Little is known of their origin, though tradition states that they came from the east. According to Nacirema mythology, their nation was originated by a culture hero, Notgnishaw, who is otherwise known for two great feats of strength—the throwing of a piece of wampum across the river Pa-To-Mac and the chopping down of a cherry tree in which the Spirit of Truth resided.

Nacirema culture is characterized by a highly developed market economy which has evolved in a rich natural habitat. While much of the people's time is devoted to economic pursuits, a large part of the fruits of these labors and a considerable portion of the day are spent in ritual activity. The focus of this activity is the human body, the appearance and health of which loom as a dominant concern in the ethos of the people. While such a concern is certainly not unusual, its ceremonial aspects and associated philosophy are unique.

The fundamental belief underlying the whole system appears to be that the human body is ugly and that its natural tendency is to debility and disease.

Incarcerated in such a body, man's only hope is to avert these characteristics through the use of the powerful influences of ritual and ceremony. Every household has one or more shrines devoted to this purpose. The more powerful individuals in the society have several shrines in their houses and, in fact, the opulence of a house is often referred to in terms of the number of such ritual centers it possesses. Most houses are of wattle and daub construction, but the shrine rooms of the more wealthy are walled with stone. Poorer families imitate the rich by applying pottery plaques to their shrine walls.

While each family has at least one such shrine, the rituals associated with it are not family ceremonies but are private and secret. The rites are normally only discussed with children, and then only during the period when they are being initiated into these mysteries. I was able, however, to establish sufficient rapport with the natives to examine these shrines and to have the rituals described to me.

The focal point of the shrine is a box or chest which is built into the wall. In this chest are kept the many charms and magical potions without which no native believes he could live. These preparations are secured from a variety of specialized practitioners. The most powerful of these are the medicine men, whose assistance must be rewarded with substantial gifts. However, the medicine men do not provide the curative potions for their clients, but decide what the ingredients should be and then write them down in an ancient and secret language. This writing is understood only by the medicine men and by the herbalists who, for another gift, provide the required charm.

The charm is not disposed of after it has served its purpose, but is placed in the charm-box of the household shrine. As these magical materials are specific for certain ills, and the real or imagined maladies of the people are many, the charm-box is usually full to overflowing. The magical packets are so numerous that people forget what their purposes were and fear to use them again. While the natives are very vague on this point, we can only assume that the idea in retaining all the old magical materials is that their presence in the charm-box, before which the body rituals are conducted, will in some way protect the worshiper.

Beneath the charm-box is a small font. Each day every member of the family, in succession, enters the shrine room, bows his head before the charm-box, mingles different sorts of holy water in the font, and proceeds with a brief rite of ablution. The holy waters are secured from the Water Temple of the community, where the priests conduct elaborate ceremonies to make the liquid ritually pure.

In the hierarchy of magical practitioners, and below the medicine men in prestige, are specialists whose designation is best translated "holy-mouth-men." The Nacirema have an almost pathological horror and fascination with the mouth, the condition of which is believed to have a supernatural influence on all social relationships. Were it not for the rituals of the mouth, they believe that their teeth would fall out, their gums bleed, their jaws shrink, their friends desert them, and their lovers reject them. (They also believe that a strong relationship exists between oral and moral characteristics. For example, there is a ritual ablution of the mouth for children which is supposed to improve their moral fiber.)

The daily body ritual performed by everyone includes a mouth-rite. Despite the fact that these people are so punctilious about care of the mouth, this rite involves a practice which strikes the uninitiated stranger as revolting. It was reported to me that the ritual consists of inserting a small bundle of hog hairs into the mouth, along with certain magical powders, and then moving the bundle in a highly formalized series of gestures.

In addition to the private mouth-rite, the people seek out a holy-mouth-man once or twice a year. These practitioners have an impressive set of paraphernalia, consisting of a variety of augers, awls, probes, and prods. The use of these objects in the exorcism of the evils of the mouth involves almost unbelievable ritual torture of the client. The holy-mouth-man opens the client's mouth and using the above-mentioned tools, enlarges any holes which decay may have created in the teeth. Magical materials are put into these holes. If there are no naturally occurring holes in the teeth, large sections of one or more teeth are gouged out so that the supernatural substance can be applied. In the client's view, the purpose of these ministrations is to arrest decay and to draw friends. The extremely sacred and traditional character of the rite is evident in the fact that the natives return to the holy-mouth-men year after year, despite the fact that their teeth continue to decay.

It is to be hoped that, when a thorough study of the Nacirema is made, there will be a careful inquiry into the personality structure of these people. One has but to watch the gleam in the eye of a holy-mouth-man, as he jabs an awl into an exposed nerve, to suspect that a certain amount of sadism is involved. If this can be established, a very interesting pattern emerges, for most of the population shows definite masochistic tendencies. It was to these that Professor Linton referred in discussing a distinctive part of the daily body ritual which is performed only by men. This part of the rite involves scraping and lacerating the surface of the face with a sharp instrument. Special women's rites are performed only four times during each lunar month, but what they lack in frequency is made up in barbarity. As part of this ceremony, women bake their heads in small ovens for about an hour. The theoretically interesting point is that what seems to be a preponderantly masochistic people have developed sadistic specialists.

The medicine men have an imposing temple, or *latipso,* in every community of any size. The more elaborate ceremonies required to treat very sick patients can only be performed at this temple. These ceremonies involve not only the thaumaturge but a permanent group of vestal maidens who move sedately about the temple chambers in distinctive costume and headdress.

The *latipso* ceremonies are so harsh that it is phenomenal that a fair proportion of the really sick natives who enter the temple ever recover. Small children whose indoctrination is still incomplete have been known to resist attempts to take them to the temple because "that is where you go to die." Despite this fact, sick adults are not only willing but eager to undergo the protracted ritual purification, if they can afford to do so. No matter how ill the supplicant or how grave the emergency, the guardians of many temples will not admit a client if he cannot give a rich gift to the custodian. Even after one has gained admission and survived the ceremonies, the guardians will not permit the neophyte to leave until he makes still another gift.

The supplicant entering the temple is first stripped of all his or her clothes. In every-day life the Nacirema avoids exposure of his body and its natural functions. Bathing and excretory acts are performed only in the secrecy of the household shrine, where they are ritualized as part of the body-rites. Psychological shock results from the fact that body secrecy is suddenly lost upon entry into the *latipso*. A man, whose own wife has never seen him in an excretory act, suddenly finds himself naked and assisted by a vestal maiden while he performs his natural functions into a sacred vessel. This sort of ceremonial treatment is necessitated by the fact that the excreta are used by a diviner to ascertain the course and nature of the client's sickness. Female clients, on the other hand, find their naked bodies are subjected to the scrutiny, manipulation, and prodding of the medicine men.

Few supplicants in the temple are well enough to do anything but lie on their hard beds. The daily ceremonies, like the rites of the holy-mouth-men, involve discomfort and torture. With ritual precision, the vestals awaken their miserable charges each dawn and roll them about on their beds of pain while performing ablutions, in the formal movements of which the maidens are highly trained. At other times they insert magic wands in the supplicant's mouth or force him to eat substances which are supposed to be healing. From time to time the medicine men come to their clients and jab magically treated needles into their flesh. The fact that these temple ceremonies may not cure, and may even kill the neophyte, in no way decreases the people's faith in the medicine men.

There remains one other kind of practitioner, known as a "listener." This witch-doctor has the power to exorcise the devils that lodge in the heads of people who have been bewitched. The Nacirema believe that parents bewitch their own children. Mothers are particularly suspected of putting a curse on children while teaching them the secret body rituals. The counter-magic of the witch-doctor is unusual in its lack of ritual. The patient simply tells the "listener" all his troubles and fears, beginning with the earliest difficulties he can remember. The memory displayed by the Nacirema in these exorcism sessions is truly remarkable. It is not uncommon for the patient to bemoan the rejection he felt upon being weaned as a babe, and a few individuals even see their troubles going back to the traumatic effects of their own birth.

In conclusion, mention must be made of certain practices which have their base in native esthetics but which depend upon the pervasive aversion to the natural body and its functions. There are ritual fasts to make fat people thin and ceremonial feasts to make thin people fat. Still other rites are used to make women's breasts large if they are small, and smaller if they are large. General dissatisfaction with breast shape is symbolized in the fact that the ideal form is virtually outside the range of human variation. A few women afflicted with almost inhuman hypermammary development are so idolized that they make a handsome living by simply going from village to village and permitting the natives to stare at them for a fee.

Reference has already been made to the fact that excretory functions are ritualized, routinized, and relegated to secrecy. Natural reproductive functions are similarly distorted. Intercourse is taboo as a topic and scheduled as an act. Efforts are made to avoid pregnancy by the use of magical materials or by limiting intercourse to certain phases of the moon. Conception is actually very infrequent. When pregnant, women dress so as to hide their condition. Parturition takes place in secret, without friends or relatives to assist, and the majority of women do not nurse their infants.

Our review of the ritual life of the Nacirema has certainly shown them to be a magic-ridden people. It is hard to understand how they have managed to exist so long under the burdens which they have imposed upon themselves. But even such exotic customs as these take on real meaning when they are viewed with the insight provided by Malinowski when he wrote (1948: 70):[3]

> Looking from far and above, from our high places of safety in the developed civilization, it is easy to see all the crudity and irrelevance of magic. But without its power and guidance early man could not have mastered his practical difficulties as he has done, nor could man have advanced to the higher stages of civilization.

Notes

1. Ed. note. George P. Murdock, *Social Structure*. New York: Macmillan, 1949.
2. Ed. note. Ralph Linton, *The Study of Man*. New York: Appleton-Century, 1936.
3. Ed. note. Bronislaw Malinowski, *Magic, Science, and Religion*. Glencoe, IL: Free Press, 1948.

2

KENNETH L. PIKE, *Etic and Emic Standpoints for the Description of Behavior*

৵৵

It proves convenient—though partially arbitrary—to describe behavior from two different standpoints, which lead to results which shade into one another. The etic viewpoint studies behavior as from outside of a particular system, and as an essential initial approach to an alien system. The emic viewpoint results from studying behavior as from inside the system. (I coined the words etic and emic from the words phonetic and phonemic, following the conventional linguistic usage of these latter terms. The short terms are used in an analogous manner, but for more general purposes.)

Characteristics of the Two Standpoints

The principal differences between the etic and emic approaches to language and culture can be summarized as follows:

Cross-Cultural versus Specific

The etic approach treats all cultures or languages—or a selected group of them—at one time. It might well be called "comparative" in the anthropological sense (cf. Mead 1952: 344)[1] were it not for the fact that the phrase "comparative linguistics" has a quite different usage already current in linguistic circles, in reference to comparing related languages with a view to reconstructing parent forms. The emic approach is, on the contrary, culturally specific, applied to one language or culture at a time.

Units available in advance versus [units] determined during analysis: Etic

28

units and classifications, based on prior broad sampling or surveys (and studied in training courses) may be available before one begins the analysis of a further particular language or culture. Regardless of how much training one has however, emic units of a language must be determined during the analysis of that language; they must be discovered, not predicted—even though the range of kinds of components of language has restrictions placed upon it by the physiology of the human organism, and these restrictions are to some degree reflected in the events of the observed range of language phenomena.

Creation versus discovery of a system: The etic organization of a world-wide cross-cultural scheme may be created by the analyst. The emic structure of a particular system must, I hold, be discovered. (But here I am assuming a philosophy of science which grants that in the universe some structures occur other than in the mind of the analyst himself. If one adopts a view that no structure of language or culture is present in the universe, except as a theoretical construct created by the analyst, then the paragraph must be restated in a different way, to preserve its usefulness in such a context. Specifically, the linguist who denies structure to a naive sentence or to a sonnet must settle for having his own statements, descriptions, or rules about these phenomena as also being without a publicly available structure or ordering. Linguistic statement comprises a subvariety of language utterance, and hence can have no structure if language has no structure.)

External versus internal view: Descriptions or analyses from the etic standpoint are "alien" in view, with criteria external to the system. Emic descriptions provide an internal view, with criteria chosen from within the system. They represent to us the view of one familiar with the system and who knows how to function within it himself.

External versus internal plan: An etic system may be set up by criteria or "logical" plan whose relevance is external to the system being studied. The discovery or setting up of the emic system requires the inclusion of criteria relevant to the internal functioning of the system itself.

Absolute versus relative criteria: The etic criteria may often be considered absolute, or measurable directly. Emic criteria are relative to the internal characteristics of the system, and can be usefully described or measured relative to each other.

Non-integration versus integration: The etic view does not require that every unit be viewed as part of a larger setting. The emic view, however, insists that every unit be seen as somehow distributed and functioning within a larger structural unit or setting, in a hierarchy of units and hierarchy of settings as units.

Sameness and difference as measured versus systemic: Two units are different etically when instrumental measurements can show them to be so. Units are different emically only when they elicit different responses from people acting within the system.

Partial versus total data: Etic data are obtainable early in analysis with partial information. In principle, on the contrary, emic criteria require a knowledge of the total system to which they are relative and from which they ultimately draw their significance.

Preliminary versus final presentation: Hence, etic data provide access into the system—the starting point of analysis. They give tentative results, tentative units. The final analysis or presentation, however, would be in emic units. In the total analysis, the initial etic description gradually is refined, and is ultimately—in principle, but probably never in practice—replaced by one which is totally emic.

If, furthermore, it is desired to present the emic—structural—units not only as algebraic points relative to a system, but also as elements physically described, the emic notation must be supplemented by etic, physical description.

The penalty for ignoring the etic/emic distinction, and of attempting to utilize (without knowing it) an etic description when an emic one is needed, is best stated in the words of Sapir, who anticipated this position years ago:

> It is impossible to say what an individual is doing unless we have tacitly accepted the essentially arbitrary modes of interpretation that social tradition is constantly suggesting to us from the very moment of our birth. Let anyone who doubts this try the experiment of making a painstaking report [i.e., an etic one] of the actions of a group of natives engaged in some activity, say religious, to which he has not the cultural key [i.e., a knowledge of the emic system]. If he is a skillful writer, he may succeed in giving a picturesque account of what he sees and hears, or thinks he sees and hears, but the chances of his being able to give a relation of what happens, in terms that would be intelligible and acceptable to the natives themselves, are practically nil. He will be guilty of all manner of distortion; his emphasis will be constantly askew. He will find interesting what the natives take for granted as a casual kind of behavior worthy of no particular comment, and he will utterly fail to observe the crucial turning points in the course of action that give formal significance to the whole in the minds of those who do possess the key to its understanding (1927, in his *Selected Writings*, 546–547).[2]

An illustration remote from human behavior may be helpful: in an emic approach, the analyst might describe the structural functioning of a particular car as a whole, and might include charts showing the parts of the whole car as they function in relation one to another; in an etic approach he might describe the elements one at a time as they are found in a stock room, where bolts, screws, rims, fenders and complex parts, such as generators and motors from various models and makes of cars, have been systematically "filed" according to general criteria.

Physical Nature, Response, and Distribution

Certain physical events must be kept in mind for an emic analysis of verbal materials. They include at least two types, neither of which, in the view presented here, can be ignored at any level of language structure without ultimate loss of some relevant data, or distortion of the system being studied. These two types of events are (a) linguistic—i.e., verbal, and (b) extra-linguistic—i.e., nonverbal. Every emic unit of language behavior must be studied in reference to its distribution—distribution in reference to verbal behavior, and distribution in reference to nonverbal cultural behavior. Within the study of the distribution of language units in nonverbal contexts is included the consideration of the nonverbal responses of individuals to speech addressed to them. Just as the verbal replies of a speaker help one determine meanings of elements of communication, so the nonverbal ones do likewise. To attempt to analyze or describe language without reference to its function in eliciting responses—verbal and nonverbal—is to ignore one of the crucial kinds of evidence which is essential if the emic structure of language is to be determined, whether one is dealing with the larger units of that structure, such as the sentence, or smaller ones, such as some of the emic units of the sound system.

This analytical dependence can be in part ignored at the presentation of the material after the language structure has been analyzed. But this theory maintains that in the analytical process there is tacit or explicit reference to cultural distribution, nonverbal as well as verbal. If one is working through a second language, by interpretation, it is easy to succumb to the illusion that there is no such dependence, since one may appear to be using 'words,' only, to get data and to determine its function and structure. With a monolingual approach the direct dependence upon nonverbal contexts is more easily seen. In either case, once the analyst notes his ultimate reliance upon cultural distribution of nonverbal as well as verbal types, he is ready to appreciate, in further detail ... that a theory of language is needed which is not discontinuous with a theory of other phases of human activity.

Value of Standpoints

Both etic and emic approaches are of great value for special phases of behavioral analysis. The etic approach to behavior is of especial value, first, in giving to a beginning student a broad training as to the kinds of behavior occurring around the world, so that he may be the more prepared to recognize quickly the different kinds of events observed, and to help him see slight differences between similar events. Second, during this process he may obtain a technique and symbolism (say a phonetic alphabet) for recording the events of a culture. Third, even the specialist, coming from one culture to a sharply different one, has no other way to begin its analysis than by starting with a rough, tentative (and inaccurate) etic description of it. No matter how skillful an emicist he may be, he can complete his emic description only after the analysis is complete—not before—and that analysis must be begun by recording data etically in terms of his prior experience (systematic training, or unclassified knowledge gained in terms of his own culture). Fourth, in studies of the geographical occurrence or diffusion of single kinds of activity, or of a pre-selected list of activities within an area, the analyst may not choose (because of financial limitations, pressure of time, and so on) to make a complete emic study of each local culture or dialect; under such circumstances an etic comparison may be used—or, better, a widespread etic sampling of many local areas with additional intensive emic studies of a few strategically located areas.

The value of emic study is, first, that it leads to an understanding of the way in which a language or culture is constructed, not as a series of miscellaneous parts, but as a working whole. Second, it helps one to appreciate not only the culture or language as an ordered whole, but it helps one to understand the individual actors in such a life drama—their attitudes, motives, interests, responses, conflicts, and personality development. In addition, it provides the only basis upon which a predictive science of behavior can be expected to make some of its greatest progress, since even statistical predictive studies will in many instances ultimately prove invalid, except as they reflect samplings and classifications which are homogeneous—but homogeneity in behavior must for many of these purposes be emically defined.

Caution—Not a Dichotomy

A caution needs to be given at this point: in many instances, an etic and an emic description may appear to be almost alike—so much so, in fact, that the unwary reader may say that there is "no difference," say, between the phonetic and phonemic descriptions of the system of sounds of a language, or that the difference is so slight as not to warrant the extra effort an emic description requires.

To be sure, much of the data is the same, and the general content looks much alike. Yet this is also true of the two separate pictures which go into a stereoscopic viewer; an untrained person usually sees them as identical, but the three dimensional effect evoked by seeing simultaneously through the stereoscope the two views of the same scene—taken at the same time, under the same lighting conditions, but with viewpoints scant inches apart—makes this added perception startling indeed. And so it can be with the two viewpoints of etics and emics. Through the etic "lens" the analyst views the data in tacit reference to a perspective oriented to all comparable events (whether sounds, ceremonies, activities), of all peoples, of all parts of the earth; through the other lens, the emic one, he views the same events, at the same time, in the same context, in reference to a perspective oriented to the particular function of those particular events in that particular culture, as it and it alone is structured. The result is a kind of "tridimensional understanding" of human behavior instead of a "flat" etic one.

It must be further emphasized that etic and emic data do not constitute a rigid dichotomy of bits of data, but often present the same data from two points of view. Specifically, for example, the emic units of a language, once discovered by emic procedures, may be listed for comparative purposes with the similar emic units from other languages so studied. The moment that this has been done, however, the emic units have changed into etic units, since they are divorced from the context of the structure of the language from which they have come, and are viewed as generalized instances of abstract stereotypes, rather than as living parts of an actual sequence of behavior events within a particular culture. Similarly, if a person working in one dialect moves to a very similar neighboring dialect, his first transcription is an etic one, perforce, because he is alien to that dialect, but it may actually be very close to the final emic transcription which he will produce: many of his tentative etic units will turn out to be emic units as well.

We turn, now, to illustrations of differences in outlook on particular events where a camera recording of the physical event would not be enough—but where other data must also be used.

Illustrations of Purposive Emic Differences Within a Culture

Within a particular culture there are many events which on the surface appear to be similar or identical, but which function very differently. This difference often consists in the different purpose of the actors. This purpose is frequently obvious to the outside observer or other participants; at other times it is obscure both to the outside observer and to the participant. When the difference of purpose is easily seen, it is detected in terms of the kind of observable larger sequence of events within which the smaller event occurs (i.e., its distribution)—and in terms of the response which it immediately receives. When the purpose is temporarily hidden from the other participants, the choice of alternate responses may be delayed until after other events have made the purposive difference clear, or a response may be given which the participants may later judge to have been inappropriate.

In the United States Senate a camera and recorder on different occasions might register two speeches which were physically similar. The first, let us say, is intended to affect the attitude of listeners, such as to convince them of the necessity of the course of action being presented. The second is discussing the same course of action, with the same words, but without any such purpose. It is a filibuster designed not to affect that irrelevant issue which happens to provide the words, but is calculated so to delay the course of business as to force the speaker's opponents to give up the attempt to pass a measure unpalatable to him. Some of the immediate reactions to a filibuster (such as inattention by the audience) may be quite different from that of the same data given as part of a different address.

A partial small-scale parallel with such an instance would be the speaking of any pair of homophones such as *pare, pair; rite, write; seal* (animal, noun), *seal* (of wax, noun), *seal* (verb). Here, too, the outward visible form may be the same, whereas the words as a whole must be considered different because of the responses which they elicit from the hearers, and the kind of verbal sequences into which they enter.

Units of size intermediate between a filibuster and single words may occur which must be similarly differentiated. Note such items as mimicry, where a child is trying to learn to speak by repeating sentences after adults; the homonymous repeated sentence is often inappropriate to normal conversation since the child may fail, for example, to change *you* to *I*, or to replace question with answer. A lie is homophonous with a parallel normal sentence, but they must be considered different emically, in spite of the identity of their internal structures. Even the immediate responses—and hence their apparent meanings—may be the same. In order to detect the essential difference between them, the observer must be prepared to notice reactions (say, a spanking) delayed for a much longer time. In lying, therefore, we have an illustration of an emic difference, where the natives themselves cannot immediately detect that difference—or it may go permanently undetected by the hearers. Here, then, there is some temporary or permanent indeterminacy of meaning.

Irony brings us a different type of homophony which includes, usually, the intention of having at least part of the audience to so detect it; if that purpose fails, the irony will be "lost on" the receiver of it—though it may cause the amusement of onlookers. Mimicry of the lisping character of someone's speech is similar to such irony—and quite different from the mimicry of an adult by a child learning to talk. An adult in learning a foreign language may be badly inhibited from adequate mimicry by reacting to his own learning process as if it were the kind of socially inacceptable mimicry rather than the other.

Nonverbal mimicry shows a similar patterning: a child utilizes small-scale implements to *do like Daddy*, in raking the lawn, digging a hole, or fishing. With his father gone from the scene, and the mimicry purpose removed, the child may not finish raking the lawn.

On an adult scale, the working activity may be quite similar, whether the regular workers or strike breakers are performing it, but the reaction to the first is one of normal community relations, whereas reaction to the second may include violent attempts by the strikers to interrupt the work of the strike breakers. The killing of a single fly by a Western adult might be an act of cleanliness, but by a Hindu might have implications of profound, religious significance, because of their beliefs concerning the possibility of the reincarnation of human souls into animal bodies. Tea drinking at 4.30 p.m. in some parts of the USA would imply a somewhat formal social gathering; in Australia it often means little more than quenching one's thirst. In meetings of the United Nations, the circumstances (i.e., distribution) and purpose of activities affect the reaction of people—to seeing one of, e.g., the participants "walk out" as a political measure to indicate disapproval (rather than to go to the toilet).

In our culture there are, furthermore, specific legal procedures which are used in an attempt to differentiate between events which are physically similar but emically different, with sharply different cultural penalties: Was the man carrying a pistol when he robbed the house? Did the driver run through a red light when he hit the man? Was the violence premeditated or the result of sudden anger? Was the author of it insane or was he deliberately cruel? Was the prisoner really trying to escape, or did the guard misunderstand, or pretend to do so, or even stage the event under orders? Nonlegal activity similarly attempts to apply criteria to determine such matters: Is this explanation the real reason, or is it just an excuse to mask laziness or irresponsibility or viciousness? Was the plate really cracked?

In nonverbal activity as in verbal activity there may be temporary ambiguities which can only be resolved by a study of a larger context. For example: Do the people of Country X know the issues which lead to their activity and choose that activity deliberately, or are they following the lead of someone else blindly or under compulsion?

Perhaps the illustration of such emic differences best known to linguistic circles is one given by Sapir (1925, in his *Selected Writings*, 34). A candle-blowing *wh*, though physically similar to the *wh* of *which* or *why*, in some dialects of English is, nevertheless, "entirely distinct" from it in the series of kinds of events to which it belongs. For both of them the lips are puckered up, and air is blown out of the mouth with a slight friction sound. In the first, the purpose is to blow out a candle, and the event is part of a series, such as "going to bed"; in the second, the sound becomes part of a word, and the word becomes part of a sentence, and the sentence becomes part of a conversation.

An emic approach would treat as significantly different the preceding pairs of events. One kind of etic approach—one which ignored meaning or purpose—might treat them as nearly identical pairs. In between these two approaches would be a different etic classification of these emic types, listing them in relation to differential purpose, meaning, or response, but not in relation to the full systems from which they were abstracted. . . .

Notes

1. Ed. note. Margaret Mead, "The Training of the Cultural Anthropologist," *American Anthropologist* 54 (1952): 343–346.
2. Ed. note. Edward Sapir, *Selected Writings of Edward Sapir in Language, Culture, and Personality*. David G. Mandelbaum (ed.). Berkeley: University of California Press, 1949.

3

ALASDAIR MACINTYRE, *Is Understanding Religion Compatible With Believing?*[1]

ৼৼ

Begin with an elementary puzzlement. In any discussion between sceptics and believers it is presupposed that, even for us to disagree, it is necessary to understand each other. Yet here at the outset the central problem arises. For usually (and the impulse to write "always" is strong) two people could not be said to share a concept or to possess the same concept unless they agreed in at least some central applications of it. Two men may share a concept and yet disagree in some of the judgments they make in which they assert that objects fall under it. But two men who disagreed in *every* judgment which employed the concept—of them what could one say that they shared? For to possess a concept is to be able to use it correctly—although it does not preclude mishandling it sometimes. It follows that unless I can be said to share your judgments at least to some degree I cannot be said to share your concepts.

Yet sceptic and believer disagree *in toto* in their judgments on some religious matters; or so it seems. So how can they be in possession of the same concepts? If I am prepared to say *nothing* of what you will say about God or sin or salvation, how can my concepts of God, sin, and salvation be the same as yours? And if they are not, how can we understand each other? There are parties to the discussion who would cut it short precisely at this point, both Protestants who believe that only saving grace can help us to understand the concepts of the Scriptures or the creeds, and sceptics who believe that religious utterances are flatly senseless. But each of these is presently convicted of paradox. For the Protestant will elsewhere deny what is entailed by his position, namely that nobody ever rejects Christianity (since anyone who thinks he has rejected it must have lacked saving grace and so did not understand Christianity and so in fact rejected something else); and the sceptic of this kind has to explain the meaning of religious utterances in order to reject them (that is, he never says—as he would have to if they were flatly senseless—"I can't understand a word of it"). So it seems that we do want to say that a common understanding of religious concepts by sceptics and by believers is both necessary and impossible. This dilemma constitutes my problem.

Someone might argue that this dilemma is an entirely artificial construction on the grounds that the concepts used in religion are concepts also used outside religion and that sceptics and believers agree in the non-religious judgments which make use of such concepts. Since I have said that it is far from necessary for two men who share a concept to agree in every judgment which they make in which they make use of the concept, there can be no objection to saying that sceptics and believers share the same concept and, *a fortiori* no difficulty in mutual understanding. But this objection rests upon two mistakes. First of all it ignores those specifically religious concepts which have no counterpart in nonreligious contexts; and the concepts I have already cited such as those of God, sin, and salvation belong to this class. Secondly, when secular predicates such as "powerful" and "wise" are transferred to a religious application, they undergo a change. Certainly they are used analogically; but just this is the point. A new element is introduced with the analogical adaptation of the concept. The transition from "powerful" to "omnipotent" is not merely quantitative. For the notion of "supreme in this or that class" cannot easily be transferred to a being who does not belong to a class (as God does not).[2] And thus a new concept has been manufactured. But if the understanding of this new concept can lead theologians to make one set of judgments and the understanding of what is apparently the same concept can lead sceptics to make quite another set of judgments, then how can it be the same concept which is in question? The dilemma stands. If by any chance examples were to be produced from religions which turned out to use no specifically religious concepts, and only to use secular predicates, without change of meaning, then certainly we should have no problems of meaning with them. And with them for that very reason I am not concerned.

An indirect way of approaching this dilemma as it arises for the philosophy of religion would be to enquire whether the same dilemma arises in any other field; and at once it is clear that there is at least one field in which it *ought* to arise, namely the study of so-called primitive societies. For anthropologists and sociologists (I intend to use these terms interchangeably) claim to understand concepts which they do not share. They identify such concepts as *mana*, or *tabu*, without themselves using them—or so it seems. If we could discover what anthropological understanding consisted in therefore, we might be in a stronger position to restate the problem. And if, as I shall claim, we could also show that the variety of positions taken up by anthropologists reproduce a variety of positions already taken up in the philosophy of religion, the sense of relevance would be even stronger. I want to distinguish four different positions, each of which has defects.

(a) There is the now unfashionable view of Lévy-Bruhl that primitive thought is pre-logical. When Australian aborigines asserted that the sun is a white cockatoo[3] Lévy-Bruhl concluded that he was faced with a total indifference to inconsistency and contradiction. From the standpoint of rational discourse we can study primitive thought much as we study natural phenomena. It obeys laws as particles obey laws; but in speaking, primitives do not follow rules as we do. Therefore we cannot elucidate the rules that they use. In an important sense therefore, although we can describe what primitives say, we cannot grasp their concepts. For they do not possess concepts in the sense of recognizing that some uses of expression conform to and others break with rules for the use of such expressions. It is of course consistent with this view that we might by a kind of empathy imagine ourselves to be primitives and in this sense "understand"; but we might equally understand by imaginative sympathy what it is to be a bear or a squirrel.

The counterpart in philosophy of religion to Lévy-Bruhl is the kind of position which wants to interpret religious language[4] as expressive of attitudes rather than as affirming or denying that anything is the case. On this view religious language simply does not function as *language*; for it is used either causally to evoke or aesthetically to express feelings or attitudes, and Carnap thinks that language can do these things in precisely the same way in which "movements" can. We can thus study religious language, as in Lévy-Bruhl's writings, only as a natural phenomenon; we cannot grasp its concepts for they cannot, on this view, be conceptual. The problem for writers like Lévy-Bruhl and Carnap is that they have to treat their own conclusions as palpably false in order to arrive at them. For unless Lévy-Bruhl had grasped that "white cockatoo" and "sun" were being used with apparently normal referential intentions, he could not have diagnosed the oddity of asserting that the sun is a white cockatoo; and unless Carnap had grasped the assertive form of religious or metaphysical statement, he would not have had to argue that this language is not assertive but expressive. That is, in Lévy-Bruhl and Carnap we find a tacit acknowledgment that primitive *language* and religious *language* are *language*. And that therefore something is there to be construed and not merely described or explained.

(b) At the opposite extreme from Lévy-Bruhl is the practice of Professor E. E. Evans-Pritchard in his book *Nuer Religion*, which is of course offered as an explicit refutation of Lévy-Bruhl. Like the Australian aborigines, the Sudanese Nuer appear to fly in the face of ordinary rules of consistency and contradiction. "It seems odd, if not absurd, to a European when he is told that a twin is a bird as though it were an obvious fact, for Nuer are not saying that a twin is like a bird but that he is a bird."[5] Evans-Pritchard begins from the Nuer concept of the divine, *kwoth*. The difficulties in the notion of *kwoth* spring from the fact that *kwoth* is asserted both to be sharply contrasted with the material creation and to be widely present in it. It is both one and many:

and the many, as aspects of *kwoth*, are one with each other. In order to tease out the notion Evans-Pritchard has to allow full weight to the social context of practice in which the assertions about *kwoth* are used. By doing this he is able to show that the utterances of the Nuer are rule-governed, and on this rests his claim to have refuted Lévy-Bruhl. But Evans-Pritchard takes this to be the same as having made the utterances of the Nuer intelligible. Certainly he has shown us what the Nuer idea of intelligibility is. He has shown why the Nuer think their religion makes sense. But this is not to have shown that the Nuer are right. "When a cucumber is used as a sacrificial victim Nuer speak of it as an ox. In doing so they are asserting something rather more than that it takes the place of an ox."[6] When we have grasped the whole of Nuer practice have we grasped what more this could be? Or is there anything left over that we have not understood? Evans-Pritchard would have to answer this last question by "No." In doing so he brings out the parallels between his position and the kind of Wittgensteinianism in philosophy of religion exemplified by Mr. Peter Winch.[7]

Winch argues that "intelligibility takes many and varied forms"; that there is no "norm for intelligibility in general."[8] He argues that "criteria of logic are not a direct gift of God, but arise out of, and are only intelligible" in the context of ways of living or modes of social life as such. For instance, science is one such mode and religion is another; and each has criteria of intelligibility peculiar to itself. So within science or religion actions can be logical or illogical; in science, for example, it would be illogical to refuse to be bound by the results of a properly carried out experiment; in religion it would be illogical to suppose that one could pit one's own strength against God's; and so on. But we cannot sensibly say that either the practice of science itself or that of religion is either illogical or logical; both are non-logical.[9] It follows from this that anything that counts as a "way of living" or a "mode of social life" can only be understood and criticized in its own terms. Winch indeed argues that so far as religion is concerned, a sociologist can only identify religious actions under their religious descriptions and if he answers any questions about them of the form "Do these two acts belong to the same kind of activity?" the answer will have to be "given according to criteria which are not taken from sociology, but from religion itself. But if the judgments of identity—and hence the generalizations—of the sociologist of religion rest on criteria taken from religion, then his relation to the performers of religious activity cannot be just that of observer to observed. It must rather be analogous to the participation of the natural scientist with fellow-workers in the activities of scientific investigation."[10] That is, you can only understand it from the inside.

Winch therefore points to a theoretical justification for Evans-Pritchard's practice, and in so doing exposes its weakness. For there are not two alternatives: *either* embracing the metaphysical fiction of one over-all "norm for intelligibility in general" *or* flying to total relativism. We can elicit the weakness of this position by considering the conceptual self-sufficiency claimed for "ways of living" and "modes of social life." The examples given are "religion" and "science." But at any given date in any given society the criteria in current use by religious believers or by scientists will differ from what they are at other times and places.[11] Criteria have a history. This emerges strikingly if we ask how we are to think of magic on Winch's view. Is magic a mode of social life"? Or is it primitive religion? Or perhaps primitive science? For we do want to reject magic, and we want to reject it—in the terms which Winch has taken over for polemical purposes from Pareto—as illogical because it fails to come up to our criteria of rationality. An excellent case here is that of the witchcraft practiced by the Azande.[12] The Azande believe that the performance of certain rites in due form affects their common welfare; this belief cannot in fact be refuted. For they also believe that if the rites are ineffective it is because someone present at them had evil thoughts. Since this is always possible, there is never a year when it is unavoidable for them to admit that the rites were duly performed, but that they did not thrive. Now the belief of the Azande is not unfalsifiable in principle (we know perfectly well what would falsify it—the conjunction of the rite, no evil thoughts and disasters). But in fact it cannot be falsified. Does this belief stand in need of rational criticism? And if so by what standards? It seems to me that one could only hold the belief of the Azande rationally *in the absence of* any practice of science and technology in which criteria of effectiveness, ineffectiveness, and kindred notions had been built up. But to say this is to recognize the appropriateness of scientific criteria of judgment from our standpoint. The Azande do not intend their belief either as a piece of science or as a piece of non-science. They do not possess these categories. It is only *post eventum*, in the light of later and more sophisticated understanding that their belief and concepts can be classified and evaluated at all.

This suggests strongly that beliefs and concepts are not merely to be evaluated by the criteria implicit in the practice of those who hold and use them. This conviction is reinforced by other considerations. The criteria implicit in the practice of a society or of a mode of social life are not necessarily coherent; their application to problems set within that social mode does not always yield *one* clear and unambiguous answer. When this is the case people start questioning their own criteria. They try to criticize the standards of intelligibility and rationality which they have held hitherto. On Winch's view it is difficult to see what this could mean. This is to return to the point that criteria and concepts have a history; it is not just activities which have a history while the criteria which govern action are timeless.

What I am quarrelling with ultimately is the suggestion that agreement in following a rule is sufficient to guarantee making sense. We can discriminate different types of example here. There are the cases where the anthropologist, in order to interpret what people say, has to reconstruct imaginatively a possible past situation where expressions had a sense which they no longer bear. Consider theories about what taboo is. To call something taboo is to prohibit it, but it is not to say that it is prohibited. To say that something is taboo is to distinguish it from actions which are prohibited but are not taboo. We could say that it is to give a reason for a prohibition, except that it is unintelligible what reason can be intended. So some theorists have constructed[13] from the uses of taboo a sense which it might once have had and a possible history of how this sense was lost. One cannot take the sense from the use, for the use affords no sense, although the temptation to tell anthropologists that taboo is the name of a non-natural quality would be very strong for any Polynesian who had read G. E. Moore.

In the case of "taboo" we can imagine lost sense for the expression. What about cases, however, where the sense is not lost, but is simply incoherent? According to Spencer and Gillen some aborigines carry about a stick or a stone which is treated *as if* it is or embodies the soul of the individual who carries it. If the stick or stone is lost, the individual anoints himself as the dead are anointed. Does the concept of "carrying one's soul about with one" make sense? Of course we can re-describe what the aborigines are doing and transform it into sense, and perhaps Spencer and Gillen (and Durkheim who follows them) mis-describe what occurs. But if their reports are not erroneous, we confront a blank wall here, so far as meaning is concerned, although it is easy to give the rules for the use of the concept.

What follows from this is quite simply that there are cases where we cannot rest content with describing the user's criteria for an expression, but we can criticize what he does. Indeed, unless we could do this we could not separate the case where there are no problems of meaning, the case where now there is no clear sense to an expression, but where once there may well have been one (as with "taboo") and the case where there appears never to have been a clear and coherent sense available. What matters for our present purposes is that these examples suggest that sometimes to understand a concept involves not sharing it. In the case of "taboo" we can only grasp what it is for something to be taboo if we extend our insight beyond the rules which govern the use of the expression to the point and purpose which these rules once had, but no longer have, and can no longer have in a different social context. We can only understand what it is to use a thoroughly incoherent concept—such as that of a soul in a stick—if we understand what has to be absent from the criteria of practice and of speech for this incoherence not to appear to the user of the concept. In other words we are beginning to notice requirements for the elucidation of concepts which are necessarily absent from the kind of account given by Evans-Pritchard or by Winch.

We have not only to give the rules for the use of the relevant expressions, but to show what the point could be of following such rules, and in bringing out this feature of the case one shows also whether the use of this concept is or is not a possible one for people who have the standards of intelligibility in speech and action which we have. But do we have to be thus self-centered in our application of criteria? Can we, as it might appear from this, only understand what makes sense to us already? Can we learn nothing from societies or modes of social life which we cannot understand within our present framework? Why dismiss what does not fit easily into that framework? Why not revise the framework? To find a clue to the answering of these questions let us examine yet a third doctrine of intelligibility in anthropology.

(c) Dr. E. R. Leach[14] commits himself to a version of the philosophical theory that the meaning of an expression is nothing other than the way in which the expression is used. Myth is to be understood in terms of ritual, saying in terms of doing. To interpret any statement made by primitive people which appears unintelligible, ask what the people in question do. So Leach writes that "myth regarded as a statement in words 'says' the same thing as ritual regarded as a statement in action. To ask questions about the content of belief which are not contained in the content of ritual is nonsense." Leach, that is, adopts an opposite standpoint to Evans-Pritchard. Evans-Pritchard insists that the anthropologist has to allow the Nuer to make sense in the Nuer's own terms; Leach insists that his Burmese society must be made sense of in Leach's own terms. What is impressive here is that both Evans-Pritchard and Leach have written anthropological classics and this may be thought to be inconsistent with what I have just said. But the reason why we get insight both into Evans-Pritchard's Nuer and Leach's *Kachin* is that both are so explicit in presenting us both with their philosophical assumptions and with the field-material to which they apply those assumptions. Each furnishes us not merely with a finished interpretation but with a view of the task of interpretation while it is being carried out.

In Leach's case, although his attitude is the opposite of that of Evans-Pritchard, the results are oddly similar. In the case of the Nuer everything made sense, for the Nuer were judged on their own terms. In the case of the Kachin everything makes sense, for the rules of interpretation provide that every statement which appears not to make sense is to be translated into one that does. So Leach insists that metaphysical questions about the spirits in whom the Kachin believe (*nats*) are out of place. We cannot ask if *nats* eat or where they live for we are not to treat statements about *nats* as statements at all, but as ritual performances which can be performed properly or improperly, but which are scarcely true or false.

The counterpart to Leach in the philosophy of religion is perhaps Professor R. B. Braithwaite's reinterpretation of the meaning of religious utterances. Braithwaite sets out a classification of utterances derived from his philosophical empiricism and asks where religion can be fitted in.[15] The answer is that the room left for religion is in providing a specification and a backing for ways of life. I do not want to discuss Braithwaite's position in this paper. I only want to point out that Braithwaite's way of giving a sense to religious utterances distracts us from the question, What sense do these utterances have for those who make them? And because Braithwaite deprives us of this question, he makes it unintelligible that anyone should cease to believe, on the grounds that he can no longer find a sense in such utterances. So also it seems difficult to see what view Leach could take of a Kachin who was persuaded, for example by a Christian missionary, that his belief in *nats* was false and idolatrous.

It is therefore true that if the criteria of intelligibility with which we approach alien concepts are too narrow we may be liable not only erroneously to dismiss them as senseless but even more misleadingly we may try to force them to a sense which they do not possess. It must seem at this point that my attempt to illuminate the original dilemma has merely led to the formulation of the second one. For it seems that we cannot approach alien concepts except in terms of our own criteria, and that yet to do this is to be in danger of distortion. But in fact if we are careful we shall be able to set out some of the necessary prerequisites for an adequate understanding of beliefs and concepts without this inconsistency.

Against Winch and Evans-Pritchard I have argued that to make a belief and the concepts which it embodies intelligible I cannot avoid invoking my own criteria, or rather the established criteria of my own society. Against Braithwaite and Leach I have argued that I cannot do this until I have already grasped the criteria governing belief and behavior in the society which is the object of enquiry. And I only complete my task when I have filled in the social context so as to make the transition from one set of criteria to the other intelligible. These requirements can be set out more fully as follows:

(1) All interpretation has to begin with detecting the standards of intelligibility established in a society. As a matter of fact, no one can avoid using clues drawn from their own society; and as a matter of exposition analogies from the anthropologist's society will often be helpful. But we have to begin with the society's implicit forms of self-description. Malinowski is contemptuous of the account which, so he says, a Trobriander would give of his own society; but Malinowski's own account of the Trobrianders is curiously like that which he puts in the mouth of his imagined Trobriand informant. And, had it not been, there would have been something radically wrong with it, since how a man describes himself is partially constitutive of what he is. It does not follow from this, as I have already suggested, that the descriptions used or the standards of intelligibility detected will always be internally coherent. And, if they are not, a key task will be to show how this incoherence does not appear as such to the members of the society or else does appear and is somehow made tolerable.

(2) But in detecting incoherence of this kind we have already invoked our standards. Since we cannot avoid doing this it is better to do it self-consciously. Otherwise we shall project on to our studies, as Frazer notoriously did, an image of our own social life. Moreover, if we are sufficiently sensitive we make

it possible for us to partially escape from our own cultural limitations. For we shall have to ask not just how we see the Trobrianders or the Nuer, but how they do or would see us. And perhaps what hitherto looked intelligible and obviously so will then appear opaque and question-begging.

(3) We can now pass on to the stage at which the difficult and important question can be put. How is it that what appears intelligible in one social context can appear not to make sense in another? What has to be underlined is that answers to this question are not necessarily all going to be of the same form.

There is the type of case where a concept works very well, so long as certain questions are not asked about it, and it may be that for a long time in a given society there is no occasion for raising such questions. The concept of the divine right of kings will undergo a strain which reveals internal incoherences only when rival claimants to sovereignty appear, for it contains no answer to the question, Which king has divine right? Then there is the type of case where incoherence and intelligibility are to some extent manifest to the users of the concept. But the use of the concept is so intimately bound up with forms of description which cannot be dispensed with if social and intellectual life is to continue that any device for putting up with the incoherence is more tolerable than dispensing with the concept. A third type of case is that in which the point of a concept or group of concepts lies in their bearing upon behavior. But changed patterns of social behavior deprive the concept of point. So that although there is no internal incoherence in the concept, the concept can no longer be embodied in life as it once was, and it is either put to new uses or it becomes redundant. An example of this would be the concept of honor detached from the institutions of chivalry. "It is difficult," a British historian once wrote, "to be chivalrous without a horse." And the change in the importance of the horse in war can turn *Don Quixote* from a romance into a satire.

(d) I must seem to have come a very long way round. And it is therefore perhaps worth trying to meet the charge of irrelevance by saying what I hope the argument has achieved. I first posed the question: in what sense, if any, can sceptic and believer be said to share the same concepts, and so to understand one another? I then tried to show how the anthropologist might be said to grasp concepts which he does not share, in the sense that he does not make the same judgments employing them as do the people whom he studies. I now want to use my answer on this point to pose a new question which will begin the journey back to the original enquiry. This is still an anthropological question. Up to the seventeenth century we should in our society all have been believers and indeed there would be no question of our being anything else. We should not merely have believed that God existed and was revealed in Christ but we should have found it obvious and unquestionable that this was so. Since the seventeenth century, even for those who believe, the truth and intelligibility of their beliefs is not obvious in the same sense. What accounts for the fact that what was once obvious is now not so? What accounts for the fact that nobody now believes in God in the way that mediaeval men did, simply because men are aware of alternatives? And more importantly still, what makes some of the alternatives appear as obvious to modern sceptics as belief in God did for pre-seventeenth-century Christians?

I pose this question as a background to another. If we can understand why one group of men in the past found Christian beliefs obviously true and intelligible and another group now find them opaque, and we can locate the difference between these two groups, perhaps we shall also be able to locate the difference between contemporary believers and contemporary sceptics. And if we do this we shall have solved our original problem. This brief excursus may make clear the relevance of my apparently rambling procedure. So it becomes urgent to attempt an answer, at least an outline, to the anthropological question. And the form of this answer will be to ask which of the different types of answer to the question, How is it that what appears intelligible in one social context can appear not to make sense in another?, is applicable in the case of the transition from mediaeval belief to modern scepticism.

It is obvious that the internal incoherences in Christian concepts did not go unnoticed in the Middle Ages. The antinomies of benevolent omnipotence and evil, or of divine predestination and human freedom, were never more clearly and acutely discussed. But it is not the case in general that mediaeval thinkers who were dissatisfied with the solutions offered to these antinomies differed in their attitude to belief in God or belief in Christ from thinkers who believed that they or others had offered satisfactory solutions. So the problem becomes: why do the same intellectual difficulties at one time appear as difficulties but no more, an incentive to enquiry but not a ground for disbelief, while at another time they appear as a final and sufficient ground for scepticism and for the abandonment of Christianity? The answers to this question are surely of the second and third types which I outlined in the last section. That is, apparent incoherence of Christian concepts was taken to be tolerable (and treated as apparent and not real) because the concepts were part of a set of concepts which were indispensable to the forms of description used in social and intellectual life. It is the secularization of our forms of description, constituting part of the secularization of our life, that has left the contradictions high and dry. To take an obvious example, Christianity does not and never has depended upon the truth of an Aristotelian physics in which the physical system requires a Prime Mover, and consequently many sceptics as well as many believers have treated the destruction of the Aristotelian argument in its Thomist form as something very little germane to the question of whether or not Christianity is true. But in fact the replacement of a physics which requires a Prime Mover by a physics which does not secularizes a whole area of enquiry. It weakens the hold of the concept of God on our intellectual life by showing that in this area we can dispense with descriptions which have any connection with the concept.

Some Christian theologians such as Paul Tillich have welcomed this process of secularization, describing it in Tillich's terms as a transition from heteronomous to autonomous reason. But the counterpart to secularization is that the specific character of religion becomes clearer at the cost of diminishing its content. Primitive religion is part of the whole form of human life. Durkheim in *The Elementary Forms of the Religious Life* tried to show, and had at least some success in showing, that the most primitive modes of our categorical grasp of the world are inextricably embedded in religion. Thus it is even difficult to talk of "religion" in this context, as though one could identify a separate and distinct element. But it is just this distinctiveness which can be identified in our culture. Religious apologists, not sceptics, stress the uniqueness of religious utterance. The slogan "Every kind of utterance has its own kind of logic" finds a ready response from theologians.

The counterpart to this is an easy toleration for contradiction and incoherence, through the use of such concepts as "the absurd" (Kierkegaard), "paradox" (Barth) or "mystery" (Marcel). We can in fact reach a point at which religion is made logically invulnerable. The attempt in the controversy over the falsification of religious assertions to show that if religion were irrefutable religious utterances would be deprived of sense failed for the same reason that attacks on Azande witchcraft would fail. Religious believers do know what would have to occur for their beliefs to be falsified—they can specify some occurrences with which the existence of omnipotent benevolence is incompatible ("utterly pointless evil" is one commonly used example). But just as the Azande can state what would falsify their assertions about witchcraft—but we could never know that such an occurrence had taken place—so the Christian will leave us in the same difficulty. For the after-life, that which we do not see, may always lend a point to otherwise pointless evil, or absurd happenings. This line of argument is certainly open to attack; but the invocation of concepts such as "mystery" or "paradox" is always there in the background. Thus the logical invulnerability of Christianity seems to me a position that can be maintained.[16] But only at a cost. The cost is emptiness.

I have already produced reasons to explain why incoherences which only presented problems to an Occam could present insuperable obstacles to a T. H. Huxley or a B. Russell. But now I want to argue that the form of Christian apologetic on moral questions itself exhibits Christian concepts as irrelevant in the modern world in much the way in which the concepts of chivalry became irrelevant in the seventeenth century. For what Christian apologists try to show is that unless we live in a certain way certain ill consequences will follow (broken homes and delinquency, perhaps). But this turns Christianity into a testable nostrum. For we can always ask empirically: do particular religious practices in fact produce higher standards of behavior? Again we return to the very simple point—are Christians in fact different from other people in our society, apart from their ritual practices? And if they are not what is the point of Christian belief, insofar as it issues an injunction? Now, whether Christians are different or not is an empirical question. Certainly empirical enquiry cannot tell us whether Christianity is true or not. But if Christian beliefs belong now to a social context in which their connection with behavior has ceased to be clear (as it was clear in the Roman empire, say) the question of the truth of Christianity is put into a different perspective.

Christians here will perhaps want to point to the distinctively Christian forms of behavior of the Confessional Church under Hitler, and this is certainly relevant. For the regressive primitivism of National Socialism with its idols provided a context sufficiently alike to that of early Christianity to make Christianity once more relevant. The Nazis desecularized society with a vengeance. But while to be asked to choose for Christ has a clear meaning when the practical choices are those of the Nazi society, does this injunction have a clear meaning also in our society? And if it had would we not in fact find Christians united on ways of behaving in a way that they are not?

From a historical point of view, of course, it is most unfair to present Christianity as only the victim of secularization. Christianity, especially Protestant Christianity, was itself a powerful secularizing agent, destroying in the name of God any attempt to deify nature, and so helping to rid the world of magic and making nature available for scientific enquiry. The kind of negative theology which refuses to identify any object with the divine (God is not this, not that) has its final fruit in the kind of atheism which Simone Weil and Tillich both see as a recognition of the fact that God cannot be identified with any particular existing object. But what is left to Simone Weil or Tillich is in fact a religious vocabulary without any remaining secular content. Hegel's irreligion consists in his insight into the possibility of extracting truth from its religious husks. Kierkegaard's answer to Hegel is the assertion of a religion defined entirely in its own religious terms, uncriticizable *ab externo*. Together Hegel and Kierkegaard reflect accurately the status of religion in a secularized environment.

(e) For a sceptic to grasp the point of religious belief, therefore, he has to supply a social context which is now lacking and abstract a social context which is now present, and he has to do this for the mediaeval Christian, just as the anthropologist has to do it for the Azande or the aborigines. But in dialogue with contemporary Christians the sceptic is forced to recognize that they see a point in what they say and do although they lack that context. And therefore either he or they are making a mistake, and not a mistake over God, but a mistake over criteria of intelligibility. What is at issue between sceptic and Christian is the character of the difference between belief and unbelief as well as the issue of belief itself. Thus the sceptic is committed to saying that he understands the Christian's use of concepts in a way that the Christian himself does not, and presumably *vice versa*. The discussion is therefore transferred to another level, and a Christian refutation of this paper would have to provide an alternative account of intelligibility. If I am right, understanding Christianity is incompatible with believing in it, not because Christianity is vulnerable to sceptical objections, but because its peculiar invulnerability belongs to it as a form of belief which has lost the social context which once made it comprehensible. It is now too late to be mediaeval and it is too empty and too easy to be Kierkegaardian. Thus sceptic and believer do not share a common grasp of the relevant concepts any more that anthropologist and Azande do. And if the believer wishes to he can always claim that we can only disagree with him because we do not understand him. But the implications of this defense of belief are more fatal to it than any attack could be.

Notes

1. This paper was originally published in John Hick (ed.), *Faith and the Philosophers*. London: Macmillan, 1964. I owe a great deal to conversations with Professor Ernest Gellner and Mr. Peter Winch, neither of whom will agree with the use I have made of what I have learned from them.
2. Thomas Aquinas, *Summa Theologica*, Part I, Q. 3, Art. 5.
3. Lucien Lévy-Bruhl, *Les Fonctions mentales dans les sociétés inférieures*, 76.
4. Or metaphysical language—see R. Carnap, *Philosophy and Logical Syntax*. London: Kegan Paul, 1935.
5. E. E. Evans-Pritchard, *Nuer Religion*. Oxford: Clarendon Press, 1956: 131.
6. *Nuer Religion*, 128.
7. Peter Winch, *The Idea of a Social Science and Its Relation to Philosophy*. London: Routledge & Kegan Paul, 1958.
8. *The Idea of a Social Science*, 102.
9. *The Idea of a Social Science*, 100–101.
10. *The Idea of a Social Science*, 87–88.
11. Consider Kepler using as a criterion in selecting from possible hypotheses what could be expected from a perfect God whose perfection included a preference for some types of geometrical figure as against others.
12. E. E. Evans-Pritchard, *Witchcraft, Oracles, and Magic Among the Azande*. Oxford: Oxford University Press, 1937.
13. See F. Steiner, *Taboo*. Harmondsworth: Penguin Books, 1968.
14. Edmund Leach, *The Political Systems of Highland Burma*. London: Bell, 1954.
15. R. B. Braithwaite, "An Empiricist's View of the Nature of Religious Belief," The Eddington Memorial Lecture, Cambridge University Press, 1955.
16. As I myself did maintain it in "The Logical Status of Religious Beliefs," *Metaphysical Beliefs*. Alasdair MacIntyre (ed.). SCM Press, 1957.

4

CLIFFORD GEERTZ, *"From the Native's Point of View": On the Nature of Anthropological Understanding*

❧❧

I

Several years ago a minor scandal erupted in anthropology: one of its ancestral figures told the truth in a public place. As befits an ancestor, he did it posthumously, and through his widow's decision rather than his own, with the result that a number of the sort of right-thinking types who are with us always immediately rose to cry that she, an in-marrier anyway, had betrayed clan secrets, profaned an idol, and let down the side. What will the children think, to say nothing of the layman? But the disturbance was not much lessened by such ceremonial wringing of the hands; the damn thing was, after all, already printed. In much the same fashion as James Watson's *The Double Helix* exposed the way in which biophysics in fact gets done, Bronislaw Malinowski's *A Diary in the Strict Sense of the Term*[1] rendered established accounts of how anthropologists work fairly well implausible. The myth of the chameleon fieldworker, perfectly self-tuned to his exotic surroundings, a walking miracle of empathy, tact, patience, and cosmopolitanism, was demolished by the man who had perhaps done most to create it.

The squabble that arose around the publication of the *Diary* concentrated, naturally, on inessentials and missed, as was only to be expected, the point. Most of the shock seems to have arisen from the mere discovery that Malinowski was not, to put it delicately, an unmitigated nice guy. He had rude things to say about the natives he was living with, and rude words to say it in. He spent a great deal of his time wishing he were elsewhere. And he projected an image of a man about as little complaisant as the world has seen. (He also projected an image of a man consecrated to a strange vocation to the point of self-immolation, but that was less noted.) The discussion was made to come down to Malinowski's moral character or lack of it, and the genuinely profound question his book raised was ignored; namely, if it is not, as we had been taught to believe, through some sort of extraordinary sensibility, an almost preternatural capacity to think, feel, and perceive like a native (a word, I should hurry to say, I use here "in the strict sense of the term"), how is anthropological knowledge of the way natives think, feel, and perceive possible? The issue the *Diary* presents, with a force perhaps only a working ethnographer can fully appreciate, is not moral. (The moral idealization of fieldworkers is a mere sentimentality in the first place, when it is not self-congratulation or a guild pretense.) The issue is epistemological. If we are going to cling—as, in my opinion, we must—to the injunction to see things from the native's point of view, where are we when we can no longer claim some unique form of psychological closeness, a sort of transcultural identification, with our subjects? What happens to *Verstehen* [understanding] when *Einfühlen* [intuition or empathy] disappears?

As a matter of fact, this general problem has been exercising methodological discussion in anthropology for the last ten or fifteen years; Malinowski's voice from the grave merely dramatizes it as a human dilemma over and above a professional one. The formulations have been various: "inside" versus "outside," or "first person" versus "third person" descriptions; "phenomenological" versus "objectivist," or "cognitive" versus "behavioral" theories; or, perhaps most commonly "emic" versus "etic" analyses, this last deriving from the distinction in linguistics between phonemics and phonetics, phonemics classifying sounds according to their internal function in language, phonetics classifying them according to their acoustic properties as such. But perhaps the simplest and most directly appreciable way to put the matter is in terms of a distinction formulated, for his own purposes, by the psychoanalyst Heinz Kohut, between what he calls "experience-near" and "experience-distant" concepts.

An experience-near concept is, roughly, one that someone—a patient, a subject, in our case an informant—might himself naturally and effortlessly use to define what he or his fellows see, feel, think, imagine, and so on, and which he would readily understand when similarly applied by others. An experience-distant concept is one that specialists of one sort or another—an analyst, an experimenter, an ethnographer, even a priest or an ideologist—employ to forward their scientific, philosophical, or practical aims. "Love" is an experience-near concept, "object cathexis" is an experience-distant one. "Social stratification" and perhaps for most peoples in the world even "religion" (and certainly "religious system") are experience-distant; "caste" and "nirvana" are experience-near, at least for Hindus and Buddhists.

Clearly, the matter is one of degree, not polar opposition—"fear" is experience-nearer than "phobia," and "phobia" experience-nearer than "ego dyssyntonic." And the difference is not, at least so far as anthropology is concerned (the matter is otherwise in poetry and physics), a normative one, in the sense that one sort of concept is to be preferred as such over the other. Confinement to experience-near concepts leaves an ethnographer awash in immediacies, as well as entangled in vernacular. Confinement to experience-distant ones leaves him stranded in abstractions and smothered in jargon. The real question, and the one Malinowski raised by demonstrating that, in the case of "natives," you don't have to be one to know one, is what roles the two sorts of concepts play in anthropological analysis. Or, more exactly, how, in each case, ought one to deploy them so as to produce an interpretation of the way a people lives which is neither imprisoned within their mental horizons, an ethnography of witchcraft as written by a witch, nor systematically deaf to the distinctive tonalities of their existence, an ethnography of witchcraft as written by a geometer.

Putting the matter this way—in terms of how anthropological analysis is to be conducted and its results framed, rather than what psychic constitution anthropologists need to have—reduces the mystery of what "seeing things from the native's point of view" means. But it does not make it any easier, nor does it lessen the demand for perceptiveness on the part of the fieldworker. To grasp concepts that, for another people, are experience-near, and to do so well enough to place them in illuminating connection with experience-distant concepts theorists have fashioned to capture the general features of social life, is clearly a task at least as delicate, if a bit less magical, as putting oneself into someone else's skin. The trick is not to get yourself into some inner correspondence of spirit with your informants. Preferring, like the rest of us, to call their souls their own, they are not going to be altogether keen about such an effort anyhow. The trick is to figure out what the devil they think they are up to.

In one sense, of course, no one knows this better than they do themselves; hence the passion to swim in the stream of their experience, and the illusion afterward that one somehow has. But in another sense, that simple truism is simply not true. People use experience-near concepts spontaneously, unself-consciously, as it were colloquially; they do not, except fleetingly and on occasion, recognize that there are any "concepts" involved at all. That is what experience-near means—that ideas and the realities they inform are naturally and indissolubly bound up together. What else could you call a hippopotamus? Of course the gods are powerful, why else would we fear them? The ethnographer does not, and, in my opinion, largely cannot, perceive what his informants perceive. What he perceives, and that uncertainly enough, is what they perceive "with" or "by means of," or "through" ... or whatever the word should be. In the country of the blind, who are not as unobservant as they look, the one-eyed is not king, he is spectator.

Now, to make all this a bit more concrete, I want to turn for a moment to my own work, which, whatever its other faults, has at least the virtue of being mine—in discussions of this sort a distinct advantage. In all three of the societies I have studied intensively, Javanese, Balinese, and Moroccan, I have been concerned, among other things, with attempting to determine how the people who live there define themselves as persons, what goes into the idea they have (but, as I say, only half-realize they have) of what a self, Javanese, Balinese, or Moroccan style, is. And in each case, I have tried to get at this most intimate of notions not by imagining myself someone else, a rice peasant or a tribal sheikh, and then seeing what I thought, but by searching out and analyzing the symbolic forms—words, images, institutions, behaviors-in terms of which, in each place, people actually represented themselves to themselves and to one another.

The concept of person is, in fact, an excellent vehicle by means of which to examine this whole question of how to go about poking into another people's turn of mind. In the first place, some sort of concept of this kind, one feels reasonably safe in saying, exists in recognizable form among all social groups. The notions of what persons are may be, from our point of view, sometimes more than a little odd. They may be conceived to dart about nervously at night shaped like fireflies. Essential elements of their psyches, like hatred, may be thought to be lodged in granular black bodies within their livers, discoverable upon autopsy. They may share their fates with *doppelgänger* beasts,[2] so that when the beast sickens or dies they sicken or die too. But at least some conception of what a human individual is, as opposed to a rock, an animal, a rainstorm, or a god, is, so far as I can see, universal. Yet, at the same time, as these offhand examples suggest, the actual conceptions involved vary from one group to the next, and often quite sharply. The Western conception of the person as a bounded, unique, more or less integrated motivational and cognitive universe, a dynamic center of awareness, emotion, judgment, and action organized into a distinctive whole and set contrastively both against other such wholes and against its social and natural background, is, however incorrigible it may seem to us, a rather peculiar idea within the context of the world's cultures. Rather than attempting to place the experience of others within the framework of such a conception, which is what the extolled "empathy" in fact usually comes down to, understanding them demands setting that conception aside and seeing their experiences within the framework of their own idea of what selfhood is. And for Java, Bali, and Morocco, at least, that idea differs markedly not only from our own but, no less dramatically and no less instructively, from one to the other.

II

In Java, where I worked in the fifties, I studied a small, shabby inland county-seat sort of place; two shadeless streets of whitewashed wooden shops and offices, and even less substantial bamboo shacks crammed in helter-skelter behind them, the whole surrounded by a great half-circle of densely packed rice-bowl villages. Land was short, jobs were scarce, politics was unstable, health was poor, prices were rising, and life was altogether far from promising, a kind of agitated stagnancy in which, as I once put it, thinking of the curious mixture of borrowed fragments of modernity and exhausted relics of tradition that characterized the place, the future seemed about as remote as the past. Yet in the midst of this depressing scene there was an absolutely astonishing intellectual vitality, a philosophical passion really, and a popular one besides, to track the riddles of existence right down to the ground. Destitute peasants would discuss questions of freedom of the will, illiterate tradesmen discoursed on the properties of God, common laborers had theories about the relations between reason and passion, the nature of time, or the reliability of the senses. And, perhaps most importantly, the problem of the self—its nature, function, and mode of operation—was pursued with the sort of reflective intensity one could find among ourselves in only the most recherché settings indeed.

The central ideas in terms of which this reflection proceeded, and which thus defined its boundaries and the Javanese sense of what a person is, were arranged into two sets of contrasts, at base religious, one between "inside" and "outside," and one between "refined" and "vulgar." These glosses are, of course, crude and imprecise; determining exactly what the terms involved signified, sorting out their shades of meaning, was what all the discussion was about. But together they formed a distinctive conception of the self which, far from being merely theoretical, was the one in terms of which Javanese in fact perceived one another and, of course, themselves.

The "inside"/"outside" words, *batin* and *lair* (terms borrowed, as a matter of fact, from the Sufi tradition of Muslim mysticism, but locally reworked) refer on the one hand to the felt realm of human experience and on the other to the observed realm of human behavior. These have, one hastens to say, nothing to do with "soul" and "body" in our sense, for which there are in fact quite other words with quite other implications. *Batin*, the "inside" word, does not refer to a separate seat of encapsulated spirituality detached or detachable from the body, or indeed to a bounded unit at all, but to the emotional life of human beings taken generally. It consists of the fuzzy, shifting flow of subjective feeling perceived directly in all its phenomenological immediacy but considered to be, at its roots at least, identical across all individuals, whose individuality it thus effaces. And similarly, *lair*, the "outside" word, has nothing to do with the body as an object, even an experienced object. Rather, it refers to that part of human life which, in our culture, strict behaviorists limit themselves to studying—external actions, movements, postures, speech—again conceived as in its essence invariant from one individual to the next. These two sets of phenomena—inward feelings and outward actions—are then regarded not as functions of one another but as independent realms of being to be put in proper order independently.

It is in connection with this "proper ordering" that the contrast between *alus*, the word meaning "pure refined," "polished," "exquisite ethereal subtle," "civilized," "smooth," and *kasar*, the word meaning "impolite rough," "uncivilized," "coarse," "insensitive," "vulgar," comes into play. The goal is to be *alus* in both the separated realms of the self. In the inner realm this is to be achieved through religious discipline, much but not all of it mystical. In the outer realm, it is to be achieved through etiquette, the rules of which here are not only extraordinarily elaborate but have something of the force of law. Through meditation the civilized man thins out his emotional life to a kind of constant hum; through etiquette, he both shields that life from external disruptions and regularizes his outer behavior in such a way that it appears to others as a predictable, undisturbing, elegant, and rather vacant set of choreographed motions and settled forms of speech.

There is much more to all this, because it connects up to both an ontology and an aesthetic. But so far as our problem is concerned, the result is a bifurcate conception of the self, half ungestured feeling and half unfelt gesture. An inner world of stilled emotion and an outer world of shaped behavior confront one another as sharply distinguished realms unto themselves, any particular person being but the momentary locus, so to speak, of that confrontation, a passing expression of their permanent existence, their permanent separation, and their permanent need to be kept in their own order. Only when you have seen, as I have, a young man whose wife—a woman he had in fact raised from childhood and who had been the center of his life—has suddenly and inexplicably died, greeting everyone with a set smile and formal apologies for his wife's absence and trying, by mystical techniques, to flatten out, as he himself put it, the hills and valleys of his emotion into an even, level plain ("That is what you have to do," he said to me, "be smooth inside and out") can you come, in the face of our own notions of the intrinsic honesty, of deep feeling and the moral importance of personal sincerity, to take the possibility of such a conception of selfhood seriously and appreciate, however inaccessible it is to you, its own sort of force.

III

Bali, where I worked both in another small provincial town, though one rather less drifting and dispirited, and, later, in an upland village of highly skilled musical instruments makers, is of course in many ways similar to Java, with which it shared a common culture to the fifteenth century. But at a deeper level, having continued Hindu while Java was, nominally at least, Islamized, it is quite different. The intricate, obsessive ritual life—Hindu, Buddhist, and Polynesian in about equal proportions—whose development was more or less cut off in Java, leaving its Indic spirit to turn reflective and phenomenological, even quietistic, in the way I have just described, flourished in Bali to reach levels of scale and flamboyance that have startled the world and made the Balinese a much more dramaturgical people with a self to match. What is philosophy in Java is theater in Bali.

As a result, there is in Bali a persistent and systematic attempt to stylize all aspects of personal expression to the point where anything idiosyncratic, anything characteristic of the individual merely because he is who he is physically, psychologically, or biographically, is muted in favor of his assigned place in the continuing and, so it is thought, never-changing pageant that is Balinese life. It is dramatis personae, not actors, that endure; indeed, it is dramatis personae, not actors, that in the proper sense really exist. Physically men come and go, mere incidents in a happenstance history, of no genuine importance even to themselves. But the masks they wear, the stage they occupy, the parts they play, and, most important, the spectacle they mount remain, and comprise not the facade but the substance of things, not least the self. Shakespeare's old-trouper view of the vanity of action in the face of mortality— all the world's a stage and we but poor players, content to strut our hour, and so on—makes no sense here. There is no make-believe; of course players perish, but the play does not, and it is the latter, the performed rather than the performer, that really matters.

Again, all this is realized not in terms of some general mood the anthropologist in his spiritual versatility somehow captures, but through a set of readily observable symbolic forms—an elaborate repertoire of designations and titles. The Balinese have at least a half-dozen major sorts of labels, ascriptive, fixed, and absolute, which one person can apply to another (or, of course, to himself) to place him among his fellows. There are birth-order markers, kinship terms, caste titles, sex indicators, teknonyms, and so on and so forth, each of which consists not of a mere collection of useful tags but a distinct and bounded, internally very complex, terminological system. When one applies one of these designations or titles (or, as is more common, several at once) to someone, one therefore defines him as a determinate point in a fixed pattern, as the temporary occupant of a particular, quite untemporary, cultural locus. To identify someone, yourself or somebody else, in Bali is thus to locate him within the familiar cast of characters—"king," "grandmother," "third-born," "Brahman"—of which the social drama is, like some stock company roadshow piece—*Charley's Aunt* or *Springtime for Henry*—inevitably composed.

The drama is of course not farce, and especially not transvestite farce, though there are such elements in it. It is an enactment of hierarchy, a theater of status. But that, though critical, is unpursuable here. The immediate point is that, in both their structure and their mode of operation, the terminological systems conduce to a view of the human person as an appropriate representative of a generic type, not a unique creature with a private fate. To see how they do this, how they tend to obscure the mere materialities—biological, psychological, historical—of individual existence in favor of standardized status qualities would involve an extended analysis. But perhaps a single example, the simplest further simplified, will suffice to suggest the pattern.

All Balinese receive what might be called birth-order names. There are four of these, "first-born," "second-born," "third-born," "fourth-born," after which they recycle, so that the fifth-born child is called again "first-born," the sixth "second-born," and so on. Further, these names are bestowed independently of the fates of the children. Dead children, even stillborn ones, count, so that in fact, in this still high-birthrate, high-mortality society, the names do not really tell you anything very reliable about the birth-order relations of concrete individuals. Within a set of living siblings, someone called "first-born" may actually be first, fifth, or ninth-born, or, if somebody is missing, almost anything in between, and someone called "second-born" may in fact be older. The birth-order naming system does not identify individuals as individuals, nor is it intended to; what it does is to suggest that, for all procreating couples, births form a circular succession of "firsts," "seconds," "thirds," and "fourths," an endless four-stage replication of an imperishable form. Physically men appear and disappear as the ephemerae they are, but socially the acting figures remain eternally the same as new "firsts," "seconds," and so on emerge from the timeless world of the gods to replace those who, dying, dissolve once more into it. All the designation and title systems, so I would argue, function in the same way: they represent the most time-saturated aspects of the human condition as but ingredients in an eternal, footlight present.

Nor is this sense the Balinese have of always being on stage a vague and ineffable one either. It is, in fact, exactly summed up in what is surely one of their experience-nearest concepts: *lek. Lek* has been variously translated or mistranslated ("shame" is the most common attempt); but what it really means is close to what we call stage fright. Stage fright consists, of course, in the fear that, for want of skill or self-control, or perhaps by mere accident, an aesthetic illusion will not be maintained, that the actor will show through his part. Aesthetic distance collapses, the audience (and the actor) lose sight of Hamlet and gain it, uncomfortably for all concerned, of humbling John Smith painfully miscast as the Prince of Denmark. In Bali, the case is the same: what is feared is that the public performance to which one's cultural location commits one will be botched and that the personality—as we would call it but the Balinese, of course, not believing in such a thing, would not—of the individual will break through to dissolve his standardized public identity. When this occurs, as it sometimes does, the immediacy of the moment is felt with excruciating intensity and men become suddenly and unwillingly creatural, locked in mutual embarrassment, as though they had happened upon each other's nakedness. It is the fear of faux pas, rendered only that much more probable by the extraordinary ritualization of daily life, that keeps social intercourse on its deliberately narrowed rails and protects the dramatistical sense of self against the disruptive threat implicit in the immediacy and spontaneity even the most passionate ceremoniousness cannot fully eradicate from face-to-face encounters.

IV

Morocco, Middle Eastern and dry rather than East Asian and wet, extrovert, fluid, activist, masculine, informal to a fault, a Wild West sort of place without the barrooms and the cattle drives, is another kettle of selves altogether. My work there, which began in the mid-sixties, has been centered around a moderately large town or small city in the foothills of the Middle Atlas, about twenty miles south of Fez. It's an old place, probably founded in the tenth century, conceivably even earlier. It has the walls, the gates, the narrow minarets rising to prayer-call platforms of a classical Muslim town, and, from a distance anyway, it is a rather pretty place, an irregular oval of blinding white set in the deep-sea-green of an olive grove oasis, the mountains, bronze and stony here, slanting up immediately behind it. Close up, it is less prepossessing, though more exciting: a labyrinth of passages and alleyways, three quarters of them blind, pressed in by wall-like buildings and curbside shops and filled with a simply astounding variety of very emphatic human beings. Arabs, Berbers, and Jews; tailors, herdsmen, and soldiers; people out of offices, people out of markets, people out of tribes; rich, superrich, poor, superpoor; locals, immigrants, mimic Frenchmen, unbending medievalists, and somewhere, according to the official government census for 1960, an unemployed Jewish airplane pilot—the town houses one of the finest collections of rugged individuals I, at least, have ever come up against. Next to Sefrou (the name of the place), Manhattan seems almost monotonous.

Yet no society consists of anonymous eccentrics bouncing off one another like billiard balls, and Moroccans too have symbolic means by which to sort people out from one another and form an idea of what it is to be a person. The main such means—not the only one, but I think the most important and the one I want to talk about particularly here—is a peculiar linguistic form called in Arabic the *nisba*. The word derives from the triliteral root, *n-s-b*, for "ascription," "attribution imputation relationship affinity," "correlation," "connection," "kinship." *Nsīb* means "in-law"; *nsab* means "to attribute or impute to"; *munāsaba* means "a relation," "an analogy," "a correspondence"; *mansūb* means "belonging to," "pertaining to"; and so on to at least a dozen derivatives, from *nassāb* ("genealogist") to *nīsbīya* ("[physical] relativity").

Nisba itself, then, refers to a combination morphological, grammatical, and semantic process that consists in transforming a noun into what we would call a relative adjective but what for Arabs is just another sort of noun by adding *ī* (f., *īya*): Sefrū/Sefrou—*Sefrūwī*/native son of Sefrou; *Sūs*/region of southwestern Morocco—*Sūsī*/man coming from that region; *Beni Yazga*/a tribe near Sefrou—*Yazgī*/a member of that tribe; *Yahūd*/the Jews as a people, Jewry—*Yahūdī*/a Jew; *'Adlun*/surname of a prominent Sefrou family—*'Adlūnī*/a member of that family. Nor is the procedure confined to this more or less straightforward "ethnicizing" use, but is employed in a wide range of domains to attribute relational properties to persons. For example, occupation (*hrār*/silk—*hrārī*/silk merchant); religious sect (*Darqāwā*/a mystical brotherhood—*Darqāwī*/an adept of that brotherhood or spiritual status), (*'Ali*/The Prophet's son-in-law—*'Alawī*/descendant of the Prophet's son-in-law, and thus of the Prophet).

Now, as once formed, nisbas tend to be incorporated into personal names—Umar Al-Buhadiwi/Umar of the Buhadu Tribe; Muhammed Al-Sussi/Muhammed from the Sus Region—this sort of adjectival attributive classification is quite publicly stamped onto an individual's identity. I was unable to find a single case where an individual was generally known, or known about, but his or her nisba was not. Indeed, Sefrouis are far more likely to be ignorant of how well-off a man is, how long he has been around, what his personal character is, or where exactly he lives, than they are of what his nisba is—Sussi or Sefroui, Buhadiwi or Adluni, Harari or Darqawi. (Of women to whom he is not related that is very likely to be all that he knows—or, more exactly, is permitted to know.) The selves that bump and jostle each other in the alleys of Sefrou gain their definition from associative relations they are imputed to have with the society that surrounds them. They are contextualized persons.

But the situation is even more radical than this; nisbas render men relative to their contexts, but as contexts themselves are relative, so too are nisbas, and the whole thing rises, so to speak, to the second power: relativism squared. Thus, at one level, everyone in Sefrou has the same nisba, or at least the potential of it—namely, Sefroui. However, within Sefrou such a nisba, precisely because it does not discriminate, will never be heard as part of an individual designation. It is only outside of Sefrou that the relationship to that particular context becomes identifying. Inside it, he is an Adluni, Alawi, Meghrawi, Ngadi, or whatever. And similarly within these categories: there are, for example, twelve different nisbas (Shakibis, Zuinis, and so forth) by means of which, among themselves, Sefrou Alawis distinguish one another.

The whole matter is far from regular: what level or sort of nisba is used and seems relevant and appropriate (to the users, that is) depends heavily on the situation. A man I knew who lived in Sefrou and worked in Fez but came from the Beni Yazgha tribe settled nearby—and from the Hima lineage of the Taghut subtraction of the Wulad Ben Ydir fraction within it—was known as a Sefroui to his work fellows in Fez, a Yazghi to all of us non-Yazghis in Sefrou, an Ydiri to other Beni Yazghas around, except for those who were themselves of the Wulad Ben Ydir fraction, who called him a Taghuti. As for the few other Taghutis, they called him a Himiwi. That is as far as things went here, but not as far as they can go, in either direction. Should, by chance, our friend journey to Egypt, he would become a Maghrebi, the nisba formed from the Arabic word for North Africa. The social contextualization of persons is pervasive and, in its curiously unmethodical way, systematic. Men do not float as bounded psychic entities, detached from their backgrounds and singularly named. As individualistic, even willful, as the Moroccans in fact are, their identity is an attribute they borrow from their setting.

Now as with the Javanese inside/outside, smooth/rough phenomenological sort of reality dividing, and the absolutizing Balinese title systems, the nisba way of looking at persons—as though they were outlines waiting to be filled in—is not an isolated custom, but part of a total pattern of social life. This pattern is, like the others, difficult to characterize succinctly, but surely one of its outstanding features is a promiscuous tumbling in public settings of varieties of men kept carefully segregated in private ones—all-out cosmopolitanism in the streets, strict communalism (of which the famous secluded woman is only the most striking index) in the home. This is, indeed, the so-called mosaic system of social organization so often held to be characteristic of the Middle East generally: differently shaped and colored chips jammed in irregularly together to generate an intricate overall design within which their individual distinctiveness remains nonetheless intact. Nothing if not diverse, Moroccan society does not cope with its diversity by sealing it into castes, isolating it into tribes, dividing it into ethnic groups, or covering it over with some common-denominator concept of nationality, though, fitfully, all have now and then been tried. It copes with it by distinguishing, with elaborate precision, the contexts—marriage, worship, and to an extent diet, law, and education—within which men are separated by their dissimilitudes, and those—work, friendship, politics, trade—where, however warily and however conditionally, they are connected by them.

To such a social pattern, a concept of selfhood which marks public identity contextually and relativistically, but yet does so in terms—tribal, territorial, linguistic, religious, familial—that grow out of the more private and settled arenas of life and have a deep and permanent resonance there, would seem particularly appropriate. Indeed, the social pattern would seem virtually to create this concept of selfhood, for it produces a situation where people interact with one another in terms of categories whose meaning is almost purely positional, location in the general mosaic, leaving the substantive content of the categories, what they mean subjectively as experienced forms of life, aside as something properly concealed in apartments, temples, and tents. Nisba discriminations can be more specific or less, indicate location within the mosaic roughly or finely, and they can be adapted to almost any changes in circumstance. But they cannot carry with them more than the most sketchy, outline implications concerning what men so named as a rule are like. Calling a man a Sefroui is like calling him a San Franciscan: it classifies him, but it does not type him; it places him without portraying him.

It is the nisba system's capacity to do this—to create a framework within which persons can be identified in terms of supposedly immanent character-istics (speech, blood, faith, provenance, and the rest)—and yet to minimize the impact of those characteristics in determining the practical relations among such persons in markets, shops, bureaus, fields, cafes, baths, and roadways that makes it so central to the Moroccan idea of the self. Nisba-type categorization leads, paradoxically, to a hyperindividualism in public relationships, because by providing only a vacant sketch, and that shifting, of who the actors are—Yazghis, Adlunis, Buhadiwis, or whatever—it leaves the rest, that is, almost everything, to be filled in by the process of interaction itself. What makes the mosaic work is the confidence that one can be as totally pragmatic, adaptive, opportunistic, and generally ad hoc in one's relations with others—a fox among foxes, a crocodile among crocodiles—as one wants without any risk of losing one's sense of who one is. Selfhood is never in danger because, outside the immediacies of procreation and prayer, only its coordinates are asserted.

V

Now, without trying to tie up the dozens of loose ends I have not only left dangling in these rather breathless accounts of the senses of selfhood of nearly ninety million people but have doubtless frazzled even more, let us return to the question of what all this can tell us, or could if it were done adequately, about "the native's point of view" in Java, Bali, and Morocco. Are we, in describing symbol uses, describing perceptions, sentiments, outlooks, experiences? And in what sense? What do we claim when we claim that we understand the semiotic means by which, in this case, persons are defined to one another? That we know words or that we know minds?

In answering this question, it is necessary, I think, first to notice the characteristic intellectual movement, the inward conceptual rhythm, in each of these analyses, and indeed in all similar analyses, including those of Malinowski—namely, a continuous dialectical tacking between the most local of local detail and the most global of global structure in such a way as to bring them into simultaneous view. In seeking to uncover the Javanese, Balinese, or

Moroccan sense of self, one oscillates restlessly between the sort of exotic minutiae (lexical antitheses, categorical schemes, morphophonemic transformations) that make even the best ethnographies a trial to read and the sort of sweeping characterizations ("quietism," "dramatism," "contextualism") that make all but the most pedestrian of them somewhat implausible. Hopping back and forth between the whole conceived through the parts that actualize it and the parts conceived through the whole that motivates them, we seek to turn them, by a sort of intellectual perpetual motion, into explications of one another.

All this is, of course, but the now familiar trajectory of what Dilthey called the hermeneutic circle, and my argument here is merely that it is as central to ethnographic interpretation, and thus to the penetration of other people's modes of thought, as it is to literary, historical, philological, psychoanalytic, or biblical interpretation, or for that matter to the informal annotation of everyday experience we call common sense. In order to follow a baseball game one must understand what a bat, a hit, an inning, a left fielder, a squeeze play, a hanging curve, and a tightened infield are, and what the game in which these "things" are elements is all about. When an *explication de texts* critic like Leo Spitzer attempts to interpret Keats's "Ode on a Grecian Urn," he does so by repetitively asking himself the alternating question "What is the whole poem about?" and "What exactly has Keats seen (or chosen to show us) depicted on the urn he is describing?," emerging at the end of an advancing spiral of general observations and specific remarks with a reading of the poem as an assertion of the triumph of the aesthetic mode of perception over the historical. In the same way, when a meanings-and-symbols ethnographer like myself attempts to find out what some pack of natives conceive a person to be, he moves back and forth between asking himself, "What is the general form of their life?" and "What exactly are the vehicles in which that form is embodied?," emerging in the end of a similar sort of spiral with the notion that they see the self as a composite, a persona, or a point in a pattern. You can no more know what *lek* is if you do not know what Balinese dramatism is than you can know what a catcher's mitt is if you do not know what baseball is. And you can no more know what mosaic social organization is if you do not know what a nisba is than you can know what Keats's Platonism is if you are unable to grasp, to use Spitzer's own formulation, the "intellectual thread of thought" captured in such fragment phrases as "Attic shape," "silent form," "bride of quietness," "cold pastoral," "silence and slow time," "peaceful citadel," or "ditties of no tone."

In short, accounts of other people's subjectivities can be built up without recourse to pretensions to more-than-normal capacities for ego effacement and fellow feeling. Normal capacities in these respects are, of course, essential, as is their cultivation, if we expect people to tolerate our intrusions into their lives at all and accept us as persons worth talking to. I am certainly not arguing for insensitivity here, and hope I have not demonstrated it. But whatever accurate or half-accurate sense one gets of what one's informants are, as the phrase goes, really like does not come from the experience of that acceptance as such, which is part of one's own biography, not of theirs. It comes from the ability to construe their modes of expression, what I would call their symbol systems, which such an acceptance allows one to work toward developing. Understanding the form and pressure of, to use the dangerous word one more time, natives' inner lives is more like grasping a proverb, catching an allusion, seeing a joke—or, as I have suggested, reading a poem—than it is like achieving communion.

Notes

1. Ed. note. James D. Watson, *The Double Helix: A Personal Account of the Discovery of the Structure of DNA*. New York: New American Library, 1969; Bronislaw Malinowski, *A Diary in the Strict Sense of the Term*. New York: Harcourt, Brace & World, 1967.
2. Ed. note. A *Doppelgänger* is a person's ghostly double or shadow figure.

Part II

The Autonomy of Religious Experience

INTRODUCTION

⤜⤛

The Enlightenment's Critique of Religion

Much of the modern study of religion traces itself back to the Enlightenment, a period of time in European history, roughly associated with the eighteenth century, when the "canons of reason and the human intellect" were thought to triumph over what were considered to be the mere superstitions and ignorance connected with religion (the next part will explore this in more detail). By placing the power to know the world in each individual's own use of their intellect, as opposed to placing this power in the mind of a deity, in a church tradition, or in a supposedly sacred text, the Enlightenment laid the foundations necessary for conceiving of religion as but one human institution among others. In other words, because religious claims and behaviors came to be considered as simply misguided, deluded, or irrational claims and behaviors, those involved in their analysis have no reason to trust the judgments of the people who are making these claims and practising these irrational behaviors.

Therefore, the Enlightenment provides the foundation of a strong outsider position in the study of religion. Such a study of religion consists in submitting the irrational aspects of human behavior to rational analysis. There may be no better example than that of the Scottish philosopher David Hume (1711–1776) who argues, in his significantly titled *A Natural History of Religion* (1757), that religious behaviors and beliefs can be traced to certain basic fears and hopes shared by all human beings. To study religion as something fundamentally religious—something studied only in terms of the religious person's own expectations and criteria—is, therefore, to fail to study its actual causes, these assorted hopes and fears of historically embedded human beings. Religion is none other than a human creation.

Friedrich Schleiermacher and the Feeling of Absolute Dependence

For those who wished to advocate the importance of religion in the life of an individual, let alone a nation, such an emphasis on human reason and intellect as the highest and final judge in all matters of knowledge left little or no room for expressing religious faith. It was in just such a climate that the young Friedrich Schleiermacher (1768–1834) attempted to persuade his enlightened and rational peers that there was indeed a role for religion and religious commitment in their lives. Schleiermacher was a German Protestant preacher who, in 1799, published his *On Religion: Speeches to Its Cultured Despisers* in an attempt to redress the heavy toll taken on religion and the religious life by the Enlightenment emphasis on the use of individual reason. Simply put, Schleiermacher attempted to persuade his readers (the so-called "cultured despisers" of religion) that religion did not conflict with their own interest in matters of rationality; if anything, he argued that religion, or religious feelings, lay deep within our own most basic experiences of what it is to be a sentient, living being.

Contrary to the rationalist emphasis that characterized many of his contemporaries, Schleiermacher represented the romantic tradition, arguing that religion eluded the critique of reason for in its essence it is not rational *or* irrational; instead, religion is an emotional state that possessed as much reality as did our experiences of the material world around us. Just as the material or natural world had to be understood in terms of rationality and conceptual thought, so too religious experiences had to be understood in terms of intuition and feeling. For example, just as a completely rational person can simultaneously feel happiness without becoming irrational, so too a rational person can have religious feelings. Schleiermacher's definition of religion, then, which he elaborated in subsequent works which made him one of, if not *the* most influential Protestant theologian of the modern era, is that religion is a highly personal feeling, an immediate consciousness, of absolute dependence on something other than oneself. That thing upon which human beings are absolutely (as opposed to relatively dependent) he called "God."

In response to the rationalist, Enlightenment critique of religion, Schleiermacher firmly placed religion within the interior, private, and personal realm of experience, emotion, and feeling. Religious feeling, he argued, is an aspect of what it is to be human, just as reason and aesthetic judgments are fundamental to human experiences of the world. The implication for the insider/outsider problem is that religious feelings are preeminently a matter for the insider; any attempt to translate, or to *reduce* these private feelings and emotions to such exterior causes as politics or psychoses is bound to misinterpret and misconstrue them. The essence of religion, this feeling of being absolutely dependent on God, can therefore only be understood from the inside, through a direct intuition. The outsider, the one who emphasizes the role to be played by rationality, simply misses the point if they think that one can study religion objectively from afar. Simply put, religion cannot be reduced to something other than a religious impulse! Understandably, then, the study of such phenomena as mystical experiences becomes attractive to such scholarship. Many writers in this tradition are therefore indebted to Schleiermacher's attempt to restore to religion what the Enlightenment had seemingly taken from it.

To Feel is to Know

With regard to the utter priority of personal religious experience, the influential works of Rudolf Otto (1869–1937) in Germany, Joachim Wach (1898-1955) in Germany and then America, and Mircea Eliade (1907–1986) first in Romania and eventually in America at the University of Chicago, can all be placed within this same school of thought. Each places emphasis on the private and emotional quality of religion, thereby necessitating that the scholar of religion be religious to avoid studying what Schleiermacher had earlier characterized as the mere externals of religion which amount to a dead thing without the immediate experience of religious feelings. Accordingly, each of these subsequent writers figure prominently in a scholarly tradition that attempted to develop methods of research capable of bridging the gap between the inquiring scholar and the insider's private religious feeling by understanding both to be capable of experiencing the same religious emotions.

There may be no better example of placing emphasis on the authority of the religious insider than the opening to the third chapter of Rudolf Otto's famous work *Das Heilige* (*The Idea of the Holy*, 1917). After defining the experience of religion as the feeling of a tremendous and fascinating mystery (the *mysterium tremendum et fascinans*) which simultaneously compels and repels (after all that which is holy is often as attractive as it is frightening), Otto recommends bluntly that those who have never known such a religious feeling should stop reading his book. One cannot discuss such matters of religious psychology, he goes on to suggest, with those who know what it is like to be hungry but have never known such a "deeply-felt religious experience."

We find here the legacy of Schleiermacher who wrote that religious feelings "must be indubitably your own feelings, and not mere stale descriptions of the feelings of others, which could at best issue in a wretched imitation." In the history of the study of religion there may be no more explicit statement of the insider's authority than Otto's. Much like artists who claim their work to possess a creative essence, an essence that exceeds the grasp of the art critic for example, so too, Otto argues, the essence of religion, a feeling of the *mysterium*, slips through the fingers of the outsider.

An Affinity to the Subject: Understanding and Interpreting

Expelled from his teaching position at Leipzig by the Nazis in 1935, Joachim Wach eventually headed up the University of Chicago's soon to be influential History of Religions program until his unexpected death in 1955 (Mircea Eliade followed Wach as head of the program). In this essay (originally published in German in 1935 and subsequently translated and published in English in 1967), Wach makes it quite clear that the study of religion requires that scholars not only learn to describe accurately but also employ their imagination and creative intuition, based on their own sense of the numinous, when attempting to interpret the meaning of other people's religious claims and behaviors. For Wach, as it was for Otto, the study of religion is, by definition, limited to one group of insiders talking to another group of insiders by means of imaginative leaps. Or, as Wach wrote in the first chapter to his book on the sociology of religion, the "inquirer must feel an affinity to his subject, and he must be trained to interpret his material with sympathetic understanding." Moreover, such a study actually serves to enhance the scholar's own religious faith. Clearly, nonreligious scholars of religion cannot make such leaps and, therefore, have little access to their subjects' experiences.

We must be clear to recognize the emphasis placed on the word "understand"—what we find here is none other than the notion of *Verstehen* that was discussed in the General Introduction. To understand in this sense implies that one re-experiences the feelings of others (empathy) and comes to appreciate their meanings as if they were one's own. For Wach, the study of religion (or *Religionswissenschaft* in German, meaning, literally, the science of religion), then, comprises the interpretive art of discerning the meaning of other people's subjective experiences.

Insights into "Human Nature" as the Basis of Socio-Political Claims

One of the more important implications of this emphasis on re-experiencing other people's subjective experiences, meanings, and intentions is that scholarship believed to capture such meanings can form the basis of other claims, sometimes claims with social relevance. This may indeed have been what Wach meant when, in his essay, he discussed the "practical significance of *Religionswissenschaft*." On a number of occasions, the historian of religions Mircea Eliade used his conclusions concerning what he saw as the common nature of all human religious experiences to authorize his own practical claims concerning how scholars of religion should reinvigorate so-called secular Western culture by reintroducing what he labelled as sacred values housed in the texts and peoples they study. His essay, "A New Humanism" (1961) makes this practical, social relevance of scholars of religion quite clear. However, their input into current social issues is only as authoritative as their insights into the human condition. If Eliade's claims concerning human nature are not as universal as he believes, then we should seriously question the social and political relevance and authority of scholarship based on these insights.

The Theoretical, Social, and Gendered Context of the Scholar

Rosalind Shaw's critique concerns the suspect basis of all scholarship that presumes religion to be an essentially private experience, as opposed to an item of public debate and analysis. As a feminist anthropologist, she studies the manner in which social, economic, and political power and privilege are generated, granted, and denied to people based on their gender. Therefore, she critiques the way in which scholars often presume religion to be *sui generis*: a Latin phrase meaning, simply, that religion is one of a kind, self-caused, and cannot be reduced to such things as culture, politics, or society. Or, as Eliade put it, because religion is utterly unique and therefore incomparable, it must be understood *on its own plan of reference*. Shaw understands the assumption that religion is *sui generis*, or irreducible, to be at the heart of scholarly attempts to protect historical, human data from the kind of critical analysis carried out by scholars who, like Raymond Firth, see all human practices as byproducts of complex social, political, economic, historical, and psychological factors of which the insider is not necessarily aware. In particular, those scholars committed to understanding human institutions and knowledge as, in some part, influenced by such factors as gender, class, and race, will be interested in discarding the notion of *sui generis* religion as the first step toward conceiving of religion as but one aspect of human culture, to be studied in the same way in which we study other aspects of culture.

Take, for example, one of the founders of the phenomenology of religion, Gerardus van der Leeuw. In describing the insider's quest for meaning, he likens it both to a beautiful flower and to someone's knowledge "that his wife is beautiful, that she can work and bear children." By means of this process of finding hidden meaning in the events he studies, van der Leeuw maintains that "he finds the secret of the flower and of woman; and so he discovers their religious significance." It is worthwhile to speculate precisely what scholars such as Shaw would make of this claim. For in the space of a few words we learn that the pronoun "he" does indeed refer to men and not women, that women, like flowers, are understood only in terms of their utility to men (they either are beautiful or can have children), that women are used by men to make meaning in men's lives, and that such meaning-making men come to know the secrets not of historical women but the "secret of ... woman" in the abstract—not a real person but a "collective subject" as Shaw phrases it. That all of this activity has "religious significance" suggests that the categories of *sui generis* religion and privatized religious experience are busy doing some kind of work to privilege one gender over another.

Contrary to Wach and Eliade, Raymond Firth makes a compelling case that because a subject's inner states, motives, feelings, and disposition are not open to empirical analysis (analysis by means of one of the observer's five senses), the researcher cannot study them *as they really are* but only *infer* what they might be. In a way, Firth's critique might also apply to Shaw's own essay, since much feminist scholarship is just as hermeneutically based as much scholarship on religion, intent not on recovering the experiences of some male-based ideal type, known as *Homo religiosus*, but on recovering actual women's lived experiences. Instead, Firth suggests that the scholar, as outsider, has access simply to what is publicly observable, such as human behavior. From such observations scholars can attempt to infer their subject's motives and intentions but they must always be aware that such speculations are just that, imaginative, approximate speculations. Lacking Wach's faith in a universally shared basis that transcends cultural and historical context, a basis that intuitively unites insider and outsider, Firth has little choice but to presume that "complete access [to the meanings and intentions of another] is impossible."

Accordingly, Firth advocates explanation rather than interpretation (as favored by Wach), discerning causes rather than the inner meanings of people's behavior. Almost as if he had Wach in mind, Firth writes: "Claims of writers and speakers of all kinds, from poets to preachers, to 'understand' what other people think and feel, or what they mean by what they do, rest upon ... broad interpretation [that offers only varying degrees of success]." By declining complete access to other people's intentions, Firth anticipates a later essay in this anthology by immediately identifying the role played by researchers in setting the parameters of their study, what many term the reflexive aspect of scholarship—an approach which is actually highly conducive to feminist scholarship, suggesting that the essays by Firth and Shaw ultimately complement each other. In Firth's words, scholars "cannot immediately grasp or communicate reality; [they] can only mediate it" by means of categories, concepts, questions, hunches, and experiences that they bring with them to their work. In this brief quotation we have the anticipation of both the need to explicitly organize these concepts and questions into a coherent theory to direct one's research as well as the need to recognize the role researchers themselves play in shaping their own scholarship.

The initial essays in this part develop a coherent line of thought concerning the social and political autonomy of deeply felt religious experiences. From Otto to Eliade, they all agree that religion cannot be *reduced* to issues of psychology, economics, politics, gender, or sociology. Instead, religion represents a private realm, so private, in fact, that we are forced to question how it is that Otto,

Wach, and Eliade can *defend* their views in public. For, if our work in the study of religion is based simply on an intuition shared only by a few, then how do we confirm or argue against these varying insights in the public university classroom or in scholarly periodicals? Must we simply share them and experience them as Otto suggested? Precisely how do we know that we are sharing the same thing? The question Firth and Shaw force us to ask is whether such a position constitutes the *study* or the *practice* of religion.

5

RUDOLF OTTO, *The Idea of the Holy*, Chapters I–III

ॐॐ

Chapter I: The Rational and the Non-rational

It is essential to every theistic conception of God, and most of all to the Christian, that it designates and precisely characterizes deity by the attributes spirit, reason, purpose, good will, supreme power, unity, selfhood. The nature of God is thus thought of by analogy with our human nature of reason and personality; only, whereas in ourselves we are aware of this as qualified by restriction and limitation, as applied to God the attributes we use are "completed," i.e., thought as absolute and unqualified. Now all these attributes constitute clear and definite concepts: they can be grasped by the intellect; they can be analyzed by thought; they even admit of definition. An object that can thus be thought conceptually may be termed rational. The nature of deity described in the attributes above mentioned is, then, a rational nature; and a religion which recognizes and maintains such a view of God is in so far a "rational" religion. Only on such terms is belief possible in contrast to mere feeling. And of Christianity at least it is false that "feeling is all, the name but sound and smoke";[1]—where "name" stands for conception or thought. Rather we count this the very mark and criterion of a religion's high rank and superior value—that it should have no lack of conceptions about God; that it should admit knowledge—the knowledge that comes by faith—of the transcendent in terms of conceptual thought, whether those already mentioned or others which continue and develop them. Christianity not only possesses such conceptions but possesses them in unique clarity and abundance, and this is, though not the sole or even the chief, yet a very real sign of its superiority over religions of other forms and at other levels. This must be asserted at the outset and with the most positive emphasis.

But, when this is granted, we have to be on our guard against an error which would lead to a wrong and one-sided interpretation of religion. This is the view that the essence of deity can be given completely and exhaustively in such "rational" attributions as have been referred to above and in others like them. It is not an unnatural misconception. We are prompted to it by the traditional language of edification, with its characteristic phraseology and ideas; by the learned treatment of religious themes in sermon and theological instruction; and further even by our Holy Scriptures themselves. In all these cases the "rational" element occupies the foreground, and often nothing else seems to be present at all. But this is after all to be expected. All language, insofar as it consists of words, purports to convey ideas or concepts—that is what language means—and the more clearly and unequivocally it does so, the better the language. And hence expositions of religious truth in language inevitably tend to stress the "rational" attributes of God.

But though the above mistake is thus a natural one enough, it is nonetheless seriously misleading. For so far are these "rational" attributes from exhausting the idea of deity, that they in fact imply a non-rational or supra-rational Subject of which they are predicates. They are "essential" (and not merely "accidental") attributes of that subject, but they are also, it is important to notice, *synthetic* essential attributes. That is to say, we have to predicate them a subject which they qualify, but which in its deeper essence is not, nor indeed can be, comprehended in them; which rather requires comprehension of a quite different kind. Yet, though it eludes the conceptual way of understanding, it must be in some way or other within our grasp, else absolutely nothing could be asserted of it. And even mysticism, in speaking of it as 'ἄρρητον, the ineffable, does not really mean to imply that absolutely nothing can be asserted of the object of the religious consciousness; otherwise, mysticism could exist only in unbroken silence, whereas what has generally been a characteristic of the mystics is their copious eloquence.

Here for the first time we come up against the contrast between rationalism and profounder religion, and with this contrast and its signs we shall be repeatedly concerned in what follows. We have here in fact the first and most distinctive mark of rationalism, with which all the rest are bound up. It is not that which is commonly asserted, that rationalism is the denial, and its opposite the affirmation, of the miraculous. That is manifestly a wrong or at least a very superficial distinction. For the traditional theory of the miraculous as the occasional breach in the causal nexus in nature by a Being who himself instituted and must therefore be master of it—this theory is itself as massively "rational" as it is possible to be. Rationalists have often enough acquiesced in the possibility of the miraculous in this sense; they have even themselves contributed to frame a theory of it; whereas anti-rationalists have been often indifferent to the whole controversy about miracles. The difference between rationalism and its opposite is to be found elsewhere. It resolves itself rather into a peculiar difference of *quality* in the mental attitude and emotional content of the religious life itself. All depends upon this: in our idea of God is the non-rational overborne, even perhaps wholly excluded, by the rational? Or conversely, does the non-rational itself preponderate over the rational? Looking at the matter thus, we see that the common dictum, that orthodoxy itself has been the mother of rationalism, is in some measure well founded. It is not simply that orthodoxy was preoccupied with doctrine and the framing of dogma, for these have been no less a concern of the wildest mystics. It is rather that orthodoxy found in the construction of dogma and doctrine no way to do justice to the non-rational aspect of its subject. So far from keeping the non-rational element in religion alive in the heart of the religious experience, orthodox Christianity manifestly failed to recognize its value, and by this failure gave to the idea of God a one-sidedly intellectualistic and rationalistic interpretation.

This bias to rationalization still prevails, not only in theology but in the science of comparative religion in general, and from top to bottom of it. The modern students of mythology, and those who pursue research into the religion of "primitive man" and attempt to reconstruct the "bases" or "sources" of religion, are all victims to it. Men do not, of course, in these cases employ those lofty "rational" concepts which we took as our point of departure; but they tend to take these concepts and their gradual "evolution" as setting the main problem of their inquiry, and fashion ideas and notions of lower value, which they regard as paving the way for them. It is always in terms of concepts and ideas that the subject is pursued, "natural" ones, moreover, such as have a place in the general sphere of man's ideational life, and are not specifically "religious." And then with a resolution and cunning which one can hardly help admiring, men shut their eyes to that which is quite unique in the religious experience, even in its most primitive manifestations. But it is rather a matter for astonishment than for admiration! For if there be any single domain of human experience that presents us with something unmistakably specific and unique, peculiar to itself, assuredly it is that of the religious life. In truth the enemy has often a keener vision in this matter than either the champion of religion or the neutral and professedly impartial theorist. For the adversaries on their side know very well that the entire "bother about mysticism" has nothing to do with "reason" and "rationality."

And so it is salutary that we should be incited to notice that religion is not exclusively contained and exhaustively comprised in any series of "rational" assertions; and it is well worth while to attempt to bring the relation of the different "moments" of religion to one another clearly before the mind, so that its nature may become more manifest.

This attempt we are now to make with respect to the quite distinctive category of the holy or sacred.

Chapter II: "Numen" and the "Numinous"

"Holiness"—"the holy"—is a category of interpretation and valuation peculiar to the sphere of religion. It is, indeed, applied by transference to another sphere—that of ethics—but it is not itself derived from this. While it is complex, it contains a quite specific element or "moment," which sets it apart from "the rational" in the meaning we gave to that word above, and which remains inexpressible—an 'ἄρρητον or *ineffable*—in the sense that it completely eludes apprehension in terms of concepts. The same thing is true (to take a quite different region of experience) of the category of the beautiful.

Now these statements would be untrue from the outset if "the holy" were merely what is meant by the word, not only in common parlance, but in philosophical, and generally even in theological usage. The fact is we have come to use the words "holy," "sacred" (*heilig*) in an entirely derivative sense, quite different from that which they originally bore. We generally take "holy" as meaning "completely good"; it is the absolute moral attribute, denoting the consummation of moral goodness. In this sense Kant calls the will which remains unwaveringly obedient to the moral law from the motive of duty a "holy" will; here clearly we have simply the *perfectly moral* will. In the same way we may speak of the holiness or sanctity of duty or law, meaning merely that they are imperative upon conduct and universally obligatory.

But this common usage of the term is inaccurate. It is true that all this moral significance is contained in the word "holy," but it includes in addition—as even we cannot but feel—a clear overplus of meaning, and this it is now our task to isolate. Nor is this merely a later or acquired meaning; rather, "holy," or at least the equivalent words in Latin and Greek, in Semitic and other ancient languages, denoted first and foremost *only* this overplus: if the ethical element was present at all, at any rate it was not original and never constituted the whole meaning of the word. Any one who uses it today does undoubtedly always feel "the morally good" to be implied in "holy"; and accordingly in our inquiry into that element which is separate and peculiar to the idea of the holy it will be useful, at least for the temporary purpose of the investigation, to invent a special term to stand for "the holy" *minus* its moral factor or "moment," and, as we can now add, minus its "rational" aspect altogether.

It will be our endeavor to suggest this unnamed Something to the reader as far as we may, so that he may himself feel it. There is no religion in which it does not live as the real innermost core, and without it no religion would be worthy of the name. It is pre-eminently a living force in the Semitic religions, and of these again in none has it such vigor as in that of the Bible. Here, too, it has a name of its own, viz. the Hebrew *qādôsh*, to which the Greek αγιος and the Latin *sanctus*, and, more accurately still, *sacer*, are the corresponding terms. It is not, of course, disputed that these terms in all three languages connote, as part of their meaning, *good, absolute goodness*, when, that is, the notion has ripened and reached the highest stage in its development. And we then use the word "holy" to translate them. But this "holy" then represents the gradual shaping and filling in with ethical meaning, or what we shall call the "schematization," of what was a unique original feeling-response, which can be in itself ethically neutral and claims consideration in its own right. And when this moment or element first emerges and begins its long development, all those expressions (*qādôsh, 'ἅγιος, sacer*, etc.,) mean beyond all question something quite other than "the good." This is universally agreed by contemporary criticism, which rightly explains the rendering of *qādôsh* by "good" as a mistranslation and unwarranted "rationalization" or "moralization" of the term.

Accordingly, it is worth while, as we have said, to find a word to stand for this element in isolation, this "extra" in the meaning of "holy" above and beyond the meaning of goodness. By means of a special term we shall the better be able, first, to keep the meaning clearly apart and distinct, and second, to apprehend and classify connectedly whatever subordinate forms or stages of development it may show. For this purpose I adopt a word coined from the Latin *numen*. *Omen* has given us "ominous," and there is no reason why from *numen* we should not similarly form a word "numinous." I shall speak, then, of a unique "numinous" category of value and of a definitely "numinous" state of mind, which is always found wherever the category is applied. This mental state is perfectly *sui generis* and irreducible to any other; and therefore, like every absolutely primary and elementary datum, while it admits of being discussed, it cannot be strictly defined. There is only one way to help another to an understanding of it. He must be guided and led on by consideration and discussion of the matter through the ways of his own mind, until he reach the point at which "the numinous" in him perforce begins to stir, to start into life and into consciousness. We can co-operate in this process by bringing before his notice all that can be found in other regions of the mind, already known and familiar, to resemble, or again to afford some special contrast to, the particular experience we wish to elucidate. Then we must add: "This X of ours is not precisely *this* experience, but akin to this one and the opposite of that other. Cannot you now realize for yourself what it is?" In other words our X cannot, strictly speaking, be taught, it can only be evoked, awakened in the mind; as everything that comes "of the spirit" must be awakened.

Chapter III: The Elements in the "Numinous"

Creature-Feeling

The reader is invited to direct his mind to a moment of deeply-felt religious experience, as little as possible qualified by other forms of consciousness.

Whoever cannot do this, whoever knows no such moments in his experience, is requested to read no farther; for it is not easy to discuss questions of religious psychology with one who can recollect the emotions of his adolescence, the discomforts of indigestion, or, say, social feelings, but cannot recall any intrinsically religious feelings. We do not blame such a one, when he tries for himself to advance as far as he can with the help of such principles of explanation as he knows, interpreting "aesthetics" in terms of sensuous pleasure, and "religion" as a function of the gregarious instinct and social standards, or as something more primitive still. But the artist, who for his part has an intimate personal knowledge of the distinctive element in the aesthetic experience, will decline his theories with thanks, and the religious man will reject them even more uncompromisingly.

Next, in the probing and analysis of such states of the soul as that of solemn worship, it will be well if regard be paid to what is unique in them rather than to what they have in common with other similar states. To be *rapt* in worship is one thing; to be morally *uplifted* by the contemplation of a good deed is another; and it is not to their common features, but to those elements of emotional content peculiar to the first that we would have attention directed as precisely as possible. As Christians we undoubtedly here first meet with feelings familiar enough in a weaker form in other departments of experience, such as feelings of gratitude, trust, love, reliance, humble submission, and dedication. But this does not by any means exhaust the content of religious worship. Not in any of these have we got the special features of the quite unique and incomparable experience of solemn worship. In what does this consist?

Schleiermacher has the credit of isolating a very important element in such an experience. This is the "feeling of dependence." But this important discovery of Schleiermacher is open to criticism in more than one respect.

In the first place, the feeling or emotion which he really has in mind in this phrase is in its specific quality not a "feeling of dependence" in the "natural" sense of the word. As such, other domains of life and other regions of experience than the religious occasion the feeling, as a sense of personal insufficiency and impotence, a consciousness of being determined by circumstances and environment. The feeling of which Schleiermacher wrote has an undeniable analogy with these states of mind: they serve as an indication to it, and its nature may be elucidated by them, so that, by following the direction in which they point, the feeling itself may be spontaneously felt. But the feeling is at the same time also qualitatively different from such analogous states of mind. Schleiermacher himself, in a way, recognizes this by distinguishing the feeling of pious or religious dependence from all other feelings of dependence. His mistake is in making the distinction merely that between "absolute" and "relative" dependence, and therefore a difference of degree and not of intrinsic quality. What he overlooks is that, in giving the feeling the name "feeling of dependence" at all, we are really employing what is no more than a very close analogy. Anyone who compares and contrasts the two states of mind introspectively will find out, I think, what I mean. It cannot be expressed by means of anything else, just because it is so primary and elementary a datum in our psychical life, and therefore only definable through itself. It may perhaps help him if I cite a well-known example, in which the precise "moment" or element of religious feeling of which we are speaking is most actively present. When Abraham ventures to plead with God for the men of Sodom, he says (Genesis 18:27): "Behold now, I have taken upon me to speak unto the Lord, which am but dust and ashes." There you have a self-confessed "feeling of dependence," which is yet at the same time far more than, and something other than, *merely* a feeling of dependence. Desiring to give it a name of its own, I propose to call it "creature-consciousness" or creature-feeling. It is the emotion of a creature, submerged and overwhelmed by its own nothingness in contrast to that which is supreme above all creatures.

It is easily seen that, once again, this phrase, whatever it is, is not a *conceptual* explanation of the matter. All that this new term, "creature-feeling," can express, is the note of submergence into nothingness before an overpowering, absolute might of some kind; whereas everything turns upon the *character* of this overpowering might, a character which cannot be expressed verbally, and can only be suggested indirectly through the tone and content of a man's feeling-response to it. And this response must be directly experienced in oneself to be understood.

We have now to note a second defect in the formulation of Schleiermacher's principle. The religious category discovered by him, by whose means he professes to determine the real content of the religious emotion, is merely a category of *self*-valuation, in the sense of self-depreciation. According to him the religious emotion would be directly and primarily a sort of *self*-consciousness, a feeling concerning oneself in a special, determined relation, viz. one's dependence. Thus, according to Schleiermacher, I can only come upon the very fact of God as the result of an inference, that is, by reasoning to a cause beyond myself to account for my "feeling of dependence." But this is entirely opposed to the psychological facts of the case. Rather, the "creature-feeling" is itself a first subjective concomitant and effect of another feeling-element, which casts it like a shadow, but which in itself indubitably has immediate and primary reference to an object outside the self.[2]

Now this object is just what we have already spoken of as "the numinous." For the "creature-feeling" and the sense of dependence to arise in the mind the "numen" must be experienced as present, a *numen praesens*, as is in the case of Abraham. There must be felt a something "numinous," something bearing the character of a "numen," to which the mind turns spontaneously; or (which is the same thing in other words) these feelings can only arise in the mind as accompanying emotions when the category of "the numinous" is called into play.

Notes

1. Goethe, *Faust*.
2. This is so manifestly borne out by experience that it must be about the first thing to force itself upon the notice of psychologists analyzing facts of religion. There is a certain naïveté in the following passage from William James's *Varieties of Religious Experience*, where, alluding to the origin of the Grecian representations of the gods, he says: "As regards the origin of the Greek gods, we need not at present seek an opinion. But the whole array of our instances leads to a conclusion something like this: It is as if there were in the human consciousness *a sense of reality, a feeling of objective presence, a perception* of what we may call '*something there,*' more deep and more general than any of the special and particular 'senses' by which the current psychology supposes existent realities to be originally revealed." (The italics are James's own.) James is debarred by his empiricist and pragmatist standpoint from coming to a recognition of faculties of knowledge and potentialities of thought in the spirit itself, and he is therefore obliged to have recourse to somewhat singular and mysterious hypotheses to explain this fact. But he grasps the fact itself clearly enough and is sufficient of a realist not to explain it away. But this "feeling of reality," the feeling of a "numinous" *object* objectively given, must be posited as a primary immediate datum of consciousness, and the "feeling of dependence" is then a consequence, following very closely upon it, viz. a depreciation of the *subject* in his own eyes. The latter presupposes the former.

6

JOACHIM WACH, *The Meaning and Task of the History of Religions (Religionswissenschaft)*[1]

❧❧

On special occasions a discipline has the right and the duty to look about and to examine the correctness of its path, to ask about the well-being of its method, and to ascertain what shall be the purpose of its task. What is the meaning of *Religionswissenschaft*? There is an old traditional discipline already concerned with religion, namely, theology. Why need there be a *Religionswissenschaft* at its side? When this discipline took shape during the nineteenth century in a very fascinating process of development, there were many—and they still may be found now and then—who thought that *Religionswissenschaft* was called to supplant theology. Recent *Religionswissenschaft*, insofar as it need be taken seriously, has definitely departed from this error. At this point it is widely separated from the work of a meritorious scholar such as Ernst Troeltsch. Theology has its own task in identifying its own confessional norms, and none may take this task from it. Theology is concerned with understanding and confirming its own faith. Foreign religions, to a certain and not inconsequential degree, belong to its realm of study; namely, as they exhibit close or distant relationships in their respective histories or in their concerns. But this can never be the reason for ascribing to theology the immense task of studying and describing the foreign religions in their manifold fulness. At the same time, the development of religious studies tells us that the proposition "he who knows one religion knows all" is false. Thus, theology has every reason to show and to cultivate a lively interest in the results of studying other religions. It nevertheless leaves the study itself to the discipline which has come into existence especially for this purpose. Quantitatively and qualitatively *Religionswissenschaft* thus has a field of study distinct from that of theology: not our own religion but the foreign religions in all their manifoldness are its subject matter. It does not ask the question "what must I believe?" but "what is there that is believed?" According to this definition, it may now seem that the question raised by *Religionswissenschaft* is a superfluous, idle, even harmful curiosity—for the satisfaction of which we can waste neither time, nor energy, nor motivation today—especially at this juncture when we ought to concentrate on what is absolutely necessary. It is good that difficult times now and then compel people to recognize the superfluous for what it is and to throw it overboard and then to limit themselves to what is essential. For us this means that if *Religionswissenschaft* is only an aesthetically interesting or purely academic matter, then, indeed, it has no right to exist today.

The religions of exotic or primitive peoples have often, as has their art, been regarded as curiosities. This is an insufficient, as well as an improper, motive for occupying oneself with them. But even the pure, academic study of foreign religions, which ethically can be justified inasmuch as it rests on a broad desire for truth, must today be prepared to defend its right to exist. It cannot be denied that many a recent attempt in *Religionswissenschaft* is more or less exposed to the threefold criticism of lifelessness, intellectualism, and historicism. This accusation is often brought against the scientific disciplines in our own time. But it is an empirical, not a basic, shortcoming. *Religionswissenschaft* can as little do without learned research as can any other discipline. Nevertheless, this purely learned pursuit stands in the servitude of a higher purpose. Where research in religions, as a consequence of individual inability or from a basically false attitude, appears in the guise of a herbarium—a collection of and for linguists, ethnologists, and historiographers of religions—and where it appears as an occupation with theoretical and abstract formations of thought which dissolve values in unlikely comparisons, there it misses the purpose of *Religionswissenschaft*.

Religionswissenschaft, as we think of it, is alive; moreover, it is positive and practical. It is a living concern to the extent that it remains aware that the religion with which it deals is the deepest and the noblest in the realm of spiritual and intellectual existence, although, to be sure, it is difficult to see into the dark depth of that inwardness. *Religionswissenschaft* is alive, further, in that it recognizes the dynamic nature of religion, in that it knows that its goal will never be reached, and in that it can never sufficiently express that which it hopes to express. For the study of religious expressions, this means a never-ending task. *Religionswissenschaft* is also positive. A rather justified suspicion to the contrary has repeatedly been expressed—and not on the part of insignificant people. This suspicion has been nourished by the sounding from within our own realm of negative, overly critical, destructive, and nihilistic opinions. These tendencies could not help but produce justified defensive reactions since the enemies of religion disguised themselves as scholars.

However, *Religionswissenschaft* in its true intention does not dissolve values but seeks for values. The sense for the numinous is not extinguished by it, but on the contrary, is enriched by it. And as research in religions discloses religious feeling, desire, and action, it helps to reveal more fully the depth and breadth to which religiosity may radiate. A history of religions (*Religionsgeschichte*) which is inwardly connected with the history of cultures can accomplish much in this respect. When we have at last stated that *Religionswissenschaft* has a practical aspect, we must however protect this assertion against a possible misunderstanding. The practical benefit which justifiably is to some degree also demanded of all scientific disciplines must not be seen and sought too directly—which happens now as ever and which is supported by the spokesmen of contemporary need. How far-reaching in its often broad and indirect effects has been what appeared at first to be a very abstract philosophical investigation! The practical aspect must not be understood too narrowly. *Religionswissenschaft* cannot and must not serve the current moment in this bad sense.

What then is the practical significance of *Religionswissenschaft*? It broadens and deepens the *sensus numinis*, the religious feeling and understanding; it prepares one for a deeper conception of one's own faith; it allows a new and comprehensive experience of what religion is and means. This is as true of the religious experience as such as it is of the doctrinal and dogmatic aspect of religion, of its practice in the cult, and of the organization of the congregation. The effectiveness of the religious genius, the power and the formation of the religious community, the shaping of culture by religion—all these are experienced in new and manifold ways which do not paralyze but rather strengthen and fortify religious impulses.

Let us here remember the comparative approach; it has been much too overworked in the past, and too great expectations have been held concerning it. Now, in turn, it is easily underestimated. To observe the multiplicity of religious life and of religious expression, to discover similarities and relation-ships, need not, as some fear, have a sobering or paralyzing effect on one's own religiosity. On the contrary, it could become a support and an aid in the battle against the godless and estranged powers; it ought to lead to the examination and preservation of one's own religious faith. The value and significance of this may be recognized more clearly through that which is related but not identical. As Christians we have no reason at all to shy away from comparison—at any rate, not insofar as the idea and the impulse of our religion is concerned, although more, perhaps, in regard to practice. But there, precisely, the results of *Religionswissenschaft* could have very enlivening and encouraging effects. Precisely because the young person of our time has often very little living knowledge of the final and decisive religious experiences, the detour through examples and analogies from other religions may serve many a purpose.

Personally, I have many times seen young and open-minded students, in the study of the great subjects of *Religionswissenschaft*, attain, to their own surprise, a new understanding of the essentials of their own faith. The study of our various creeds—not as the dry enumeration of various doctrinal opinions, but as actual introductions into the piety of particular Christian movements—may accomplish something new. For example, in understanding the meaning of the cultic [i.e., ritual] expressions of Catholicism, we may effect a richer and more forceful unfolding of our own religious life. As an instance from the general history of religions, the understanding of the immense role which the ethical aspect plays in the life of Buddhists will in theory and in practice lead increasingly to a more intensive unfolding of the motives contained in the imperative of the Christian ethic. Out of life and for life—even though it is to be understood in the above-described sense—is the motto of every scientific discipline and consequently also of *Religionswissenschaft*.

It is of course especially clear that the discipline concerned with religion must be inwardly alive (more, perhaps than the disciplines concerned with economics, law, language, and art), that it can proceed finally only with the austerity and sacred depth appropriate to its great subject matter, with an ever renewing openness, with enthusiasm and thoroughness. It is an exaggeration, but nevertheless understandable, when some people in principle and because of the depth and delicacy of religious matters question the possibility of a *Religionswissenschaft* or of "understanding" religion. Perhaps there is here a greater justification than there is for those who seek to interpret the documents of religious life no differently from documents of a business nature or than there is for those who cast judgment from the ivory tower of a modern intellectual enlightenment upon the customs and beliefs of the primitives. In any case, *Religionswissenschaft* would choose to assert rather less than too much. Happily, at least among us, it has freed itself from the pathos of optimistic positivism.

However much the work of *Religionswissenschaft*, as research will always be careful about particulars—for here the meditation on the insignificant, of which Jakob Grimm spoke, cannot be thorough enough—the goal of *Religionswissenschaft* remains to understand and to present as living totalities the religions studied. After they have been disclosed and studied, its desire will always be to place the individual beliefs and ideas, the customs and communal modes, into that context in which alone they live; to connect them and to show them together with the spirit of the entire religion, with the basic intention that animates them, and with the creative religious intuition at their source.

Schleiermacher has said that every religion represents one aspect of the divine and develops a certain attitude toward it, an attitude which unfolds within the major spheres of religious expression, in doctrine, and in community. It is the task of *Religionswissenschaft* to show how strong, how weak, how enduring, the spirit (*Geist*) of a religion is, or how, in ever new beginnings it manifests itself externally. In this the hermeneutic circularity need not frighten us. This spirit must be understood by means of its dogmatic, cultic, and sociological expressions so that it may then be presupposed in the interpretation of these same manifestations. Religious language in the broader sense of "expression" (*Ausdruck*) is always a code which points beyond itself. This is the truth of the hermeneutic of depth-exegesis, which we encounter in all great religious complexes and which—however arbitrary and unprovable its interpretation of the particulars may seem—has an eternal right over against all rationalism in the understanding of religious expressions.

In a religious doctrine, or in a cultic act, there is always more intended than can be recognized (because expressions in word, pitch, and gesture always limit that which is to be expressed). And then again in excess of what is intended, there is also something in an expression of the religious totality which is represented by it and hinted at by it. The demand to do justice always to all these relationships is put on the student of religions. It is exactly the decisive trend, the central motivation of a given religiosity, which is often very difficult to grasp, to trace, and to describe. And still, this apparently theoretical and abstract undertaking is of special practical significance. It is significant for missions; they are just as much entitled to make use of the work of *Religionswissenschaft* as the latter will always thankfully accept for study—and this does not exclude criticism—the results of missionary reports about other religions. For the sake of contact (*Anknüpfung*), it will be very important to recognize the primary motivating forces of the religiosity which one confronts. These forces are definitely not always expressed in the ideas and beliefs of the primary official doctrine. It is important to identify them, to determine where and to what extent a religion is alive and has power to live. It is important to determine where the negative and sensitive spots are that require considerate care and to determine where positive values appear, the admiration of which is required for contact and communication to occur.

From what has been discussed, it should be clear that the central concern of *Religionswissenschaft* must be the understanding of other religions. Before we speak about this understanding proper, we shall venture yet a few words toward the further clarification of what has been said. Today, especially, the study of religions which are not our own is obliged to defend its ambitions. First, it has to defend itself against the theological objection that "he who knows one religion knows them all." Then, further, it must defend itself not only with respect to external opportunity (Can one afford to occupy oneself beyond the present concerns of our nation and our hemisphere with the religions of distant lands and times?) but also against skepticism that knowledge is possible about that which transcends one's own vital and spiritual life, feeling, thought, and will. To the point respecting opportunity, we may add that *Religionswissenschaft* in its presentations and in its research has to distinguish between what is important and what is less important, what is interesting and what is peripheral, what is necessary to know and what is worthy of knowing. But this is essentially a didactic matter. It is understandable that today in lectures and in courses it is primarily the religions which appeal to the wider public that must be discussed: those which stand prior historically to our Christianity—as for example, the Germanic religion as the early faith of our people—or, in another way, the high religions with which our own struggles today at so many places. In this, *Religionswissenschaft* will have to claim the totality of religious phenomena as the task of its research—to study them and to understand them—but it will also have to claim penetration into most distant realms. A discussion of the final reasons for this would lead us deeply into the systematic problems of philosophy of religion, on the one hand, and into the methodology of the intellectual disciplines, on the other. Therefore, in the present context we must omit such a discussion. But since again and again in the course of time the possibility of understanding other religions has been doubted, *Religionswissenschaft* has a fundamental interest in this question.

The student of religions must be clear about the difficulties to which critics have rightly pointed. We refer here to the difficulties contained in the very naive assumption that religious phenomena, if only sufficient materials were available, could readily be understood through the scientific approach. This assumption still plays a great role among the various types of positivism, as well as in that study of religions which is determined by it. Of course, a radical skepticism as a consequence of either religious indifference or of agnosticism or as a result of historical skepticism (where the history of religions, as all history, is a *fable convenue*) must be rejected just as must be any naive optimism concerning phenomenological imagery.

The difficulties in our understanding are of various types. First, they are quantitative in nature: for example, the often considerable distance in time and space, especially serious with respect to the "dead," the exotic, and the primitive religions. With the consequent lack of information, with the discontinuities and transformations among the traditions or source materials, may one still hope at all to attain a more or less true picture of the religions from the distant past and from distant realms? One need only think for instance of the religions of Egypt, Babylonia, China, and Mexico. Second, there are the qualitative difficulties that hinder our understanding: the uniqueness of foreign inwardness, which is likewise inherent in its expressions. Spengler, to name only one widely known thinker, has recently pointed especially to the uniqueness of ancient thought, feeling, and perceptivity. Who is there who has not felt the unfathomable depths that inhabit the religious representations of the Far East or the demonic so typical of African religions?

However, not only *Religionswissenschaft* is burdened with both of these types of difficulties; rather, all intellectual disciplines concerned with cultures, especially the historical disciplines, share them. In long and toilsome work they have sought to develop methods and criteria which would allow to some degree the mastery of these difficulties. If one looks to the results of these labors, one will have to admit how astonishingly and how extensively they have been crowned with success. We actually have a body of knowledge about the religions of peoples long since past as well as of distant places. This knowledge can withstand the most exacting tests and controls; it completes, broadens, and extends itself continuously, and it constitutes more than a subjective picture of particulars. Moreover, we are even able to test against the certain results of research the false pictures which are based on insufficient and one-sided information; here the error of poor subjectivity appears to be eliminated to a very great extent. Nevertheless, nobody will therefore underestimate the difficulties that have been mentioned.

We continuously have reasons to examine within an ever-extending problematic the possibilities, the chances, and the limits in understanding other religions. How difficult it is even to obtain a clear picture of the religiosity of a person near to us—still within the realm of common faith and familiarity. How difficult it is to comprehend the piety of our predecessors of perhaps only a few decades, of the faiths of neighboring lands, of the faith of Islamic peoples who still have certain religious influences in common with Europe, and finally of the people of India and China.

With this we actually have arrived at the third major difficulty with which the understanding of other religions must struggle. This difficulty is unique in that it concerns the nature of the religious. It will certainly be less difficult to obtain a picture of the legal customs and of the linguistic and artistic expressions of a people than of their religion. The last is above everything else kept in high esteem. It may even be fearfully hidden from foreign eyes and guarded as an arcanum. And even when it is possible to look into it, it is really not easy to grasp its meaning. A simple example will point this out: a Roman Catholic mass, in which so much is interrelated and unfamiliar, even foreign, to the Protestant who attends. If it is a church service according to the Greek, the Coptic, or the Armenian rite, the strangeness is immediately greater. This foreignness grows again as we encounter no longer a Christian but, for example, a Jewish, or an Islamic, or even a Buddhist worship service. How difficult for consequent understanding are the religious root-conceptions and root-customs of taboo, totem, nagual, and others. How different the baroque mythology of Japanese Shinto, the orgiastic cults of certain Indian Shiva sects, the fanaticism of the Islamic Shi'ah, appear to us. Here our discussion closes in on a great and serious problem: the secret of plurality among religious experiences. We can only lead up to this problem, for its consideration is a concern for philosophy of religion and for theology. Here we shall deal only with the question whether and how it is possible for *Religionswissenschaft* to understand other religions. We have already seen that many practical proofs of its possibility are available. Hermeneutically, on what does this possibility rest?

We have spoken above of what is generally representative of spiritual, and therefore also of religious, expressions. The expression then becomes transparent; it allows something to shine through of the specific and perhaps unique spirit (*Geist*) of a certain religious context. Thus it is that views into the depths (*Tiefenblicke*) become possible. Not always and not to everybody do they open themselves. But it is amazing how much a small and peripheral aspect, taken from the conceptions and customs of a faith, can disclose to a gifted and trained mind. Actual intuition (*Divination*) here, as always, is the exception. Synthesis (*Kombination*) stands in the foreground of all intellectual endeavors, as it does in *Religionswissenschaft*. If then, perhaps, in a happy and fruitful interplay of both avenues to knowledge, some decisive characteristics of a foreign religiosity have emerged for the researcher, he may then dare to grasp and describe its basic intention. In this it is a great help for the human understanding that in the structure of spiritual expressions (of such great and deep experiences as are the productively religious ones) there is inherent an amazing continuity (*Folgerichtigkeit*). Nor is this continuity absent in the structures of the historical religious systems.

It is not very difficult for one who has really comprehended the central intuition of Islam, its experience of the deity, as this is expressed in the original revelation to the prophet Muhammed, to discover it again in the doctrine, theology, cosmology, anthropology, soteriology, and cult. In spite of all other influences, this central intuition develops within the framework of these expressions. The experience of suffering within a world of change, fundamental for Buddhism, is displayed with such a continuity in its doctrine, is presented in its symbols, and is shaped within its ethic, so that the understanding of this may, like a great key, unlock an otherwise strange-appearing world of expressions.

Such considerations certainly ought not minimize the difficulties; they ought not delude us about the levels and degrees of understanding, about the differences involved among its various risks. But by considering and by honoring differences, an old truth must not be forgotten. As Goethe and Wilhelm have formulated it, in every man there dwell all the forms of humanity. Novalis asked at one time: How can a man have an understanding of something of which he does not have the seed within himself? This insight in no way implies the lack or the weakness of him who does the understanding; rather, it implies the conviction that in all of us is contained more than becomes manifest in the co-operation of circumstances and fate.

Only very recently Eduard Spranger in his illustrative investigation of the primary levels of reality-consciousness (*Abhandlungen der Akademie der Wissenschaften* [Berlin], 1934) has proven that in all of us there are latently present certain more, primeval structures of consciousness. What is called "mind" has the ability to activate these and to understand, so to speak, the atavistic and distant expressions of our soul, the expressions which are alien to our present consciousness. Novalis again says: we stand in relationship with all parts of the universe, with the future and with the past. What relationship we shall primarily develop and what relationship for us shall become primarily effective and important depend only on the direction and duration of our attentiveness. This means that in principle there could resound in each of the ecstatic, the spectral, the unusual—something of that which to us, the children of another age, of another race, and of other customs, appears strange among the religious expressions of distant lands. Where this natural disposition is developed through training, there also the prerequisite for an actual understanding of foreign religiosity exists.

This can be illustrated through the example of myth. In myth, religious experience is expressed in unique categories. As recent ethnological and psychological research has shown, our logical norms are not necessarily valid for these categories. Thus the myths of primitive peoples with their identifications, their theriomorphisms, and so on, at first seem abstruse to the uninformed, contemporary reader or listener. And still, it does not seem impossible to sense something of the intended reality of the myth. Such immersions into archaic modes of consciousness are generally more easily attained by young people. Such modes of consciousness are almost self-evident and present for them. I am reminded of our youth associations and their experience, their symbolism and their customs; in them the world of primitive man (*Naturmensch*) is not only imitated externally but actually felt in participation, and it becomes clear that their experience of it is not a purely intellectual affair.

In the human understanding, as the excellent hermeneutics of Wilhelm Dilthey has shown, the totality of mind and soul (*Totalität des Gemüts*) is effective. Concretely stated, the religious content of myth cannot be found alone in a careful and thorough, though necessary, analysis of its ideological elements and motives; rather, the entire personality of him who studies and understands is spoken to. If he wishes to understand the attitude from which the mythological faith and custom have issued, he must respond. An inner aliveness and broadness is necessary if we actually wish to understand other religions. In this connection it should be stated explicitly that the one-sided advancement of a particular point of view is bad for the understanding. As justified and fruitful as may be the co-operative approaches of psychology, sociology, and typology, pure psychological, pure sociological, and pure typological answers do not help us to understand foreign religiosity. Unfortunately, our discipline is rich in one-sided attempts that have been based on false, narrow, and oblique conceptions of the nature of religion.

It appears to be a truism to say that hermeneutics demands that he who wishes to understand other religions must have a sense (*Organ*) for religion and in addition the most extensive knowledge and training possible. Many still think that one of these two prerequisites is sufficient. While all sorts of dilettantes (a famous example is the interpretation of Lao-tse's *Tao Te Ching*) err in one of these directions, often philologists, ethnologists, and other specialists go amiss in the other. The first demand is stated by some in a still more strict and narrow sense. Well aware of the above-mentioned difficulties in understanding other religions they think that one must actually belong to a community of believers if one wishes to grasp its actual concern. This is a significant assertion, and it must be seriously examined. If it proves to be fully correct, the ground on which *Religionswissenschaft* builds will have been withdrawn. Here, too, a glance at the results of a century rich in religious studies of the most varied kinds will reveal in fact that even those who have not studied another religion as a member of that particular religious community may be successful. The same can likewise hardly be denied of knowledge concerning the entire realm of expressions, that is, of the doctrine, cult, and constitution of the religious community concerned.

But the matter gets more difficult when we are dealing with the inner experience, the understanding and intention to which such expressions bear witness. There can be no question that growing up within a tradition, belonging to the community of faith, can be a favorable precondition. However, the effect of habit, the absence of distance, and so on, may certainly also be negative influences. Standing within a tradition is nevertheless important. It could perhaps be an advantage in certain situations for the convert over the outsider. It could enable him to grasp the conscious ambition of the community which he joins. But one would want to ask, with respect to understanding Buddhism, for example, whether he who through conversion has been accepted into the community actually has a greater insight than the outsider, perhaps a Westerner, who for a long time has immersed himself in Buddhist studies. We may admit without reservation that standing in a tradition is something that is difficult to replace and that—provided the other prerequisites which we have found necessary, are also present—the chances for understanding the actual intention of a religious community are increased. But in practical confrontation with the multiplicity of phenomena, with which the student of religions must deal, such a participation will not be possible. Thus, the demand that one belong to the religious community which one wishes to understand cannot be made a prerequisite—not to speak of the new errors which could arise under these circumstances. The problem of knowledge and faith, of faith and understanding, cannot be discussed here. Only this much must be summarized: being rooted in a personal faith—a faith which may well blind one to other things but which, in contrast to the opinion of many, need not do so—does not necessarily mean a disadvantage for him who seeks to understand. The demand of a *tabula rasa* has long been recognized as utopian; and even though such objectivity might be desirable, it is actually impossible. Schleiermacher has seen that we must learn from our personal religious life in order to encounter the foreign. We need not a blank sheet but an impregnated one, one that will preserve the pictures projected onto it.

Is it at this point that *tout comprendre c'est tout pardonner*? In other words—and in connection with the above—is not the result of *Religionswissenschaft*, then, a hopeless relativism? Is it of such a nature that in its own best interests the Christian mission should be warned against a closer touch with *Religionswissenschaft*? I hope that with the foregoing I have succeeded in showing that contemporary *Religionswissenschaft* no longer pays obeisance to the historicist fallacy which in its time has fettered the so-called *Religions-geschichtliche Schule*, namely, that norms may be attained from history itself. If history of religions were supposed to tell us what we ought to believe, we would wait for such information for a long time. No, since it no longer thinks about giving such advice and since it has recognized that its field of study is sufficiently large as it is and that it has many concrete tasks that can ambitiously be attacked, we would be doing it a grave injustice to have this sort of suspicion. Certainly, it seeks to understand foreign religiosity. We have also seen that its motivation for this is ethically beyond reproach. How does it stand now with respect to forgiveness? Does the study of *Religionswissenschaft* weaken the sense of value, the courage and the ability to decide?

The ability to decide "what must I believe?" lies—and this we have repeatedly emphasized here—outside the sphere of a scientific discipline. We no longer are good enough rationalists and positivists to believe that an intellectual discipline can replace religion, not even that it necessarily limits it. In practice, it is, however, still the case, as we can see among those peoples who have not yet emerged from their susceptibility to the scientific faith, that an Eastern student graduated from a Western university returns to his home region and deems himself toweringly exalted above the "superstition" which "still" prevails there. As we have said, with us this is no longer the case. It is not a good sign for a faith if it allows itself to be shaken by an intellectual discipline. True decision for a faith, I would like to say, is not only not impaired but is aided and depended by *Religionswissenschaft*. But what about the sense of value? Nietzsche, who must be understood not only as a dogmatist but also as a critic, has said in his famous discussion of the advantages and disadvantages of historiography, on behalf of the life of the concrete force (*plastische Kraft*), that it would be impaired if the great museum of human history—and thus also that of history of religions—were spread out without choice and distinctions before the people of today. The nineteenth century, to which Nietzsche held up the mirror, was stuck deeply in historicism; its anarchy of values was destined to have its full effects only at the beginning of the twentieth century.

We now have again found the right and the courage to evaluate. *Religionswissenschaft* will seek to grasp with understanding all that foreign religions produce of faith, cult, custom, and community. It will seek to grasp the actual meaning the religious intention, out of which spring all these: otherwise, and this it knows well, it will have only empty shells to tinker with. *Religionswissenschaft* does not abstain from using scales and standards; on the contrary, it makes much use of them. It seeks to overcome all superficial presuppositions, all the binding tendencies; it attempts to see the phenomena of other religious life; it tries to understand and honor this life in its actuality. For once, the student of religions looks at a particular religion immanently, from within. He asks himself what a conception or a characteristic looks like, how it integrates within the totality of the religion concerned. He asks further—and here the reference to value in his study becomes quite clear—about the amount of religious productivity and vitality which speaks from within the specific phenomenon. If, for example, we consider the faith in a god (*Gottesglauben*) of a certain African tribe, we must determine the degree of perfection to which this belief in a god is expressed by this particular community; then we must honor the level of theistic experience which appears attained therein. This certainly is no easy task. Good sense, manners, and experience are needed in order to appraise correctly, to appraise, beyond all naive absolutizing of one's own personal beliefs and feelings, the religious quality among the particular phenomena of religious life. This is so precisely because standards which are taken from elsewhere, from the realm of aesthetic and ethical evaluation, very easily creep into the place of the only decisive religious point of view. It is understandable that from a didactic point of view, the more history of religions increases the amount of data and the more data it pushes into our horizon, the more the separation of the important from the unimportant, the great from the small, will have to be worked out.

An introduction to *Religionswissenschaft* should not consist of a non-selective enumeration of encyclopedic facts—as is said to be the case occasionally in academic presentations. Rather, it should be concerned with describing the great and classic figures in the history of religions, and of these, again—for each, of these great inspirations, too, represents something typical—there should be pointed out the typical and the significant, the personal and the characteristic. The world religions have a claim to a special and thorough consideration. To this introduction also belongs the study of the history of a particular religion, perhaps the history of a significant one from among the more advanced as well as one from among the primitive cultures; then, further, the structure of that religion (its central point of doctrine, the major aspects of the cult, the hinge-point of the organization) and the major phases in its development must be identified clearly enough to make a comparison possible. For this, the role of the leading religious personalities, as well as the transformation of the official religion by popular piety, must also be presented. In all this the decisive thing is to make visible that in which true religiosity is present—a religiosity which may further be cultivated to determine secondary formations, for example where petrification and degeneration have set in. An exemplary model for training oneself to grasp the significant from the fulness of the materials of *Religionswissenschaft* is still Rudolf Otto's *Das Heilige* [*The Idea of the Holy*]. This study, besides being important for the phenomenology of religion, also has great methodological significance.

We have spoken of scales and of choice. It becomes readily clear that here again there is an important starting point with practical consequences. The missionary will find it valuable to have worked out for himself scales of the type hinted at here. From his point of view, he will know well the religion of the nation or tribe with whom he primarily deals. But he gladly and in addition would also like to acquire the greater background against which he can still more deeply understand this religion. In this context we cannot talk in detail about the various relationships between *Religionswissenschaft* and the study of missions. To cultivate and to deepen this knowledge, has already been the special task of this periodical. The more the insight spreads and deepens—as has happened especially in recent times—the more in all Christian missions one motive must stand decisively in the foreground: that behind the religious motive all other motives must retreat to the background, and that the people whom we missionize ought to be led to a religiosity appropriate to themselves and to their uniqueness. So the thorough study of their uniqueness becomes an increasingly important task; to this, too, *Religionswissenschaft* can contribute its share.

I invite you to observe every faith which human beings have ever confessed, every religion which you have designated by a certain name or label and which perhaps has long since degenerated into a codex of empty customs, into a system of abstract concepts and theories; and when you investigate it at its source and through its more original constituents, you will discover that all this dead slag at one time was a red-hot pouring of the inner fire, the fire which is contained to a greater or lesser degree in all religions; you will discover in their true nature that, as I have presented it, each of these unique formations has been the one which the eternal and never-ceasing Religion had necessarily to assume among finite and limited characteristics.[2]

Notes

1. This article was first published in *Zeitschrift für Missionskunde und Religionswissenschaft* 50/5 (1935). It has been translated by Karl W. Luckert with the help of Alan L. Miller.
2. Friedrich Schleiermacher, *Über die Religion. Reden an die Gebildeten unter ihren Verächtern*. 3rd ed. Berlin: G. Reimer, 1821: 364–365.

7

MIRCEA ELIADE, *A New Humanism*[1]

❧

Despite the manuals, periodicals, and bibliographies today available to scholars, it is progressively more difficult to keep up with the advances being made in all areas of the history of religions.[2] Hence it is progressively more difficult to become a historian of religions. A scholar regretfully finds himself becoming a specialist in *one* religion or even in a particular period or a single aspect of that religion.

This situation has induced us to bring out a new periodical. Our purpose is not simply to make one more review available to scholars (though the lack of a periodical of this nature in the United States would be reason enough for our venture) but more especially to provide an aid to orientation in a field that is constantly widening and to stimulate exchanges of views among specialists who, as a rule, do not follow the progress made in other disciplines. Such an orientation and exchange of views will, we hope, be made possible by summaries of the most recent advances achieved concerning certain key problems in the history of religions, by methodological discussions, and by attempts to improve the hermeneutics of religious data.

Hermeneutics is of preponderant interest to us because, inevitably, it is the least-developed aspect of our discipline. Preoccupied, and indeed often completely taken up, by their admittedly urgent and indispensable work of collecting, publishing, and analyzing religious data, scholars have sometimes neglected to study their meaning. Now, these data represent the expression of various religious experiences; in the last analysis they represent positions and situations assumed by men in the course of history. Like it or not, the scholar has not finished his work when he has reconstructed the history of a religious form or brought out its sociological, economic, or political contexts. In addition, he must understand its meaning—that is, identify and elucidate the situations and positions that have induced or made possible its appearance or its triumph at a particular historical moment.

It is solely insofar as it will perform this task—particularly by making the meanings of religious documents intelligible to the mind of modern man—that the science of religions will fulfill its true cultural function. For whatever its role has been in the past, the comparative study of religions is destined to assume a cultural role of the first importance in the near future. As we have said on several occasions, our historical moment forces us into confrontations that could not even have been imagined fifty years ago. On the one hand, the peoples of Asia have recently reentered history; on the other, the so-called primitive peoples are preparing to make their appearance on the horizon of greater history (that is, they are seeking to become *active subjects* of history instead of its *passive objects*, as they have been hitherto). But if the peoples of the West are no longer the only ones to "make" history, their spiritual and cultural values will no longer enjoy the privileged place, to say nothing of the unquestioned authority, that they enjoyed some generations ago. These values are now being analyzed, compared, and judged by non-Westerners. On their side, Westerners are being increasingly led to study, reflect on, and understand the spiritualities of Asia and the archaic world. These discoveries and contacts must be extended through dialogues. But to be genuine and fruitful, a dialogue cannot be limited to empirical and utilitarian language. A true dialogue must deal with the central values in the cultures of the participants. Now, to understand these values rightly, it is necessary to know their religious sources. For, as we know, non-European cultures, both oriental and primitive, are still nourished by a rich religious soil.

This is why we believe that the history of religions is destined to play an important role in contemporary cultural life. This is not only because an understanding of exotic and archaic religions will significantly assist in a cultural dialogue with the representatives of such religions. It is more especially because, by attempting to understand the existential situations expressed by the documents he is studying, the historian of religions will inevitably attain to a deeper knowledge of man. It is on the basis of such a knowledge that a new humanism, on a world-wide scale, could develop. We may even ask if the history of religions cannot make a contribution of prime importance to its formation. For, on the one hand, the historical and comparative study of religions embraces all the cultural forms so far known, both the ethnological cultures and those that have played a major role in history; on the other hand, by studying the religious expressions of a culture, the scholar approaches it from within, and not merely in its sociological, economic, and political contexts. In the last analysis, the historian of religions is destined to elucidate a large number of situations unfamiliar to the man of the West. It is through an understanding of such unfamiliar, "exotic" situations that cultural provincialism is transcended.

But more is involved than a widening of the horizon, a quantitative, static increase in our "knowledge of man." It is the meeting with the "others"—with human beings belonging to various types of archaic and exotic societies—that is culturally stimulating and fertile. It is the personal experience of this unique hermeneutics that is creative. It is not beyond possibility that the discoveries and "encounters" made possible by the progress of the history of religions may have repercussions comparable to those of certain famous discoveries in the past of Western culture. We have in mind the discovery of the exotic and primitive arts, which revivified modern Western aesthetics. We have in mind especially the discovery of the unconscious by psychoanalysis, which opened new perspectives for our understanding of man. In both cases alike, there was a meeting with the "foreign," the unknown, with what cannot be reduced to familiar categories in short, with the "wholly other."[3] Certainly this contact with the "other" is not without its dangers. The initial resistance to the modern artistic movements and to depth psychology is a case in point. For, after all, recognizing the existence of "others" inevitably brings with it the relativization, or even the destruction, of the official cultural world. The Western aesthetic universe has not been the same since the acceptance and assimilation of the artistic creations of cubism and surrealism. The "world" in which preanalytic man lived became obsolete after Freud's discoveries. But these "destructions" opened new vistas to Western creative genius.

All this cannot but suggest the limitless possibilities open to historians of religions, the "encounters" to which they expose themselves in order to understand human situations different from those with which they are familiar. It is hard to believe that experiences as "foreign" as those of a paleolithic hunter or a Buddhist monk will have no effect whatever on modern cultural life. Obviously such "encounters" will become culturally creative only when the scholar has passed beyond the stage of pure erudition—in other words, when, after having collected, described, and classified his documents, he has also made an effort to understand them *on their own plane of reference*. This implies no depreciation of erudition. But, after all, erudition by itself cannot accomplish the whole task of the historian of religions, just as a knowledge of thirteenth-century Italian and of the Florentine culture of the period, the study of medieval theology and philosophy, and familiarity with Dante's life do not suffice to reveal the artistic value of the *Divina Commedia*. We almost hesitate to repeat such truisms. Yet it can never be said often enough that the task of the historian of religions is not completed when he has succeeded in reconstructing the chronological sequence of a religion or has brought out its social, economic, and political contexts. Like every human phenomenon, the religious phenomenon is extremely complex. To grasp all its valences and all its meanings, it must be approached from several points of view.

It is regrettable that historians of religions have not yet sufficiently profited from the experience of their colleagues who are historians of literature or literary critics. The progress made in these disciplines would have enabled them to avoid unfortunate misunderstandings. It is agreed today that there is continuity and solidarity between the work of the literary historian, the literary sociologist, the critic, and the aesthetician. To give but one example: If the work of Balzac can hardly be understood without a knowledge of nineteenth-century French society and history (in the broadest meaning of the term—political, economic, social, cultural, and religious history), it is nonetheless true that the *Comédie humaine* cannot be reduced to a historical document pure and simple. It is the work of an exceptional individual, and it is for this reason that the life and psychology of Balzac must be known. But the working-out of this gigantic *oeuvre* must be studied in itself, as the artist's struggle with his raw material, as the creative spirit's victory over the immediate data of experience. A whole labor of exegesis remains to be performed after the historian of literature has finished his task, and here lies the role of the literary critic. It is he who deals with the work as an autonomous universe with its own laws and structure. And at least in the case of poets, even the literary critic's work does not exhaust the subject, for it is the task of the specialist in stylistics and the aesthetician to discover and explain the values of poetic universes. But can a literary work be said to be finally "explicated" when the aesthetician has said his last word? There is always a secret message in the work of great writers, and it is on the plane of philosophy that it is most likely to be grasped.

We hope we may be forgiven for these few remarks on the hermeneutics of literary works. They are certainly incomplete,[4] but they will, we believe, suffice to show that those who study literary works are thoroughly aware of their complexity and, with few exceptions, do not attempt to "explicate" them by reducing them to one or another origin—infantile trauma, glandular accident, or economic, social, or political situations, etc. It serves a purpose to have cited the unique situation of artistic creations. For, from a certain point of view, the aesthetic universe can be compared with the universe of religion. In both cases, we have to do at once with *individual experiences* (aesthetic experience of the poet and his reader, on the one hand, religious experience, on the other) and with *transpersonal realities* (a work of art in a museum, a poem, a symphony; a Divine Figure, a rite, a myth, etc.). Certainly it is possible to go on forever discussing what meaning one may be inclined to attribute to these artistic and religious *realities*. But one thing at least seems obvious: Works of art, like "religious data," have a mode of being that is peculiar to themselves; they *exist on their own plane of reference*, in their particular universe. The fact that this universe is not the physical universe of immediate experience does not imply their nonreality. This problem has been sufficiently discussed to permit us to dispense with reopening it here. We will add but one observation: A work of art reveals its meaning only insofar as it is regarded as an autonomous creation; that is, insofar as we accept its mode of being—*that of an artistic creation*—and do not reduce it to one of its constituent elements (in the case of a poem, sound, vocabulary, linguistic structure, etc.) or to one of its subsequent uses (a poem which carries a political message or which can serve as a document for sociology, ethnography, etc.).

In the same way, it seems to us that a religious datum reveals its deeper meaning when it is considered on its plane of reference, and not when it is reduced to one of its secondary aspects or its contexts. To give but one example: Few religious phenomena are more directly and more obviously connected with sociopolitical circumstances than the modern messianic and millenarian movements among colonial peoples (cargo-cults, etc.). Yet identifying and analyzing the conditions that prepared and made possible such messianic movements form only a part of the work of the historian of religions. For these movements are equally creations of the human spirit, in the sense that they have become what they are—*religious movements*, and not merely gestures of protest and revolt—through a creative act of the spirit. In short, a religious phenomenon such as primitive messianism must be studied just as the *Divina Commedia* is studied, that is, by using all the possible tools of scholarship (and not, to return to what we said above in connection with Dante, merely his vocabulary or his syntax, or simply his theological and political ideas, etc.). For, if the history of religions is destined to further the rise of a new humanism, it is incumbent on the historian of religions to bring out the autonomous value—the value as *spiritual creation*—of all these primitive religious movements. To reduce them to sociopolitical contexts is, in the last analysis, to admit that they are not sufficiently "elevated," sufficiently "noble," to be treated as creations of human genius like the *Divina Commedia* or the *Fioretti* of St. Francis.[5] We may expect that sometime in the near future the intelligentsia of the former colonial peoples will regard many social scientists as camouflaged apologists of Western culture. Because these scientists insist so persistently on the sociopolitical origin and character of the "primitive" messianic movements, they may be suspected of a Western superiority complex, namely, the conviction that such religious movements cannot rise to the same level of "freedom from sociopolitical conjuncture" as, for instance, a Gioachino da Fiore or St. Francis.

This does not mean, of course, that a religious phenomenon can be understood outside of its "history," that is, outside of its cultural and socioeconomic contexts. There is no such thing as a "pure" religious datum, outside of history, for there is no such thing as a human datum that is not at the same time a historical datum. Every religious experience is expressed and transmitted in a particular historical context. But admitting the historicity of religious experiences does not imply that they are reducible to nonreligious forms of behavior. Stating that a religious datum is always a historical datum does not mean that it is reducible to a nonreligious history—for example, to an economic, social, or political history. We must never lose sight of one of the fundamental principles of modern science: *the scale creates the phenomenon.* As we have recalled elsewhere,[6] Henri Poincaré asked, not without irony, "Would a naturalist who had never studied the elephant except through the microscope consider that he had an adequate knowledge of the creature?" The microscope reveals the structure and mechanism of cells, which structure and mechanism are exactly the same in all multicellular organisms. The elephant is certainly a multicellular organism, but is that all that it is? On the microscopic scale, we might hesitate to answer. On the scale of human vision, which at least has the advantage of presenting the elephant as a zoological phenomenon, there can be no doubt about the reply.

We have no intention of developing a methodology of the science of religions here. The problem is far too complex to be treated in a few pages.[7] But we think it useful to repeat that the *homo religiosus* represents the "total man"; hence, the science of religions must become a total discipline in the sense that it must use, integrate, and articulate the results obtained by the various methods of approaching a religious phenomenon. It is not enough to grasp the meaning of a religious phenomenon in a certain culture and, consequently, to decipher its "message" (for every religious phenomenon constitutes a "cipher"); it is also necessary to study and understand its "history," that is, to unravel its changes and modifications and, ultimately, to elucidate its contribution to the entire culture. In the past few years a number of scholars have felt the need to transcend the alternative *religious phenomenology* or *history of religions*[8] and to reach a broader perspective in which these two intellectual operations can be applied together. It is toward the integral conception of the science of religions that the efforts of scholars seem to be orienting themselves today. To be sure, these two approaches correspond in some degree, to different philosophical temperaments. And it would be naive to suppose that the tension between those who try to understand the *essence* and the *structures* and those whose only concern is the *history* of religious phenomena will one day be completely done away with. But such a tension is creative. It is by virtue of it that the science of religions will escape dogmatism and stagnation.

The results of these two intellectual operations are equally valuable for a more adequate knowledge of *homo religiosus*. For, if the "phenomenologists" are interested in the meanings of religious data, the "historians," on their side, attempt to show how these meanings have been experienced and lived in the various cultures and historical moments, how they have been transformed, enriched, or impoverished in the course of history. But if we are to avoid sinking back into an obsolete "reductionism," this history of religious meanings must always be regarded as forming part of the history of the human spirit.[9]

More than any other humanistic discipline (i.e., psychology, anthropology, sociology, etc.), history of religions can open the way to a philosophical anthropology. For the sacred is a universal dimension and ... the beginnings of culture are rooted in religious experiences and beliefs. Furthermore, even after they are radically secularized, such cultural creations as social institutions, technology, moral ideas, arts, etc., cannot be correctly understood if one does not know their original religious matrix, which they tacitly criticized, modified, or rejected in becoming what they are now: secular cultural values. Thus, the historian of religions is in a position to grasp the permanence of what has been called man's specific existential situation of "being in the world," for the experience of the sacred is its correlate. In fact, man's becoming aware of his own mode of being and assuming his *presence* in the world together constitute a "religious" experience.

Ultimately, the historian of religions is forced by his hermeneutical endeavor to "relive" a multitude of existential situations and to unravel a number of presystematic ontologies. A historian of religions cannot say, for example, that he has understood the Australian religions if he has not understood the Australians' *mode of being in the world*. And ... even at that stage of culture we find the notion of a plurality of modes of being as well as the awareness that the singularity of the human condition is the result of a primordial "sacred history."

Now, these points cannot be successfully realized if the investigator does not understand that every religion has a *"center,"* in other words, a central conception which informs the entire corpus of myths, rituals, and beliefs. This is evident in such religions as Judaism, Christianity, and Islam, notwithstanding the fact that the modifications introduced in the course of time tend, in some cases, to obscure the "original form." For example, the central role of Jesus as Christ is transparent no matter how complex and elaborated some contemporary theological and ecclesiastical expressions may seem in comparison to "original Christianity." But the "center" of a religion is not always so evident. Some investigators do not even suspect that there is a "center"; rather, they try to articulate the religious values of a certain type of society in compliance with a fashionable theory. Thus, for almost three-quarters of a century the "primitive" religions were understood as illustrating one of the dominant theories of the day: animism, ancestor cult, *mana*, totemism, and so on. Australia, for example, was considered almost the territory par excellence of totemism, and because of the supposed archaism of the Australians, totemism was even proclaimed the most ancient form of religious life.

Whatever one may think of the various religious ideas and beliefs brought together under the name of "totemism," one thing seems evident today, namely, that totemism does *not* constitute the *center* of Australian religious life. On the contrary, the totemic expressions, as well as other religious ideas and beliefs, receive their full meaning and fall into a pattern only when the *center* of religious life is sought where the Australians have untiringly declared it to be: in the concept of the "Dreaming Time," that fabulous primordial epoch when the world was shaped and man became what he is today. We have discussed this problem at length elsewhere and it is unnecessary to take it up again here.[10]

This is only one example among many others, and perhaps not even the most illuminating, for the Australian religions do not present the complexity and the variety of forms that confront the student of Indian, Egyptian, or Greek religions. But it is easy to understand that the failure to search for the real center of a religion may explain the inadequate contributions made by the historians of religions to philosophical anthropology.... [S]uch a shortcoming reflects a deeper and more complex crisis. But on the other hand, there are also signs that this crisis is in the process of being resolved....

Notes

1. This chapter is a revised and expanded version of an article originally entitled "History of Religions and a New Humanism," which was first published in *History of Religions* 1 (1961): 1–8 (© 1961 by The University of Chicago).
2. Since *Religionswissenschaft* is not easily translatable into English, we are obliged to use "history of religions" in the broadest sense of the term, including not only history properly speaking but also the comparative study of religions and religious morphology and phenomenology.
3. Rudolf Otto described the sacred as the *ganz andere*. Although occurring on the nonreligious plane, the encounters with the "wholly other" brought about by depth psychology and modern artistic experiments can be reckoned as parareligious experiences.
4. It is also necessary to consider, for example, the vicissitudes of the work in the public consciousness, or even "unconscious." The circulation, assimilation, and evaluation of a literary work present problems that no discipline can solve *by itself*. It is the sociologist, but also the historian, the moralist, and the psychologist, who can help us to understand the success of *Werther* and the failure of *The Way of All Flesh*, the fact that such a difficult work as *Ulysses* became popular in less than twenty years, while *Senilità* and *Coscienza di Zeno* are still unknown, and so on.
5. We may even wonder if, at bottom, the various "reductionisms" do not betray the superiority complex of Western scholars. They have no doubt that only science— *an exclusively Western creation*—will resist this process of demystifying spirituality and culture.
6. *Traité d'histoire des religions*. Paris, 1949: ii. English translation: *Patterns in Comparative Religion*. New York, 1958: xi.
7. Certain preliminary suggestions will be found in some of our preceding publications. See especially *Patterns in Comparative Religion*, 1–33; *Images et symboles*. Paris, 1951: 33–52, 211–235 (English translation: *Images and Symbols*. New York, 1961: 27–41, 16–78); *Mythes, rêves et mystères*. Paris, 1957: 7–15, 133–164 (English translation: *Myths, Dreams and Mysteries*. New York, 1961: 13–20, 99–122); "Methodological Remarks on the Study of Religious Symbolism," *The History of Religion: Essays in Methodology*. Mircea Eliade and Joseph M. Kitagawa (eds.). Chicago, 1959: 86–107.
8. These terms are used here in their broadest sense, including under "phenomenology" those scholars who pursue the study of structures and meanings, and under "history" those who seek to understand religious phenomena in their historical context. Actually, the divergences between these two approaches are more marked. In addition there are a certain number of differences—sometimes quite perceptible—within the groups that, for the sake of simplification, we have termed "phenomenologists" and "historians."

9. In one of his last works, the great historian of religions Raffaele Pettazzoni reached similar conclusions. "Phenomenology and history complement each other. Phenomenology cannot do without ethnology, philology, and other historical disciplines. Phenomenology, on the other hand, gives the historical disciplines that sense of the religious which they are not able to capture. So conceived, religious phenomenology is the religious understanding (*Verständniss*) of history; it is history in its religious dimension. Religious phenomenology and history are not two sciences but are two complementary aspects of the integral science of religion, and the science of religion as such has a well-defined character given to it by its unique and proper subject matter" ("The Supreme Being: Phenomenological Structure and Historical Development," *The History of Religion: Essays in Methodology.* Mircea Eliade and Joseph Kitagawa (eds.). Chicago, 1959: 66).

10. "Australian Religion: An Introduction," *History of Religions* 6 (1966): 108–134, 208–237.

8

ROSALIND SHAW, *Feminist Anthropology and the Gendering of Religious Studies*

પ્રૐ

Feminist projects of disciplinary transformation may be caught up in contradictions arising from the histories of the disciplines in which change is sought. In the history and phenomenology of religions, problems of disciplinary transformation appear to extend far beyond the difficulties of eradicating "male bias" or of including women's standpoints. Such transformation may entail nothing less than the dissolution and reconstruction of the discipline itself. In anthropology, attempts to effect a feminist metamorphosis in the 1970s and early 1980s were subject to contradictions whose identification and critique by Strathern (1981, 1987) assisted scholars in rethinking the relationship between feminism and anthropology. Strathern's characterization of the "awkward relationship" between anthropology and feminism finds important parallels in the history of religions, and her critiques may usefully be applied to certain forms of feminist religious studies today.

Strathern (1987) characterizes feminism and anthropology as close neighbors, enmeshed in a relationship of mutual mockery. They do not so much contradict as "mock" each other, she argues, because each so nearly attains the ideal which eludes the other. On the one hand, anthropologists have a comparative perspective which can give them a critical distance from dominant Euro-American understandings of gender and women's power—a distance which is highly valued in much of feminist thought. On the other hand, anthropologists are striving to reform anthropology from the conditions of its production, in which knowledge has been constituted within unequal power relationships between white Western anthropologists and colonized peoples of the Third World, among whom most anthropologists have worked. Anthropologists' struggles to effect a shift from a "view from above" in order to reinvent anthropology contrast sharply with the apparent ease with which feminist scholars have assumed a "view from below," in which relations of domination are analyzed from a subordinate standpoint.

While anthropology "mocks" feminism from its advantaged position for cultural critiques of Western social forms, then, feminism—from its own assumed standpoint of the subordinate's perspective—mocks anthropology. Anthropology can never really achieve its desired perspective of the "view from below" until non-Western anthropologists have a stronger voice in its reinvention (see Moore 1989). Because of this mutual mockery, "feminist anthropology" is, for Strathern, not quite an oxymoron, but a hybrid beast. The awkwardness between feminism and anthropology thus involves disjunctions which extend beyond the problems of introducing women's perspectives into a discipline with a history of "male bias." This is because other forms of domination—in particular those of colonialism and racism—are just as central as that of gender inequality to the relationship between feminist thought and anthropology.

The same could be said of those forms of domination implicit in the relationship between feminism and the history of religions, but the mockery here is one-sided. Like anthropology, the history of religions has a long tradition of a perspective which is valued highly in feminist scholarship. A hermeneutic approach which makes empathy with lived religious experience central to interpretation and comparison was developed in the history and phenomenology of religions when other disciplines were working through their positivist phases (see, for example, Dudley 1977; Allen 1978). Since critiques of positivism have been prominent in many strands of feminist epistemology, the history of religions could be said to have had at its core an interpretive standpoint which many have seen as central to feminist scholarship.

But in practice, the history/phenomenology of religions is an apt illustration that a hermeneutic of empathy and experience is far from being automatically feminist. The question of whose subjective experience is being empathized with is crucial. All too typically, it is not that of real persons but of a "collective subject" whose supposedly authoritative experience is either undifferentiated by gender, race, class or age, or defined explicitly as male. In particular, the writings of Eliade and his followers are premised upon this collective subject, usually known as "*Homo religiosus*": "Eliade understood that religious man will take a wife, build a house, make love, raise children, eat, sleep, go to war, make peace, and prepare for death out of [a] felt relationship to the gods, and what he believes they expect of him" (Idinopulos 1994: 72).

What does "lived religious experience" mean when it is located in a purportedly universal subject? And how universal can this impersonal subject be when represented through such unabashedly gender-specific depiction? In this totalizing but exclusionary empathy for a reified *Homo religiosus*, the mockery of feminism by the history of religions—like the mockery of feminism by anthropology—falls flat.

This mockery, moreover, is not reciprocated. Those in mainstream history of religions have not typically striven for ideals represented by feminist scholarship. Allen, for example, draws attention to feminist critiques of Eliade (such as Saiving 1976), and observes that "one would never guess from Eliade's treatment that androcentrism and a theologically misogynist tradition, that patriarchal structures of exploitation and oppression, were key notions in the interpretation of witchcraft" (Allen 1978: 117–118). Yet he does so merely to make a point about the perspectival nature of knowledge; he cites such critiques "not ... so much ... to show that Eliade's scale is explicitly androcentric, but rather that his perspective emphasizes certain notions and overlooks or de-emphasizes other dimensions of the phenomena" (Allen 1978: 118–119). But to argue that the standpoint of mainstream history and phenomenology of religions and the standpoint of feminist critiques are merely two perspectives among many misses the point of such critiques: it is not just that all knowledge is partial, but that some perspectives represent a "view from above." In the history of religion, a "view from above" is entrenched through, first, the over-whelming emphasis given to religious texts and, second, the concept of the *sui generis* nature of religion, in which religion is treated as a discrete and irreducible phenomenon which exists "in and of itself." Feminist scholarship can only collide with, rather than mock, mainstream history of religions: not only has the latter had a very poor record of overhauling itself in terms of critiques "from below," but its central *sui generis* argument is incompatible with the very basis of such critiques.

The "Distinctively Religious" and the Distinctly Apolitical

Both the textual and the *sui generis* definitions emphasized in religious studies scholarship are, in practice, "bracketing" devices which support each other in representing religion as socially decontextualized and ungendered. Under-standings of "religion as scripture" tend, for example, to privilege (a) religions with texts, and (b) scholarly elites within scriptural religious traditions who claim the authority to interpret texts (and from whom women are usually debarred). The religious understandings of those excluded from authorizing discourses of textual interpretation are implicitly discounted and relegated to a "lower" level. To "saby book," as the Nigerian participants in [Rosalind] Hackett's essay ... put it, has indeed been used to define the center of religious traditions—as well as of the discipline concerned with their study—and to relegate women to the periphery. That strand of women's scholarship which simply presents accounts of "women who wrote texts too" thus does little to recast this dominant focus. This orthodoxy has recently been challenged, however, by feminist studies which explore innovative ways of reading and critically interrogating scriptures and other texts (e.g., Fiorenza 1983; Atkinson *et al.*, 1985).

Like the understanding of "religion as text," the concept of the *sui generis* nature of religion also entails the decontextualization of religion. In mainstream history of religions, understandings of "the uniquely religious" are usually constituted by excluding or peripheralizing social and political content in defining what really counts as "religion." Historians of religion who make the *sui generis* claim do not suggest that "pure religious" phenomena can exist empirically, but that "certain experiences or phenomena exhibit a fundamental religious character and that our method must be commensurate with the nature of our subject-matter. From the perspective of the History of Religions, the sociological, economic, or anthropological dimensions of the phenomena are "secondary" (Allen 1978: 83–84).

Thus desocialized, "the uniquely religious" is deemed interpretable only "on its own terms": studies of religion which entail social or political analysis are typically dismissed as reductionist. Eliade, who more than anyone else has defined this dominant "antireductionist" discourse in the history of religions, offers the following axiom: "[A] religious phenomenon will only be recognized as such if it is grasped at its own level, that is to say, if it is studied as something religious. To try to grasp the essence of such a phenomenon by means of physiology, psychology, sociology, economics, linguistics, art or any other is false (Eliade 1963: xiii). As some of the contributors to a recent volume on reductionism and religion (Idinopulos and Yonan 1994) point out, such essentializing assumptions close off the potentially awkward question of what "the nature of religion" is:

> If I am right about the intellectual history of the notion of religion, it has shifted several times in the last hundred years already.... Eliade slams the door shut on possible competitors to his own "spiritualist" position. Instead, he just insists on the identity of religious phenomena by appeal to "what they are ..." But "what they are" is or should be an open question; Eliade's anti-reductionist (by replacement) stance rejects alternatives out of hand. (Strenski 1994: 101; see also Segal 1989, 1994)

Since "religion" as a category is not indigenous to most parts of the world, moreover, the *sui generis* concept often involves the imposition of "the irreducibly religious" upon a landscape of human practices and understandings which do not divide up into the categories cherished by Western scholars.

As part of its discouragement of debates about "the nature of religion," the discourse of irreducibility also deflects questions of power and inequality: the "distinctively religious" is constituted as distinctly apolitical. Eliade writes, for example:

> Few religious phenomena are more directly and more obviously connected with socio-political circumstances than the modern messianic and millenarian movements among colonial people (cargo-cults, etc.). Yet

identifying and analyzing the conditions that prepared and made possible such messianic movements form only a part of the work of the historian of religions. For these movements are equally creations of the human spirit, in the sense that they have become what they are—religious movements, and not merely gestures of protest and revolt—through a creative act of the spirit. (Eliade 1969: 6)

Eliade leaves us in no doubt that for him "mere gestures of protest and revolt" are not part of the creative repertoire of "the human spirit." But for those within millenarian movements, politics and protest are implicated in the very constitution of their religious practice. Their experience of colonial power is "interior" to—not somehow detachable from—their lived religious experience. Power, then, cannot simply be bracketed off as a "dimension" or "aspect" of religion (see Shaw and Stewart 1994).

To take another example, attempting to understand a woman's experience of religion in terms of (not just "in the context of") her position within a male-dominated religious tradition is reductionist only if we have severed "religion" from "power" in the first place. On the contrary, it would be a "reduction"—in the rather different sense of a diminished and distorted representation of her experience—to bracket off "male dominance" and "gender asymmetry" as a mere biographical backdrop to, but not really part of, experiences which she calls "religious." With power and social organization detached from the analysis of gender and religion, we are left either with meaningless accounts of "religious gender roles" ("the men do this; the women do that"), or with disconnected descriptions of female deities ("add goddesses and stir").

The *sui generis* concept thus stands in a contradictory relationship to the premises of feminist scholarship. By making power irrelevant to "the nature of religion," it denies the scholar of religion a language with which to make a critique "from below," relegating the very basis of a distinction between a "view from above" and a "view from below" to the realm of crass reductionism. By making it central to their discourse, scholars in the history of religions are effectively insulated from uncomfortable questions about standpoint and privilege—questions upon which feminist scholarship is based. The relationship between feminism and mainstream history of religions is not merely awkward; it is mutually toxic.

Institutional Embattlement and the Politics of Interpretation

The concept of the irreducibility of religion was not, of course, intentionally formulated as a bulwark against feminist critiques (even if this is, in fact, a consequence). Its hegemony has to be understood within the politics of disciplinary identity, in the embattled institutional position of the history of religions within the academy. Like feminist scholarship and women's studies, religious studies is ambiguously situated as both a distinct discipline and a multidisciplinary field analogous to American studies or science studies. As such, in many universities it has been in constant danger of being demoted from a department to a sub-department or an interdisciplinary program. In other institutions it is perceived to be subsumed by—and hence institutionally indistinct from—theology: in British universities in particular, the era of cuts euphemistically described as "rationalization" in the late 1970s and throughout the 1980s saw the closure of most departments of religious studies which were not sheltered within departments of theology. In public, secular American universities, on the other hand, religious studies is often attacked as an apparent anomaly. As Idinopulos writes:

> we who taught in the Department of Religion were faced with difficult questions from our colleagues about the appropriateness of such a department in a tax-supported, public university: Why teach religion in a secular university? Does the study of religion really warrant a separate department? What are the special credentials which attach to a professor of religion that differ from the credentials of any social scientist who takes an interest in the study of religion and offers courses based on his research? (Idinopulos 1994: 65)

In addition to this institutional embattlement, mainstream history of religions has for several decades been intellectually marginalized, consistently out of phase with broader debates and paradigm-shifts which cut across disciplines, such as feminism, structuralism, postmodernism, reflexivity, and cultural critique. It has been so ignored by scholars in other disciplines who are concerned with religion that any attention from the latter tends to bring forth a spate of published reactions—witness Dudley's (1977) response to an anthropologist's attack upon Eliade in a mere book review (Leach 1966). Up to the 1960s, the strong phenomenological strand of the history of religions placed it, in many ways, ahead of its time. This also placed it beyond the pale, however, during the positivist and scientistic phase of anthropology and other social sciences during their structural-functionalist and structuralist eras. In the 1960s and 1970s, however, anthropological interests shifted towards a concern with meaning and interpretation which took the form of symbolic anthropology in the USA (e.g., Geertz 1966) and semantic anthropology in the UK (e.g., Crick 1976). These shifts entailed a reawakening of interest in religion and in phenomenology, but this took place for the most part as if the phenomenology of religion had never existed.

It has been in response to the double threat of institutional embattlement and intellectual marginalization that the boundary-defending argument of the *sui generis* nature of religion—and accompanying claims for the unique interpretive privilege of the history of religions—have been developed into a kind of disciplinary creed. "Antireductionist" arguments, usually reiterated as a counter-critique of a structural-functionalist anthropology which has not existed for thirty years, are still part of the prevailing discourse of the history of religions today (when many anthropologists, ironically, can scarcely remember what structural-functionalism was).

The "straw discipline" argument of antireductionism may sometimes be tactically useful in institutional battles over departmental autonomy and resources, but at the ultimately self-defeating cost of continued intellectual marginalization. "By imagining a continuing struggle between religious studies and the social sciences," one scholar of religion observes sadly, "we can be encouraged that someone is taking us seriously, even if that someone is mostly only we ourselves" (Elzey 1994: 94). The high disciplinary walls which scholars of religion have created have cut them off from many new intellectual directions, debates and discourses, thereby transforming mainstream history of religions from an exciting approach ahead of its time in the 1950s and 1960s to a broken record endlessly rehearsing thirty-year-old debates in the 1990s. Some scholars in religious studies, aware of the missed opportunities entailed by Eliade's exaggerated claims of autonomy, argue for an end to "all those interminable arguments about the transcendental reality of religion" (Strenski 1994: 107): "... despite the real risks of reconceptualization, we must resist looking on reduction like our cry-baby colleagues.... Reconceptualization also promises renewal and revival.... We have to begin accepting conceptual change as a normal part of trading in the world of knowledge (Strenski 1994: 104–105).

The Gendering of Religious Studies

By reconceptualizing power as integral to—as opposed to a detachable "dimension" of—religion, feminist religious studies has the potential to generate conceptual change and renewal. Yet its capacity for disciplinary transformation is currently cramped by hangovers from mainstream religious studies which some forms of feminist religious studies have carried with them. In this way, these (fairly dominant) strands of feminist religious studies are in a position analogous to that of feminist anthropology in the 1970s, which responded to the marginalizing of women in the discipline's mainstream by an essentializing discourse which placed it securely in a feminist "ghetto." Another article by Strathern (1981) consists of a critique of such writings, which eventually enabled feminist anthropology to reconceptualize itself, leave its ghetto and acquire a more audible voice in the discipline.

Particularly important here was Strathern's critique of the assumption of a unitary and essentialized category of "woman" which unites the female researcher with the women in the (different) social and cultural context she is researching. Strathern's scepticism helped to sensitize white feminist anthropologists to criticisms of Western feminism by non-Western women and women of color, who pointed out that their race and their history of colonization make a difference which makes it impossible to talk of a universal "women's nature." Currently, few feminist scholars in any discipline assume a universal "female reality." That many scholars in feminist religious studies are an exception to this derives, I believe, from the universalizing and essentializing tendencies of the discipline's mainstream.

In a recent critique of the "transubstantiation" of women's experience into images of goddesses and cyborgs in some forms of feminist theory, Hewitt (1993) examines recent writings in feminist spirituality, best exemplified in the work of Carol Christ (e.g., Christ 1985, 1987; Christ and Plaskow 1979). As its alternative name of "thealogy" suggests, feminist spirituality is directed against—yet implicitly shaped by—patriarchal traditions of Christian theology and practice. Thus God the Father is replaced by the Goddess as Mother, the embodiment of a cosmic femininity which "refers back to a feminine ontology that is little more than the inverse of masculinist conceptualizations" (Hewitt 1993: 138).

Although Christ is highly critical of Eliade (Christ 1991), moreover, her methodology is closer to his than her criticism would suggest. Where Eliade proposed a universalized (but male) *Homo religiosus* as the true subject of religious experience, Christ proposes a universalized female spiritual essence in which all women participate. Eliade felt free to construct his version of this collective subject, unhampered by the self-representations of real religious participants:

> "It does not matter in the least," says Eliade beginning his dismissal of any Dilthey-like advocacy of the native's point of view, "whether or not the 'primitives' of today realize that immersion in water is the equivalent both of the deluge and of the submerging of a continent in the sea".... Instead, Eliade proposes nothing less than a total theory of religion, and thus one which *replaces* old meanings with (his) new ones. This "totalizing" ambition explains why, in the end, Eliade does not care about what the "natives" say or think. (Strenski 1994: 102–103; see also Idinopulos 1994: 75–78)

Christ's approach—to use her own experiences of reconstructed goddess rituals as the basis for her interpretation of prehistoric goddess worship (e.g., Christ 1985: 123)—is no less totalizing. With the aid of these experiences, she adapts Elisabeth Schüssler Fiorenza's method of "imaginative reconstruction of reality." Yet Fiorenza's method:

> is not easily adaptable to non-linguistic evidence from Neolithic times, which is where Christ ultimately wishes to apply it.... Without acknowledging the complexities involved, Christ uses Schüssler Fiorenza's

method of "imaginative reconstruction" as license for mythic and literary invention. By doing this, Christ hopes to avoid having to differentiate between the religious, symbolic meaning of the Goddess in her own spiritual life, and the public, historical claims that seek to establish the prevalence of Goddess worship, including the higher status of women, in prehistoric times. (Hewitt 1993: 147)

Through such appropriation of the experience of women in other times and places, a feminized *Homo religiosus* lives on. A feminist religious studies which does not incorporate differences between women—in particular between the researcher and the women she writes about—will merely invoke the concept of power without applying it to its own colonizing discourse. That sensitivity to these differences does not, of course, mean "objectivity" is clear in examples of feminist studies of women's religion which demonstrate such sensitivity (e.g., Boddy 1989; Brown 1991). Quite the reverse: it requires more reflexivity rather than less; more attention to intersubjectivity; more attention to the voices of other women as personal actors that one cannot speak for; and more attention to the web of social relationships and cultural practices through which their power and experience are constituted.

References

Allen, Douglas 1978. *Structure and Creativity in Religion: Hermeneutics in Mircea Eliade's Phenomenology and New Directions*. The Hague: Mouton.

Atkinson, C. *et al.* (eds.) 1985. *Immaculate and Powerful: The Female in Sacred Image and Social Reality*. Boston: Beacon Press.

Boddy, Janice 1989. *Wombs and Alien Spirits: Women, Men and the Zar Cult in Northern Sudan*. Madison: University of Wisconsin Press.

Brown, Karen McCarthy 1991. *Mama Lola: A Vodou Priestess in Brooklyn*. Berkeley: University of California Press.

Christ, Carol 1985. "Discussion: What are the Sources of My Theology," *Journal for Feminist Studies in Religion* 1: 120–123.

—— 1987. *Laughter of Aphrodite: Reflections on a Journey to the Goddess*. San Francisco: Harper & Row.

—— 1991. "Mircea Eliade and the Feminist Paradigm Shift," *Journal for Feminist Studies in Religion* 7: 75–94.

Christ, Carol and Judith Plaskow (eds.) 1979. *Womanspirit Rising: A Feminist Reader in Religion*. San Francisco: Harper & Row.

Crick, Malcolm 1976. *Explorations in Language and Meaning: Towards a Semantic Anthropology*. London: Malaby Press.

Dudley, Guilford 1977. *Religion on Trial: Mircea Eliade and his Critics*. Philadelphia: Temple University Press.

Eliade, Mircea 1963. *Patterns in Comparative Religion*. New York: Meridian Books.

—— 1969. *The Quest: History and Meaning in Religion*. Chicago: University of Chicago Press.

Elzey, Wayne 1994. "Mircea Eliade and the Battle Against Reductionism," *Religion and Reductionism*, 82–94. Thomas Idinopulos and Edward Yonan (eds.). Leiden: E. J. Brill.

Fiorenza, Elisabeth Schüssler 1983. *In Memory of Her: A Feminist Theological Reconstruction of Christian Origins*. New York: Crossroad.

Geertz, Clifford 1966. "Religion as a Cultural System," *Anthropological Approaches to the Study of Religion*, 1–46. Michael Banton (ed.). New York: Praeger.

Hewitt, Marsha A. 1993. "Cyborgs, Drag Queens, and Goddesses: Emancipatory-Regressive Paths in Feminist Theory," *Method & Theory in the Study of Religion* 5: 135–154.

Idinopulos, Thomas A. 1994. "Must Professors of Religion be Religious? Comments on Eliade's Method of Inquiry and Segal's Defense of Reductionism." *Religion and Reductionism*, 65–81. Thomas Indinopulos and Edward Yonan (eds.). Leiden: E. J. Brill.

Idinopulos, Thomas and Edward Yonan (eds.) 1994. *Religion and Reductionism: Essays on Eliade, Segal, and the Challenge of the Social Sciences for the Study of Religion*. Leiden: E. J. Brill.

Leach, Edmund 1966. "Sermons by a Man on a Ladder," *New York Review of Books*, October 20: 28–31.

Moore, Henrietta 1989. *Feminism and Anthropology*. London: Polity Press.

Saiving, Valerie 1976. "Androcentrism in Religious Studies," *Journal of Religion* 56: 177–197.

Segal, Robert A. 1989. *Religion and the Social Sciences: Essays on the Confrontation*. Atlanta: Scholars Press.

—— 1994. "Reductionism in the Study of Religion," *Religion and Reductionism*, 4–14. Thomas Indinopulos and Edward Yonan (eds.). Leiden: E. J. Brill.

Shaw, Rosalind and Charles Stewart 1994. "Introduction: Problematizing Syncretism," *Syncretism/Anti-Syncretism: The Politics of Religious Synthesis*. Charles Stewart and Rosalind Shaw (eds.). London and New York: Routledge.

Strathern, Marilyn 1981. "Culture in a Netbag: On the Manufacture of a Subdiscipline in Anthropology," *Man* 16: 665–688.

—— 1987. "An Awkward Relationship: The Case of Feminism and Anthropology," *Signs* 12: 276–292.

Strenski, Ivan 1994. "Reduction Without Tears," *Religion and Reductionism*, 95–107. Thomas Idinopulos and Edward Yonan (eds.). Leiden: E. J. Brill.

9

RAYMOND FIRTH, *An Anthropological Approach to the Study of Religion*

ও৲ও৲

A major problem in modern thought is the existence and survival of religion. In a world of rapidly developing technology and radically changing social and political institutions, is religion in peril? Opinions on this vary greatly. Some people hold that secularism and rationalism are sweeping irresistibly across the world of belief. In many Western countries they see organized church congregations greatly shrunk, and the forces of modernism and the international market threatening to reduce religious institutions to a negligible dimension. Events in communist countries seemed for a time to bear out this view also. But an opinion which now seems better founded is that organized religion can be eliminated only in special cases, and diffuse religious belief may continue in the absence of overt ritual practice. Belief and ritual relating to the transcendent, it is thought therefore, will not only survive in the face of adversity and indifference, but may even develop in protest against the materialistic thrust of secular values.

Yet bitter controversy has arisen regarding the relation of religion to the secular world, even among religious people themselves. Animosity has also been manifest between followers of different religions, and even of members of sects, denominations, churches within any particular religion. Sometimes these come to expression in continued acts of violence, as between Catholics and Protestants in Northern Ireland. Sometimes they are evident in struggles for adherents, as in the wasteful duplication of missionary efforts of Christianity and Islam in Africa. Often argument about ideas has been deeply divisive within religious bodies, as entrenched positions on say the teaching of religion in school; the ordination of women to priesthood; the dominance of religious or secular law in a nation-state.

Many theories about the nature and origin of religion try to account for the persistence of faith and ritual. They also explore reasons for the changes that religions have undergone in the course of their history. Two contrasted positions are common. Believers argue that their religion is simply accounted for by the existence of God or whatever spiritual entities they worship. Sceptics hold that religion is just a human illusion. But clearly the matter is more complex. Religion cannot be understood simply as a response of men to divine revelation, or alternatively as a case of mistaken perception. For religions show enormous variety, in types of belief, degrees of belief, kinds of ritual procedures, spiritual concepts and symbolic imagery. Religions also vary greatly in the kind of relationship they bear to the social, economic and political structures of the communities in which they are practiced. Any "theory" then has to be many-armed, multi-factorial, to take account of this range of variation. Ideally, the theory should be explanatory, showing why the given forms and processes originated. But the ultimate "Why?" of any religion may be thought to be too elusive. Any simple affirmation of divine presence and revelation will not do; assertion has to stand the test of evidence. Metaphysical problems enter here at every turn.

All that may be possible in a theory of religion may be interpretation, a demonstration of the nature and meaning of rites and beliefs for those people who hold and practice them, of their value for the people in the context of their lives. As part of the interpretation, the theory must deal with nonrational as well as rational elements in belief patterns and practice.

Anthropologists have contributed in a unique way to theories of the operations and meaning of religions, over a wide comparative range. In earlier times the work of Edward Burnett Tylor, Robertson Smith, James Frazer, R. R. Marett, Jane Harrison and E. O. James was of pioneering character. More recently Edward Evans-Pritchard, Godfrey Lienhardt, S. E. Nadel, John Middleton, Victor Turner, Monica Wilson—to mention only a few Africanists—have provided detailed analytical studies of particular religious systems. They and many other anthropologists in other regions have examined notions of God; concepts of the soul, ghosts, ancestral and other spirits; cults of the dead; the operations of priests and prophets; shrines, offerings, sacrifices; purification and pollution; ideas of sin and salvation. My own studies in the religious field have included a demonstration of the close fit between economic and religious operations in the traditional seasonal ritual cycles of a western Polynesian community (Firth 1967) and a more general examination of the relation between the political structure and the religion of these people (Firth 1970).

Though anthropologists have focused largely on the comparative study of the small-scale so-called "primitive" religions of the technically less developed peoples, many of us have also examined aspects of the major universalistic religions. Following a lead of E. O. James in his historical study of Christian myth and ritual (1933), Victor Turner has written of Christianity, S. J.

Tambiah of Buddhism, Dale F. Eickelman, Clifford Geertz and Ernest Gellner of Islam. Nearly all the dozen anthropological contributions to a book on religious organization and religious experience edited by John Davis (1982) dealt with aspects of the great religions. My own studies of religious symbolism (1973) have included comment upon the ethnicity of Jesus, the concept of the Sacred Heart of Jesus, and the Eucharist.

The value of any theory of religion depends not only on the logical development of the argument, but also upon the validity of the evidence produced in support. The approach of social anthropologists to the study of religion, unlike that of historian, theologian, psychologist or even sociologist, has been based largely upon unique experience, that of field enquiry. This has consisted in personal observation, often involving actually taking part in the religious practices of the people being studied, and systematic discussion of their religious beliefs with them. This has also involved studying the religion in its social setting and noting the economic and political parameters to religious ideas and operations. Combined with a training in the comparative scholarship of religious belief and institutions, this has given social anthropologists a special perspective and a powerful body of evidence for examining religion.

Since the study is so unfamiliar to many people, in the next part of this chapter I give an outline of a social anthropological approach, its aims, its difficulties and the kind of results it hopes to get. But social anthropologists have approached the subject of religion and formulated their theories about it with many different interests and diverse assumptions about the reality of the phenomena studied. Hence in the latter part of this chapter I describe my own personal position, as a preface to the general theoretical statements of the book as a whole.

General Character of Social Anthropology

Anthropology, from the Greek, means the study of man. Social anthropology, my own specialism, was the latest main branch of the subject to develop explicitly, about seventy years ago. It is concerned with men's and women's relationships to one another in society, with the behavior patterns, institutions and beliefs which characterize people in different types of society. Social anthropology has two important features which distinguish it from other fields of social study. It is essentially comparative, studying human behavior in all forms of society in any part of the world, its variations and the meaning of such variants. In such comparisons social anthropology tends to take a wider range than sociology, with which it has shared a considerable theoretical history. Social anthropology is also distinguished by the directness and intensity of the relationship of its fieldworkers to the people among whom they work. Often described as "participant observation," the situation of the fieldworker is apt to be unique, living in a hunter's camp, village or urban ward among the people, sharing food with them, attending their marriage ceremonies, initiation rites and funerals, speaking their vernacular tongue. The anthropologist is in communication with them throughout the day—and often well into the night— listening to their gossip and tales of joy or woe, getting to understand their loves, their jealousies and rivalries, their expectations and their fears, their religious beliefs and forms of symbolic behavior. Such experiences, even if lasting for only a year or so, but sometimes repeated periodically, can be very significant for the anthropologist, with aesthetic and emotional as well as intellectual values. Vividly meaningful, the record of these experiences forms the basis for much analytical anthropological study.

There is another feature of peculiar importance in an anthropological study of religion. Unlike many of those, such as missionaries or government officials, who have been in contact with members of an alien society, anthropologists have been trained not to attach a moral evaluation to their record of what they see and hear. Personally, any anthropologist may feel approval or revulsion at some religious practice or belief, but his/her job is to describe it and reveal its meaning, not to class it on some moral scale. One may expect from an anthropologist then a more compassionate, more neutral, perhaps more sympathetic and more understanding account of a religious system than that provided by another outside observer.

Considering the unique character of the anthropological experience in studying religion, some questions may arise about the methods and the validity of the findings.

A general question in all fieldwork, not particularly in a study of religion, is how far an anthropologist can really have access to the ways of thinking and feeling of the alien, often "exotic" people studied? Complete access is impossible. One can observe, even share another person's overt behavior. One cannot observe, let alone directly experience another person's thoughts and emotions; one can only infer them. An anthropologist may watch a Polynesian religious ritual of offering a libation of *kava* (an infusion of pepper root) liquid, where the officiating chief-priest raises the coconut shell cup to his brow before pouring out the liquid upon the ground before him. The anthropologist infers that the act is an offering to invisible spirits of gods and ancestors, and this is confirmed by statements of priest and other elders, and by the behavior of respect shown to symbols of the spirits. The lifting of the cup to the brow is then clearly an act of obeisance, of acknowledgment of dependence upon the spirits, and such an interpretation fits into the whole passage of the ritual. But it is impossible for the anthropologist to know *exactly* what is passing through the mind of the priest as he lifts the cup to his brow. There are various possibilities known to the anthropologist—the chief is thinking with respect to the spirits, he is anxious about food supplies for the rite, he is worried about the health of his family which depends upon the goodwill of the spirits, or he is concerned with some more mundane problem such as to whom will be distributed the food brought as offering, once the rite is over. Later discussion with the priest may let the anthropologist check as to whether such thoughts may have been in the priest's mind. This means that anthropological inferences about religious belief, as distinct from accounts of religious behavior, must always be approximate. But this is not a situation confined to anthropology; it is so with all forms of human encounter and communication. In every phase of everyday life we have to make an effort at interpreting what is being thought by others, or felt, with varying degrees of success. Claims of writers and speakers of all kinds, from poets to preachers, to "understand" what other people think and feel, or what they do, rest upon such broad interpretation.

The question of how far an anthropologist's findings are governed by his or her personality, temperament and experience is important for any study of religion. There has been much professional emphasis in recent years upon the "reflexive" or "autobiographical" components of an anthropological inter-pretation. The idea of objectivity has been scorned. It has been held that all anthropological accounts are subjective, reflections of the self of the investigator, as imaginative constructs.

But recognition of such personal elements in anthropological findings is not new. Some thirty years ago I myself wrote that the observer's experience is always viewed through his personal lens; that if one wished to use Cassirer's terms there is no content which is not construed according to some form which is supplied by the human understanding at the start of apprehension. The experience is itself form-selected. A scientist cannot immediately grasp or communicate reality; he can only mediate it. In knowledge, truth itself must be in accord with the form of understanding. But while we may grant that the form-giving and symbolizing activities of consciousness mean that we can never reproduce the "crude facts" of Malay or Tikopia social life, this does not justify intellectual retreat (Firth 1964: 41). We can continually learn from experience, and the field experience of the anthropologist is continually being built into his/her framework of ideas. So these ideas are continually being modified, not simply emerging as a kind of pre-formed straitjacket upon the construction and interpretation of what is observed, thought and felt in the field. Too much preoccupation with the anthropologist's own role and state of mind can blur the observation of record.

There is undoubtedly some relation, however faint, between the tempera-ment and personality of an anthropologist and his/her interpretation of the data gathered. But it may be hard to identify this relation adequately; even in a study of religion I think I can identify some aspects of my own early religious and moral upbringing in my writings about religion. But what about aesthetic make-up? In the attraction which Romanesque painting and sculpture have for me, with their grotesque, hieratic and symbolic forms, I can perceive a kind of general link with some of the more idiosyncratic, bizarre religious practices of people studied by anthropologists. But not so in my preference for Western "early music." It has a curious appeal for me, from Machaut's first setting of the Mass through Dufay's lament for the fall of Constantinople and the work of Josquin des Prés, Ockeghem, Dunstable, Tallis, Byrd, Schütz, Monteverdi to the supreme beauty of J. S. Bach. This musical commitment clearly fits into a historical interest in Christian religion. But I cannot trace its effect in any of my interpretation of the religious sayings and doings of the Tikopia or of the Kelantan Malays. What I am arguing is that the elements of temperament and experience of any anthropologist are so complex, so subtly composed and intertwined that only at a most superficial level can any identification of them be usually seen in his or her professional work. In judging such work the primary criteria are those of internal validity—amount and quality of evidence, degree of checking manifest, systematic approach in putting counter-questions to see if the propositions formulated can be falsified, consistence of inference from the record.

What I am defending is the claim of social anthropology to present an acceptable ethnography of religion, not a fictionalized, fantasized account of what has been studied. But, ... when it comes to more general interpretation of religious matters, the personal assumptions of the anthropologist may be highly significant. An important set of problems in any anthropological study of religion involves language. The treachery of language as a mode of reference is well-known. To express thought in language often creates great difficulties. A Slav poet, Fyodor Tyutchev, has said "A thought when uttered is a lie," in despair at the inadequacies of language to convey the intricacies of mental process. For an anthropologist there is the problem of rendering in verbal form, in words, images many of which have been presented to the fieldworker in non-verbal, visual, or aural terms. There is also the special problem of glossing in one language utterances which have originally been made in another language. Anthropologists are now generally expected to "speak the vernacular." But there are many stages or levels of being able to handle an alien vernacular tongue. During my time in Malaya I became fairly competent in speaking and understanding the Kelantan dialect of Malay, carrying on extensive conversations with fishermen and rice farmers, and local magicians, on a variety of topics from net-making and catching fish to shadow-play drama and beliefs about the bounty of Allah. But I was not equipped to deal easily either with the linguistic niceties of court etiquette or the more abstract theological and philosophical discussions with the more learned men of the neighborhood. Over the years, I have become highly competent in the Tikopia language. Uncommonly for an anthropologist, I have published a dictionary (Tikopia–English), in which I have been able to gloss Tikopia words very extensively in terms of their social context of use. Yet I would never claim that I have had the complete fluency of a native Tikopia speaker. Deep questions, including those relating to unstated philosophical and religious assumptions, lie behind the anthropologist's choice of glosses in his/her translations of many esoteric vernacular terms. From the linguistic angle, then, I insist on the approximate, illustrative nature of any ethnographic account of a religious system.

Granted these qualifications, I would still contend that an anthropologist is probably better equipped than most observers to give an account of an alien religious system, and to offer an original, comparative theoretical view of religion in general.

Personal Standpoint

I now turn to my own more personal standpoint in anthropological analysis, with particular reference to the ideas and practices of religion. In my collection and interpretation of anthropological data I have been guided by a basic curiosity about the nature of the human condition, with all its complexities of individual belief and action as affected by a network of social relationships, norms and obligations. In shaping my enquiries I have been led by two themes which to a degree have marked my work off from that of some of my colleagues. These are empiricism and humanism.

It has been a fashion in much modern or "post-modern" social anthropology to decry what has been termed a positivist, empiricist approach. By contrast, I call myself an empiricist, accepting in general the validity of sensory experience as a guide to knowledge. I reject claims to knowledge by revelation. But I am a modified empiricist, a neo-empiricist. I accept the possibility that ultimately the results of sensory experience may be illusory, that their unreality is a logical alternative. As J. N. Findlay and others have pointed out, there is always a possibility of error in any material-object statements, including those about the nature of material existence itself (Findlay 1963: 36). I also accept as significant in thought what may be called "intuition," a cohering activity of the mind not apparently due to any action of the senses. (But what is called "intuition" in my view is often only an unconscious inference from subliminal observation, often relying on previous experience, or an analogy in experience.) My empiricist position has been closely bound to my conviction of the importance of evidence in anthropological propositions. I am sceptical of assertions of knowledge not backed up by empirical evidence; in religious matters they are often no more than assertions of privilege or claims to power. That the evidence must be open to critical scrutiny applies to any study of religion as to that of any other social phenomenon.

My approach to religion has been distinguished from that of some of my colleagues by my humanism. There are alternative approaches to the recognition of reality. Some Western anthropologists have clearly professed a Christian faith, while others elsewhere have adhered to Hinduism, Buddhism,

Judaism, or Islam. The term "humanism" is rather suspect in Western intellectual circles, since it suggests an old-fashioned rationalism. But some other social anthropologists such as Ernest Gellner and the late Edmund Leach, as I myself, have been honorary associates of the Rationalist Press Association, the major humanist association in Britain, as well as other distinguished thinkers such as Karl Popper and Joseph Needham. In social anthropology other colleagues are probably of much the same temper, though preferring not to bear the humanist label. (Philosophers who share the same general trend of thought may call themselves "realists," such as "internal realists" or "scientific realists.")

Any social anthropologist studying religion must have some basic assumptions about the nature of the phenomena. My own assumptions are humanistic, based on the view that a central part of reality for people everywhere lies in the existence of human individuals in their social matrix, and that it is comprehensible only by human cognition and expressible only in human language. The universe holds many mysteries, from the behavior of quasars in space, to the sexual attraction between two persons. Many human problems are obscure, and the fate of individuals unpredictable. But I assume that whatever be the nature of the external world, there is no reality of another order beyond that world, no revelation of divine plan or divine values, no creative supersensible transcendent mind that can give meaning and sense to human experience and human endeavors.

To an anthropologist such as myself, therefore, religion, including ideas of God, is clearly a human construct. It grows and is maintained by the wish to have answers to fundamental human problems. Religion supplies reasons for the forms of nature, for human existence. It faces questions of pain and suffering and the ultimate fate of the human personality. According to its particular tenets, it encourages love, charity and respect for others. It can also provide a great pillar of strength, both by the alleged certainty of the propositions it proclaims, and by a body of faithful who support one another. But religion is a human art. It has produced, like other arts, some of the greatest literary and intellectual constructs, analyses of thought and emotion, and stirring aesthetic experiences of a creative order in painting, poetry and music. But it has also been treated as a ladder to personal and group advancement, as an instrument of manipulation in ideas and behavior, the purveyor of ready-made solutions to traumatic issues of human conduct. In its corporate aspect, a church can be a sociological force of great impact. It can be of positive value in helping to maintain moral standards. But it can also offer a field for controversy about doctrine and ritual, for divisive sectarian activity and opposition. It can even act as a force of destruction, as violent collisions of religious wars have demonstrated in many faiths.

A humanist approach to religion, within an anthropological framework, of enquiry, means that rational study can go much further than religious people are often prepared to allow. "Science" may be able to give no final answers to such problems as the origin of the universe, the nature and fate of a soul, the occurrence of miracles. The answers of religion are assertions, no more capable of proof. But if the answers given by either science or religion are untestable, one can speak in terms of probabilities. On this basis, the asserted existence of an invisible, transcendent, omniscient, omnipotent being known as God is highly improbable. It is much more probable that such an assertion fits the highly complex world of human imagining, and serves an array of human purposes not always consciously realized by people themselves. It corresponds in figurative and symbolic language to an attempt to meet basic human problems involved in mental and physical anxiety and pain, the certainty of death, the uncertainties of life in the complicated relations with other human beings. The propositions of religion, despite claims to any divine origin, are all formulated by human beings. Its asserted transcendental origins do not mean that these propositions are true in any external, objective sense. One does not speak of a musical composition as true (unless in a highly technical sense) but as beautiful, powerful, aesthetically and emotionally satisfying. And so it should be with the imaginative creations of religion.

Such a humanist viewpoint is unpalatable to many religious people. Most theologians object to what they have termed such a reductionist, projectionist approach to religion. A professor of theology, John Kent, has singled out Emile Durkheim, author of a book on what he called the elementary forms of religious life, and an early proponent of a humanist view of religion, for critical treatment (in Richardson and Bowden 1983, "Reductionism"). "When Durkheim, the French sociologist, attempted to 'reduce' the idea of God to society's sense of its own oneness, he did so, the historian may say, because he was a frightened moralist anxious to detect social forces which might be relied upon to unite what he saw as a disintegrating French society in the early twentieth century." But to anyone familiar with Durkheim's work this interpretation seems an odd paraphrase of his own statement of his objective: "to lead to an understanding of the religious nature of man, that is to say, to show us an essential and permanent aspect of humanity." Durkheim's proposition that God is society divinized can be criticized on various grounds, as over-simplified. But striking examples of how it may apply in some conditions do occur. In some aspects of Israeli fundamentalism, the modern concept of Eretz Israel—"a land promised to the Jews by Abraham"—claims that God Himself is the author of the sanction for settlement in Palestinian lands. Such an interpretation by the extreme nationalist group Gush Emunim clearly identifies God as the justificatory sanctified projection of their own sense of pressing community territorial needs. The crude community drive is given spiritual cloak.

The following chapters deal with selected aspects of religion, from a broad comparative point of view. They combine the results of deep analysis by anthropologists, including myself, with the critical use of documentary sources. They include examination of individual and corporate religious beliefs and ritual forms. They range in evidence from relatively simply organized "primitive" religious systems to the highly sophisticated complex "universalistic" religious systems. And above all, they demonstrate how "pure" religion hardly exists; how closely religion is bound to a social, economic and political framework in an essentially human construction....

References

Davis, John (ed.) 1982. *Religious Organization and Religious Experience*. London: Academic Press.

Findlay, J. N. 1963. *Language, Mind, and Value*. London: Allen & Unwin.

Firth, Raymond 1964. "Essays on Social Organization and Values," London School of Economics Monograph, *Social Anthropology* 28. London: Althone Press.

—— 1967. *Tikopia Ritual and Belief*. London: Allen & Unwin.

—— 1970. *Rank and Religion in Tikopia*. London: Allen & Unwin.

—— 1973. *Symbols Public and Private*. London: Allen & Unwin.

James, E. O. 1933. *Christian Myth and Ritual*. London: Murray.

Richardson, Alan and John Bowden 1983. *A New Dictionary of Christian Theology*. London: SCM Press.

Part III

REDUCTIONISM AND THE STUDY OF RELIGION

INTRODUCTION

❧❧

Naturalism in the Study of Religion

In the previous part we saw how the notion of *sui generis* religion privileged religious phenomena, ensuring that they could not be studied or explained in the same manner as so-called non-religious, or secular aspects of human history. However, the critiques of Shaw and Firth suggested that, like all human constructs, religious narratives, practices, and institutions can just as easily be involved in the messy world where power is routinely contested. In fact, such a criticism supports the idea that we might be able to develop a coherent approach to the study of religion that does not presume, as did Otto and Eliade, that there is a fundamental distinction between the sacred and the profane, a distinction that necessitates the development of special skills in the study of each aspect of human history.

Just such an approach has existed for some time: as we already saw, the Enlightenment laid the foundations for it. It has gone by such names as the scientific or the naturalistic study of religion. By "naturalistic" one does not mean that this approach is more natural but simply that it presumes from the outset that religion is not *sui generis*, not a special case. Instead, it presumes that when religious people claim to have had supernatural experiences that defy rational explanation they are mistaken in some way. Although such people could be lying (and because we do not have access to their inner thoughts we must always be prepared to entertain this), they may quite innocently not realize or recognize the actual cause of their emotions, perceptions, and behaviors. Because we all have had occasion to realize that our perceptions can sometimes be mistaken (as in the case of optical illusions), why should we trust the religious devotee to be communicating the actual cause of their experiences, feelings, actions, and institutions?

Not only does the naturalistic approach to the study of religion presume that religious systems are but one aspect of historical, psychological, sociological, political, and cultural systems, it also presumes that the behavior and beliefs of human beings can be studied in much the same way as the behavior of other aspects of the natural world. Contrary to the tradition represented by Schleiermacher, which presumed that humans are fundamentally different from other parts of the natural world, this tradition models itself after the natural sciences in attempting to generate universal theories of human behavior from the analysis of specific cases, asking not what religion means but why it is that human beings sometimes invoke such things as gods in their analysis of the worlds in which they live.

The Idols Which Beset Our Minds

The assumption that human behavior, like the workings of the natural world, is governed by law-like regularities that outside observers can determine, if only they look hard enough, is apparent in the writings of Francis Bacon (1561–1626). Bacon's name, much like that of René Descartes (1596–1650), is associated with some of the earliest European attempts to develop an ordered analysis of the natural world, what we would today simply call scientific method. Although scientific analysis today has developed significantly beyond the time of Bacon and Descartes, what is still assumed is that the behavior of such things as cells, rocks, clouds, animals, insects, planets, and even human beings are governed by certain orderly laws that can be discerned through careful observation. The inductive method (arriving at general conclusions based on a specific number of particular observations), as well as the comparative method, forms the basis of Bacon's scientific method, a method that he maintained could dispel the "idols and false notions" that have come to occupy our minds. We must start our analyses of the world around us with the study of specific empirical cases (what Bacon termed "true induction"), instead of beginning with general claims and axioms for which we have little or no empirical evidence (such fantasies as Fortune or the Prime Mover). Although Descartes too put stock in the inductive method (or, as he described it, one should not accept anything as true unless one has first-hand knowledge of the evidence), the method of doubt was far more important for establishing anything as knowable. In other words, to arrive at sure knowledge of anything, Descartes argued that we must begin by doubting everything we had previously accepted as known or even knowable. For example, knowing that our senses can sometimes be fooled (think of an optical illusion), we can easily doubt the veracity of our sensory perceptions; if they can be mistaken, then our sensory observations can hardly be the starting place for certain knowledge. Descartes argued that only that which can stand up to our most ardent doubt could provide for us a sure and secure starting point in our attempt to determine the order and regularity of the world around us.

But why is it that the insider cannot determine the supposed regularities and laws that the scientific, outsider observer supposedly sees? In part we could simply say that insiders are under the influence of what Bacon termed the idols, especially the Idol of the Den, or Cave, which "refracts and discolors the light of nature." Our social worlds limit and restrict what we are able to perceive. By using the image of "the cave" Bacon brings to mind Plato's (427–347 BCE) widely known story from the *Republic*, a story of how the philosopher is the only one capable first of breaking the chains that normally govern our experiences and then leaving the dim cave that we usually take to comprise the real world. Whereas his or her peers remain in the depths of the cave, seeing only faint shadows that move across its back wall, it is the philosopher whose eyes can eventually become accustomed to the brighter light of the world outside the cave. It is therefore the philosopher who can return to the darkness of the cave to help enlighten his or her still chained, deluded peers—an effort that, for the philosopher, will not necessarily be successful nor safe for challenging the limits that constrain thought and perceptions is never an easy task. At least this is one of the lessons Plato draws from his story, a lesson that must have been based, at least in part, on his memories of his own teacher, Socrates (470?–399 BCE), who was executed by the Athenian state for corrupting the youth of Athens.

The Enlightenment: "Dare to Know"

It is significant that Plato's philosopher was described above as gaining enlightenment upon leaving the shadows of the cave; the Enlightenment happens to be the name generally used to describe a complex and diverse series of intellectual, social, and political changes that took place in seventeenth- and eighteenth-century Europe. Building on the work of, among others, such writers as Bacon and Descartes, a philosophical movement gradually arose that emphasized the role played by the individual over that of the group, rationality over unthinking submission to the seemingly arbitrary rule of authority or tradition, and the inevitable social progress that occurred when individuals used their reason. The earliest attempts to explain religion as simply one aspect of the natural world, as a human construct no different from such other human constructs as culture or society, can be traced to the Enlightenment.

One example of an Enlightenment thinker is the German philosopher Immanuel Kant (1724–1804). Although best known for his attempts to determine how it was that human reason worked (what categories or principles are employed when we come to know the world around us, what are the limits of reason, etc.), Kant's brief essay, "What is Enlightenment?" (German: *Was ist Aufklärung* [1784]) is perhaps one of the best examples of an Enlightenment thinker attempting to articulate the key features of this influential movement. Kant's answer to the question in his title is sharply stated in his opening sentence and explained throughout the remainder of the essay: "Enlightenment is man's release from his self-incurred tutelage. Tutelage is man's inability to make use of his understanding without direction from another. Self-incurred is this tutelage when its cause lies not in lack of reason but in lack of resolution and courage to use it without direction from another. *Sapere aude!* [Dare to know!] 'Have courage to use your own reason!'—that is the motto of enlightenment."

"We are placed in this world, as in a great theater, where the true springs and causes of every event are entirely concealed from us.... We hang in perpetual suspense between life and death, health and sickness, plenty and want." So begins the third chapter of David Hume's *The Natural History of Religion* (1755), a book that offers a fine example of the Enlightenment's approach to studying religion as a form of mistaken human reasoning. Hume, a Scottish philosopher born about a decade prior to Kant, is today widely known as one of the first European scholars to develop a coherent, naturalistic approach to the study of religion. As should be clear from his book's title, Hume attempted to determine the historical origins or natural (as opposed to supernatural) causes of religion. He found this origin not in the revelation of a deity or the inspiration of scripture—places where many religious insiders might find the origin. Rather, Hume argued that the origin of religion was to be found in the pre-history of the human species itself: human fears and uncertainty about their place in the natural world. Whereas religious insiders might offer a supernatural history of religion (such as the intervention of a deity in human history), Hume therefore offered a completely natural history that anticipated twentieth-century psychological theories of religion.

Two aspects of Hume's theory of religion's origins are worth mentioning. First, although he wrote long before evolutionary theories had been developed and popularized in the nineteenth century, Hume, like many Europeans of his day, generally presumed that complex things developed from earlier, simpler things. Hence, what he took to be the more complex notion of one deity controlling all parts of creation (monotheism) developed, or so he argued, from the simpler notion of a variety of deities each controlling distinct aspects of the created world (polytheism). Second, he was forced to inquire where polytheism came from in the first place. To answer this Hume suggested that human beings have the in-built tendency to "conceive all beings like themselves, and to transfer to every object those qualities, with which they are familiarly acquainted, and of which they are intimately conscious." In other words, human beings have no choice but to personify or anthropomorphize (from the Greek words *anthropos* meaning human and *morphe* meaning form): in our attempts to understand and thereby control the world around us we routinely apply human forms, qualities, and traits to what are actually its non-human aspects. We see faces in the moon, we talk about the sea being angry, and we mistake shadows for people. His naturalistic theory, then, is that early human beings, unsure of the workings of the natural world, easily became fearful and personified the world around them in an attempt to cope with the anxiety and stress of not knowing the causes of things. Although by no means a completely satisfying account of religion's origins (in part because speculations about the pre-historic origin of anything are just that, sheer speculation since no one has access to empirical evidence to confirm or disconfirm them), Hume's theory is an early example of scholarship that tries to account for religious behavior by observing lawlike regularities (such as the human penchant to anthropomorphize) of which the insider is not necessarily aware.

Reductionism Defended

One of the most outspoken modern proponents of the outsider's privilege in the modern study of religion is Robert Segal. In a number of essays he has vigorously argued in favor of the right of scholars of religion to explain the religious beliefs and behaviors they study in light of such factors as Marx's economics or Freud's psychology. In his essay, "In Defense of Reductionism," Segal largely critiques Eliade's view of the field and concludes that whereas reductionistic interpretations of religion are inevitable for outsiders, they are impossible for insiders, a position that firmly supports a clear division between insider and outsider scholarship on religion.

Along with Segal's defense, Terry Godlove explains why it is that scholars of religion are particularly apt to suspend the insider's right to interpret their own experiences and actions and, in place of such interpretations, offer their own theories. Using an example drawn from Hume's writings, Godlove explains how, when it comes to claims made about such nonempirical beings as gods, the insider and outsider do not necessarily share a common set of experiences of the external world. Without such common experiences there is nothing that can be used as a reference for the insider's claims. If, for example, you were to ask a friend, "Please pass me the bottle," you could presume that the shared set of assumptions that united you and your friend, coupled with an object in your environment that you both agreed to recognize by the name "bottle," would lead to your friend handing you the bottle. But what if you made a claim to someone such as, "God loves me"? Unlike the bottle, there is no empirical object to which you can point as a reference for your term "God." If outsiders do not necessarily share your set of assumptions concerning beings such as gods, what are they to make of your claim? Suspending the authority of your interpretation of such claims, and offering their own, seems inevitable when insiders and outsiders meet.

Throwing the Baby Out With the Bathwater?

In their attempts to redescribe and, eventually, explain the behavior of other
_le_ scholars may be accused of ignoring or minimalizing what the insider
important and meaningful. Some scholars accuse reductionists of
heir data or "throwing the baby out with the bathwater"—
_to reduce and explain religion, the very thing they
study disa_____ced by economy, society, gender, or politics.
Where did religio_____g, some scholars argue that our role is not to
"explain away" religion ___ _"guard_ what is sacred to the common culture
against [the kind of] displacement" that takes place when insider claims are
redescribed by outsiders. At least this is the claim of Tony Edwards who, much
like Kenneth Pike, identifies the degree to which etic categories inevitably fail to
overlap completely with emic categories. According to Edwards, it is the
scholar's responsibility not to minimalize the emic but to represent it faithfully.

Somewhat like Edwards, Daniel Pals is critical of the reductionist's emphasis
on outsider categories and theories when it comes to studying religion. His
essay surveys a number of influential nonreductionist studies of religion and
focuses specifically on critiquing Segal's position. In fact, based on these essays
by Segal and Pals, a significant debate began that lasted for several years and
involved a number of different authors. Attempting to avoid explaining away
religion, and thereby leaving the scholar of religion with nothing to study, Pals
maintains that the autonomy of religion is nothing more than a disciplinary
axiom in the field, a necessary assumption somewhat akin to the literary critic
presuming that such a thing as literature exists.

Surely this part will not settle the debate on reductionism—a debate which
floats in and out of many of the essays in this anthology. But readers should
now at least be aware of what is at stake in a debate that continues to appear in
the pages of scholarly periodicals.

10

IMMANUEL KANT, *What is Enlightenment?*[1]

෨෨

Enlightenment is man's release from his self-incurred tutelage. Tutelage is man's inability to make use of his understanding without direction from another. Self-incurred is this tutelage when its cause lies not in lack of reason but in lack of resolution and courage to use it without direction from another. *Sapere aude!*[2] "Have courage to use your own reason!"—that is the motto of enlightenment.

Laziness and cowardice are the reasons why so great a portion of mankind, after nature has long since discharged them from external direction (*naturaliter maiorennes*), nevertheless remains under lifelong tutelage, and why it is so easy for others to set themselves up as their guardians. It is so easy not to be of age. If I have a book which understands for me, a pastor who has a conscience for me, a physician who decides my diet, and so forth, I need not trouble myself. I need not think, if I can only pay—others will readily undertake the irksome work for me.

That the step to competence is held to be very dangerous by the far greater portion of mankind (and by the entire fair sex)—quite apart from its being arduous—is seen to by those guardians who have so kindly assumed superintendence over them.[3] After the guardians have first made their domestic cattle dumb and have made sure that these placid creatures will not dare take a single step without the harness of the cart to which they are tethered, the guardians then show them the danger which threatens if they try to go alone. Actually, however, this danger is not so great, for by falling a few times they would finally learn to walk alone. But an example of this failure makes them timid and ordinarily frightens them away from all further trials.

For any single individual to work himself out of the life under tutelage which has become almost his nature is very difficult. He has come to be fond of this state, and he is for the present really incapable of making use of his reason, for no one has ever let him try it out. Statutes and formulas, those mechanical tools of the rational employment or rather misemployment of his natural gifts, are the fetters of an everlasting tutelage. Whoever throws them off makes only an uncertain leap over the narrowest ditch because he is not accustomed to that kind of free motion. Therefore, there are few who have succeeded by their own exercise of mind both in freeing themselves from incompetence and in achieving a steady pace.

But that the public should enlighten itself is more possible; indeed, if only freedom is granted, enlightenment is almost sure to follow. For there will always be some independent thinkers, even among the established guardians of the great masses, who, after throwing off the yoke of tutelage from their own shoulders, will disseminate the spirit of the rational appreciation of both their own worth and every man's vocation for thinking for himself. But be it noted that the public, which has first been brought under this yoke by their guardians, forces the guardians themselves to remain bound when it is incited to do so by some of the guardians who are themselves capable of some enlightenment—so harmful is it to implant prejudices, for they later take vengeance on their cultivators or on their descendants. Thus the public can only slowly attain enlightenment. Perhaps a fall of personal despotism or of avaricious or tyrannical oppression may be accomplished by revolution, but never a true reform in ways of thinking. Rather, new prejudices will serve as well as old ones to harness the great unthinking masses.

For this enlightenment, however, nothing is required but freedom, and indeed the most harmless among all the things to which this term can properly be applied. It is the freedom to make public use of one's reason at every point.[4] But I hear on all sides, "Do not argue!" The officer says: "Do not argue but drill!" The tax collector: "Do not argue but pay!" The cleric: "Do not argue but believe!" Only one prince in the world says, "Argue as much as you will, and about what you will, but obey!" Everywhere there is restriction on freedom.

Which restriction is an obstacle to enlightenment, and which is not an obstacle but a promoter of it? I answer: The public use of one's reason must always be free, and it alone can bring about enlightenment among men. The private use of reason, on the other hand, may often be very narrowly restricted without particularly hindering the progress of enlightenment. By the public use of one's reason I understand the use which a person makes of it as a scholar before the reading public. Private use I call that which one may make of it in a particular civil post or office which is entrusted to him. Many affairs which are conducted in the interest of the community require a certain mechanism through which some members of the community must passively conduct themselves with an artificial unanimity, so that the government may direct them to public ends, or at least prevent them from destroying those ends. Here argument is certainly not allowed—one must obey. But so far as a part of the mechanism regards himself at the same time as a member of the whole community or of a society of world citizens, and thus in the role of a scholar who addresses the public (in the proper sense of the word) through his writings, he certainly can argue without hurting the affairs for which he is in part responsible as a passive member. Thus it would be ruinous for an officer in service to debate about the suitability or utility of a command given to him by his superior; he must obey. But the right to make remarks on errors in the military service and to lay them before the public for judgment cannot equitably be refused him as a scholar. The citizen cannot refuse to pay the taxes imposed on him; indeed, an impudent complaint at those levied on him can be punished as a scandal (as it could occasion general refractoriness). But the same person nevertheless does not act contrary to his duty as a citizen when, as a scholar, he publicly expresses his thoughts on the inappropriateness or even the injustice of these levies. Similarly a clergyman is obligated to make his sermon to his pupils in catechism and his congregation conform to the symbol of the church which he serves, for he has been accepted on this condition. But as a scholar he has complete freedom, even the calling, to communicate to the public all his carefully tested and well-meaning thoughts on that which is erroneous in the symbol and to make suggestions for the better organization of the religious body and church. In doing this there is nothing that could be laid as a burden on his conscience. For what he teaches as a consequence of his office as a representative of the church, this he considers something about which he has no freedom to teach according to his own lights; it is something which he is appointed to propound at the dictation of and in the name of another. He will say, "Our church teaches this or that; those are the proofs which it adduces." He thus extracts all practical uses for his congregation from statutes to which he himself would not subscribe with full conviction but to the enunciation of which he can very well pledge himself because it is not impossible that truth lies hidden in them, and, in any case, there is at least nothing in them contradictory to inner religion. For if he believed he had found such in them, he could not conscientiously discharge the duties of his office; he would have to give it up. The use, therefore, which an appointed teacher makes of his reason before his congregation is merely private, because this congregation is only a domestic one (even if it be a large gathering); with respect to it, as a priest, he is not free, nor can he be free, because he carries out the orders of another. But as a scholar, whose writings speak to his public, the world, the clergyman in the public use of his reason enjoys an unlimited freedom to use his own reason and to speak in his own person. That the guardians of the people (in spiritual things) should themselves be incompetent is an absurdity which amounts to the eternalization of absurdities.

But would not a society of clergymen, perhaps a church conference or a venerable classis (as they call themselves among the Dutch), be justified in obligating itself by oath to a certain unchangeable symbol in order to enjoy an unceasing guardianship over each of its members and thereby over the people as a whole, and even to make it eternal? I answer that this is altogether impossible. Such a contract, made to shut off all further enlightenment from the human race, is absolutely null and void even if confirmed by the supreme power, by parliaments, and by the most ceremonious of peace treaties. An age cannot bind itself and ordain to put the succeeding one into such a condition that it cannot extend its (at best very occasional) knowledge, purify itself of errors, and progress in general enlightenment. That would be a crime against human nature, the proper destination of which lies precisely in this progress; and the descendants would be fully justified in rejecting those decrees as having been made in an unwarranted and malicious manner.

The touchstone of everything that can be concluded as a law for a people lies in the question whether the people could have imposed such a law on itself. Now such a religious compact might be possible for a short and definitely limited time, as it were, in expectation of a better. One might let every citizen, and especially the clergyman, in the role of scholar, make his comments freely and publicly, i.e., through writing, on the erroneous aspects of the present institution. The newly introduced order might last until insight into the nature of these things had become so general and widely approved that through uniting their voices (even if not unanimously) they could bring a proposal to the throne to take those congregations under protection which had united into a changed religious organization according to their better ideas, without, however, hindering others who wish to remain in the order. But to unite in a permanent religious institution which is not to be subject to doubt before the public even in the lifetime of one man, and thereby to make a period of time fruitless in the progress of mankind toward improvement, thus working to the disadvantage of posterity—that is absolutely forbidden. For himself (and only for a short time) a man may postpone enlightenment in what he ought to know, but to renounce it for himself and even more to renounce it for posterity is to injure and trample on the rights of mankind.

And what a people may not decree for itself can even less be decreed for them by a monarch, for his lawgiving authority rests on his uniting the general public will in his own. If he only sees to it that all true or alleged improvement stands together with civil order, he can leave it to his subjects to do what they find necessary for their spiritual welfare. This is not his concern, though it is incumbent on him to prevent one of them from violently hindering another in determining and promoting this welfare to the best of his ability. To meddle in these matters lowers his own majesty, since by the writings in which his subjects seek to present their views he may evaluate his own governance. He can do this when, with deepest understanding, he lays upon himself the reproach, *Caesar non est supra grammaticos* [Caesar is not above the law]. Far more does he injure his own majesty when he degrades his supreme power by supporting the ecclesiastical despotism of some tyrants in his state over his other subjects.

If we are asked, "Do we now live in an *enlightened age?*" the answer is, "No, but we do live in an *age of enlightenment*".[5] As things now stand, much is lacking which prevents men from being, or easily becoming, capable of correctly using their own reason in religious matters with assurance and free from outside direction. But, on the other hand, we have clear indications that the field has now been opened wherein men may freely deal with these things and that the obstacles to general enlightenment or the release from self-imposed tutelage are gradually being reduced. In this respect, this is the age of enlightenment, or the century of Frederick.[6]

A prince who does not find it unworthy of himself to say that he holds it to be his duty to prescribe nothing to men in religious matters but to give them complete freedom while renouncing the haughty name of *tolerance*, is himself enlightened and deserves to be esteemed by the grateful world and posterity as the first, at least from the side of government, who divested the human race of its tutelage and left each man free to make use of his reason in matters of conscience. Under him venerable ecclesiastics are allowed, in the role of scholars, and without infringing on their official duties, freely to submit for public testing their judgments and views which here and there diverge from the established symbol. And an even greater freedom is enjoyed by those who are restricted by no official duties. This spirit of freedom spreads beyond this land, even to those in which it must struggle with external obstacles erected by a government which misunderstands its own interest. For an example gives evidence to such a government that in freedom there is not the least cause for concern about public peace and the stability of the community. Men work themselves gradually out of barbarity if only intentional artifices are not made to hold them in it.

I have placed the main point of enlightenment—the escape of men from their self-incurred tutelage—chiefly in matters of religion because our rulers have no interest in playing the guardian with respect to the arts and sciences and also because religious incompetence is not only the most harmful but also the most degrading of all. But the manner of thinking of the head of a state who favors religious enlightenment goes further, and he sees that there is no danger to his lawgiving in allowing his subjects to make public use of their reason and to publish their thoughts on a better formulation of his legislation and even their open-minded criticisms of the laws already made. Of this we have a shining example wherein no monarch is superior to him whom we honor.

But only one who is himself enlightened, is not afraid of shadows, and has a numerous and well-disciplined army to assure public peace, can say: "Argue as much as you will, and about what you will, only obey!" A republic could not dare say such a thing. Here is shown a strange and unexpected trend in human affairs in which almost everything, looked at in the large, is paradoxical. A greater degree of civil freedom appears advantageous to the freedom of mind of the people, and yet it places inescapable limitations upon it; a lower degree of civil freedom, on the contrary, provides the mind with room for each man to extend himself to his full capacity. As nature has uncovered from under this hard shell the seed for which she most tenderly cares—the propensity and vocation to free thinking—this gradually works back upon the character of the people, who thereby gradually become capable of managing freedom; finally, it affects the principles of government, which finds it to its advantage to treat men, who are now more than machines, in accordance with their dignity.[7]

Königsberg, Prussia
September 30, 1784

Notes

1. Ed. note. Apart from the last note, which is Kant's, notes lacking the "Ed. note" opening are those of the essay's translator, Lewis White Beck.
2. "Dare to know!" (Horace, *Ars poetica*). This was the motto adopted in 1736 by the Society of the Friends of Truth, an important circle in the German Enlightenment.
3. Ed. note. That Kant, like virtually all writers from this period, is open to a resounding feminist critique at this point should be more than obvious to the attentive reader.
4. It is this freedom Kant claimed later in his conflict with the censor, deferring to the latter in the "private" use of reason, i.e., in his lectures.
5. "Our age is, in especial degree, the age of criticism, and to Criticism everything must submit" (Immanuel Kant, *Critique of Pure Reason*, Preface to first edition [N. Kemp Smith trans.]).
6. Ed. Note. The Emperor of Prussia, Frederick the Great (1712–1786), sometimes known as an enlightened despot, is remembered for having put into place various economic, legal, political, religious, and educational reforms.
7. Today I read in the *Büchingsche Wöchentliche Nachrichten* for September 13 an announcement of the *Berlinische Monatsschrift* for this month, which cites the answer to the same question by Herr Mendelssohn.* But this issue has not yet come to me; if it had, I would have held back the present essay, which is now put forth only in order to see how much agreement in thought can be brought about by chance. (*Ed. note. Mendelssohn's answer was that enlightenment lay in intellectual cultivation, which he distinguished from the practical. Kant, quite in line with his later essay on theory and practice, refuses to make this distinction fundamental.)

11

ROBERT A. SEGAL, *In Defense of Reductionism*

෮෮෮

However crude the generalization, twentieth-century interpretations of human phenomena often differ sharply from nineteenth-century ones. Far more than their predecessors, contemporary anthropologists, sociologists, psychologists, historians, and philosophers seek to understand those phenomena in the participant's own terms.[1] Whether earlier interpreters were less tolerant of the participant's point of view or simply less interested in it, they were not the least reluctant to understand human beliefs and actions in their own terms rather than his. Indeed, they were not averse to evaluating those beliefs and actions, frequently pronouncing them false or foolish. What contemporary sociologist J. D. Y. Peel says of his nineteenth-century predecessors holds for other disciplines as well: "Early attempts to understand social phenomena were so tied to the peculiar interests of the social world of the sociologist himself, that he only tried to understand what seemed odd, deluded, perverse or unusual; and his understanding consisted in showing how the odd, deluded, etc., came to be believed, in contrast to the true and usual—what his own society believed" (1969: 70).

By contrast, contemporary interpreters typically strive to overcome their own professed biases and to "appreciate" the participant's point of view. What Mircea Eliade says of the interpretation of myth in particular applies to the interpretation of human phenomena in general: "For the past fifty years at least, Western scholars have approached the study of myth from a viewpoint markedly different from, let us say, that of the nineteenth century. Unlike their predecessors, who treated myth in the usual meaning of the word, that is, as 'fable,' 'invention,' 'fiction,' *they have accepted it as it was understood in the archaic societies*, where, on the contrary, 'myth' means a 'true story' and, beyond that, a story that is a most precious possession because it is sacred, exemplary, significant" (1968a: 1; italics added).

It is surely not coincidental that Eliade is widely regarded as at once one of the leading contemporary interpreters of religion and one of the leading defenders of its irreducibility. For by its irreducibility he means the inability to understand religion in other than its own terms, by which he means the terms of believers themselves. According to Eliade, religion is understandable in only religious rather than, say, psychological or sociological terms because for believers it is. Eliade's popularity among interpreters of religion surely reflects in part the popularity of his position.

The Believer's Point of View

Exactly what Eliade means by the believer's own terms must first be determined. Eliade might mean simply the recapitulation of a believer's conscious view of religion. He might, that is, intend to be only describing, or transcribing, a believer's conscious view of the origin, function, and meaning of religion. In actuality, Eliade does much more than report the believer's conscious view, an approach that better characterizes the work of Wilfred Cantwell Smith.[2] To begin with, Eliade does not hesitate to discuss dead religions, whose adherents are scarcely available for consultation. His chief sources of information for living and dead religions alike are, furthermore, not informants themselves but their sacred texts.

More important, Eliade clearly exceeds and probably even violates the conscious view of most believers: in regarding the sacred phenomena of all religions as manifestations of an impersonal sacred realm beyond all gods; in interpreting the exclusive aim of all religions as a return, spatially and temporally, to that sacred realm; and above all in considering the sacred phenomena of individual religions to be only instances of universal religious phenomena—for example, considering specific trees to be only instances of the Cosmic Tree.[3] Presumably, many, if not most, believers postulate no impersonal sacred realm beyond all gods, deem the aim of religion more or other than a return to that realm, and above all consider only their own religion true.[4] Eliade's equation of his own interpretation of religion with the believer's point of view therefore becomes arbitrary.

Still, in the broader sense of deeming the referent of religion transcendent, Eliade might be said to be describing the conscious view of believers. Against the argument that believers, especially in primitive societies, may have no idea of the significance of religion for them, so that there may be no believer's point of view, Eliade could maintain that for all believers the significance of religion is at least its irreducibility to human or natural terms. Against the argument that believers may differ considerably over the interpretation of religion, so that there may be no one believer's point of view, Eliade could maintain that all believers agree on at least the transcendent nature of religion.

Yet even when defined as simply the belief in the reality of the transcendent, the believer's point of view is not for Eliade limited to his conscious one. As Eliade says of the significance of religious symbols: "we do not have the right to conclude that the message of the symbols is confined to the meanings of which a certain number of individuals are fully conscious, even when we learn from a rigorous investigation of these individuals what they think of such and such a symbol belonging to their own tradition. Depth psychology has taught us that the symbol delivers its message and fulfills its function even when its meaning escapes awareness" (1959b: 106–107). Eliade's equation of his interpretation of religion with the believer's point of view thus remains arbitrary.

Moreover, Eliade asserts that despite the widespread conscious atheism of modern man, all mankind is truly religious: "For, as we said before, non-religious man *in the pure state* is a comparatively rare phenomenon, even in the most [consciously] desacralized of modern societies. The majority of the 'irreligious' still behave religiously, even though they are not aware of the fact.... [T]he modern man who feels and claims that he is nonreligious still retains a large stock of camouflaged myths and degenerated rituals" (1968b: 204–205). When Eliade imputes to the beliefs and actions of self-professed atheists a significance of which they are not just partly but wholly unconscious and which not just exceeds but outright contradicts their own conscious one, his equation of the actor's point of view with an irreducibly religious one proves entirely arbitrary. Indeed, it becomes hard to see why his interpretation of the actor's point of view is any less reductionistic than the interpretations of religion he opposes as reductionistic.

The Irreducibly Religious Interpretation of Religion

What Eliade means by an "interpretation" of religion, irreducibly religious or otherwise, may be no less clear than what he means by the believer's own view of religion. Occasionally, he equates an "interpretation," which he uses interchangeably with an "understanding," with a causal, or genetic, account. An irreducibly religious interpretation of religion would therefore ascribe religion to an irreducibly religious source: "I do not mean to deny the usefulness of approaching the religious phenomenon from various different angles; but it must be looked at first of all in itself, in that which belongs to it alone and can be explained in no other terms" (1963: xiii).

More often, Eliade associates an interpretation with an account of not the origin but the function and, more, the meaning of religion. As, indeed, he says in criticizing past interpreters for their preoccupation with the origin of religion: "we must not confuse the historical circumstances which make a human existence what it actually is with the fact that there is such a thing as a human existence. For the historian of religions the fact that a myth or a ritual is always historically conditioned does not explain the very existence of such a myth or ritual. In other words, the historicity of a religious experience does not tell us what a religious experience ultimately *is*" (1969: 53). The irreducibly religious meaning and origin of religion are, however, closely tied: both postulate above all the reality of the transcendent.

Assume, for convenience's sake, that by an "interpretation" of religion Eliade means an account of its meaning, not of its origin or function. Even assume, to advance the argument, that Eliade is dealing with the interpretation of religion of only self-professed believers. Assume most of all that, if only in the broad sense of deeming the object of religion transcendent, his interpretation of religion for them matches their own conscious interpretation. For the central issue is not whether Eliade truly describes believers' conscious interpretation of religion but whether, even if he does, their conscious interpretation of religion is for him the true interpretation of religion.

On the one hand Eliade usually restricts himself to the irreducibly religious meaning of religion for believers themselves, not necessarily to the meaning of it in fact: "A sacred stone remains a stone; apparently (or, more precisely from the profane point of view), nothing distinguishes it from all other stones. *But for those to whom a stone reveals itself as sacred*, its immediate reality is transmuted into a supernatural reality. In other words, *for those who have a religious experience* all nature is capable of revealing itself as cosmic sacrality" (1968b: 12; italics added). Interpreting religion religiously thus means presenting its irreducibly transcendent meaning for believers. Eliade is therefore merely describing, or transcribing, the believer's own view of the meaning of religion for him.

On the other hand Eliade sometimes implies strongly that in interpreting religion religiously he is presenting its irreducibly transcendent meaning in fact, not just for believers. He would therefore be not merely describing but outright endorsing their interpretation, which, conversely, would simply coincide with the true one: "A religious phenomenon will only be recognized as such if it is grasped at its own level, that is to say, if it is studied as something religious. To try to grasp the essence of such a phenomenon by means of physiology, psychology, sociology, economics, linguistics, art or any other study is false; it misses the one unique and irreducible element in it—the element of the sacred" (1963: xiii).

On the one hand Eliade continually says or implies that, as a historian of religion, he is only conveying, not evaluating, the believer's point of view: "The ultimate aim of the historian of religions is to understand, and to make understandable to others, religious man's behavior and mental universe" (1968b: 162). In contrast to the theologian, from whom he repeatedly distinguishes himself, he relies on scientific evidence, not revelation, for his explication: "The procedure of the historian of religions is just as different from that of the theologian. All theology implies a systematic reflection on the content of religious experience, aiming at a deeper and clearer understanding of the relationships between God-creator and man-creature. But the historian of religions uses an empirical method of approach. He is concerned with religio-historical facts which he seeks to understand and to make intelligible to others" (1959b: 88).[5]

On the other hand Eliade far more regularly pits his interpretation of religion against all reductionistic ones, as his objection to those who "try to grasp the essence" of religion "by means of physiology, psychology, sociology," and so on evinces. If he intends to be only presenting the conscious meaning of religion for believers, he need logically have no objection to those who intend to do more. Not only would, or could, his erstwhile antagonists surely agree that the conscious meaning of religion for believers is irreducibly religious, but they themselves would surely distinguish a concern with merely conveying the believer's view of the meaning of religion from a concern with determining the actual meaning of it. For Eliade to be countering real opponents, he must, then, be saying that the actual meaning of religion is irreducibly religious. Whatever he himself "consciously believes" he is doing, his argument logically commits him to much more.

Any distinction between the true meaning of religion and the true meaning of it for believers, as if Eliade might somehow be restricting himself to only the true meaning of religion for believers, is fallacious. The true meaning of religion is its true meaning for believers. For what meaning can religion have except one for believers? The issue is whether believers are aware of the true meaning of religion for them. If Eliade were saying only that the conscious, irreducibly religious meaning of religion for believers is religious, he would be uttering a tautology, with which no one, including his reductionistic adversaries, would disagree. What he must therefore be saying, despite his profession of modesty, is that the conscious, irreducibly religious meaning of religion for believers is its true one, which means at once its true one for them and its true one in itself. Indeed, Eliade's willingness to exceed and even violate believers' particular conscious views of the meaning of religion for them suggests that he is concerned with more than its truth for them.

Put another way, Eliade means to be either a humanist or a social scientist. If he means to be a humanist, he is seeking only to describe the irreducibly religious meaning of religion for believers. As a humanist, he is necessarily nonreductionistic. If, however, he means to be a social scientist, he is seeking to explain, not merely to describe, that irreducibly religious meaning, if not also origin and function. As a social scientist, he can be either nonreductionistic or reductionistic. The point is that a humanist and even a reductionistic social scientist run askew, not contrary, to each other: in seeking only to describe the conscious meaning of religion for believers the humanist is not asserting that that conscious meaning is necessarily the true one for believers, and in seeking to explain the true meaning of religion for believers the reductionistic social scientist is not denying that the conscious meaning is irreducibly religious. In order, then, for Eliade to be confronting real antagonists he must be "operating" as a social scientist—of a nonreductionistic variety. He must be seeking the actual meaning of religion for believers, not just the conscious meaning of it for them.

Seemingly, Eliade is dismissing nonreligious interpretations altogether. Seemingly, he is maintaining that nonreligious, reductionistic interpretations, which means those of the social sciences above all, are wholly irrelevant. Thus, he warns his fellow historians of religion against continuing "to submit to the audacious and irrelevant interpretations of religious realities made by psychologists, sociologists, or devotees of various reductionist ideologies" (1969: 70).

Yet occasionally Eliade grants these disciplines a secondary role. They can, he sometimes says, delineate the background to religion, though still not illuminate its true origin, function, or meaning: "In sum, a religious phenomenon cannot be understood outside of its 'history,' that is, outside of its cultural and socioeconomic contexts. There is no such thing outside of history as a 'pure' religious datum. For there is no such thing as a human datum that is not at the same time a historical datum. Every religious experience is expressed and transmitted in a particular historical context. But admitting the historicity of religious experiences does not imply that they are reducible to nonreligious forms of behavior. Stating that a religious datum is always a historical datum does not mean that it is reducible to a nonreligious history— for example, to an economic, social, or political history" (1968c: 250–251). As he illustrates: "Few religious phenomena are more directly and more obviously connected with sociopolitical circumstances than the modern messianic and millenarian movements among colonial peoples (cargo-cults, etc.). Yet identifying and analyzing the conditions that prepared and made possible such messianic movements form only a part of the work of the historian of religions. For these movements are equally creations of the human spirit, in the sense that they have become what they are—religious movements, and not merely gestures of protest and revolt—through a creative act of the spirit" (1963: viii).[6]

Because Eliade considers only earlier social scientific interpretations of religion, his rejection or curtailed acceptance of them is not inconsistent with the trend within the social sciences toward nonreductionism. In fact, it is scarcely clear that Eliade himself recognizes this trend. The trend toward a nonreductionistic approach to myth which he notes probably refers to the increased study of myth by historians of religion rather than by contemporary social scientists, who probably remain for him incorrigibly reductionistic.

Eliade's Defense of Nonreductionism

Eliade does not merely announce his nonreductionistic stance but attempts to prove it. He attempts to prove that the believer's conscious view of not the origin but the function and, more, the meaning of religion is the true one. He appeals to what he considers the evidence: the conscious, irreducibly religious significance of religion for believers. He argues unceasingly that only as a spiritual enterprise does religion give value to believer's lives. It does so by providing divine counterparts, or "archetypes," to virtually all things in the world. The archetypes of physical objects exist somewhere in the heavens. The archetypes of human activities are the activities of the gods described in myths. Archetypes are not the causes of the phenomena they parallel but, like Platonic Forms, the models for them. The knowledge of archetypes confers meaning on phenomena, and so on life, by transforming those phenomena from merely human or natural entities into manifestations of divinity.[7] The value religion provides is exactly the knowledge that divinity underlies the world. Through ritual, religion also provides a means of escaping from one's present, fallen state of separation from the gods and returning to the Edenic state of nearness to them.

The issue at hand is not whether Eliade's irreducibly religious interpretation of the meaning, not to say origin and function, of religion for believers is their own conscious one. That it is it has been assumed. The issue is whether the conscious meaning of religion for believers is the true meaning for them. The issue is not whether the true meaning of religion for believers is the true meaning of religion itself. That it is has been explained. The issue is whether the true meaning of religion is its conscious meaning for believers.

Eliade systematically fails to prove that it is. All he does is continually assert, as cited, that reductionistic interpretations of religion are either irrelevant or secondary because they skirt the conscious, irreducibly religious meaning of religion for believers. But he thereby begs, not answers, the key question: whether the conscious, irreducibly religious meaning of religion for believers is the true meaning of religion, which means the true one for them. In the light of, if nothing else, discoveries by modern psychology, sociology, anthropology, and other disciplines, Eliade can hardly contend that a human being knows all the possible meanings of any of his beliefs and actions, not just of his religious ones. He can contend only that a participant knows all the true ones, but that contention is precisely what requires justification. In the absence of any noncircular justification for a nonreductionistic interpretation alone, a reductionistic interpretation of human phenomena proves no less proper.

Other Defenses of Nonreductionism

Eliade's failure to provide a sturdy defense of nonreductionism does not, of course, mean that none exists. At least three possible defenses have commonly been offered: the comparative method, the process of *Verstehen*, and the phenomenological approach. Eliade himself invokes one or two of them. When

Eliade says that "it is impossible to understand the meaning of the Cosmic Tree by considering only one or some of its variants" and that "it is only by the analysis of a considerable number of examples that the structure of a symbol can be completely deciphered" (1959b: 94), he is presenting the standard argument of many comparativists: that only a comparison of many instances of any phenomenon, religious or nonreligious, discloses its true meaning.[8] At first glance this assertion might seem self-evident, but it is in fact questionable.[9]

In the first place it is not clear that a survey of the instances of a phenomenon provides a unique source of even hypotheses about the phenomenon. The meticulous scrutiny of a single instance might well prove as revealing "heuristically" as a presumably more cursory scrutiny of many instances. Moreover, if one does not understand a single instance, on what basis can one understand other instances? What is objectionable is the claim not that the comparative method *may* be useful in "generating" hypotheses but that it is indispensable to doing so.

In the second place it is certainly not the case that, even if the comparative method were an indispensable *source* of hypotheses, those hypotheses would be self-validating. What is objectionable here is the implicit claim that the comparative method provides not merely a unique source of hypotheses but an automatic validation of them. Surely the hypotheses derived from comparative study, like those derived from any other source, must be tested in turn—by the application of them to as many further instances as possible. Surely even hypotheses derived from the study of all instances of a phenomenon would not therefore be automatically correct.

In the third place it is hardly the case that even if the comparative method yielded both unique and self-validating hypotheses, those hypotheses would necessarily be nonreductionistic. For all theorists of religion, like all other theorists of classes of phenomena, are by definition comparativists: they seek the universal origin, function, and meaning of religion. Reductionistic theorists of religion use the comparative method as fully as Eliade, in which case he can scarcely appeal to it to support his approach. In short, the comparative method yields no defense of nonreductionism.

The concept of *Verstehen*, or "understanding," offers a weightier possible defense of nonreductionism. The understanding sought is, purportedly, the conscious meaning of phenomena for participants themselves. Underlying the concept is the conviction that human beings are different in kind from natural phenomena and that the brand of understanding sought by the humanities and the social sciences, which study human beings exclusively, must therefore be different in kind from that sought by the natural sciences, which study human beings as part of nature.

Where, it is said, the "actions" of natural objects are merely caused, those of human beings are motivated. Where natural objects "act" merely in response to a cause, human beings act for a purpose as well. To understand human behavior is thus necessarily to understand the purposes, motives, or reasons behind it—the differences among purposes, motives, and reasons aside.

Like the comparative method, the notion of *Verstehen* raises various problems in its own right, over and above its bearing on nonreductionism.[10] In the first place it is not self-evident that the distinction between human beings and natural phenomena is as sharp as proponents of *Verstehen* assume. In the second place it is not clear that even if human beings are different in kind from natural phenomena, it is necessary to understand them in terms of reasons rather than causes. In the third place it is not clear that even if it is necessary to understand human beings in terms of reasons rather than causes, it is sufficient.

In the fourth place it is simply not true that, even if it were both necessary and sufficient to understand human beings in terms of reasons rather than causes, the act of *Verstehen* would provide more than a source of hypotheses about human beings. In that case those hypotheses would still have to be tested. For how can one be sure that he has discovered the actor's true reasons for his behavior unless he sees them borne out by his behavior, which goes beyond the act of *Verstehen* itself?

In the fifth place it is uncertain whether *Verstehen* is even meant to be a *method* of understanding human beings and not simply the *aim* of understanding. In that case not only would the aim still have to be justified, but a method for practicing it would still be needed.

In the sixth and final place it is by no means the case that even if *Verstehen* provided an incontestable method or aim for understanding human beings, it, any more than the comparative method, would offer automatic support for nonreductionism. For to say that the reasons which alone make sense of an actor's actions are his own is not, for advocates of *Verstehen*, to say that they must be his conscious ones. The alternative to conscious reasons need not be causes. It can be unconscious reasons.

Certainly in the fields of history,[11] sociology,[12] and anthropology,[13] where the practice of *Verstehen* has been particularly widespread, the actor's reasons have not necessarily meant his conscious ones. For example, R. G. Collingwood, one of the chief proponents of *Verstehen* in history, contrasts it to the sheer duplication of the agent's consciousness, which he dismisses as "psychologism." [14] Advocates of *Verstehen* in history and the social sciences tend to reduce the actor's reasons for his actions to some basic, typically unconscious universal need—for an orderly world, for example. Religion gets reduced to simply one means of fulfilling that larger, secular need instead of, as for Eliade, remaining the exclusive means of fulfilling an exclusively religious need. Even if, for some advocates, religion is the best and possibly even the sole means of fulfilling that need, the need itself is still secular. Because human actions still get explained in terms of reasons rather than causes and because the reasons are usually intellectual rather than, say, psychological or economic, as for Freud and Marx, the practice of *Verstehen* comes closer to the actor's presumably conscious point of view. The increasing popularity of this approach in history and the social sciences as a whole does, then, represent a move toward reductionism, though in reducing, say, religious reasons to nonreligious ones it nevertheless stops short.

Where proponents of *Verstehen* in history and the social sciences assert only that human actions must be understood from the actor's point of view, proponents of *Verstehen* in philosophy—notably, Wittgensteinians—assert that the actor's point of view is true.[15] Where, that is, historians and social scientists by nature seek to determine the reasons for human behavior, philosophers seek to evaluate those reasons. Wittgensteinian practitioners of *Verstehen*, dubbed "fideists," maintain not merely that human beings know the true reasons for which they act but that their reasons are true. The reasons with which the Wittgensteinians are concerned are not reasons for any actions but reasons for actions involving beliefs about the world. Since a believer's reasons for acting religiously surely involve beliefs about the world, the Wittgensteinian approach would seemingly support Eliade's.

In actuality, it does not, and in part because the Wittgensteinians, like their counterparts in history and the social sciences, do not equate the actor's reasons, and so his beliefs, with his conscious reasons. The disparity between Peter Winch's existentialist interpretation of Azande witchcraft and the Azande's own conscious, very likely proto-scientific interpretation typifies the point.[16]

But there is an additional and more important reason for Eliade's presumed failure to find support here: the Wittgensteinians, whether or not faithful to Wittgenstein himself, are in fact ultimately relativists. Truth for them means internal coherence, not correspondence to external reality. In asserting that an actor's beliefs are true they are asserting simply that all would-be criticisms of his beliefs reflect merely the critic's own beliefs. Only internal, not external, criticism is permissible. Where, then, Eliade declares that a believer's belief in the transcendent is true because it corresponds to external reality, Wittgensteinian fideists would declare that that belief is true only because it is as coherent as a nonbeliever's.

The utility of the Wittgensteinian position for nonreductionism aside, there are at least as many objections to it as to the concept of *Verstehen* in general. It has been argued not only, as with *Verstehen* generally, that acceptance of the actor's own account of his behavior is unnecessary, insufficient, and untestable but also that his account is subject to being proved false, irrational, or unintelligible. Whether or not valid, these criticisms must surely be met before Wittgensteinian fideism can be used to bolster Eliade's views.

Three issues closely related to *Verstehen* turn out to have no bearing on nonreductionism: the issues of teleological explanations, rationality, and methodological individualism. The debate over teleological explanations is well-nigh identical with that over *Verstehen*: it is between those who assert and those who deny that human actions must be explained in terms of purposes as well as causes.[17] The debate over rationality is also almost identical with that over *Verstehen*: it is between those who assert and those who deny that the actor alone can determine the rationality of his beliefs and actions.[18] The debate over methodological individualism is somewhat different: it is between those who assert and those who deny that human actions are explicable in terms of individuals alone rather than necessarily in terms of collective entities like the state as well.[19] Whatever the cogency of their arguments, teleologists, "rationalists," and methodological individualists, in arguing for the actor's point of view, are not identifying it with his conscious point of view and so with nonreductionism.

The third and final appeal which Eliade might make in defense of nonreductionism is to phenomenology—specifically, the phenomenology of religion. Although phenomenologists of religion can also be historians of religion, by definition phenomenologists deal with religions collectively, not, like historians, individually, and deal with them in the abstract, not, like historians, in their "living" contexts.

The goal of the phenomenology of religion is ambiguous.[20] Minimally, the aim is sheer description: an accurate recording of the irreducibly religious nature of religion for believers. Because phenomenologists deal with religions collectively, description invariably means classification. As W. Brede Kristensen, a leading phenomenologist, says: "its [i.e., phenomenology's] task is to classify and group the numerous and widely divergent data in such a way that an over-all view can be obtained of their religious content and the religious values they contain" (1960: 1). The data to be classified are the various expressions of religious beliefs and practices—for example, varying conceptions of God or varying forms of prayer.

To the extent that the goal of the phenomenology of religion is mere description, it offers no help to Eliade, who, again, is committed to defending, not merely describing, the irreducibly religious meaning of religion for believers. Maximally, however, the aim is the same as his. As C. Jouco Bleeker, another prominent phenomenologist, asserts: "From the studies of its [i.e., phenomenology of religion's] adherents it appears that nobody is any longer content with a pure description of the religious facts. People want to understand their significance and structure.... The scholars ... wanted to penetrate deeper into their object than is possible with a simple description. They aimed at the understanding of the spirit, the *essence*, the structure of the religions which they treated" (1959: 101; italics added).

The meaning of the "essence" of religion is, however, ambiguous in turn. For the essence sought is apparently only the essence of religion for the believer, not in fact. As Kristensen says: "History of Religion and Phenomenology do not have as their object the formulation of our conception of the essence of religious data. This is the task of the philosopher. They must, on the contrary, investigate what religious value the believers ... attached to their faith, what religion meant for them" (1960: 13). Characterized in this way, the phenomenology of religion provides anew only a description, not an endorsement, of the believer's point of view and so lends Eliade no aid.

Even if the aim of phenomenologists of religion were the unraveling of the essence of religion in fact, they would obviously have to justify their claim that its essence is irreducibly religious. Presumably, they would cite the insights yielded by the three procedures they employ: the comparative method, the *epoché*, and the "eidetic vision."

All three procedures are, to say the least, moot. The comparative method, which is so tightly tied to phenomenology that the term "comparative religion" is often used synonymously with the phenomenology of religion, has already been discussed. The *epoché*, according to Bleeker, means "the suspension of judgment. In using the *epoché* one puts oneself into the position of the listener, who does not judge according to preconceived notions" (1959: 98). But then the *epoché*, as the bracketing of biases toward religion, secures only an appreciation of its significance for believers, not an assessment of its significance in fact, which necessarily involves a bias toward religion.

Even if the *epoché* were intended to reveal the significance of religion in fact, not just for believers, phenomenologists of at least religion invariably neglect to explain how to practice it. To prescribe the suspension of biases is one thing. To achieve it is quite another. Until the actual means of ridding oneself of all biases gets explained, the *epoché* must remain only a forlorn ideal.

The "eidetic vision," according to Bleeker, "has as its aim the search of the eidos, that is the essentials of religious phenomena" (1959: 99). Here the phenomenological aims seems to be, as earlier, to decipher the essence of religion in fact, in which case it would fit Eliade's aim. But the secondary objection to the *epoché* proves the primary one here: the absence of a means just as phenomenologists of religion fail to explain how to exorcize biases, so they fail to explain how to grasp intuitively the essence of religious phenomena. Is it by will? Is it by training? If so, of what kind? How does one know when one has succeeded? Can one validate one's vision? If not, then, as Willard Oxtoby concludes: "There is nothing outside one's intuitive grasp of a pattern which validates that pattern. The phenomenologist is obliged simply to set forth his understanding as a whole, trusting that his reader will enter into it. But there is no procedure stated by which he can compel a second phenomenologist to agree with the adequacy and incontrovertibility of his analysis, unless the second phenomenologist's eidetic vision happens to be the same as the first's. For this reason phenomenological expositions of religion are in fact very personal appreciations of it, akin more to certain forms of literary and aesthetic criticism than to the natural or even the social sciences" (1968: 597). But where, then, is the dividing line between a personal appreciation of religion and the bias which phenomenologists strive to expunge?

Finally, the essence of religion constitutes metaphysical knowledge, and it is far from evident that any empirical method, which the phenomenology of religion purports to be, can provide it. A phenomenologist can certainly try to prove empirically that an irreducibly religious interpretation of religion either is more nearly adequate than any other one or captures a dimension of religion missed by all other ones, but when he maintains that his interpretation uncovers the essence of religion he exceeds the bounds of empirical evidence. He exceeds not simply the meaning of religion for believers but also its provable meaning in fact.[21] In seeking both the meaning of religion in fact and the irreducibly religious meaning of it the phenomenological method may, in sum, provide more support for Eliade's ends than either the comparative method or the practice of *Verstehen*, but it proves at least as tenuous as they.[22]

The Superiority of Reductionism

In the wake of the failure of any of these arguments to justify an exclusively nonreductionistic interpretation of human phenomena, a reductionistic one proves no less proper. Yet, in addition, a reductionistic interpretation of religious phenomena in particular is the only one possible, at least for a nonbelieving interpreter. For if Eliade fails to prove that a nonreductionistic interpretation is alone proper, he also fails to prove that, for a nonbeliever, it is even possible. Indeed, he does not even try. He simply assumes that it is. Like his assumption of the superiority of nonreductionistic interpretations, his assumption of their possibility for nonbelievers is typical of religious studies.

In fact, it is impossible for a nonbeliever to accept a believer's own interpretation of religion as even the believer's own true one. The issue is not whether a nonbeliever can accept a believer's interpretation of religion as the *nonbeliever's* own. By definition he cannot. The issue is whether he can accept, or "appreciate," a believer's interpretation of religion as merely the *believer's* own. "Nonbeliever" here means not simply atheist but also agnostic. "Appreciation" here means not simply acknowledging but grasping the believer's point of view: it means not simply describing the believer's point of view, which a nonbeliever can do as readily as a believer, but explaining it— in the believer's own terms.

Undeniably, a nonbeliever can appreciate some aspects of a believer's point of view. He can probably appreciate the secular functions of religion for the believer—for example, the serenity or the security religion provides. Perhaps he can appreciate as well a secular origin of religion for the believer. The decisive issue is whether he can appreciate the *reality* of religion for the believer. For how can he do so except by considering the divine real himself? What else can appreciating the reality of the divine mean except accepting it? But then, of course, the nonbeliever would have to be a believer. To the extent that the nonbeliever cannot appreciate the reality of the divine for the believer he cannot fully appreciate the believer's point of view.

Take the conventional statement that a nonbeliever can appreciate religion in a believer's own terms. As what can he appreciate it? is the fundamental question. As a response to the divine? But what can the divine mean to him when he does not accept its reality? Unless he reduces it to something else, can it mean anything to him? If he does reduce it to something else, can he be appreciating what a believer says it means? Would not a *believer* say that the meaning of the divine is above all that it is real? Would not a *believer* say that to appreciate its meaning is to accept it? How, then, can a nonbeliever profess to be appreciating its reality for a believer without accepting it himself?

To say that a nonbeliever cannot appreciate the meaning of religion for a believer would be imprecise. What he cannot do is appreciate its meaning in a believer's own, or own conscious, terms. That he need not do so is what has been argued till now. That he cannot do so is what is being argued now. The argument is a logical, not an empirical, one: it appeals to the necessary consequences of the definitions of "appreciation" and "nonbeliever."

Of course, a nonbeliever can refuse to reduce religion to other terms and can do so in the name of appreciating, or "respecting," it. But such respect is self-deceptive. One cannot respect what one cannot accept. One cannot will respect or grant it blindly. The purported respect would be doubly self-deceptive. For one would be left not only with something that one could not accept in its own purported terms but with something that one could likely accept quite well in other terms, be they psychological, sociological, or other. A nonbeliever would be left with something that he probably not only would *have* to reduce in order to make sense of it but would *want* to reduce in order to make sense of it. Yet his espousal of nonreductionism would prohibit him from reducing it. He would be left not with an incomprehensible phenomenon but with a phenomenon which he had barred himself from comprehending. He would be left not agape but gagged.

In arguing that modern man's acceptance of modern science precludes his acceptance of the *Bible* on at least the literal level Rudolf Bultmann best describes the self-deception that any attempt to do so involves:

> Can Christian preaching expect modern man *to accept the mythical* [*= literal] view of the world as true*? To do so would be both senseless and impossible. It would be senseless, because there is nothing specifically Christian in the mythical view of the world as such. It is simply the cosmology of a prescientific age. Again, it would be impossible, because no man can adopt a view of the world by his own volition—it is already determined for him by his place in history.... [I]t is impossible to revive an obsolete view of the world by a mere fiat, and certainly not by a mythical view. For all our thinking today is shaped irrevocably by modern

science. A blind acceptance of the New Testament mythology would be arbitrary, and to press for its acceptance as an article of faith would be to reduce faith to works.... It would involve a sacrifice of the intellect which could have only one result—a curious form of schizophrenia and insincerity. It would mean accepting a view of the world in our faith and religion which we should deny in our everyday life. (1961: 3–4)

Whether Bultmann or others like him[23] are correct is not the point. Whether Eliade, who interprets all religions and all religious texts almost literally, must confront the difficulties posed by modern science and, more, modern culture and modern scholarship is [the point]. Yet he considers none of them. He never questions whether the acceptance of the believer's point of view requires more than willingness on the interpreter's part.

To say that a nonbeliever cannot accept what he does not believe might seem to be confusing appreciation with endorsement. Why, one might ask, can a nonbeliever not simply imagine what the belief of others is like? Is he not likely to use his imagination to conceive of other states of mind which he himself does not share? Does he not daily use his imagination to grasp myriad beliefs and actions of other individuals and societies, past and present, native and foreign? Undeniably, a nonbeliever, like anyone else, uses his imagination to comprehend others in countless ways. The issue, however, is not whether he is capable of employing his imagination in other circumstances but whether he is capable of employing it in the case of religion. The point is exactly that appreciating religion is different from appreciating other beliefs and actions.

A nonbeliever seeking to appreciate, say, the economy of another society might well disapprove of it. But the appreciation required would be of only the utility of the economy, not of its truth. One might prefer one's own economy as more efficient or flexible but not as more nearly true. By contrast, a nonbeliever seeking to appreciate the religion of a believer must appreciate the truth, not merely the origin or function, of a belief, and must appreciate the truth of a belief which, even as an agnostic, he not merely does not happen to share but cannot accept.

Still, one might ask, what prevents a nonbeliever from granting that the divine is real for a believer even if not for him himself? The answer is two-fold. First, appreciating the believer's point of view as even the believer's own means, as argued, more than merely acknowledging or describing the reality of the divine for the believer. It means making sense of that reality in the believer's own terms. Second, appreciating the reality of the divine for the believer means truly appreciating the reality of it oneself, which by definition a nonbeliever cannot do. A believer's "attitude" toward the divine is that it is real. A nonbeliever's nonbelief bars him from duplicating that attitude. The difference between his appreciation of other phenomena and his appreciation of religious ones is exactly that his appreciation of other phenomena does, or need, not challenge any present beliefs about the world.

Suppose, however, that a nonbeliever nevertheless sought to appreciate religion in a believer's own terms. How would he go about securing that appreciation? The most direct way would be to ask a believer. A less direct way would be to observe a believer or, in the case of dead religions, to read the sacred texts left by believers. But immediately the prior problem recurs: how would a nonbeliever be able to appreciate the believer's point of view? How, directly or indirectly, would a believer be able to convey the meaning of a reality which a nonbeliever could not accept? How could a believer explain what the divine meant when by definition a nonbeliever could not accept that the divine meant what a believer said it meant? A nonbeliever would not question a believer's sincerity. He would not doubt that the believer was sure that the divine was real. He would simply doubt that the divine was in fact real and so would appreciate the divine, and the believer's belief in the divine, in other terms. He not only *could* not appreciate the reality of the divine for the believer. He would not *wish* to do so.

But suppose a nonbeliever *did* wish to do so, the reply would go. Could he not then suspend what would be literally his disbelief and proceed to appreciate the reality of the divine for a believer? To say that he would not wish to do so would seem to load the issue from the start—the issue being whether a nonbeliever *could* appreciate religion in a believer's own terms, not whether he would wish to do so. Indeed, the assumption is that he would very much wish to do so.

Suppose, then, that a nonbeliever did wish to appreciate religion from the believer's point of view. Again, how would he be able to grasp that point of view? The common answer is: through "empathy," or the recreation in his mind of the believer's own. But recreating the believer's own mind is no different from appreciating a believer in his own terms, so that to say that through empathy a nonbeliever appreciates a believer in his own terms is to speak tautologically. Empathy merely redescribes the end sought by the nonbeliever. It provides no means. *How* to "empathize" is the question—the original one.

The means typically offered are open-mindedness, sincerity, and willpower. Unfortunately, they are of little help. They are emotional solutions to a logical problem: how to appreciate in its own terms that which one can appreciate only in other terms. Open-mindedness, sincerity, and willpower may be necessary to appreciating religion in the believer's own terms, but they are not sufficient. Were the problem one of persuading a nonbeliever to *want* to appreciate the believer's point of view, they might be helpful, but this problem has been ruled out. The nonbeliever, it is taken for granted, wants to appreciate religion in the believer's own terms. The problem is that he logically, rather than psychologically, cannot, and all the open-mindedness, sincerity, and willpower he can muster are therefore to no avail.[24]

If, then, no means exist by which a nonbeliever can appreciate religion in a believer's own terms, appreciating religion in a believer's own terms proves a forlorn goal—unless one happens to be a believer. Doubtless many believers would agree,[25] but few academic interpreters of religion, including Eliade, would do so. If they did, not only would they thereby be saying that interpreters who are nonbelievers cannot appreciate religion in a believer's own terms. They would be saying that no interpreter can make nonbelievers appreciate religion in those terms in turn. Contemporary academic interpreters may argue that religion is "appreciable" in only a believer's own terms, but they rarely argue that only a believer can appreciate those terms. If in actuality only a believer can appreciate religion in a believer's own terms, then many academic interpreters and their audiences cannot. Moreover, even if all interpreters and their audiences were believers, religion in its own terms would remain a problematic subject of inquiry, not because it would still elude appreciation but because it would still be prerequisite to that appreciation.

✳ Not everyone seeks to appreciate religion in its own terms, however. Many earlier interpreters did not. Perhaps only contemporary ones do. The reason may lie in the alien nature of the phenomena they, or at least the nonbelievers among them, encounter and in their subsequent desire to surmount it by accepting those phenomena in their own terms. Since, however, their predecessors encountered the same phenomena, the alien nature of them cannot itself account for the kind of appreciation they seek. Yet it can perhaps account for the extreme character of the interpretation they seek and the equally extreme character of the interpretation often sought by their predecessors: the resolve of contemporary interpreters to appreciate religious phenomena wholly in their own terms and the frequent determination of their predecessors to understand them wholly in ours.

For the phenomena which nonbelieving interpreters confront are not just mildly alien but radically alien, so radically alien that they permit no compromise. To appreciate them in other terms is to appreciate them in ruthlessly other terms, and to appreciate them in their own terms is necessarily to appreciate them in solely their own terms, lest the barest admission of other terms admit ruthlessly other ones. Interpreters must make an either/or choice, and contemporary interpreters, in rejecting the choice of their predecessors, have necessarily been left with its opposite.

Their failure, like any other failure, is sad, but their particular failure is particularly sad. For if it is in the effort to overcome the alien nature of religious phenomena that contemporary interpreters strive to appreciate them in their own terms, it is exactly their refusal to dispense with those terms that makes the phenomena all the more inscrutable and therefore all the more alien. Contemporary interpreters see correctly that to reduce the terms of a religious phenomenon is to fail to appreciate it in its own terms and is in that respect to keep it alien. What they overlook is that to retain those terms is, for nonbelievers, to fail to appreciate the phenomenon in any terms and is therefore to keep it far more alien.

It may well be that no reductionistic interpretation developed so far has been adequate, let alone has met any of the other criteria for truth. Perhaps all have failed to make, sense of some, if not much, of religion. But then they have failed not, as Eliade would say, because they have been unable to encompass the religious meaning of religion for believers but because they have been unable to reduce that meaning to another one. They have failed not because they have been reductionistic at all but because they have not been reductionistic enough.

Their failure, moreover, is that of individual interpretations. It is not, like that of nonreductionistic interpretations for nonbelievers, the failure of the approach itself. Where all nonreductionistic interpretations are doomed for nonbelievers, future reductionistic ones, whether from existing or from new social sciences, may yet succeed.

There are several issues which it is not the purpose of this article to consider. First, it is not the purpose here to consider whether reductionistic interpretations of religion are true. The purpose is to argue only that their truth is an open rather than closed question, an empirical rather than a *priori* one. Whether or not they ultimately prove true empirically, reductionistic interpretations are not, it has been argued, *a priori* inadequate—inadequate on the grounds that they are reductionistic.

Second, the purpose of this article is not to consider whether nonbelievers can become believers or vice versa. To deny that a nonbeliever can appreciate a believer's view of religion because he does not accept the reality of the divine is not to deny that he can become a believer. Indeed, it is not even to deny that he can become a believer by concluding that reductionistic interpretations of religion are inadequate and that only nonreductionistic ones, which presuppose the reality of the divine, are adequate. The purpose here is to argue only that as long as he is a nonbeliever he cannot accept the reality of the divine and so appreciate the believer's point of view. Put conversely, conversion is prerequisite to his accepting the believer's point of view—a claim contrary to that of Eliade and other contemporary academic interpreters of religion, who almost uniformly assume that a nonbeliever as well as a believer can, with sufficient dedication and effort, appreciate religion from the believer's point of view.

Third, the purpose of this article is most certainly not to argue that believers alone can understand religion. On the contrary, it is the purpose of the first half of this article to argue that believers, like human beings generally, have no automatic, privileged, incorrigible *entrée* to the true nature of their behavior. The fact that they are the subject of their behavior is almost coincidental. It scarcely entails that they are the best, let alone sole, judge of it. Their own view may in fact prove the correct one, but not simply because it is their view.

The purpose of the second half of this article is to argue that, in the case of religion in particular and not of human behavior in general, believers alone can understand not their behavior itself but simply their own views of it. If their own views of religion were the sole ones to be considered, interpretations of religion would be confessional exclusively. Because views askew and even contrary to their own are to be considered as well, interpretations of religion can be social scientific as well.

If Eliade is wrong to oppose reductionistic interpretations of religion on the grounds that they misinterpret religion, he is right to oppose them on the grounds that they threaten, or may threaten, it. For what underlies, if hardly justifies, his abhorrence of reductionistic interpretations is his fear that they reduce God to a delusion. Eliade insists on a nonreductionistic interpretation of religion in order to preserve the reality of God.

His effort might, however, appear to be unnecessary. For, as philosophers of science continually note, a scientific explanation of a phenomenon does not dissolve the phenomenon itself but only accounts for it. A neurological explanation of pain, for example, specifies the neurological conditions under which pain occurs but does not reduce pain to, say, the stimulation of nerve endings. The stimulation may cause the pain but is surely not the pain itself. Indeed, a neurological explanation must presuppose the reality of pain in order to have something to explain. As Carl Hempel illustrates: "The kinetic theory of gases plainly does not show that there are no such things as macroscopic bodies of different gases that change volumes under changing pressure, diffuse through porous walls at characteristic rates, etc., and that there 'really' are only swarms of randomly buzzing molecules. On the contrary, the theory takes for granted that there are those macroscopic events and uniformities, and it seeks to account for them in terms of the microstructure of the gases and the microprocesses involved in their various changes" (1966: 78).

What, it is commonly said, a scientific explanation can dissolve is not the phenomenon being explained but alternative explanations of it. If, for example, a chemical explanation of pain were able to account for all the aspects of pain presently accounted for biologically, it could reduce the biological terms to chemical ones. The biological explanation would thereby become superfluous, but pain itself would not. This distinction between the reducibility of one theory to another and the irreducibility of one phenomenon to another has recently been invoked by Hans Penner and Edward Yonan against Eliade.[26] They argue that he, together with other nonreductionists, wrongly rejects reductionistic explanations of religion because he wrongly fears that they reduce God to a delusion. Were he to realize that reductionistic explanations of religion challenge only nonreductionistic explanations, not God himself, he would have no reason to oppose them: "As we have shown, reduction is an operation concerned with theories or systems of statements, not with phenomena, data, or the properties of the phenomena.... None of the scholars we have examined ... states that reduction wipes out, levels, or demeans the phenomena or data being explained. On the contrary, reduction in the sciences implies an *explanation* of one *theory* by the use of another in the same discipline (or, different disciplines)" (1972: 130–131).

Unfortunately, God is not, like pain, a reality to be explained but is rather, like atoms, an explanation itself of reality. The reality to be explained is religion, or its object. Where God is the explanation offered by nonreductionists, nature, society, and the psyche are among the explanations offered by social scientific reductionists. Those explanations, as rival ones to God, do challenge the reality of God, so that Eliade is justified in fearing them, even if he is not justified in rejecting them.[27] These explanations may not refute the existence of God, but, if accepted, they may well render his existence superfluous—and in that sense threaten the reality of God.

Just as the purpose of this article was to argue earlier that reductionistic interpretations of religion are alone possible for nonbelievers, so the purpose of the end of this article has been to argue that reductionistic interpretations may be impossible for believers. At the same time the purpose of this article is not, primarily, to consider whether reductionistic interpretations do challenge the reality of God. The purpose is to note, rather, that even if they do not, nonbelievers are by definition obliged to use them. Whether or not reductionistic interpretations themselves refute the reality of God, nonbelievers, as long as they are nonbelievers, can use only them. Nonbelievers are scarcely, barred from rejecting reductionistic interpretations for nonreductionistic ones, but they can do so only by becoming believers themselves. Whether or not reductionistic interpretations themselves preclude the reality of God, nonbelievers by definition do not accept that reality and so cannot employ interpretations which presuppose it.

Notes

1. Some examples are symbolic anthropologists, cognitive anthropologists, phenomenological and existential sociologists, ethnomethodologists, cognitive psychologists, existential and humanistic psychologists, historians of "mentalities," phenomenologists generally, and Wittgensteinian philosophers. Admittedly, the generalization is crude. On the one hand behaviorism and structuralism, for example, are twentieth-century movements which conspicuously spurn understanding human phenomena in their participants' own terms. On the other hand romanticism and nationalism, for example, were nineteenth-century movements which equally conspicuously sought to understand human phenomena in their participants' own terms.
2. See above all Smith.
3. See above all Eliade 1959a, 1965, 1968a, 1968b.
4. For other criticisms of Eliade's interpretation of believers' conscious view of religion see Saliba (ch. 4) and Allen (208–212).
5. As Ricketts, one of Eliade's self-proclaimed defenders, states: "Eliade has mislead some readers by his definition of the sacred as the 'real.' Some have thought that

this means that Eliade himself regards the sacred as Reality: that is, that he is making a theological statement. Eliade would deny this. All he means here is that for the believer, that which is sacred for him is the Real, the True, the meaningful in an ultimate sense. As for what the Real 'really' is, Eliade never ventures an answer: such a question lies beyond the methodology of the history of religions. To answer that question one must go beyond the limits of the history of religions—and speak as philosopher, theologian or perhaps psychologist" (28).

6. For further examples see Allen (134–136).

7. See above all Eliade 1959a and 1968b.

8. See, for example, Campbell (24, 216).

9. See Segal (105–106).

10. On the practice of *Verstehen* generally see, pro, above all Weber, Schutz, MacIver, Hayek. See, con, above all Abel, Nagel (1963: 200–206; 1961: 473–485), Penner and Yonan (123–127, 131–133). See, both pro and con, above all Brodbeck (part I), Natanson (part III), Dallmayr and McCarthy (parts I–II).

11. On the practice of *Verstehen* in history see, pro, above all Collingwood (introduction; part V), Dray. See, con, above all Hempel (1942, 1963), Gardiner.

12. On the practice of *Verstehen* sociology see, pro, above all Garfinkel, Roy Turner, Sudnow, Jack Douglas. See, con, above all Durkheim, Gellner (1956), Denzin.

13. On the practice of *Verstehen* in anthropology see, pro, above all Tyler, Geertz, Mary Douglas, Victor Turner. See, con, above all Radcliffe-Brown, Harris.

14. See Collingwood (172, 215–216, 230–231, 305).

15. On the Wittgensteinian practice of *Verstehen* see, pro, above all Winch, Louch, Phillips. See, con, above all Nielsen, MacIntyre, Gellner (1975), Richards, Shepherd. See, pro and con, above all Borger and Cioffi (231–269).

16. See Winch (1964: 322–324).

17. On teleological explanations see, pro, above all Taylor, Wright. See, con, above all Braithwaite (ch. 10), Nagel (1961: ch. 12). See, pro and con, above all Borger and Cioffi (49–95).

18. On rationality see, pro and con, above all Wilson, Benn and Mortimore, Borger and Cioffi (167–230).

19. On methodological individualism see, pro, above all Popper (1945: ch. 14; 1957: chs. 7. 23–24, 31), Hayek (chs. 4, 6, 8), Wrong, Homans, Watkins. See, con, above all Mandelbaum, Gellner (1956), Goldstein, Lukes. See, pro and con, above all O'Neil, Borger and Cioffi (271–311), Brodbeck (part IV).

20. On the ambiguity of the phenomenologists' goal see Saliba (30–31), Smart (19–21), Allen (57–96).

21. For comparable criticisms of the phenomenology of religion see Oxtoby (595-599), Baird (89–91), Dudley (119–221).

22. Whether or not as a phenomenologist of religion, Eliade gets faulted on the same basic grounds as one. See Saliba (ch. 4), Baird (74–91), Dudley (chs. 3–4). In defense of Eliade see Allen (ch. 7).

23. See, notably, Ricoeur (3–24, 151–157, 161–174, 347–357).

24. The confusion of a logical problem with an emotional, or psychological, one occurs in attempts not only to understand religious belief but also to acquire it. When, to cite the grandest instance, Soren Kierkegaard demands that faith resolutely affirm what reason can, and should, not, he is not just offering but demanding a

psychological solution to a logical problem: the problem of the incompatibility of religion with reason.

25. To be sure, many believers would probably demand that one be not just a believer of any kind but a believer in the particular religion he wants to understand.

26. See Penner and Yonan (117–122, 130–131).

27. Where Penner and Yonan seek a reconciliation between religion and the social sciences on the grounds that the social sciences cannot reduce religion to all illusion, Saliba (ch. 5) and Fenton, among others, seek reconciliation on the grounds that the social sciences cannot do so entirely—there remaining aspects of religion unexplained by the social sciences. Whether or not Saliba and Fenton confuse the reduction of religious explanations with the reduction of religious phenomena themselves, as Penner and Yonan would charge, they do confuse the present, admittedly incomplete state of social scientific explanations of religion with a future, potentially complete one.

References

Abel, Theodore 1948. "The Operation Called Verstehen," *American Journal of Sociology* 54: 211–218.

Allen, Douglas 1978. *Structure and Creativity in Religion*. Religion and Reason Series, No. 14. The Hague: Mouton.

Baird, Robert 1971. *Category Formation and the History of Religions*. Religion and Reason Series, No. 1. The Hague: Mouton.

Benn, S. I. and G. W. Mortimore (eds.) 1976. *Rationality and the Social Sciences*. London: Routledge & Kegan Paul.

Bleeker, C. Jouco 1959. "The Phenomenological Method," *Numen* 6: 96–111.

Borger, Robert and Frank Cioffi (eds.) 1970. *Explanation in the Behavioral Sciences*. Cambridge: Cambridge University Press.

Braithwaite, R. B. 1953. *Scientific Explanation*. Cambridge: Cambridge University Press.

Brodbeck, May 1968. *Readings in the Philosophy of the Social Sciences*. New York: Macmillan.

Bultmann, Rudolf 1961. "New Testament and Mythology," *Kerygma and Myth*, 1–44. Hans Werner Bartsch (ed.) and Reginald H. Fuller (trans.). New York: Harper Torchbooks.

Campbell, Joseph 1972. *Myths to Live By*. New York: Viking.

Collingwood, R. G. 1946. *The Idea of History*. T. M. Knox (ed.). New York: Oxford University Press.

Dallmayr, Fred R. and Thomas A. McCarthy (eds.) 1977. *Understanding and Social Inquiry*. Notre Dame: University of Notre Dame Press.

Denzin, Norman K. 1969. "Symbolic Interactionism and Ethnomethodology," *Sociological Review* 34: 922–934.

Douglas, Jack D. 1970. *Understanding Everyday Life*. Chicago: Aldine.

Douglas, Mary 1966. *Purity and Danger*. London: Routledge & Kegan Paul.

—— 1970. *Natural Symbols*. New York: Pantheon.

—— 1975. *Implicit Meanings*. London and Boston: Routledge & Kegan Paul.

Dray, William 1957. *Laws and Explanation in History*. Oxford: Clarendon Press.

—— 1963. "The Historical Explanation of Actions Reconsidered," *Philosophy and History*, 105–135. Sydney Hook (ed.). New York: New York University Press.

Dudley, Guilford, III 1977. *Religion on Trial*. Philadelphia: Temple University Press.

Durkheim, Emile 1915. *The Elementary Forms of the Religious Life*. Joseph Ward Swain (ed.). New York: Macmillan.

—— 1938. *The Rules of Sociological Method*. George Catlin (ed.) and Sarah A. Solovay and John H. Mueller (trans.). Glencoe, IL: Free Press.

—— 1951. *Suicide*. George Simpson (ed.) and John A. Spaulding (trans.). Glencoe, IL: Free Press.

Eliade, Mircea 1959a. *Cosmos and History*. Willard R. Trask (ed.). Bollingen Series XLVI. New York: Harper Torchbooks.

—— 1959b. "Methodological Remarks on the Study of Religious Symbolism," *The History of Religions*, 86–107. Mircea Eliade and Joseph Kitagawa (eds.). Chicago: University of Chicago Press.

—— 1963. *Patterns in Comparative Religion*. Rosemary Sheed (trans.). Cleveland: Meridian Books.

—— 1968a. *Myth and Reality*. Willard R. Trask (trans.). New York: Harper Torchbooks.

—— 1968b. *The Sacred and the Profane*. Willard R. Trask (trans.). New York: Harvest Books.

—— 1968c. "Comparative Religion: Its Past and Future," *Knowledge and the Future of Man*, 245–254. Walter J. Ong (ed.). New York: Holt, Rinehart.

—— 1969. *The Quest*. Chicago: University of Chicago Press.

Fenton, John Y. 1970. "Reductionism in the Study of Religions," *Soundings* 53: 61–76.

Gardiner, Patrick 1952. *The Nature of Historical Explanation*. Oxford: Clarendon Press.

Garfinkel, Harold 1967. *Studies in Ethnomethodology*. Englewood Cliffs: Prentice-Hall.

Geertz, Clifford 1960. *The Religion of Java*. Glencoe, IL.: Free Press.

—— 1968. *Islam Observed*. New Haven: Yale University Press.

—— 1973. *The Interpretation of Cultures*. New York: Basic Books.

—— 1980. *Negara*. Princeton: Princeton University Press.

Gellner, Ernest 1956. "Explanations in History," *Aristotelian Society Supplementary* 30: 157–176.

—— 1975. "A Wittgensteinian Philosophy of (or Against) the Social Sciences," *Philosophy of the Social Sciences* 5: 173–199.

Goldstein, Leon J. 1956. "The Inadequacy of the Principle of Methodological Individualism," *Journal of Philosophy* 53: 801–813.

Harris, Marvin 1968. *The Rise of Anthropological Theory*. New York: Crowell.

—— 1979. *Cultural Materialism*. New York: Random House.

Hayek, F. A. 1952. *The Counter-Revolution of Science*. Glencoe, IL: Free Press.

Hempel, Carl G. 1942. "The Function of General Laws in History," *Journal of Philosophy* 39: 35–48.

—— 1963. "Reasons and Covering Laws in Historical Explanation," *Philosophy and History*, 143–163. Sidney Hook (ed.). New York: New York University Press.

—— 1966. *Philosophy of Natural Science*. Foundations of Philosophy Series. Englewood Cliffs: Prentice-Hall.

Homans, George 1964. "Bringing Men Back In," *American Sociological Review* 29: 809–818.

Kristensen, W. Brede 1960. *The Meaning of Religion*. John B. Carman (trans.). The Hague: Martinus Nijhoff.

Louch, A. R. 1966. *Explanation and Human Action*. Oxford: Blackwell.

Lukes, Steven 1968. "Methodological Individualism Reconsidered," *British Journal of Sociology* 19: 119–129.

MacIntyre, Alasdair 1964. "Is Understanding Religion Compatible With Believing?" *Faith and Philosophers*, 115–133. John Hick (ed.). New York: St. Martin's Press.

—— 1967. "The Idea of a Social Science," *Aristotelian Society Supplementary* 41: 95–114.

MacIver, R. M. 1942. *Social Causation*. Boston: Ginn.

Mandlebaum, Maurice 1955. "Societal Facts," *British Journal of Sociology* 6: 305–317.

Nagel, Ernest 1961. *The Structure of Science*. New York: Harcourt, Brace.

—— 1963. "Problems of Concept and Theory Formation in the Social Sciences," *Philosophy of the Social Sciences*, 189–209. Maurice Natanson (ed.). New York: Random House.

Natanson, Maurice (ed.) 1963. *Philosophy of the Social Sciences*. New York: Random House.

Nielsen, Kai 1967. "Wittgensteinian Fideism," *Philosophy* 42: 191–207.

—— 1971. *Contemporary Critiques of Religion*. New York: Herder & Herder.

O'Neil, John 1973. *Modes of Individualism and Collectivism*. New York: St. Martin's Press.

Oxtoby, Willard G. 1968. "*Religionswissenschaft* Revisited," *Religions in Antiquity*, 590–608. Jacob Neusner (ed.). Supplements to *Numen*, No. 14. Leiden: E. J. Brill.

Peel, J. D. Y. 1969. "Understanding Alien Belief System," *British Journal of Sociology* 20: 69–84.

Penner, Hans H. and Edward A. Yonan 1972. "Is a Science of Religion Possible?" *Journal of Religion* 52: 107–133.

Phillips, D. Z. 1965. *The Concept of Prayer*. London: Routledge & Kegan Paul.

—— 1967. "Faith, Skepticism, and Religious Understanding," *Religion and Understanding*, 63–79. D. Z. Phillips (ed.). New York: Macmillan.

—— 1970. *Faith and Philosophical Enquiry*. London: Routledge & Kegan Paul.

—— 1976. *Religion Without Explanation*. Oxford: Oxford University Press.

Popper, Karl 1945. *The Open Society and Its Enemies*. London: Routledge.

—— 1957. *The Poverty of Historicism*. Boston: Beacon Press.

Radcliffe-Brown, A. R. 1922. *The Andaman Islanders*. Cambridge: Cambridge University Press.

—— 1952. *Structure and Function in Primitive Society*. Glencoe, IL: Free Press.

Richards, Glyn 1978. "A Wittgensteinian Approach to the Philosophy of Religion: A Critical Evaluation of D. Z. Phillips," *Journal of Religion* 58: 288–302.

Ricketts, Mac Linscott 1973. "In Defense of Eliade," *Religion* 3: 13–34.

Ricoeur, Paul 1969. *The Symbolism of Evil*. Emerson Buchanan (trans.). Boston: Beacon Press.

Saliba, John A. 1976. "*Homo Religiosus*" *in Mircea Eliade*. Supplements to *Numen*,

Altera Series V. Leiden: E. J. Brill.

——— Alfred 1962. "Concept and Theory Formation in the Social Sciences," *ʌcted Papers*, Vol. 1, 48–66. Maurice Natanson (ed.). The Hague: Martinus ̱off.

——— Robert A. 1978 "Joseph Campbell's Theory of Myth: An Essay Review of His ̱vre," *Journal of the American Academy of Religion Supplement* 44: 97–114.

Shepherd, William C. 1974. "On the Concept of 'Being Wrong' Religiously," *Journal of the American Academy of Religion* 42: 66–81.

Smart, Ninian 1977. *The Science of Religion and the Sociology of Knowledge.* Princeton: Princeton University Press.

Smith, Wilfred C. 1963a. *The Meaning and End of Religion.* New York: Macmillan.

——— 1963b. *The Faith of Other Men.* New York: Mentor Books.

——— 1979. *Faith and Belief.* Princeton: Princeton University Press.

Sudnow, David (ed.) 1972. *Studies in Social Interaction.* New York: Free Press.

Taylor, Charles 1964. *The Explanation of Behavior.* London: Routledge & Kegan Paul.

Turner, Roy (ed.) 1970. *Ethnomethodology.* Harmondsworth: Penguin.

Turner, Victor 1967. *The Forest of Symbols.* Ithaca: Cornell University Press.

——— 1969. *The Ritual Process.* Chicago: Aldine.

——— 1974. *Dramas, Fields, and Metaphors.* Ithaca: Cornell University Press.

——— 1975. *Revelation and Divination of Ndembu Ritual.* Ithaca: Cornell University Press.

Tyler, Stephen A. (ed.) 1969. *Cognitive Anthropology.* New York: Holt, Rinehart.

Watkins, J. W. N. 1952. "Ideal Types and Historical Explanation," *British Journal for Philosophy of Science* 3: 22–43.

——— 1949. "'Objectivity' in Social Science and Social Policy," *The Methodology of the Social Sciences*, 49–112. Edward A. Shils and Henry A. Finch (eds. and trans.). New York: Free Press.

Wilson, Bryan (ed.) 1970. *Rationality.* Oxford: Blackwell.

Winch, Peter 1958. *The Idea of a Social Science.* London: Routledge & Kegan Paul.

——— 1964. "Understanding a Primitive Society," *American Philosophical Quarterly* 1: 307–324.

Wright, Larry 1976. *Teleological Explanation.* Berkeley and Los Angeles: University of California Press.

Wrong, Dennis, H. 1961. "The Oversocialized Conception of Man in Modern Sociology," *American Sociological Review* 26: 183–193.

12

TERRY F. GODLOVE, JR., *Religious Discourse and First Person Authority*

&∂∼&∂∼

The study of religion, as I understand it, shares the basic aim of the other branches of the human sciences. It aims, as they do, to understand the beliefs, actions, and values of persons. What makes the study of religion distinctive—if perhaps not unique—is that the beliefs, actions, and values at stake typically have to do with, in David Hume's apt phrase, "invisible, intelligent powers"— with angels, ancestors, demons, spirits, gods, goddesses, and all the rest.

Many times "have to do" cashes out without remainder as poetry, song, dance, myth, metaphysics, or metaphor. But religious people very often seem to speak as if they believe these creatures do exist, and therein lies a problem, for as far as we observers can tell, they do not. Not that all disagreement or apparent error leads to interpretive problems. There is no problem—to take one of Wayne Proudfoot's examples (1985: 216)—about interpreting the hiker's exclamation, "There's a bear!," although we can see he is looking at a partially obscured log. By contrast, many people—perhaps most influentially, Ludwig Wittgenstein—have felt that there often is a problem in attributing to someone the belief that voodoo really works or that the king is related by kinship to a grove of trees or that God became man.

Recently, philosophers, linguists, and social scientists have had much to say about the attribution of error. This subject's cross-disciplinary appeal is unsurprising, for it naturally falls at the intersection of interpretation theory and epistemology. While I will shortly take up aspects of this debate, for now, I simply want to observe that many scholars of religion seem to have aligned themselves with Wittgenstein in tending to construe what sound like straightforward assertions about invisible, intelligent powers as neither true nor false. The question becomes: What do religious people really mean when they seem to be talking about invisible, intelligent beings? Or: What are they really doing?

Today we have plenty of theoretical perspectives from which to choose when attempting to answer these questions. To mention only a few, we have continuing contributions from various forms of critical theory (Bataille 1989; Blumenberg 1983), functionalism (Douglas 1966; Turner 1967), psychoanalysis (Jones 1991; Meisner 1984), structuralism (Penner 1989: part 2), ethnology (Staal 1989), deconstruction (Taylor 1987), cognitive linguistics (Sperber 1975; Lawson and McCauley 1990; for a discussion of important differences between these two works see Godlove 1993), social ecology (Smith 1987; Bell 1992), Kantian-style and other comparative moral theories (for the former see Green 1978; 1988; for the latter, Little and Twiss 1978), socio-biology (Wilson 1978: chapter 8), a newly resurgent, sophisticated verificationism (Martin 1990), and from neo-Wittgensteinian theologians who urge us to treat religious traditions as "language-games" (Lindbeck 1984). Perhaps the only important feature which these diverse approaches share is the assumption that, in the nature of the case, religious people are often not talking about what they claim or appear to be talking about, namely, invisible, intelligent powers. In fact, the common assumption is that we interpreters are often in a better position than they are to know the true significance of their words. To use the phrase common in the current literature, all these theories often seem to deny persons their usual "first person authority" (see, for example, Burge 1979, 1982, 1986; Davidson 1984b, 1987).

From the standpoint of theory and method, the apparent widespread denial of first person authority seems to me to be one of the most striking aspects of the contemporary study of religion. In what follows, I discuss the nature and ground of first person authority, and ask why scholars of religion appear to deny it with such regularity.

The Edible God

Ordinarily, competent speakers are authoritative about the meaning of their own words. This fact seems to be traceable in some way to the directness of the evidence language-users have concerning their own speech. We do not normally have to listen to our words in order to interpret them. This immediacy sets us apart from our audience. Our listeners must gather evidence through their senses—their interpretations are based on a complex set of hypotheses and background assumptions that undergo constant, if generally unnoticed, revision. And, of course, such listeners can only marshal their evidence after witnessing each successive speech act. By contrast, the insight competent speakers have into the meaning of their own speech-behavior is, as a rule, neither so hypothetical nor so tardy. As competent speakers, we are authoritative about the meaning of the vast bulk of our words. As competent interpreters, we ordinarily presume and do our best, all things being equal, to preserve one another's first person authority.

To note this common phenomenon is of course not to explain or justify it. What, then, is its basis, and why is it so often allowed to lapse in the academic study of religion?

Hume was perhaps first in pointing the way toward a serious treatment of these issues. In his *Natural History of Religion* (1957: 55–56), he tells the story of a young Turkish prisoner, who was taken to the Sorbonne for instruction. It seems that some of the priests

> solicited Mustapha very hard to turn Christian, and promised him, for his encouragement, plenty of good wine in this world, and paradise in the next. These allurements were too powerful to be resisted; and therefore, having been well instructed and catechized, he at last agreed to receive the sacraments of baptism and the Lord's supper. The priest, however, to make everything sure and solid, still continued his instructions, and began the next day with the usual question, *How many Gods are there? None at all,* replies Benedict; for that was his new name. *How? None at all!* cries the priest. To be sure, said the honest proselyte. *You have told me all along that there is but one God and yesterday I eat him.*

Nearly everyone—including Hume—would agree that, whatever the priest meant by the term "God," he did not mean the wafer. And probably a majority would even say that the boy made a mistake in taking that as the priest's intended meaning. But the second judgment is, I think, just what Hume wants to put in doubt.

Let us ask how the boy has arrived at his humorous interpretation of the priest's discourse. We may imagine some such scene as this: the boy is seated before the priest, who is explaining the significance of the sacrament. In the course of his explanation, the priest now and then makes this sound, "God." Further, at those times when the priest makes this sound—for simplicity's sake, let us say at only those times—he handles and directs his attention to the holy wafer. In time, the boy comes to take this pairing as more than coincidental; that is, he comes to hold the sound "God" applicable when—and only when—in the presence of the wafer. And this is as much as to say that he learns that the word "God" refers to, and means, the wafer.

Accepting something like this reconstruction, we may now reconsider whether the boy has made a mistake in interpreting the priest's "God." Whatever our eventual verdict, certainly some such learning process—one involving the pairing of verbal behavior to publicly observable objects and events—does play a crucial role in our everyday assignments of reference and meaning. This point has recently been emphasized by a number of philosophers, including Hilary Putnam (1975: 227), whose thought experiments are designed to show that, as he has famously put it, "meanings just ain't in the head." Writing in the same spirit, Donald Davidson (1987: 450) notes that "a sentence someone is inspired (caused) to hold true by and only by sightings of the moon is apt to mean something like 'there's the moon'; the thought expressed is apt to be that the moon is there." Davidson's claim is that, at least in "basic cases," we must take the cause of a belief also to be its object.

With Putnam's slogan in mind—that "meanings just ain't in the head"—we can mount a pretty fair defense of the boy's interpretation. He has focused, after all, on the one aspect of the environment that he can see—and that he has every reason to think that the priest also sees—is reliably tied to the priest's discourse. In his approach to interpretation Mustapha is a good behaviourist, and, as Quine has long emphasized (1992: 38), in that he joins the rest of us.

> As long as our command of the language fits all external checkpoints, where our utterance or our reaction to someone else's utterance can be appraised in light of some shared situation, all is well. Our mental life between checkpoints is indifferent to our rating as master of the language. There is nothing in linguistic meaning beyond what is to be gleaned from overt behavior in observable circumstances.

As far as Mustapha could tell, his own wafer-talk was behaviorally indistinguishable from the priest's God-talk.[1] And, for Mustapha and Quine, that exhausts the notion of sameness of meaning.

But we can further sharpen the boy's defense. We can well imagine that the priest's verbal behavior cannot be correlated with *any* change in the environment *except* that involving the wafer. Some such result would be no surprise. For it is a matter of orthodoxy in Judaism, Christianity, and Islam that speech about God cannot be paired with an actual, physical appearance; though intelligent and powerful, God is immaterial. But more radically, there is not even any *indirect* correlation to be had; the deity leaves no trace, at least no public trace, and, in the context of interpretation, such traces are what we require—they allow us to infer its properties. God is, so to speak, more invisible than a magnetic field or a sub-atomic particle.

These considerations should, it seems to me, generate no little sympathy for the boy's interpretation, even if we do not want to go so far as to conclude that the priest's use of "God" really meant wafer (that the boy was flat-out right). But some will be unmoved. Surely, they will say, the boy has just failed in his attempt to grasp correctly the meaning of "God" operative within the priest's linguistic community. Since the priest was a competent member of that community, and intended his words to be understood in the way he knew to be standard within that community, his words are correctly interpreted only when understood in that standard sense. Whatever that standard sense is, *that* is both what the priest's words meant and (given his intentions) what the priest meant by his words, and *that* is what the boy—perhaps through no fault of his own— failed to master.

At issue here is the difficult question of whether speakers' words must always be given the meaning they have in their own speech community. We may agree that speakers must intend to be understood as they want, and that this will promote uniformity in interpretation, since competent speakers know from experience that they cannot typically interpret other speakers from scratch (Davidson 1987: 449; Burge 1982: 289) (and competent hearers know that competent speakers know this, and also know that competent speakers know that competent hearers know that competent speakers know this). Further, speakers can only have this intention if they expect their listeners to grasp how they (the speakers) want to be interpreted. (I assume that a speaker cannot intend to be understood as he wishes by a hearer he knows or believes cannot so interpret him—that, more generally, we cannot intend to do what we know or believe to be impossible.) What, then, has gone awry between the priest and Mustapha—if anything has?

We must distinguish between three points of view. From the priest's vantage point, he may justly claim to be authoritative about what his words mean. He is a member in good standing of a speech community within which the words he used carry just the standard meaning that he intended them to inspire (assuming of course that his "God-talk" has a standard intra-community meaning, that it is not, for example, a deliberate misuse of language). From Mustapha's point of view, Mustapha can only appeal to the best principles of interpretation he knows in decoding both the meaning of the speaker's sounds and what the speaker meant by making those sounds then and there. I have already suggested that it is at least plausible that Mustapha has fully discharged that obligation. While it would not be plausible to hold that the boy's interpretive resources should *confer* a non-standard meaning to the priest's words (that they could somehow reach out and override the speaker's intentions), it does not follow that the boy has violated the priest's first person authority by interpreting his words in (from the priest's point of view) a nonstandard way. If, in forming his interpretation of the priest's words, the boy has appealed to principles of interpretation that are, under the circumstances, defensible, what sense can there be in concluding that he has made a mistake or that he has violated anything?

Lastly, we come to our own point of view as—relative to the exchange between Mustapha and the priest—well-informed observer-interpreters. We can see that the priest's expectation that the boy would understand his words in the standard (intended) sense was spectacularly ill-founded. The priest expected to be understood in a way that he should have known was, at the very least, unlikely. Further, it was unlikely for the apparent reason that he had not given the boy sufficient clues to prompt the understanding that he intended (here assuming that we have somehow gleaned clues sufficient to enable our appreciation of a gap between the two). The priest's theory about the boy's theory about the priest's theory of meaning was wildly mistaken. If anyone has failed, it is the priest.

Having beaten Hume's little story pretty well to a pulp, let me extract three morals. First, the prime casualty of Mustapha's collision with the priest is the notion that there exists one correct interpretation of a speaker's words, a notion associated with the further thesis that words have meaning in themselves, apart from the conditions, mental and physical, surrounding their use. These two ideas in turn go hand in hand with the thought that linguistic meaning is somehow in the heads of speakers, and that the interpreter's job is somehow to get inside the speaker's head in order to extract it with a minimum of distortion. Hume's story illustrates, on the contrary, Putnam's slogan that "meanings just ain't in the head." For here, a bit of the world (the wafer), a speaker, and an interpreter clever enough to notice a connection between the first two have all conspired to produce a defensible interpretation. It may be objected that Mustapha worked from an evidential base that was simply too thin—that, while he may be epistemically justified in his interpretation, it is simply false. But that would be to miss the deeper point that, under even optimal conditions, the interpretation of speech (and non-linguistic behavior) will always involve balancing the same sorts of considerations that Mustapha had to consider, according to maxims that often must undergo continual adjustment.[2] Far from having direct access to a speaker's beliefs and theory of meaning, we must construct each of them on the basis of the other. From an interpreter's point of view, the product of this constructive activity is all there *is* to the notion of a speaker's beliefs and meanings. In that sense, there simply was no fact of the matter for Mustapha to get right or wrong.[3] I take it that this is one way to approach Quine's thesis of the indeterminacy of translation or Davidson's variation on it, the indeterminacy of interpretation.

Second, discourse ostensibly about an invisible, intelligent power is hard to interpret because its component sentences are held true under any and all observable circumstances. Whatever goes on in the world, still, "the Redeemer liveth," and, "there is but one God." With respect to environmental change, the discourse of (at least) abstract monotheism is indifferent. But this very indifference flaunts what is apparently basic to the interpretation of verbal behavior—namely, our ability to identify the object or event which systematically prompts an utterance with what that utterance is about. By refusing to be paired, even indirectly, with an aspect of the environment, discourse about invisible, intelligent powers tries to be meaningful exclusively "in the head."

Third, and finally, reflection on Hume's tale suggests a first, rough answer to the question concerning why scholars of religion often appear to run roughshod over first person authority. For why are competent speakers generally authoritative about the meaning of their words? If we agree to the externalist position and take the meaning of a word to be fixed (at least in basic cases) by the aspect of the world that prompts the word's use, then the answer is clear. Speakers can be certain of the meaning of their words because whatever they regularly apply them to gives them their meaning. Then, to doubt the general validity of first person authority is to doubt that competent speakers generally know what is prompting them to use the words they are using. But, for all but the Cartesian sceptic, that doubt will seem far-fetched.[4]

Taking, then, the basis of first person authority to be "outside the head" in something like the way that I have outlined, our question is whether it extends to talk of invisible, intelligent power. We must ask: What aspect of the world prompts, directly or indirectly, use of the word "God" ? In the limiting case of the thoroughly abstract, immaterial deity, the answer is: nothing, no-thing. But, on the line we are pursuing, it is just this prompting that makes for first person authority. Thus, by eschewing a semantic natural history—by trying to purchase its meaning strictly "in the head"—talk of an abstract, immaterial deity denies itself the very basis of first person authority. While these remarks are in many respects incomplete,[5] they suggest, I believe, why scholars of religion often seem not to let religious people speak for themselves.

The Natural History of "God"

I have so far referred to the thoroughly abstract god—perhaps Tillich's "God above the God of theism"—as a limiting case. But of course most gods and goddesses, devils and demons, are more substantial than this. In part to drive home just this contrast, Hume's *Natural History* traces the ironic degeneration of religion from polytheistic nature-worship to abstract monotheism. Hume's point is that belief in, for example, the solar god can be understood because it has a specifiable natural history—that is, a causal trail traceable outside the head of the worshiper. Thus, we notice that worshipers turn toward the sun when they utter the word "sun." Here we can easily make the sort of connection between speaker and world that in turn tends to make for the strongest first person authority. By contrast, the field linguist out to interpret speech about a thoroughly abstract god does not have this advantage—that was what made for Mustapha's predicament and what called for his ingenuity. An invisible, intelligent power cannot have a causal history that identifies it as an invisible, intelligent power—and so interpretation of speech about it is, if perhaps not impossible, inherently problematic.

For my purposes, Hume's contrast between polytheistic nature-worship and abstract monotheism is crucial. On the line I am urging, we ought to find that theories of nature-religions rely, for interpretive purposes, on the evident causal contexts of the beliefs they aim to decode. And this is in fact the case, for each of the two main competing meta-theoretical stances found in the modern literature. Thus, the so-called intellectualist model follows Hume in making nature-worship a kind of proto-science, seeing it as primarily a means-end or instrumental mode of behavior. Champions of this view include Robin Horton and, at times, Bronislaw Malinowski. But even if we endorse the competing model—the symbolist approach—we will still not have lost sight of the literal.

The symbolist—say, Edmund Leach, Talcott Parsons, John Beattie or, in a recent book, Stanley Tambiah (1990)—counsels us to decode the symbolic significance of religious belief, the one that lies beneath the overt meaning. But then of course the symbolist has not denied the importance of the literal interpretation of the belief; in fact it is crucial, precisely as that which must be decoded.

The point is that, for both of these approaches, nature-worship is intelligible—is interpretable—because of the agent's interaction with aspects of the shared, public environment. We may and ought to let polytheistic nature worshipers speak for themselves. Or, rather than us, it is *the world,* in the form of the public objects (suitably anthropomorphized) they worship, that allows them to speak for themselves—even if, with the symbolists, we are inclined not to rest content with what they say. As before, the theme is that "meaning ain't in the head."

By contrast, it is not so clear how we are to let believers in thoroughly immaterial deities speak for themselves. Just as objective features of the world—the sun, the moon, and so on—tend to make possible the interpretation of nature religions, so their absence tends to block our understanding of, for example, classical monotheism. The problem is age-old: how to understand talk about a god who is said to be, for example, intelligent and yet completely immaterial and undetectable.

Let me emphasize that I do not say that it cannot be done. From early on, what we know today as philosophical theology has been preoccupied with showing that we finite humans can sensibly talk about an invisible, intelligent power. To this end, theologians and philosophers have constructed ingenious conceptions of God and equally ingenious accounts of linguistic reference. In the Christian tradition, one thinks of Augustine's appeal in the *Confessions* to the image of light, or of Aquinas' discussion of analogical predication; in recent times, we have the panentheistic deity of process metaphysics and the suggestion that all language is, at bottom, metaphorical. All of these theories try to show that human speech can, to some degree, bridge the gap between divinity and humanity. But let us grant these theories complete success; still, they show at most the abstract possibility of referring to an invisible, intelligent power. As Hume's tale vividly illustrates, they establish nothing about whether a given interpreter's construal of a given bit of speech behavior is justified. Put differently, philosophical theology rarely has any role to play in our understanding of religious speech and action.[6]

We should expect, then, to find that first person authority is strongest in the nature-religions and weakest in the abstract monotheisms. Now this distinction is obviously crude and far from exhaustive. The lunar god and the ineffable god above god anchor opposite ends of a spectrum filled out by a familiar cast of religious characters—what Hume calls "middle beings" angels, ancestors, demons, the holy spirit, and the like. It would be a mistake to look for a definite place where talk about such things ceases to be meaningful, for the data is too diverse and the talents of the interpreter too variable. By way of generalization, we can say only that, as religious persons ascend the scale of abstractness they tend to forfeit the right to speak for themselves; similarly, the power of speech returns to the extent that they embrace anthropomorphism and thereby supply the local deity (etc.) with an identifiable trail within the world of public objects and events.

The basic claim is that the strength of a person's authority over the meaning of his or her words varies with the interpreter's ability to appreciate their natural history, to unearth their systematic—even if subtle and indirect—ties to the world that all language-users must share. This is to be expected, for it is just such a tie that gives the words their meaning. We should find, then, what we do find—that talk of the angels is more secure than is talk of the holy spirit; speech about the continuing activity of our revered ancestors is more readily interpreted than is talk about the god beyond the god of theism. In sum, first person authority turns out to be a matter of degree. It ranges over a gradient formed, roughly, by the degree of abstractness claimed for the putative object of a belief, action, or value.

If something like this is right, then among all those pursuing one or another of the human sciences, scholars of religion are best prepared to appreciate the ebb and flow of first person authority. For they are trained to deal on a daily basis with a range of more or less abstract beings and so—in order to give religious persons their rightful semantic authority—have had to become skilled in the arts of taste, sympathy, intuition, and imaginative surmise (Davidson 1984a: 279; 1984b: 438). But no amount of training or sympathy on the part of the interpreter can confer authority to a speaker where none is warranted. If Putnam, Davidson, and others are right that "meaning just ain't in the head," then even the omniscient interpreter will stumble over talk of a thoroughly immaterial, intelligent power (even God cannot interpret god-talk). Like the boy who thought he had eaten God, of course we interpreters must do our best to understand the priest as he wishes to be understood. But, also like Mustapha, we must be ready to accept what our best evidence dictates. We cannot be blamed for appealing to interpretive principles which are themselves wholly defensible.

Reductionism and the First Person Authority

Recently, some influential voices from within the religious studies community have alleged the widespread abuse of first person authority and have called for reform. Perhaps the most eloquent and powerful of these has been Robert Wilken's, contained in his 1989 Presidential Address to the American Academy of Religion. Wilken writes (1989: 707):

When we allow the "ostensible" meaning of religious language to be taken hostage to the etiquette of disinterested secondary discourse, or to things that have only a tangential relation to things religious people care about, not only do we prune the list of things we talk about, we also narrow the circle of people we will talk to, or better, of those who will talk to us. And that is a great loss, a kind of self-imposed deafness.[7]

I shall close by considering some aspects of Wilken's charge. Wilken seems to be targeting those guilty of what Proudfoot terms "descriptive reductionism." It is one thing to assign content to a belief, something else to explain how its holder came to hold its content true. When we attempt the former, an important touchstone of success will be the subject's agreement with our assignment—vigorous protest will likely be enough by itself to make us re-think our theory of his understanding of his words (and perhaps our theory of his theory of our theory of his understanding of his words). But, having once satisfied ourselves on this score, there is no methodological reason why we cannot then pursue explanatory reductionism, that is, to explain the holding of the belief in terms that our subject may dispute just as vigorously (Proudfoot 1985: chapter 6). Insofar as Wilken is condemning descriptive reductionism, we can only add our voices to his.

However, in considering Wilken's charge, we must remember that the belief in invisible, intelligent power presents a built-in obstacle to the (from the speaker's point of view) exercise and (from the interpreter's standpoint) recognition of first person authority—or so I have been urging. This means that, before applying Proudfoot's distinction to alleged cases of abuse, we will have to be doubly sure that first person authority has already been established beyond reasonable doubt. Thus, Proudfoot notes of the person who mistakes the log for the bear that—on pain of descriptive reductionism—we must describe his fear as of a bear. The clarity and force of the example—that is, the strength and vividness of this person's first person authority—derives from our prior confidence in our ability to match up a piece of behavior (the frightened exclamation) with a piece of the world (the log). ("Meaning just ain't in the head.") For just this reason we will almost certainly want the person who worships the lunar god to speak for him or herself. This person cannot mean to be speaking of, say, society, however striking the Durkheimian correlation we observe between her belief-foundation and the gathering of her clan. For the nature of the situation in which the person learned to use the term "moon"—that is, the objective presence of the moon will exert a powerful methodological pressure to prevent us from assigning any meaning and reference to the term other than the one the speaker claims for it. (We are free, as I have noted, to pursue its symbolic significance—we may well decide that has nothing to do with the anthropomorphized moon. My comments are neutral as between the intellectualist and symbolist stances.)

On the other hand, interpreters of, for example, the abstract monotheisms do not face this methodological pressure in so potent a form. For there, as I have been suggesting, the presumption of first person authority has likely been weakened, if it has not lapsed altogether. It has likely been weakened because the causal context that grounds first person authority is in principle absent, or nearly so. At issue is not the interpreter's own belief, disbelief, or agnosticism, nor—at this point—is there any question of descriptive reductionism. Rather, the very methodology of interpretation guarantees the so-called primitive nature religions an interpretive advantage over their more abstract cousins, in the sense that devotees of the former will naturally be counted as more authoritative than those of the latter concerning the meaning of their words. While the relevance of this consideration must of course be judged case by case, this, I think, should be the basic line of defense for the interpreter of religious discourse who feels wrongly accused of violating first person authority.

Having sketched a line of defense, I would like to offer a counter-charge. There is, I think, a danger in an over-zealous respect for first person authority. The danger is that it may become what Proudfoot has called a "protective strategy," serving apologetic interests. It may be possible for humans to speak meaningfully of an invisible, intelligent power; and Wilken and others are right that the religious traditions themselves have offered ingenious theories about how that might be so. But the more resolute our allegiance to such theories, the more likely we are to become insensitive to, or even to ignore, both the often subtle and surprising causal contexts of the behavior that confronts us, and the welter of ever-present competing and complementary maxims that govern responsible interpretive practice. (One example: only when Wittgenstein [1979: 41] stopped asking whether a certain people really believe that the rain-king can make rain did he notice that they only petition for rain in the rainy season.) It would be an interesting question—though one which I cannot pursue here—to determine to what extent modern students of religion have been distracted by the effort to understand how a speaker can use a vocalization, "God," perhaps, to refer to an invisible, intelligent power. Proudfoot (1985) and Hans Penner (1989: part 1) have recently argued persuasively that the detour has been great. When we as scholars of religion insist that "God" and its kin be assigned religious content we risk forgetting what Dagfinn Follesdal (1986: 117) has called the "hypothetical element" in all our perception of human action. We risk forgetting that, with further evidence, we may be led to see a different intentional action or even a bodily movement explainable in purely physical terms. I hope to have made plausible the suggestion that religious discourse is inherently liable to being seen, in Follesdal's sense, anew. I suggest that that liability at least partially explains the apparent violation of first person authority suggested by the welter of theoretical perspectives I listed at the outset. By doggedly pursuing the presumed theological content of "god" -talk, scholars of religion risk ignoring its all too tangible natural history. But now we have come full-circle: If first person authority rests on our appreciation of just these natural-historical connections, to ignore them would be the most profound form of scholarly deafness.[8]

Notes

1. But see Davidson 1986: 318: "Communication begins where causes converge: your utterance means what mine does if belief in its truth is systematically caused by the same events and objects." It is perhaps worth emphasizing—what Quine and Davidson repeatedly note—that endorsing behaviorism in interpretation does not commit one to it in psychology or in the theory of meaning.
2. I have in mind in particular the so-called principle of charity, in all its multifaceted glory. For discussion see Gauker 1986. I have explored some of the issues that arise in incorporating charity into the interpretation of religious discourses in Godlove 1989: chapter 4; and 1992.
3. For a discussion of the nature and sources of evidence in interpretation see Follesdal 1986: 117–220. I am ignoring the question to what extent communication by means of language involves interpretation. According to Dummett, it "is of necessity an exceptional occurrence":

   > In the normal case, the speaker simply says what he means. By this I do not mean that he first has the thought and then puts it into words, but that, knowing the language, he simply speaks. In the normal case, likewise, the hearer simply understands. That is, knowing the language, he hears and thereby understands; given that he knows the language, there is nothing that his understanding the words consists in save hearing them. There are, of course, many exceptional cases. (Dummett 1986: 471)

   Those who side with Dummett here will view the encounter between Mustapha and the priest as an "exceptional case." Those who, agreeing with Davidson and Quine, see interpretation as an essential moment in linguistic communication, will generalize their encounter across the board. I pass over this issue because either position could accommodate my treatment of Mustapha's theological education.
4. The thought that we might be systematically mistaken about what features of the world, on given occasions, prompt our application of concepts, may also tempt persons who think that reference to an object is fixed by essential features of that object. Such persons may hold that, in pointing to the colorless, odorless, potable, universal solvent in the local trout stream, my "water" refers to water only if that liquid has the requisite molecular structure (H_2O). The systematic doubt might then be taken to arise because no finite language-user is in a position to verify the molecular structure of the objects around her as she speaks. These issues are beyond the scope of the present paper. For discussion see Kripke 1979.
5. In particular, I have said nothing that ought to persuade the person who thinks my position reflects nothing more than empiricist prejudice—who thinks that it is just a brute fact that lots of religious (and other) people do hold beliefs about invisible, intelligent powers. This person may feel that my error stems from the unwarranted

assumption that the content of a belief has something to do with its relation to things. (I owe this reminder to Tony Dardis.) In this paper, I am simply diagnosing some issues surrounding first person authority in the contemporary study of religion from the point of view of what seems to me a very plausible picture of linguistic interpretation. I have not defended that picture or even filled in its details.

6. "Rarely" recognizes those instances in which we require the philosophical theologian's help in understanding a conversation between philosophical theologians.

7. I have pursued other aspects of Wilken's charge in Godlove 1994.

8. I wish to thank Warren Frisina, Paul Griffiths, Bob Holland, Russell McCutcheon, and audiences at Dartmouth College and at the 1991 annual meeting of the American Academy of Religion for their helpful comments on earlier drafts of this paper.

References

Bataille, Georges 1989. *Theory of Religion*. Robert Hurley (trans.). New York: Zone Books.

Bell, Catherine 1992. *Ritual Theory, Ritual Practice*. New York: Oxford University Press.

Blumenberg, Hans 1983. *The Legitimacy of the Modern Age*. Robert M. Wallace (trans.). Cambridge, MA: MIT Press.

Burge, Tyler 1979. "Individualism and the Mental," *Midwest Studies in Philosophy*. Vol. 4: 73–124. Peter French, Theodore Uehling, and Howard Wettstein (eds.). Minneapolis: University of Minnesota Press.

—— 1982. Two Thought Experiments Reviewed. *Notre Dame Journal of Formal Logic* 23: 284–293.

—— 1986. Individualism and Psychology. *The Philosophical Review* 95: 3–45.

Davidson, Donald 1984a. Communication and Convention. *Inquiries into Truth and Interpretation,* 265–280. New York: Oxford University Press.

—— 1984b. First Person Authority. *Dialectica* 38: 101–111.

—— 1986. A Coherence Theory of Truth and Knowledge. *Truth and Interpretation: Perspectives on the Philosophy of Donald Davidson*, 307–319. Ernest LePore (ed.). New York: Blackwell.

—— 1987. "Knowing One's Own Mind," *Proceedings and Addresses of the American Philosophical Association* 60 (3): 441–458.

Douglas, Mary 1966. *Purity and Danger*. London: Routledge & Kegan Paul.

Dummett, Michael 1986. Comments on Davidson and Hacking. *Truth and Interpretation: Perspectives on the Philosophy of Donald Davidson*, 459–477. Ernest LePore (ed.). New York: Blackwell.

Follesdal, Dagfinn 1986. Intentionality and Rationality. *Rationality, Relativism and the Human Sciences*, 109–126. J. Margolis, M. Krausz, and R. M. Burian (eds.). Boston: Martinus Nijhoff.

Gauker, Christopher 1986. The Principle of Charity. *Synthese* 69 (1): 1–25.

Godlove, Terry F. 1989. *Religion, Interpretation, and Diversity of Belief: The*

Framework Model from Kant to Durkheim to Davidson. New York: Cambridge University Press.

—— 1992. Respecting Autonomy and Understanding Religion. *Religious Studies* 28: 43–60.

—— 1993. Review of Lawson and McCauley, *Rethinking Religion. Zygon* 28 (1): 115–120.

—— 1994. "The Instability of Religious Belief: Some Reductionistic and Eliminitivist Pressures," *Religion and Reductionism*, 49–64. Edward Yonan and Thomas Idinopulos (eds.). Leiden: E. J. Brill.

Green, Ronald M. 1978. *Religious Reason: The Rational and Moral Basis of Religious Belief*. New York: Oxford University Press.

—— 1988. *Religion and Moral Reason: A New Method for Comparative Study*. New York: Oxford University Press.

Hume, David 1957. *The Natural History of Religion*. H. E. Root (ed.). Stanford: Stanford University Press.

Jones, James W. 1991. *Contemporary Psychoanalysis and Religion*. New Haven: Yale University Press.

Kripke, Saul 1979. Speaker's Reference and Semantic Reference. *Contemporary Perspectives on the Philosophy of Language*, 6–27. Peter A. French, Theodore E. Uehling, and Howard K. Wettstein (eds.). Minneapolis: University of Minnesota Press.

Lawson, E. Thomas and Robert McCauley 1990. *Rethinking Religion: Connecting Cognition and Culture*. New York: Cambridge University Press.

Lindbeck, George A. 1984. *The Nature of Doctrine: Religion and Theology in a Post-Liberal Age*. New Haven: Yale University Press.

Little, David and Sumner B. Twiss 1978. *Comparative Religious Ethics*. San Francisco: Harper & Row.

Martin, Michael 1990. *Atheism: A Philosophical Justification*. Philadelphia: Temple University Press.

Meisner, W. W. 1984. *Psychoanalysis and Religious Experience*. New Haven: Yale University Press.

Penner, Hans H. 1989. *Impasse and Resolution: A Critique of the Study of Religion*. New York: Peter Lang.

Proudfoot, Wayne 1985. *Religious Experience*. Berkeley: University of California Press.

Putnam, Hilary 1975. "The Meaning of 'Meaning'," In *Philosophical Papers*. Vol. II: Mind, Language and Reality, 215–271. New York: Cambridge University Press.

Quine, W. V. 1992. *Pursuit of Truth*. Cambridge, MA: Harvard University Press.

Smith, Jonathan Z. 1987. *To Take Place: Toward Theory in Ritual*. Chicago: University of Chicago Press.

Sperber, Dan 1975. *Rethinking Symbolism*. Alice L. Morton (trans.). New York: Cambridge University Press.

Staal, Frits 1989. *Rules Without Meaning: Rituals, Mantras, and the Human Sciences*. New York: Peter Lang.

Tambiah, Stanley J. 1990. *Magic, Science, Religion, and the Scope of Rationality*. New York: Cambridge University Press.

Taylor, Mark C. 1987. *Altarity*. Chicago: University of Chicago Press.

Turner, Victor 1967. *The Forest of Symbols: Aspects of Ndembu Ritual*. Ithaca: Cornell University Press.

Wilken, Robert L. 1989. "Who Will Speak for the Religious Traditions?" *Journal of the American Academy of Religion* 57 (4): 617–717.

Wilson, E. O. 1978. *On Human Nature*. Cambridge, MA: Harvard University Press.

Wittgenstein, Ludwig 1979. *Remarks on Frazer's Golden Bough*. Rush Rhees (ed.) and A. C. Miles (trans.). Atlantic Highlands: Humanities Press.

13

DANIEL PALS, *Reductionism and Belief: An Appraisal of Recent Attacks on the Doctrine of Irreducible Religion*

ॐॐ

Scholarship, it is sometimes said, lives by its quarrels. If that is so, then the recurring debate over "reductionism" in the study of religion ensures a lonely future for the discipline. In simplest terms, reductionists are those who insist that religion is best understood by going outside religion to explain it. In various ways their theories are concerned to show that a religious phenomenon—let us say, belief in God, or an act of ritual—owes its existence to nonreligious causes. Depending on the theory, the causes put forward may be the urges of the body, the needs of the psyche, the pressures of nature or society. Around the turn of the century, reductionism claimed among its spokesmen some of the most vigorous and celebrated intellects of the age. One need only recall Freud's psychology or Haeckel's materialism, the dialectic of Marx or the potent stream of evolutionary rationalism that traced its wellsprings to Feuerbach and Comte. The intellectual disciplines born in this era, as Britain's Bryan Wilson reminds us concerning sociology, developed amid a certain tension with traditional religious belief.[1] A measure—and perhaps more—of this strain is discernible as well among those who nourished the infant science of religion. For Tylor and Frazer, for Reinach, Durkheim, and others, religion appeared less an entity than an expression. It rode the surface of hidden forces which the scholar, by diligent application of his theories, could uncover and explain.

Our own century, by contrast, has seen the emergence, even triumph, of a very different spirit. In this view religious life is something unique and irreducible, an entity all its own, not a mere expression of something else. One of the earliest and most adamant statements of this position belongs, naturally enough, to Rudolph Otto: "For if there be any single domain of human experience that presents us with something unmistakably specific and unique, peculiar to itself, assuredly it is that of the religious life.... I shall speak, then, of a unique 'numinous' category of value and of a definitely 'numinous' state of mind, which is always found wherever the category is applied. This mental state is perfectly *sui generis* and irreducible to any other." [2] Otto has drawn his critics through the years, but there can be no question that this axiom has exerted a profound guiding influence upon the study of religion in Western Europe and America over the last three generations. It has claimed the support of leading scholars on both continents, from phenomenologists such as Gerardus van der Leeuw to historians of religion such as Mircea Eliade.[3] It has attracted new and vigorous proponents in the Orient.[4] It has been virtually enshrined in the distinguished history of religions program at the University of Chicago.[5] And within the most recent decades it has won the surprising endorsements from the realm of none other than that old deluder sociology. In much discussed statements from the early 1970s, both Robert Bellah and Peter Berger announced that they could find no more appropriate avenue into religion than the classic doctrine of the irreducible sacred. Here is Bellah: "I am prepared to claim that as Durkheim said of society, religion is a reality *sui generis*. To put it bluntly, religion is true. This is not to say that every religious symbol is equally valid.... But it does mean that ... all reductionism must be abandoned."[6] And Berger: "I would recommend that the scientific study of religion return to a perspective on the phenomenon 'from within,' that is, to viewing it in terms of the meanings intended by the religious consciousness. I rather doubt that ... it will be possible to go very far beyond the contributions of the phenomenological school. Indeed, I think that one could do worse than return to Otto's starting point in this matter." [7]

The surprising thing amid all these endorsements of "irreducible religion" is that the doctrine has been so seldom subjected to thorough-going analysis. What precisely does it mean to say that religion—broadly construed as here it is—is not reducible? What, precisely, does it mean to say that religion is reducible? To be sure, the whole matter has something to do with explanations, with "accounting for" religious belief and behavior, but in what way? Is reduction the same as explanation? Is it only theories that can be reduced, or does the process apply to "things" as well? What is the relation between competing explanations? What is the relation between explanatory theories and religious (or irreligious) commitments? Is it true that nonbelief issues invariably in reductionism, and belief, on the contrary, in its denial? If so, are such things necessarily so, or merely accidents owing to the associations of particular scholars or schools of thought? In what way does reduction entail a judgment of value upon religion? Among religions (or within any one religion) are there distinctions to be made, so that some beliefs or practices may be reductively explained and others not? Finally, is there even any point in claiming that religion is irreducible? Is the entire problem perhaps an imaginary one?

For those who prefer clarity to confusion, the dense tangle of these questions is perhaps cause enough to begin some sorting out. Religious explanation certainly seems an issue in search of analysis, a topic in need of a benchmark text. But other reasons are equally compelling. Within the last decade and despite the conversions in sociology, the doctrine of irreducible religion has begun to draw fire from assailants within the camp. Theorists of religion have themselves attacked it as unnecessary, as unproductive, and still worse, as a covert agent of evangelism in the cause of belief. The debate has been marked, moreover, by occasional appeals to a sophisticated literature on explanation and reduction which has emerged from the sciences, both social and natural.[8] Unfortunately, this promising strategy has brought only mixed success, in part because the discussion has been carried on in a very general way and with insufficient heed to A. R. Peacocke's warning that those who wish to explain explanations stand at the edge of Pandora's box.[9] Here we can perhaps avoid disaster by keeping to a few recent episodes in the attack on irreducible religion and allowing general suggestions to follow only upon the appraisal of specific cases.

We can begin with a basic and nontechnical distinction. An explanation is one thing; a reduction, or reductive explanation, is another.[10] All thinking people intuitively have some notion of what an explanation is. We know as well that any phenomenon one meets can usually be explained in many ways. To the question, "What is Michelangelo's *Pietà*?" one can give multiple answers: a piece of freestanding, chiseled marble; a likeness of the human form; a commodity produced in the patron economy of bourgeois Renaissance Florence; an enduring image of the mingled suffering and innocence which lie at the heart of the Christian vision. It should be noted that all of these assertions may stand as miniature explanatory theories among which there is no necessary logical connection. Each is a different account, none necessarily at odds with any other. In defending religious explanation, Mircea Eliade in fact appeals to the analogy with art by noting the multiple levels of explanation open to those who interpret a work of literature, such as Dante's *Divine Comedy*.[11] But the comparison is not entirely helpful. To see the issue at stake in reductive explanation we need a phenomenon that presents us with a clear and close hierarchy of relationships, something which appears to invite overlapping explanations. Though one could claim a hierarchy in the *Divine Comedy* or *Pietà*, the features are clouded. How do we know, for example, that a sculpture's function as art is higher (or lower) than its function as economic commodity? What do "higher" and "lower" even mean in this context? A better and more natural parallel can be found in the sciences. To the question, "What is the human body?" one can give, again, many unrelated answers. Physiologically, however, there is a close hierarchy, so that in this vein one might respond, "The human body is an assemblage of subatomic particles formed into atoms, which are formed into molecules, which compose cells, which compose organs, which compose a complete bodily system." It is in connection with this sort of system that the prospect of reduction, or reductive explanation, makes its appearance.[12]

Since theories of a biological, chemical, or physical sort are developed to explain bodily processes at appropriate levels, and since these seem dependent on one another in descending order, it is natural to ask whether the theories explaining the higher might be reducible to those explaining the lower and more basic. The standard technical description of reduction, put forward over two decades ago by Ernest Nagel, holds that a higher theory can be reduced to a lower, providing that the concepts of the former are both connectable with and derivable from the latter.[13] A classic paradigm of reduction in the natural sciences is the attempt to reduce all biological concepts to those of physics and chemistry. No one has yet claimed such a reduction, but as Karl Popper notes, even without success such efforts are enormously fruitful. From them we learn much.[14]

Now the first thing to note about classic reductionist theory in religion is that it assumes this form drawn from the sciences. Religious beliefs are taken to stand in a close logical and hierarchical relationship to other features of the human organism, which can presumably be shown to be more basic. In the psychology of Freud, for example, religious expressions—like faith in God—are explained as arising from needs and drives planted deep in the psychic structure of individuals. Beliefs are projected outward in the attempts to resolve psychic stress.[15] In the sociology of Durkheim, group structures, such as the clan, are taken as fundamental, and religious beliefs turn out to be reducible to the "effervescence" of a certain spirit in the group, which presumably gives vent to the group's basic drives or needs.[16] In either of these cases, to understand the private psyche, or the public structure, is quite simply to understand in full why people have religious beliefs.

It is not hard to see why religious believers would find these reductionist theories disturbing. On the face of things they stand in direct contradiction to what the believer thinks of his[17] beliefs. For him they are founded on his free, personal choice, and on a perception of what is true. They are not, and certainly not merely, the product of mental neurosis or social circumstance. When, on the other hand, theorists of religion such as Otto and Eliade oppose reductionism, the matter is more complicated. If they are believers, they will share the believer's objections. But as scholars they may also be disposed to reject religious reductionism for the same reason that biologists might oppose physical-chemical reduction. They might simply feel that such explanation furnishes an inadequate description of the things under study; it misses crucial features of religion as we commonly experience it. To use a distinction found in some of the scientific literature, believers oppose "ontological reductionism," the reduction of their beliefs to something other than the result of their free personal assent to truth. Scholars oppose "theoretical reductionism," the claim that religion can be explained without any help from theories unique to the field of religious studies.[18]

While these two forms of reductionism can be distinguished, it would be misleading to suppose that they can be easily separated. In a piece often cited in reductionist debate, Hans Penner and Edward Yonan argue that the whole concern to defend irreducible religion is the product of false anxiety. Reduction, as they see it, is only a matter of theories. Drawing upon Nagel's theory of reductive explanation they write:

> Both Rudolf Otto and Mircea Eliade maintain that religion is irreducible on the grounds that the "numinous" or "sacred" is a unique category....
>
> Our analysis ... indicates that these views of reduction clearly misunderstand what is implied by that procedure. By misunderstanding reduction, they falsify what the other sciences mean by it. As we have shown, reduction is an operation concerned with theories or systems of statements, not with phenomena, data, or the properties of phenomena. For as Nagel has said, "properties," or the "nature" of something, is always stated as a theory. None of the scholars we have examined ... states that reduction wipes out, levels, or demeans the phenomena or data being explained. On the contrary, reduction in the sciences implies an *explanation* of one *theory* by the use of another.... The sole purpose of reduction is to offer adequate theoretical explanations and to provide for the continued progress of scientific knowledge.[19]

Reduction, in short, is not only harmless, but useful and necessary. It poses no threat at all to the "thing" (the assemblage of actions, beliefs, values) we call religion. Denouncing reduction in the name of irreducible religion is pointless.

Is this really so? A careful look at Nagel's argument suggests here a misreading of his actual intent. Properly—and certainly in Nagel's discussion—reduction applies to theories. But theories, after all, are about things. If I have a theory that apples fall from trees because a certain spiritual life-force urges them to do so in a certain season, and you then fully explain the same process as the product of chemical change in the stem, your theory, on proving correct, obviously has not stolen the life-force from apples. You have merely shown that my theory of apples is wrong. Your reduction has not changed the apple; it has only proved the apple is in fact not what I thought it to be. Clearly, this is what Nagel means when Penner and Yonan cite him as repudiating "'deduction' of properties from one another—as if in the reduction of one science to another one were engaged in the black magic of extricating one set of phenomena from others incommensurably different from the first." [20]

But if this is so, notice what follows. Reduction of the "life-force" theory of apples adds to our scientific knowledge—chiefly by eliminating error. So in the same way a successful reduction of religion to the epiphenomenal product of social structure also adds to knowledge—chiefly by eliminating the error of antireductionists such as Otto and Eliade. But Otto and Eliade think they are not in error about religion. Hence their opposition would hardly seem to rest on a misunderstanding.

Penner and Yonan seem to be saying that because there is such a thing as theoretical reduction, there is no such thing as ontological reduction. The current literature of explanation offers little support for such a notion.[21] It recognizes a *distinction* between ontological and theoretical, but then goes on to assume there is a connection, though there is no clear agreement on its precise nature.[22] Were things as simple as Penner and Yonan suppose, we could expect shorter bibliographies than are now the rule. So far as it claims to be an independent discipline, then, the study of religion does face at least a potential threat from reductionist theories. The reduction of biological explanations to physical-chemical ones would not put an end to living organisms, but it might well put an end to biology, at least as a separate science. Similarly, reducing faith solely to the interaction of psyche and society need not spell doom for religion, but it might well bring the demise of *Religionswissenschaft*.

Leaning in part on Penner and Yonan, Guilford Dudley argues in a similar vein and sets his focus specifically upon Mircea Eliade—understandably enough, since he is the leading current spokesman for irreducible religion. In the course of an otherwise sympathetic critique, Dudley insists, "The argument for the *sui generis* character of religious phenomena should be surrendered without further ado. A certain dogmatism ... can serve a useful function, but this particular dogma has become a stumbling block. It has been demolished by Penner and others and should be retired." [23] This demolition, as we have seen, is rather less than complete. But Dudley gives further grounds. Irreducible religion should be abandoned "not because the statement that religion is *sui generis* is false, but because it is part of a general theory that has failed to be useful." [24] It is also arbitrary: "Eliade's uncompromising opposition to what he considered 'reductionism' in explaining religious phenomena is, in effect, to insist by fiat that there are no considerations under which this particular program can be overthrown." [25] These observations are, to say the least, peculiar. On the matter of utility, it would be interesting to inquire by what standard such a judgment is made. One can hardly scan the cataract of scholarly literature that has flowed from the pens of Otto, van der Leeuw, Eliade, and other colleagues or disciples without concluding that if it were no more than an empty motto, "irreducible religion" would nonetheless have produced a flood of extraordinarily useful information. One could claim the thesis is utterly false and still concede it to be remarkably productive. As Peacocke intimates in reference to biology, such theories can be productive by merely providing a "focus of interest." [26]

In contending that irreducible religion is arbitrarily imposed by Eliade's personal fiat, Dudley's argument is even more puzzling. He borrows from Imre Lakatos the distinction between the "hard core" of any explanatory theory and its "protective belt" of hypotheses." [27] To guide a useful program of research, the former must be regarded as virtually immune to criticism or revision, while the latter, which does stand open to change, forms the realm of creative advance in knowledge. The scheme certainly seems applicable, but Dudley makes curious use of it. For him it is obvious that a doctrine such as irreducible religion can only belong to the protective belt in Eliade's theoretical system. And since it has been unproductive and effectively challenged, it ought to be forthwith dismissed, at no loss to the central core of Eliade's vision. But why? Surely if anything belongs to the hard core of a disciplinary approach, it would be the independence of the discipline. The hard core of physics is that, at bottom, things have physical explanations. The nonnegotiable core of biological theory is that living organisms require more explanation than is available solely through physics. The study of religion would seem to require the same. Nor is this, as Dudley seems to think, a leap into dogmatism. To adopt such a determinate stance is not, in religion any more than physics or biology, to decree that it cannot be overthrown. It is only to state that the involved are exceedingly broad, entangled, and complex. If irreducibility is to be discarded, it will not be on the telling of a single instance, or series or set of instances, but only after an extensive accumulation of difficulties. If indeed they are mortal, core theories such as these are to die struggling, after a long life and the frailties that accumulate with age; they are not to commit suicide at the first sight of difficulty. A declaration of religious study's independence would seem to be no less essential than in other disciplines—and just as productive.

Whatever the problems with Dudley's critique, it seems mild in comparison with the most recent renunciation of Eliade and his ways. In a strongly worded assessment, Robert Segal mounts a direct and wide-ranging assault on the doctrine of irreducible religion.[28] For him the stance of scholars such as Otto and Eliade is confused, untenable, and mistakenly designed to rescue the cause of actual religious belief. Segal's case deserves careful scrutiny, for the issues are important ones, and the scope of the indictment is large.

The first count contends that Eliade's determination to appraise religious belief "in its own terms" leads him to a curious confusion of his own stance with that of the very believers he places under study. In reading primitive myth and ritual, Eliade strongly repudiates the older rationalist tradition, which was inclined to dismiss such things as the sad product of ignorance and superstition. He sees myth instead as affirming a unique realm: the sacred. It can be fitted into archetypal patterns shared across the experience of the human race. Like modern religious beliefs, an archaic myth is "a 'true story' and beyond that, a story that is a most precious possession because it is sacred, exemplary, significant." [29] But merely to recount this, says Segal, is enough to discover a problem. Eliade thinks the thoughts of scholarship, not belief. The ordinary believer knows nothing of such abstractions as "the sacred"; his interests are centered upon things "more or other" than professorial notions like "eternal return"; and clearly he does not trouble to think of any among his beliefs as yet another instance of a universal pattern. This last point is especially important. The believer reveres his sacred stone, or cosmic tree, precisely insofar as it is the true stone or the unique tree. His claim cancels all others. Unfortunately for Eliade, the believer's commitment to a cosmic tree precludes the scholar's discovery of a cosmic forest. The one cannot be subsumed under the form of the many. "Eliade's equation of his own interpretation with the believer's point of view therefore becomes arbitrary." [30]

How could this charge be assessed? Well, if this were in fact the position of Eliade, or any other comparativist, it would not merely be arbitrary; it would be mistaken. An interpreter who assumed that understanding a religion "in the believer's terms" can only be the same thing as believing what the believer believes would be a confused specimen indeed. He would in fact find himself in the odd position of recommending conversion as the apprenticeship for proper interpretation. Obviously Eliade does not recommend this, and it is difficult to find anything in his approach which would oblige him to do so. An outside interpreter can find himself in agreement with any number of things asserted or entailed by a believer's creed without thereby committing himself to the truth of the believer's faith. Consider, for example, the following two propositions which might be uttered by any good Muslim: (1) Allah exists; (2) Islam is not the product of fear and ignorance. Among other things, understanding Islam "on its own terms" might mean something as elementary as accepting B while denying A. The distinction is really a rather basic one; most students of religion make it regularly, and properly, in the course of their work.

Segal's misunderstanding here is not entirely his own fault. In pressing their case, advocates of irreducible religion sometimes use language loosely to achieve an effect. Thus Berger in the heat of conversion speaks of this approach as treating religion "from within"—a phrase that recurs frequently in the vocabulary of scholars similarly inclined. Bellah too tells us "religion is true," presumably in the same way Eliade finds archaic myth to be a "true story." Using language strictly, these critics would doubtless agree that many of the beliefs they consider "true" are in their view actually false. The "truth" they refer to, obviously, is the claim that such beliefs cannot be reduced to the accidental product of fear or ignorance, of psychic need or social circumstance. It is true, they say, that religious beliefs are creations of the human spirit which express insights and grasp realities in a manner that cannot simply be explained away.

It does not occur to Segal that this is the chief sense in which advocates of irreducible religion may be said to endorse the beliefs of those whose faith they interpret. He chooses instead to think in terms of a simple option. Either the interpreter of religion merely describes what certain religious people think about their faith, or he actually endorses the believers' view. In other words, the interpreter either engages in a simple act of transcribing what believers believe, or he goes on to say believers are correct in so thinking. Now obviously, Segal continues, Eliade is concerned to offer more than mere description. When he insistently pits his own views against the reductionist theories of psychology, sociology, and the like, we can only conclude that he is actually taking the second path and "outright endorsing" the claims of the believer. As Segal puts it, "For Eliade to be countering real opponents, he must, then, be saying that the actual meaning of religion is irreducibly religious." "What he must therefore be saying . . . is that the conscious, irreducibly religious meaning of religion for believers is its true one, which means at once its true one for them and its true one in itself." [31]

It should now be clear that Eliade is committed to nothing of the sort. Argumentation like this wears a certain surface plausibility because of the very general conceptions it employs. But as soon as terms such as "religion" and "believer's interpretation" are broken down into the specific claims they are likely to contain, the fault lines become obvious. We can agree with the Aztec who insists he is not a Freudian neurotic and still deny that Quetzalcoatl exists.

It is unfortunate that this unspecified style of discussion survives to work further damage when we come to Segal's second charge. Eliade, he contends, endorses the believer's claim that religious phenomena are irreducible but completely fails to prove his case. "All he does is continually assert ... that reductionistic interpretations of religion are either irrelevant or secondary because they skirt the conscious, irreducibly religious meaning of religion for believers. But he thereby begs, not answers, the key question: whether the conscious, irreducibly religious meaning of religion for believers is the true meaning of religion.... In the light of, if nothing else, discoveries by modern psychology, sociology, anthropology, and other disciplines, Eliade can hardly contend that a human being knows all the possible meanings of any of his beliefs and actions, not just of his religious ones." [32] The compelling logic of these cryptic remarks is rather difficult to discern. In light of the foregoing discussion, the "key question" certainly cannot be formulated in vague language about the meaning of religion for believers. The key question is whether believer and scholar can agree in assenting to one or more nonreductionist assertions. Once placed in these terms, the key answer to the key question is, Yes, they can. It is true that neither Eliade nor any other scholar can contend that a human being knows all the possible meanings of any of his beliefs, but what does that have to do with the argument?

The question of whether Eliade (or anyone else) has "proved" religion irreducible seems to be badly framed. If it is true, as it seems to me, that such a thesis acts at a high level of abstraction as a kind of disciplinary axiom, directing our attention to a certain aspect of the world and life, then it certainly will not be provable—or refutable—in any simple way. It will function as one of those "hard-core" rationales adduced by Lakatos as essential to a program of research. Like biology's claim to be autonomous over against the reductions of chemistry and physics, it will have to prove itself over a long run by the quality of its fruits.

And fruits are not lacking. Compare, as a specific case, the evidence assembled by Eliade with a classic reductionist approach to religion such as we find in Freud's *Future of an Illusion* and *Civilization and Its Discontents*. Freud's views are not always coherent, but their central thrust is discernible. Belief in God (or the gods) springs from a deep-seated psychic wish. Facing the terrors of nature and fate; as well as the sacrifices civilization requires, mankind naturally longs for consolation and for approval of its venture. Following the model of the child who receives these things from its father, the race in its childhood draws the assurance it needs from the deities its desires have conjured. Religious belief, therefore, is the "universal obsessional neurosis of humanity." Appropriate perhaps to the adolescence of mankind, it of course becomes a pathology if it is allowed to afflict the years of our maturity. Among the atavistic few it may survive, but in general, "the more the fruits of knowledge become accessible to men, the more widespread is the decline of religious belief." [33]

The limits and merits of Freud on religion need not detain us here. That discussion has a long history and seems now at an end. Even when stripped of their polemic, Freud's views on religion in their unmodified, original form today claim few serious disciples. As an instance of reduction, however, his theory remains of considerable interest. Certainly he found the persistence of religion into modernity a bad thing. The extent to which his argument is reductive depends upon the weight one gives to what might be called its prophetic, or predictive component. Freud suggests that religious belief must decline as its tasks pass away or into better hands. But clearly that is so only if we have in fact located all the functions of religion. Should someone turn up another, not likely to be eliminated by the spread of knowledge, then of course we have no reason to suppose religion will disappear. Judicious minds have found this predictive feature of Freud's argument unnerving—and reductionist.

Assuming this is so and granting that Eliade opposes such a view, what sort of claims should we expect him to make? Well, to the extent Freud serves as an enemy we should expect judgments on religion that are positive or neutral rather than negative and we should look for functions other than psychic wish fulfillment. One need not read far into Eliade, or others in his camp to find them working closely along these lines. "The supreme function of myth is to 'fix' the paradigmatic models for all rites and all significant human activities— eating, sexuality, work, education and so on. Acting as a fully responsible human being, man imitates the paradigmatic gestures of the gods, repeats their actions, whether in the case of a simple physiological function such as eating or of a social, economic, cultural, military, or other activity." Again, "The faithful repetition of divine models has a twofold result: (1) by imitating the gods, man remains in the sacred, hence in reality; (2) by the continuous reactualization of paradigmatic divine gestures, the world is sanctified. Men's religious behavior contributes to maintaining the sanctity of the world." [34] On the face of it, Eliade would certainly seem to have here identified functions of religion which not only differ from Freud's but also deserve different judgments of value. Quite apart from assuaging our fear and covering our ignorance, belief in the gods seems to occupy itself with basic patterns of culture: how and why to hunt, or eat, or learn. And provision of these patterns is a perfectly normal and natural business. To Freud's functions we must apparently add others. Yet the moment we do, religion is of course no longer reducible exclusively to Freud's categories.

The resourceful reductionist is not left without reply on this matter. He might want to maintain that what Eliade thinks a separate function can in fact be subsumed under those cited by Freud—or those of other reductionist theories. He might insist that Eliade actually misreads his data, so that the myths he adduces do not actually do what he says.[35] Either approach might bring on a profitable discussion. But it is a discussion Segal never engages. He contents himself with a brief and general recitation of Eliade's themes, then renders the strong verdict that Eliade "systematically fails" to prove his case.[36] Unfortunately at this crucial point mere assertion will not do. Here and in numerous works laden with specific examples Eliade claims that religion has some, and probably many, functions not noticed by Freud. He has in short developed an inductive argument against Freudian reduction. His reading of the evidence may well be wrong. But if so, one must *show* it an interpretation that fails against the evidence; one must not, like Segal, simply *say* that it so fails.

The final charge laid against Eliade is the most forcible. Is irreducible religion actually the disguise under which believers smuggle their commitment into their work as scholars? Segal thinks so. "If Eliade is wrong to oppose reductionistic interpretations of religion on the grounds that they misinterpret religion, he is right to oppose them on the grounds that they threaten, or may threaten, it. For what underlies, if hardly justifies, his abhorrence of reductionistic interpretations is his fear that they reduce God to a delusion. Eliade insists on a non-reductionistic interpretation of religion in order to preserve the reality of God."[37] We should notice that this is a twofold accusation, part of which can be handled rather easily. Assuming it to be true that Eliade opposes reductionism because he is a believer, why should that make any difference? How does that make his stance unjustified? Motives are one thing, grounds another. Serious proponents of irreducible religion do not claim to have seen its truth in a vision; they adduce evidence to support it. And while all belief will oppose reduction, that is no reason to suppose that only belief will oppose it. Any interpreter, regardless of personal commitment, might wish to take the view that religious phenomena cannot be reduced.

The other side of this criticism is more complex. According to Segal, Eliade is also "wrong to oppose reductionistic interpretations of religion on the grounds that they misinterpret religion." Why? Because outside of the view held by the believer himself, reductionist explanations are all that exist. The reductionist does not merely ply his trade beside others in the avenue of religion; he claims a monopoly of the market. "A reductionist interpretation of religious phenomena in particular is the only one possible, at least for an unbelieving interpreter."[38] This view is so striking that we should pause to get a full statement of it:

> Undeniably, a nonbeliever can appreciate some aspects of a believer's point of view. He can probably appreciate the secular functions of religion for the believer—for example the serenity or the security religion provides.... The decisive issue is whether he can appreciate the *reality* of religion for the believer. For how can he do so except by considering the divine real himself? What else can appreciating the reality of the divine mean except accepting it? But then, of course, the nonbeliever would have to be a believer. To the extent that the nonbeliever cannot appreciate the reality of the divine for the believer he cannot fully appreciate the believer's point of view....
>
> Take the conventional statement that a nonbeliever can appreciate religion in a believer's own terms. As what can he appreciate it? is the fundamental question. As a response to the divine? But what can the divine mean to him when he does not accept its reality? Unless he reduces it to something else, can it mean anything to him?[39]

Again, in interpreting a religious tradition, "a nonbeliever would be left with something that he probably not only would have to reduce in order to make sense of it but would want to reduce in order to make sense of it."[40] I have quoted here at length because all who engage in the study of religion need to feel the weight of the charge. Segal challenges in the most unhesitating fashion the very axioms of comparative, sympathetic religious inquiry. He insists, in language of admirable candor, that the interpreter simply cannot go outside himself. Short of actual conversion, there is no way for anyone to escape the fence of his own convictions. In brief, reductionism is inevitable.

What is to be made of this extraordinary point of view? At the very least, it is, like so much other argument over irreducible religion, a sobering lesson in the perils of generality. Consider Segal's pointed rhetorical question: "What can the divine mean to him [the non-believer] when he does not accept its reality?" One answer might be: "It can mean everything it means to the believer, except for its reality?" What bedevils this discussion is its crippling reliance on large, loose abstractions when what we desperately need are precise and specific assertions. Instead of "religion" we here need actual claims made by believers. Instead of "the reality of the divine" we need to see actual propositions bearing claims about God or the gods. Instead of loose, multipurpose verbs such as "appreciate," we need to give the scholar a precise and specific task, to be covered in a phrase such as "assessing the truth of" definite religious claims.

Once we have done this, the consequence is most illuminating. Notice the following set of statements, which might reasonably be affirmed by any traditional Christian, Muslim, or Jew: (1) God is perfectly good. (2) God is all-powerful. (3) God exists. (4) Jesus died on the cross in the first century AD. Can the nonbeliever "appreciate" these beliefs? It seems he can do more than that. He can accept most of them as true. He can recognize, in exactly the same sense as the believer, that (1) and (2) are in fact necessarily true.[41] Perfect goodness and omnipotence follow from the very definition (traditionally understood) of the term "God." Indeed, for those nonbelievers who practice natural atheology, the truth of (1) and (2) is essential to the formulation of their proofs that God does not exist. The nonbeliever can in addition accept (4) as true, though as contingently so. Even in the case of (3), which the nonbeliever denies, he can still appreciate the assertion in the sense of understanding what it says. In fact, he must appreciate it in at least this sense if he is to deny its claim to truth.

To say the nonbeliever cannot appreciate the reality of the divine is to state in a vague way what will be far less misleading if put more precisely: some claims made by believers nonbelievers deny. The latter form allows us to understand precisely what does in fact go on all the time in the academic study of religion. I deny that Zeus, Apollo, Hermes, or Ares actually exists. But having admitted that, I am still able to appreciate almost anything I choose in the vast network of Greek religious mythology. I can recognize truths: that Zeus is not the Messenger; Hermes is. I can detect falsehoods: that Apollo is a goddess. I can understand relationships: that some gods are superior to others. And so on. I may even be able to approximate emotional states. If I have a clear understanding of who Hades is, I may, despite my disbelief, be able at least to understand how the fear of Hades has a different texture, or quality, from the Christian fear of Hell. Nor are these in any way trivial levels of understanding. By far the most important thing we want to know about another belief system is its inner logic, the way it draws conclusions from premises we personally cannot accept. Early Christians claimed that the Romans persecuted because they were possessed by devils. But if I have a grasp of classical polytheism (the actual existence of whose gods I deny), I can reach a very different, and more plausible, understanding of the imperial policy. Similarly with other traditions; we can understand, and understand fully (often better than believers themselves), all sorts of things, without for a moment committing ourselves to "appreciating the reality of the divine."

These examples take us by the way into a secondary complication, which Segal seems not to notice. The conflict he discerns is merely a two-sided one. Nonbelief, unable to accept the reality of the divine, cannot appreciate belief.

But why confine ourselves to these two? Belief in Judaism is, after all, nonbelief in Hinduism. Belief in Buddhism is nonbelief in Christianity. Belief in a living world religion of course entails disbelief in archaic or primitive religions. So if nonbelief cannot appreciate belief in its own terms, then of course no member of any religion can understand the beliefs of any other without embarking on what now would be a course of "religious" reductionism. Hinduism must somehow be "reduced" to Judaism before a Jew can understand it. Buddhism must be transformed into Christian vocabulary before its meaning becomes clear. And so on for each new interpreter and each religion under scrutiny. That a member of one religion cannot accept as true all of the beliefs held by another is of course self-evident. But there is no reason to suppose he could not understand all of them, and in fact accept as true a great many. Once again, we must at least credit Segal with candor. Faced with the logical conclusion of his view—that conversion is then necessary to true understanding of the believer's point of view—he accepts it with an unflinching embrace. The courage is admirable, but bad premises exact a heavy price.

It should further be noted that there is nothing soft-headed or sentimental about the practice of cross-cultural, or shall we say, counter-truth, understanding—as if feeling could supply what reason disallows. The procedure is a perfectly rational one, identical in fact to that which governs other disciplines. The physicist who believes that light ultimately consists of waves denies certain claims made by colleagues who think it ultimately consists of particles. Both theories rest upon an intricate network, of assumptions, evidence, inference, and perceived relationships which allow for many levels of agreement and difference. The convinced wave theorist will obviously seek to explain evidence which seems to support particle theory in accord with the principles of wave behavior. But while denying particle light in this respect, he will continually refer to data, formulas, and assumptions shared as valid by both sides. It may even happen that a crucial claim of particle theory, which he insistently denies, will turn out to be true, yet when combined with new evidence or a different assumption, will issue in a decisive refutation of the opposing view and a vindication of his own.

It follows then that there is nothing inevitable about reductive explanations of religion. Any of the elements in a system of belief can in some form be understood by the nonbelieving interpreter. If not, they could not be disbelieved. Further, a great many such elements can in fact be accepted as true by nonbelievers. And further still, even in those cases where the believer affirms what the critic denies, it is neither obvious nor automatic that sharp, antithetical differences of explanation will follow. For orthodox Christians the resurrection is the physical return of Christ from death which changed the lives of his disciples; for Rudolph Bultmann it is merely the latter—a life-changing experience of the twelve. Yet on either premise it is possible to produce virtually the same account of the apostolic mission and growth of the earliest church. Finally, even where belief and nonbelief produce different explanations, nonbelief is under no oath to produce a reductive explanation. As we noticed earlier, reduction in the clearest sense of the term is an explanation which accounts for religious belief wholly in terms of nonpurposive social or psychological (or other) forces. One can certainly give an explanation of erroneous belief without being under obligation to reduce it.

We are in a position to draw some conclusions. Despite the vigor and diversity of recent attacks, there is no present cause either to discard or revise the theory of irreducible religion insisted upon by Otto, Eliade, and others. On close scrutiny, the criticism turns out to be misplaced or unconvincing. More succinctly, we should note the following:

1. There is no reason to suppose, with Penner and Yonan, that opponents of reductionism are merely jousting with a phantom. To be sure, reductions are theories, but they are theories about things. Insofar as classic reductionists traced belief exclusively to subconscious need or social circumstance, they tended to undermine those concepts of human freedom and responsibility which anchor the claims of irreducible religion. No doubt it is true that the older reductionism of Freud and Marx and Durkheim proved unsuccessful. But however that may be, the challenge of reductionism is a real one. The quarrel cannot be dismissed as illusion.

2. There is no reason to suppose, with Dudley and Segal, that irreducible religion is little more than an arbitrary and unproductive dogma. The parallel with biology seems particularly helpful here. To claim that religion cannot be reduced is to commit oneself to what might be called a disciplinary axiom. It serves on the most basic level to provide a focus for the scholar's attention. If in the language of Lakatos we further regard it as belonging to the "hard-core" theory of a program in religious research, then it must be measured by the results it has produced. The "results" produced by four generations of *Religionswissenschaft* would seem to speak for themselves.

3. There is finally no reason to suppose, with Segal, that belief is an intruder in the discussion, or that irreducible religion is a fiction because all explanations outside those furnished by belief itself turn out to be reductive. Only with the help of generalities and considerable imprecision can such a case even begin to be made. Unquestionably there are ties to be found between any scholar's personal beliefs and the explanations he prefers. But as long as motives and grounds are kept distinct, there is nothing objectionable in such a circumstance. It would even seem to be healthy. As Nagel noted over a generation ago, there is nothing inevitable or de jure about recourse to reductive explanations, or for that matter irreducible ones. The case for reduction, like the case to be made against it, will have to stand on the evidence. If we judge by that standard, and by it the present state of the opposition, the doctrine of irreducible religion is in no immediate danger.

Notes

1. Bryan Wilson, "The Academic Position of the Sociology of Religion in Modern Science," *Japanese Journal of Religious Studies* 9/1 (1982): 9–18.
2. Rudolph Otto, *The Idea of the Holy*. John W. Harvey (trans.). New York: Galaxy Books, 1958: 4, 132. Otto rests his case at least partly on certain philosophical conceptions from Kant and the idealist thinker Jakob Friedrich Fries.
3. Gerardus van der Leeuw, *Religion in Essence and Manifestation*. J. E. Turner (trans.). New York: Harper & Row, 1963: 1: 52–53; Mircea Eliade, *Patterns in Comparative Religion*. Rosemary Sheed (trans.). Cleveland: Meridian Books, 1963: xiii.
4. Araki Michio, "Toward an Integrated Understanding of Religion and Society: Hidden Premises in the Scientific Apparatus of the Study of Religion," *Japanese Journal of Religious Studies* 9/1 (1982): 65–76.
5. See Frank E. Reynolds, "History of Religions: Condition and Prospects," *Council on the Study of Religion Bulletin* 13/5 (1982): 129, 131–133.
6. Robert Bellah, *Beyond Belief: Essays on Religion in a Post-traditional World*. New York: Harper & Row, 1970: 253.
7. Peter Berger, "Some Second Thoughts on Substantive versus Functional Definitions of Religion," *Journal for the Scientific Study of Religion* 13/2 (1974): 125–133, 129.
8. In this area the standard references have been Ernest Nagel, *The Structure of Science*. New York: Harcourt, Brace, 1961; Carl Hempel, *Philosophy of Natural Science*. Englewood Cliffs: Prentice-Hall, 1966; and for the humanistic disciplines, William Dray, *Laws and Explanation in History*. Oxford: Clarendon Press, 1957. Subsequent newer approaches can be sampled from an important work that ranges wider than its title: Francisco Jose Ayala and Theodosius Dobzhansky (eds.), *Studies in the Philosophy of Biology: Reduction and Related Problems*. New York: Macmillan, 1974; see also, in this connection, A. R. Peacocke, "Reductionism: A Review of the Epistemological Issues and Their Relevance to Biology and the Problem of Consciousness," *Zygon* 11/4 (1976): 307–334.
9. Peacocke, 314.
10. Some statement of definition is virtually a mandate of current debate over reduction and reductionism, for the term is used in widely varying senses. For some, like John Y. Fenton ("Reductionism in the Study of Religions," *Soundings* 53 [1970]: 61–76), reduction is simply a form of explanation which leans heavily on one set of categories and does not exclude others; in other cases, such as Joe E. Barnhart ("Reductionism and Religious Explanation," *Perspectives in Religious Studies* 4 [1977]: 241–252), to explain at all is to reduce, with the result that the two processes are indistinguishable. Here reduction is taken, as in the natural sciences, to mean a complete explanation in terms of one set of related categories, whether they be applied within a single discipline or from one discipline to the phenomena normally explained by means of another (see Peacocke, 313–328).
11. Mircea Eliade, "History of Religions and a New Humanism," *History of Religions* 1/1 (1961): 1–8, 6.
12. On this see Morton Beckner, "Reduction, Hierarchies, and Organicism," in Ayala and Dobzhansky (eds.), 163–177.

13. Ernest Nagel, *Structure of Science*, chap. 11.

14. Karl Popper, "Scientific Reduction and the Essential Incompleteness of All Science," in Ayala and Dobzhansky (eds.), 259–282.

15. The briefest, but often confusing, entry to Freud's view is, of course, Sigmund Freud, *The Future of an Illusion*. W. D. Robson-Scott (trans.). Garden City, NY: Doubleday, 1957. See Philip Rieff, *Freud: The Mind of the Moralist*. London: Gollancz, 1959, and thorough analysis by William Alston, "Psychoanalytic Theory and Theistic Belief," *Faith and Philosophers*, 63–110. John Hick (ed.). New York: St. Martin's Press, 1964.

16. Emile Durkheim, *The Elementary Forms of Religious Life*. London: Allen & Unwin, 1971; on Durkheim see W. S. G. Pickering, *Durkheim on Religion*. London: Routledge & Kegan Paul, 1975; also E. E. Evans-Pritchard, *Theories of Primitive Religion*. Oxford: Clarendon Press, 1965.

17. Throughout this article masculine pronouns such as "he" and "his," when not referring to someone cited in the text of the article will be used in the neuter sense to indicate a person, male or female.

18. See Peacocke, "Reductionism," 312–313. It should be noted that both Otto and Eliade insist upon considerably more than simple dissent from theoretical reductionism. Quite apart from the empirical and disciplinary claims that the phenomena we recognize as "religious" require for proper explanation a set of rational propositions not found in disciplines such as sociology and psychology, both are concerned to make an ontological case. Religion for Otto is rooted in an *a priori* mental capacity, which uniquely apprehends the "numinous"; for Eliade it reaches to a unique mental structure, which he calls the "transconscious." From these more ambitious ontological positions, it follows *a fortiori* that both scholars are committed to the claim that religion is theoretically irreducible as well. The concern of this article is not to defend the former but to refute those who deny any purpose or validity in making even the more modest claims of the latter. For a stance that seems to approximate theoretical irreducibility, while opposing ontological, see Jonathan Z. Smith, *Imagining Religion: From Babylon to Jonestown*. Chicago: University of Chicago Press, 1982: xi, 41. On Eliade's doctrine of irreducibility and the "transconscious," see Douglas Allen, *Structure and Creativity: Hermeneutics in Mircea Eliade's Phenomenology and New Directions*. The Hague: Mouton, 1978: 82–84, 218–219; also Adrian Marino, *L'hermeneutique de Mircea Eliade*. Jean Gouillard (trans.). Paris: Gallimard, 1981.

19. Hans Penner and Edward Yonan, "Is a Science of Religion Possible?" *Journal of Religion* 52 (1972): 107–133, 130–131.

20. Citied in Penner and Yonan, 119; for the original, see Ernest Nagel, "The Meaning of Reduction in the Natural Sciences," *Science and Civilization*. Robert C. Stauffer (ed.). Madison: University of Wisconsin Press, 1949: 99–135.

21. See, e.g., Peacocke, 312–313; Beckner (see n. 12 above), 163–165, 174–175; and J. S. Krüger, "'Reductionism' in Studying Religious Phenomena," *Theologica Evangelica* 15/2 (1982): 26–30.

22. Beckner, 174; also Krüger, 27.

23. Guilford Dudley, *Religion on Trial: Mircea Eliade and His Critics*. Philadelphia: Temple University Press, 1977: 144.

24. Dudley, 132.

25. Dudley, 128.
26. Peacocke, 318.
27. Imre Lakatos, "Falsification and the Methodology of Scientific Research Programmes," *The Methodology of Scientific Research Programmes*. John Worrall and Gregory Currie (eds.). Cambridge: Cambridge University Press, 8–101; for Dudley's use of the distinction, see 121–135.
28. Robert Segal, "In Defense of Reductionism," *Journal of the American Academy of Religion* 51/1 (1983): 97–124.
29. Mircea Eliade, *Myth and Reality*. Willard R. Trask (trans.). New York: Harvest Books, 1968: 1.
30. Segal, 98.
31. Segal, 101.
32. Segal, 103.
33. Freud (see n. 15 above), 69.
34. Mircea Eliade, *The Sacred and the Profane*. Willard R. Trask (trans.). New York: Harvest Books, 1968: 98, 99.
35. The approach has, in fact, been taken by Edmund Leach in an acerbic review of Eliade's *oeuvre*, "Sermons by a Man on a Ladder," *New York Review of Books* (October 20, 1966).
36. Segal, 103.
37. Segal, 115.
38. Segal, 109.
39. Segal, 109, 110.
40. Segal, 110.
41. A dissenter in this connection is Alasdair MacIntyre, "Is Understanding Compatible with Believing," *Faith and Philosophers*. John Hick (ed.). New York: St. Martin's Press, 1964: 115–133, where he advances the unconventional notion that believer and nonbeliever cannot mean the same thing when they utter a proposition about God. He seems, however, to qualify his claims (125), and they are, in any case, subjected to cogent criticism by William Alston, "On Sharing Concepts," in *Faith and Philosophers*, 154–155. For a discussion of the complex issues involved, see Bryan Wilson (ed.), *Rationality*. Oxford: Basil Blackwell, 1970, in particular, the contributions of Martin Hollis, who makes a forcible case for cross-cultural understanding.

14

Tony Edwards, *Religion, Explanation, and the* Askesis *of Inquiry*[1]

❧❧

I

In *The Mind's New Science*, Howard Gardner describes a phenomenon he calls "the computational paradox": when we try to explain human cognition using an exclusively computational model, the noncomputational features of human cognition do not disappear; instead, they are actually highlighted. "[O]nly through scrupulous adherence to computational thinking," he wrote, "could scientists discover the ways in which humans actually *differ* from the serial digital computer."[2]

The computational paradox is actually a particular instance of a more general phenomenon, a paradox of explanation. That is, when we offer a correct explanation of a phenomenon, the result is a *direct* gain in knowledge; on the other hand, when we offer a mistaken explanation of a phenomenon, there remains an *indirect* gain of the kind Gardner observes: our "mistake" draws our attention to the very counterexamples it fails to cover.[3]

Yet, if this is true, then there is nothing to fear from explanation. Moreover, there is nothing to fear from reductionist explanation. Developing and checking reductionist explanations turns out to be a no-lose enterprise: if the reduction in question is appropriate, then nothing is lost; if it is inappropriate, then there will be some remainder, some exception to the hypothesis that will lead to its refutation. We can try out explanations with perfect freedom, even reductionist ones.[4]

This is really the long and the short of the matter. Other questions about the general propriety or impropriety of reductionist agendas have to do with the institutional or personal adjustments that might be involved if some of these agendas gain favor or succeed. As such, they are questions that fall outside the scope of our concern as inquirers. If we focus only on the epistemic aspect of the problem, there is no reason *a priori* to exclude explanations of religion—even reductionist ones—from our ways of understanding religion. If some reductions are sound, that will be important to know. If none is, that will be important too, not least because it will help us to see more clearly how our subject differs from subjects that can be dealt with reductively.[5] ...

III

Once we appreciate the paradox of explanation, we see that, *along with our other ways of understanding religion*, we can pursue reductionist explanations without prejudice to the truth.[6] On this view, if a strategy succeeds in revealing the truth, then we should accept it; if a strategy fails, then we should not. This is the *askesis* of inquiry:[7] to let the better argument decide the question—for the time being.[8]

There is a kind of faith in this, a faith that may be difficult to share. In letting the chips fall where they may, we are assuming that whether reductionist strategies succeed or fail, we have nothing to lose. If some thing we believe is refuted, then it was false, so we haven't lost anything.

This, of course, is a little like saying, "The good man can't be harmed." The good man is slandered, robbed, beaten, even killed, and yet (we blithely insist) "He hasn't been harmed." Likewise when we say we haven't lost anything as the result of the success or failure of a reduction: a scholar may lose time, a research grant, his reputation as a scholar, his research paradigm, his conviction that his cultural background is superior to others', his belief that the issues of his generation are important ones—he may even lose his faith. It seems strange to say that he "hasn't lost anything." Yet however important these losses may be in other respects, within the *askesis* of inquiry they really are nothing: they cannot override considerations of evidence and argument; they simply do not count. In the *askesis* of inquiry the only loss that counts is a loss of the truth.[9]

Yet although this is correct, it also shows that the *askesis* of inquiry is actually a relatively narrow frame of reference—an ivory tower, in fact. For the "*askesis*" [or the activity] consists in prescinding from many of the interests that matter to us most. In addition to our interest in the truth, we also have interests in goodness, beauty, fun, health, happiness, and community. There is a real possibility that inquiry—specially reductionist strategies of inquiry—will harm these other interests. In short, the problem of reductionism solved by the paradox of explanation is not the only problem of reductionism we have to face. It is not that reductionism threatens the truth, but that reductionism, like other agendas of inquiry, threatens our other interests, interests that cannot be ignored.

Thus, the anti-reductionist is right in a way: there is something to be feared from reductionism. He is wrong, however, in thinking that this is because reductionism somehow falls outside the scope of honest inquiry. For reductionist agendas are a form of such inquiry—an aggressive form of it, perhaps, but a form of it nonetheless. And from this it follows also that the anti-reductionist is not the only one who has reason to be nervous. Much as we stand to gain, we all have something to lose from disciplined inquiry.

What we stand to lose, *how* we might lose it—these are questions that deserve extended sociological answers. For present purposes, an insight of Richard Rorty's will serve to bring the issue into focus. Rorty suggests that there can be harm merely in being redescribed:

> [M]ost people do not want to be redescribed. They want to be taken on their own terms—taken seriously just as they are and just as they talk. The ironist tells them that the language they speak is up for grabs by her and her kind. There is something potentially very cruel about that claim. For the best way to cause people long-lasting pain is to humiliate them by making the things that seemed most important to them look futile, obsolete, and powerless.[10]

Rorty's point holds, not only for the ironist, but for the inquirer as well. Anyone who inquires successfully into the lives of others has the power to redescribe them.

Inquiry is threatening, then, because—and when—it is likely to issue in a redescription of ourselves or our community. Moreover, inquiry in the humanities and social sciences typically results in such a redescription: the first-person, internal, or *emic* vocabulary of the people studied is redescribed in the third-person, external, or *etic* vocabulary of those who study them.[11] Although such redescriptions need not displace the previous description, often they do.[12] Thus, we have reason to be concerned in religious studies, for, except under special conditions, displacement of a sacred vocabulary is a sacrilege. It is as if, without permission, one were to tear down a neighborhood temple or church and rebuild it with different architecture a few blocks away. It is not enough to tell the people, "Look, the new one is just as good as the old one!" The point is, it is not the old one. Indeed, the threat is only slightly decreased if a religion redescribes itself—as when the Roman Catholic Mass was changed from Latin to English, or the Episcopalian *Book of Common Prayer* was translated into modern English.

IV

Thus, as inquirers, we *propose* redescriptions; as objects of inquiry, we resist them. This conflict is heightened when the agenda of inquiry is reductionist, because, in the humanities in general and in religious studies in particular, *our myth of reductionism is that, in contrast to interpretation, in explanation the redescription of the object always displaces, and thus nullifies, its original, native description.*

This, I believe, accounts for the anti-reductionism of most religious studies scholars. (1) It accounts for the anti-reductionism of scholars who are religious themselves. Such scholars are always both subject and object of inquiry, even when the religion they study is not their own. Thus, any generalization about religious people is about them as well, and they therefore believe an explanation of a common religious phenomenon (e.g., conversion) would nullify their self-description along with the self-descriptions of others.[13] (2) It also accounts for the anti-reductionism of scholars who are not religious, but who nevertheless have come to love, admire, or empathize with the religious people they study. As Aristotle said, a friend is another self, to the extent that we "go native" and befriend the people we study, we find ourselves acting on their behalf to resist the displacement of their self-description.

(3) What of the religious studies scholar who fits neither of these descriptions but is anti-reductionist nonetheless? What does he have against reductionism? In some ways, he is the most instructive case. Religious studies is largely made up of scholars of the first two types. Accordingly, it has never developed strong explanatory traditions of its own, and has no established vocabulary for proposing explanations. This in turn means that explanatory vocabularies, if used at all, must be imported from outside, and outside vocabularies for discussing religious phenomena belong to rival communities of inquiry. If these outside vocabularies were to gain dominance, it would amount to a redescription of religious studies itself.

Such verbal colonization would affect the third type of scholar no less than the first two; he fears redescription just like anyone else. Like the other two types of scholar, he shares the vocabulary of his community of inquiry, and he recognizes that an external vocabulary might displace not only that indigenous vocabulary, but also the interests that it expresses and integrates—interests with which his own personal and professional interests are deeply interwoven. Consequently, he too is an anti-reductionist. Moreover, since his anti-reductionism merely embodies the self-interest of his community, his motive for anti-reductionism is one that is shared throughout the community. Thus it also constitutes a second and unifying motive for the first two types of scholar.

There are two other motives for anti-reductionism that extend throughout the community: (4) a duty to affirm what is sacred to the common culture, and (5) a duty to protect it.[14] In the humanities in general, and in religious studies in particular, we not only *inquire* into cultural traditions but also selectively *affirm* them. There is a priestliness to our work that not only allows but requires these acts of affirmation.

A comparison with music may be useful here. In music, scholars not only analyze, compare, and explain works of music; they offer them up for appreciation. In the classroom, and in scholarly articles as well, there is amid all the evidence and argument the moment when a music historian presents the object for the wonder of her audience or readership. She does not merely *describe* the object, she does not merely *interpret* the object, she does not merely *explain* the object—she *celebrates* it. She invites wonder, admiration, "wows," "oohs," and "ahs." This is not done with just one object, of course, but neither is it done with every object—there is a canon and the canon of such objects represents and embodies those values that define us as a culture, and thus are sacred to us.

The same holds in religious studies. Just as a music historian does "music appreciation," so scholars of religion do "religion appreciation." In doing it, we serve as priests of the common culture. We even get to affirm what is sacred to us personally insofar as it belongs to this wider sense of the sacred. In joining with our colleagues to celebrate this wider sacred, we initiate students of diverse backgrounds into adulthood in the common culture, and, increasingly, into the emerging world culture as well.

Yet, having this priestlike responsibility, we also have another: it is also our job to *guard* what is sacred to the common culture against displacement.[15] As noted above, redescription of the sacred is a very touchy matter. Once it takes place, the words in which the object was sacred disappear or are no longer heard. They are replaced by other words—unfamiliar words, without the old resonance or depth. In these new words the object remains—we are told—but it no longer seems sacred in the same way. Moreover, once the sacrality of the object has been shown to be so readily negotiable, it may not seem sacred at all anymore. Consequently, one of our traditional tasks in the humanities has been to monitor the processes of cultural redescription very carefully, in order to see that the core values are preserved and passed on.

These responsibilities to affirm and guard what is sacred to the common culture find natural expression in anti-reductionism. According to our myth of reductionism, explanation in the human sciences involves a wholesale redescription of human culture, and thus a wholesale nullification of all self-descriptions; thus, since our priestlike function is to uphold at least the core of our common self-description, we find ourselves opposing reductionism.

V

Each of the motives of anti-reductionism I have mentioned assume either that redescription logically *entails* displacement or that it causally *leads* to it. Yet clearly there is no entailment: if someone redescribes us, we are free to reject the new description and retain the old one. Also, in some cases we are free to accept the new description and retain the old one as well.

And, although redescription can and often does lead to displacement, it need not do so. Consequently, the solution to the problem of reductionism is to drive a conceptual wedge between redescription and displacement. Unfortunately, in religious studies and elsewhere, the wedge used has been the distinction between *interpretation* and *explanation*.[16] To put it in the terms I have been using here, this answer assumes that interpretation can redescribe without displacing, whereas explanation cannot. Thus, this solution fails: interpretation does not avoid redescription any more than explanation does. Indeed, the only distinction we need is the distinction between redescription and displacement. Nevertheless, the distinction between interpretation and explanation contains so many important misconceptions, and is such a popular way of distinguishing acceptable from unacceptable studies of religion, that I will give it detailed treatment here.

When comparing concepts of interpretation and explanation, two phrases are especially revealing: "explained away" and "reduced." Granted, we do not really do away with an object when we provide an explanation of it.[17] Nevertheless, we do redescribe it, and this redescription, if it is accepted by or enforced upon the people redescribed, may remove the object as previously described from their language, and thus from their lives. If so, there is a real loss: a world in which the sacred object is described in a certain way and described only in that way gives place to a world in which (a) it cannot be described at all, (b) it can be described only in the old way together with a new way, or (c) it can be described only in a new way. Only of (b) might we say that the object-as-described has survived the transition, and even in that case there has been a change. Hence the expression "explained away."

The same transition can be characterized as a change from a world in which sacred events are primary to a world in which these same events are secondary and thus no longer sacred. Hence the expressions "reduced," "reductive," "reductionist," and the like.

When we turn to *interpretation*, however, we find that it is rarely, if ever, discussed in terms of "removal" or "diminution." We do not say—except in irony—"He interpreted it away," nor do we speak—except in irony—of "reductionist interpretation." In other words, even though an interpretation can replace the original language of an object with an entirely new language, we not only imagine the object surviving the process of interpretation, but we also imagine it with the same status it had prior to that process.

These differences between our understandings of explanation and interpretation can be explained as follows.[18] Whereas we see interpretation as an act of mediating an audience to an object, we see scientific explanation as an act of mediating an object to a framework. In interpretation, the object is the fixed point of reference; it is respected under its current description. In explanation, by contrast, the object is not the fixed point of reference; it is not respected as currently described, but only as redescribed. Also, in scientific explanation the audience is not the focus of interest to the same degree as in interpretation. When scientific explanation is further described as "reductionist," the redescription is seen as a reevaluation as well, and an unfair one. The object is seen as having been demoted relative to its original and proper frame of reference.[19]

Yet scientific explanation not only stands in contrast to interpretation; it also stands in contrast to the pragmatics of everyday explanation. Indeed, it can easily be taken as a violation of that pragmatics, and this contributes to the sense that it "does away with" or "reduces" its object. In everyday, nonscientific explanation, an explanation is given by a speaker at the request of a hearer: e.g., "What are your shoes doing on the table?" [20] In response to such a request, the speaker "removes" an apparent anomaly by a redescription in which the speaker tells the hearer the place of the object by invoking the hearer's frame of reference: e.g., "I was about to shine them." If the hearer accepts the explanation, then she drops the former description under which the object was anomalous.[21]

Several aspects of everyday explanation are noteworthy:

1. The description of the object changes from presenting its *"apparent"* character to presenting its *"real"* character.
2. The appearance of anomaly is thus *"removed."*
3. The object is now seen not to be *anomalous* to the assumed framework but instead to *fit* it.
4. The object is not *respected* as originally described; as originally described it is anomalous, and thus problematic.
5. The hearer, however, is respected; it is her common sense background framework to which the explanation fits the object and which is used in redescribing the object.
6. The redescription displaces the prior description of the object, else the anomaly would remain.

As lay people or humanists perceive it, scientific explanation is quite different. "Explanation" as used in regard to scientific work can be seen as a metaphorical extension of "explanation" as used in everyday life. Because metaphors are ambiguous, this extension leaves room for us to be uncertain about just how much of the everyday meaning of "explanation" carries over into scientific explanation. The first three changes remain; likewise the fourth:

1'. The description of the object changes from presenting its *"apparent"* character to presenting its *"real"* character.
2'. The appearance of anomaly is thus *"removed."*
3'. The object is now seen not to be *anomalous* but instead to *fit*.
4'. The object is not *respected* as originally described; as originally described it is anomalous, and thus *problematic*.

Yet, because the background framework is no longer the common sense framework of the hearer, the object is no longer "anomalous" in quite the same sense, and likewise it is never "fitted" to the framework in quite the same sense. The framework is now a scientific theory unfamiliar to the layperson or humanist, and the object is anomalous only in the sense in which everything in the domain of the theory is anomalous until it is given a place in the theory. Thus:

5'. The hearer is *not respected*; it is not her common sense background framework to which the explanation fits the object or which is used in redescribing the object; rather, the background framework is an unfamiliar, artificially constructed scientific theory.

On this view, then, *everything* stands in need of explanation; therefore, disturbingly, every vocabulary is subject to redescription. Finally, and importantly, the sixth feature is retained despite these differences:

6'. The redescription *displaces* the prior description of the object, else the anomaly would remain.

If this analysis is correct, it is easy to understand why scientific explanation would be offensive to some people: as they understand it, the object is not respected; the hearer is not respected; the speaker, though harmful, acts involuntarily; the framework is artificial; and the entire domain—the entire world as they know it—is viewed as if it were an embarrassment in need of excuse or justification.[22] To a fully initiated scientist, however, these features, left over from the metaphorical connection with everyday explanation, have all dropped away:

1". The shift from "apparent" to "real" is a metaphysical question on which reasonable scientists may differ.
2". The appearance of anomaly is still "*removed*," but is generally understood as an appearance, an anomaly, and the removal is relative to the theory under consideration.
3". Here also, the object is now seen not to be *anomalous* but instead to *fit*.
4". The object is *neither respected nor disrespected* as previously described. The ordinary description of the object, if any, is not the theory-relative description under which it is anomalous.
5". The hearer is respected; she, too, is an initiate, a fellow scientist. Thus, it is as much her background framework as the speaker's that is used in redescribing the object.
6". The redescription does not displace the prior, ordinary description of the object. Nor, in many cases, does it displace the prior, technical description of the object, since solutions are only understood in relation to the problems they solve, and some redescriptions are understood as solutions.

Little wonder, then, that scientific explanation offends the layperson and the academic humanist: the metaphorical interplay between everyday "explanation" and scientific "explanation" creates plenty of room for confusion and bad feeling. Because of the misunderstanding, scientific explanation not only seems more harmful than interpretation, but seems insultingly to violate the pragmatics of everyday explanation as well. If we add to this the agenda by which scientists attempt to bring all of our world under scientific laws, organize those laws hierarchically, include religion under those laws, and apply Ockham's razor to tidy things up, then antireductionism becomes an understandable response. For, because of the misunderstanding, the scientific agenda of redescription seems to be in direct conflict with the religious agenda of continuing community.

Here the crucial question is whether the "removal" of the "anomaly"—for our purposes, the religious phenomenon in the domain of explanation—requires that the prior description of the phenomenon be nullified. It does not. A scientific explanation of a phenomenon need no more nullify the prior description of a phenomenon than would an interpretation of that same phenomenon.[23] (An answer to the question, "Why do bridges ice over more quickly?", will not prevent us from reminding one another, "Bridges ice over more quickly.")

Moreover, adding "reductionist" only represents the decision—the separate decision—to let the redescription nullify the original description. This is neither natural nor inevitable; where it seems so, it is only the inappropriate metaphorical carryover from the "reducing" features of ordinary explanation: e.g., "Oh, that's *just* his wife," which *minimizes* the anomaly even as it fits the behavior to the audience's framework; or "Oh, that's *really* just his wife," which emphasizes that the anomaly was merely *apparent*. These features of ordinary explanation are in no way entailed or implicated by scientific explanation.[24]

I have spent so much time with this, our mythology of explanation, because it is really more relevant to our concern with reductionism than a more sophisticated and technical theory of explanation would be. Most of us do not know much about science; it is an "Other," a Rorschach onto which we project fears and confusions of our own. The metaphor of "explanation" supports those projections. We have thus come to understand the difference between interpretation and explanation as the difference between an approach that leaves its object intact and an approach that does not. This difference, so far as I can see, has nothing to do with scientific explanation itself, nor with the redescriptive process that takes place in science. Hence, although redescription is often understood as a conceptual displacement, the move from redescription to displacement is always a separate decision.

My point, then, is that we can have a scientific explanation of a religious phenomenon and still retain the original descriptions of it; there is no need to choose between them. The scientific explanation "redescribes" the phenomenon, but it does not "displace" either the phenomenon or its previous description.

Moreover, we do not have to decide which description is "more real." The impression that this question will be decided by scientific explanation is a carryover from everyday explanation, where the apparent anomaly must either be allowed to stand or be "removed," and where its allowance or removal determines whether or not the appearance is to be regarded as "real." In regard to actual scientific explanation, the question is not forced in this same way. The successful inquirer does not have to settle this question, and others need do so only if that is their personal choice or if it is in some way required by a norm of their community.

Thus, the only sense in which academics face a question of whether their redescriptive *explanantes* are "more real"' than the originally described *explananda* is analogous to the sense in which philosophers of science debate realist and anti-realist views of science. The work of Max Black, George Lakoff, Mark Johnson, Mary Hesse, and others suggests that scientific models can be construed as extended metaphors.[25] Lakoff emphasizes a basic-level of categorization from which more sophisticated forms are built up by metaphor and metonymy, including "idealized cognitive models" such as those used in science. The question, "Which is real, the basic-level description or the idealized cognitive model?", remains open.[26] Lakoff seems to come out in favor of the basic-level description, which corresponds to common sense. The philosopher of science Bas van Fraassen takes a similar view, emphasizing the *constructed* (though for him literal) character of scientific theory, and the reality of our common sense understanding of the world.

Thus, if we have proposed a reductionist explanation—even if that explanation has survived all challenges—we still have not settled the question of its ontological status, and we have not addressed in any way the ontological status of the other descriptions we use. These questions remain very open indeed.[27] Thus, even though explanation does not aim to direct us to the object, it leaves us free to do so, just as interpretation does.

VI

In this paper, I have suggested that our ostensibly epistemic arguments about the general viability of reductionist agendas are actually motivated by political and personal concerns—concerns about what might happen if some of those agendas should someday succeed. I have argued that reductionist agendas do not jeopardize the truth, and that they jeopardize self-description only if (a) those redescribed interpret the proposed accounts in a way that contradicts their self-description, and only if (b) they then adopt those descriptions instead of retaining their own.

For many people, I realize, reductionist agendas look like strategies designed to deprive them of that power of choice. But redescription does not entail displacement; there is scope for choice. Results in the *askesis* of inquiry do not and logically cannot entail decisions that would conjoin those results with conclusions based on our other, nonepistemic interests. If there are reductionists who believe that their work will preempt those decisions, then they are mistaken. Our freedom to redescribe others is matched by their freedom not only (a) to decide whether to accept those redescriptions but also (b) to decide whether to allow those redescriptions to replace the self-description they already have.

It may seem odd to think that the question of reductionism is basically a matter of freedom, but the failure to notice this is merely a result of our having muddied the issue by treating a large number of *a posteriori* questions— questions about the adequacy of *each and every possible explanation of religion*, no less!—as if they were a single question that could be settled *a priori*. The *a priori* epistemic question, "Are reductionist methods appropriate to the study of religion?", is a pseudo-question that can be dissolved by reflecting on the paradox of explanation. Yet the political problem that underlies this pseudo-question is an important one: how to free academic studies of religion from obscurantism without violating the rights of the people whose lives we redescribe.

As scholars, we can only be free from obscurantism if we are free to redescribe, and our redescriptive enterprise cannot begin by granting the accuracy of the self-descriptions of religious peoples.[28] Not only would this be contradictory—their self-descriptions disagree with one another—but this would make religious studies an "inquiry" that began by having its answers ahead of time. As such, it would be a form of "inquiry" that would have little to say, little to offer. In that case, we would do better simply to remain silent and let the people of the traditions speak for themselves. In fact, however, we have a great deal to say, and have begun to say it. In saying it, we often generalize; in applying these generalizations, we often explain; and through correcting and revising our explanations, we may someday succeed in understanding human religion.

Yet this freedom to redescribe people cannot preempt their freedom to choose their own self-descriptions. Thus, although the emphasis of my argument in this paper has been to resist encroachments on academic freedom of inquiry, I would argue equally that academics have no right to encroach on the freedom of belief of nonacademics. We have the benefits of an ivory tower only because we have its limitations. It is not our business to change the world by enforcing redescriptions, tempting as that may sometimes seem.[29]

In religious studies, this restraint is especially important. We, above all, need the protective preserve of academia in which to do our work, for our subject matter is intimately important to nonacademics. We have a right to be protected from *their* interference only if they have a right to be protected from *ours*. Yet the way to ensure both freedoms is not to sneak political measures into our methodological slogans, but simply to identify and assert the rights of all parties. At times this may require institutional means; certainly universities should implement policies that guarantee both freedoms. In general, however, they can be maintained most effectively simply by agreeing to make them part of the ethos of our community, as an informal condition of membership. William James spoke to the heart of the matter:

> No one of us ought to issue vetoes to the other, nor should we bandy words of abuse. We ought, on the contrary, delicately and profoundly to respect one another's mental freedom: then only shall we bring about the intellectual republic; then only shall we have that spirit of inner tolerance without which all outer tolerance is soulless, and which is empiricism's glory; then only shall we live and let live, in speculative as well as in practical things.[30]

Notes

1. This paper was first given at the annual meeting of the Eastern International Region of the American Academy of Religion on April 19, 1991. I would like to thank Bruce Alton, Mark Cladis, Dane Gordon, and Douglas Rayment for their remarks.
2. Howard Gardner, *The Mind's New Science: A History of the Cognitive Revolution.* New York: Basic, 1985: 385.
3. See Karl Popper, *The Logic of Scientific Discovery* (New York: Harper, 1958), and *Conjectures and Refutations* (New York: Basic, 1962), where this feature of inquiry is a recurrent theme. As Paul Feyerabend points out, however, the origin of this line of argument is John Stuart Mill's *On Liberty*, especially Chapter 2. See Paul K. Feyerabend, "Consolations for the Specialist," in Imre Lakatos and Alan Musgrave (eds.), *Criticism and the Growth of Knowledge* (Cambridge: Cambridge University Press, 1970): 211; John Stuart Mill, *The Philosophy of John Stuart Mill*, Marshall Cohen (ed.), (New York: Random House, 1961): 203–248.
4. Of course, there can be problems with an explanation other than direct counterevidence, such as the incompatibility of the explanation with other, well-established theoretical claims. Nevertheless, I wish to stress the importance of counterevidence here, both because counterevidence will suffice to call the adequacy of an explanation into question, and because, if a well-formulated explanation is unsound, then its refutation will come from counterevidence, one way or another. The scholar who opposes reductionism, therefore, need only insist on an explanation sufficiently well-formulated to indicate the kind of evidence that would falsify it, then find an example of such evidence. For extensive discussion of falsification, see Lakatos and Musgrave, *Criticism and the Growth of Knowledge*, especially Lakatos, "Falsification and the Methodology of Scientific Research Programmes" (91–195).

5. I should emphasize that in this paper I am arguing only for the permissibility of reductionist and other explanatory efforts in the study of religion. I am not arguing that they are *obligatory*; I am not arguing that they are ideal; I am not even arguing that there is reason to expect that some of them will be successful. I am merely arguing that there are no good epistemic reasons for obstructing such efforts, and that it is in the interest of freedom of inquiry to give them a hearing, just as we would give a hearing to literary-critical interpretations, philosophical analyses, phenomenological descriptions, historical reconstructions, and cross-cultural comparisons.

   I should also note that those who argue for and against reductionism as a general "research programme" for religious studies are addressing a different issue—a question not of the permissibility of reductionism for some researchers, but of its desirability as an agenda for us all. That is not my concern here. Hence the *laissez-faire* Popperian—even Feyerabendian—quality to my argument. Nevertheless, my argument does contradict Daniel Pals's position, which holds that non-reductionism is axiomatic for religious studies as a whole. See Daniel L. Pals, "Is Religion a 'Sui Generis' Phenomenon?" *The Journal of the American Academy of Religion* 55/2 (1987): 259–282. See also Robert A. Segal and Donald Wiebe, "On Axioms and Dogmas in the Study of Religion," *The Journal of the American Academy of Religion* 57/3 (1989): 591–605, and Daniel L. Pals, Donald Wiebe, and Lorne L. Dawson, "Colloquium: Does Autonomy Entail Theology?" *Religion* 20 (1990): 1–51. On the notion of a "research programme" see Imre Lakatos, "Falsification and the Methodology of Scientific Research Programmes," in Lakatos and Musgrave, *Criticism and the Growth of Knowledge.*

6. I use italics here to emphasize that this type of theoretical work is merely one enterprise in which we should be engaged.

7. Ed. note. *Askesis* is a Greek term meaning the practice of, or to be engaged in, an activity.

8. There is a place for tenacity, however. As Feyerabend puts it, "It seems, then, that the interplay between tenacity and proliferation which we described in our little methodological fairytale is also an essential feature of the actual development of science. It seems that it is not the puzzle-solving activity that is responsible for the growth of our knowledge but the active interplay of various tenaciously held views. Moreover, it is the invention of new ideas and the attempt to secure for them a worthy place in the competition that leads to the overthrow of old and familiar paradigms. Such inventing goes on all the time. Yet it is only during revolutions that the attention turns to it. This change of attention does not reflect any profound structural change (such as for example a transition from puzzle solving to philosophical speculation and testing of foundations). It is nothing but a change of interest and of publicity." In "The Consolations of the Specialist," in Lakatos and Musgrave, *Criticism and the Growth of Knowledge*, 209. See also 136, 173–180.

9. "[H]owever humble the sphere of her rule, yet at least, while within that sphere, criticism is subject to no intrusion and oppressed by no authority. She moves on her path unheedful of the wanting, unheedful of the clamor, of that which beyond her realm may be or may call itself religion and philosophy; her philosophy and her religion are the realization and fruition of herself, and her faith is this, that while true to herself she can never find an enemy in the truth." F. H. Bradley, *Collected Essays*, I, quoted in Van A. Harvey, *The Historian and the Believer* (Philadelphia: Westminster Press, 1966): x.

10. Richard Rorty, "Private Irony and Liberal Hope," in *Contingency, Irony, and Solidarity*, 89. Rorty has in mind a redescription that moves from one "final vocabulary" to another. He explicates "final vocabulary" as follows (73):

> All human beings carry about a set of words which they employ to justify their actions, their beliefs, and their lives. These are the words in which we formulate praise of our friends and contempt for our enemies, our long-term projects, our deepest self-doubts, and our highest hopes. They are the words in which we tell, sometimes prospectively and sometimes retrospectively, the story of our lives. I shall call these words a person's final vocabulary.
>
> It is "final" in the sense that if doubt is cast on the worth of these words, their user has no noncircular argumentative recourse. Those words are as far as he can go with language; beyond them there is only helpless passivity or a resort to force. A small part of a final vocabulary is made up of thin, flexible, and ubiquitous terms such as "true," "good," "right," and "beautiful." The larger part contains thicker, more rigid, and more parochial terms, for example, "Christ," "England," "professional standards," "decency," "kindness," "the Revolution," "the Church," "progressive," "rigorous," "creative." The more parochial terms do most of the work.

11. On the *emic/etic* distinction, see Marvin Harris, "Emics, Etics, and the New Ethnography," *The Rise of Anthropological Theory* (New York: Harper & Row, 1968): 568–604. A similar distinction is developed by Ninian Smart in *The Phenomenon of Religion* (New York: Herder & Herder, 1973): 43–44, and is discussed by Donald Wiebe in *Religion and Truth: Towards an Alternative Paradigm for the Study of Religion* (The Hague: Mouton, 1981): 72–79.

12. By "displace" here I just mean that the new description takes the place of the old, which is no longer used, even by the people redescribed. Thus, "A has redescribed B" does not entail "B's final vocabulary has been displaced by A's." In short, redescription does not entail displacement. Note, too, that neither redescription nor displacement involves a total change of "world" or "conceptual scheme." See Donald A. Schon, *Displacement of Concepts* (London: Tavistock, 1963); Donald Davidson, "On The Very Idea of a Conceptual Scheme," *Inquiries into Truth and Interpretation* (Oxford: Oxford University Press, 1984); also Terry F. Godlove, "In What Sense Are Religions Conceptual Frameworks?" *The Journal of the American Academy of Religion* 60/2 (1984), and *Religion, Interpretation, and Diversity of Belief: The Framework Model from Kant to Durkheim to Davidson* (Cambridge: Cambridge University Press, 1989).

13. See Wayne Proudfoot's admirable *Religious Experience* (Berkeley: University of California, 1985), especially 190–236. Here my account of redescription and displacement can be understood as including as a special case Proudfoot's emphasis on the conflict between the explanatory commitments of the believer and the researcher. The psychological core of conflict—the knee-jerk reaction of each party to the other—seems to derive from the prospect each faces of having his framework subsumed by the other's. This does not, however, seem to be an effect of explanation per se. Any impending displacement of final vocabulary will raise the same problems. Thus, fear of reductionism is sometimes expressed in terms that

could also be used for a people's fear of conquest, for in either case the final vocabulary is displaced.

14. See Proudfoot, *Religious Experience*, xvi–xvii:

> The insistence on describing religious experience from the subject's point of view, the stress on the reality of the object for the person who has that experience, the avoidance of reductionism, and the distinction between descriptive and explanatory tasks are all important for the study of religion. Each, however, can and has been used to block inquiry for apologetic purposes. In the following chapters we shall examine the accounts that have been given and the claims that have been made for religious experience with a view toward distinguishing the genuine insights from erroneous theories and protective strategies.

> The notion of a "protective strategy" plays an important role throughout the book.

15. I say this as a point of fact. Some may want to argue that we have no professional obligation that is as conservative as this. Yet even where the goals of education are expressly progressive, there is an understanding that nothing truly valuable should be lost in the process, and that it is our responsibility as faculty to see that nothing truly valuable is lost. Personally, I am not always happy with this responsibility, because it conflicts with the *askesis* of inquiry. But by the same token, I am not always happy about the *askesis* of inquiry, precisely because it conflicts with this other, obviously important task. If the job description were unified, things would be easier on all of us.

16. See Wilhelm Dilthey, *Selected Writings*. H. P. Rickman (ed. and trans.). Cambridge: Cambridge University Press, 1976.

17. See Hans H. Penner and Edward A. Yonan, "Is a Science of Religion Possible?" *The Journal of Religion* 52 (1972): 130–131.

18. The argument that follows is informed in part by the discussion of image schemas in Mark Johnson, *The Body in The Mind: The Bodily Basis of Reason, Imagination, and Feeling* (Chicago: University of Chicago Press, 1987), George Lakoff, *Women, Fire, and Dangerous Things* (Chicago: University of Chicago Press, 1987), and Michael J. Reddy, "The Conduit Metaphor: A Case of Frame Conflict in Our Language about Language," *Metaphor and Thought*. Note, too, that I focus on our understandings of interpretation and explanation. That is, I believe it is important at this juncture in the argument to concentrate, not on how these acts ought to take place, nor even on how they actually do take place, but rather on how we think they take place.

19. I do not have in mind a complete relativity of frames of reference, nor is any such relativity presupposed. See Davidson, "The Very Idea of a Conceptual Scheme," and Godlove, "In What Sense are Religions Conceptual Frameworks?"

20. On the role of why-questions in explanation, see Bas C. van Fraassen, *The Scientific Image* (New York: Oxford University Press, 1980): 126–157, and Wesley Salmon, "Four Decades of Scientific Explanation," *Minnesota Studies in the Philosophy of Science, XIII: Scientific Explanation*, Philip Kitcher and Wesley C. Salmon (eds.) (Minneapolis: University of Minnesota Press, 1989): 37–47, 134–154.

21. Bas van Fraassen emphasizes that acceptance, not necessarily belief, is the positive

response to a sufficient explanation. See *The Scientific Image*, 12, 18, 201–203. Ian Hacking writes, "[I]nstrumentalism is to be contrasted with van Fraassen's view, that theoretical expressions are to be taken literally—but not believed, merely 'accepted' and used" (*Representing and Intervening*. Cambridge: Cambridge University Press, 1983: 51, 63).

22. I recognize, of course, that further distinctions can be made between "explanation," "excuse," and "justification." My point, however, is that in everyday speech we do not distinguish these so sharply. The request for an explanation assumes either that something is wrong or that there is something the person making the request does not understand. These features carry over as "connotations" into popular and humanistic understandings of scientific explanation.

23. This is part of the force of van Fraassen's work. It is true that a scientific explanation involves a total redescription of the original object; but an interpretation may do likewise, as when we translate or paraphrase. We often think of interpretation as merely returning us to the phenomenon with new eyes; but an explanation, although it does more, can certainly do the same.

24. By "implicated" here I mean features that might be inferred by the semantics of explanation when taken together with pragmatic principles such as those of van Fraassen or Paul Grice. See Paul Grice, *Studies in the Way of Words* (Cambridge, MA: Harvard University Press, 1989): 3–57, and Stephen C. Levinson, *Pragmatics* (Cambridge: Cambridge University Press, 1983): 97–166.

25. George Lakoff and Mark Johnson, *Metaphors We Live By* (Chicago: University of Chicago Press, 1980); George Lakoff, *Women, Fire, and Dangerous Things*; Mark Johnson, *The Body in the Mind: The Bodily Basis of Meaning, Imagination, and Reason*. See also Richard Boyd, "Metaphor and Theory Change: What is 'Metaphor' a Metaphor for?" and Thomas S. Kuhn, "Metaphor in Science," both in *Metaphor and Thought*, 356–419.

26. Note that it also remains unclear that the question is a good one, and yet it informs the debate between realists and anti-realists in the philosophy of science, and is likely to have comparable effects in the theory of religion.

27. For a sense of the contrast, it is instructive to read Lakoff's *Women, Fire, and Dangerous Things* and *Inquiries into Truth and Interpretation* at the same time.

28. See Proudfoot, *Religious Experience*, chapters 5 and 6.

29. We hope, of course, that the world will be better for our teaching and research, but convictions about religion can easily lead to imposing redescriptions on our students. See John Searle, "The Storm Over the University," *The New York Review of Books*, December 6, 1990, and Gerald Graft's response in subsequent issues.

30. William James, "The Will to Believe," *Philosophy of Religion: An Anthology*. Louis P. Pojman (ed.). Belmont, CA: Wadsworth. 1987: 395.

Part IV

NEUTRALITY AND METHODOLOGICAL AGNOSTICISM

INTRODUCTION

❦❦

How do We Know What We Claim to Know?

Where the nonreductionist proclaims that religious believers are to be believed, for they communicate their feelings of deep realities, and the reductionist maintains that only the nonbelieving outsider can adequately study the actual reasons why believers say what they say and do what they do, there is a strong tradition in the field that opts for a mediating position: that of neutrality.

The argument goes something like this: if we were to have a conversation between a religious believer and a nonbeliever, how would either convince the other that they were wrong in their belief or disbelief. If anything, they might just end up talking past each other, with one making claims concerning the manner in which a deity guides cosmic events and the other making claims about the deluded nature of such beliefs. As far as any outside observer could tell, both positions in this debate are grounded in assumptions of the way the world, or human nature, *really* is that can neither be proved nor disproved; for, what *evidence* could the disbeliever provide to convince the believer that they were wrong, or *vice versa*? How can we prove the existence of a deity? How can we prove that someone is ideologically deluded? In a word, what we have is a question of epistemology (from the Greek *episteme*, meaning knowledge): a question of the methods by which we know what we claim to know. In other words, what standards or criteria does the believer employ to make claims to knowledge? How is it that disbelievers know what they know?

It seems that both the religious insider *and* the outsider are making unsubstantiated claims. Although one or the other may be right, some scholars have suggested that we have no way of confirming which side is right *or* wrong. Perhaps the task of the scholar of religion is not to advocate the religious insider position *or* the outsider position; instead, the scholar of religion could suspend all attempts to determine any kind of deep truth (whether they be religious or psychological) and simply describe and compare other people's attempts to make such grand claims. The position they take is known as methodological agnosticism which simply means that the methods scholars use to ask questions and compare data avoid inquiring into the truth of what the insider claims.

Agnosticism, Atheism, and Methodological Agnosticism

Before anyone enters the debate on the requirements and potential benefits of methodological agnosticism, it is worthwhile first to examine agnosticism itself. Although they are *not* to be confused, the term methodological agnosticism owes much to Thomas H. Huxley's (1825–1895) arguments concerning the limits of what is and what is not knowable. Using the limits of human perception and reason as his criteria, Huxley argues in a vein we can trace back at least to Hume and the German philosopher Immanuel Kant: from Hume he gathers that all knowledge based on past experiences is necessarily limited and uncertain (inductively based knowledge cannot predict the future with any certainty); from Kant he gathers that because the very tools with which we apprehend the world around us are of our own making, then we have little access to things as they *really might be*.

In the appendix to his book, *The Sacred Canopy* (1967), the sociologist Peter Berger argued for a position he termed methodological atheism, implying that we must "bracket the ultimate status [or truth] of religious definitions of reality." For the sociologist, religion is, by definition, a human projection; whether or not that is what it ultimately turns out to be is not the question. In Berger's words, the sociological, or for that matter the political or the psychological, perspective "can have nothing to say about the possibility that this projection may refer to something other than the being of its projector." There may be a god, there may not, but this is not what interests the sociologist. The scholar is therefore neither an insider nor an outsider but is, instead, in the middle and interested not in determining the truth of anyone's claims but in describing and comparing them accurately.

The scholar of religion Ninian Smart took issue with Berger's name for this position, insisting that the scholar is hardly a methodological atheist (using methods that presume that the gods do not exist). Instead, he refined this methodological stance and renamed it methodological agnosticism—a stance that avoids any and all stands on issues of knowledge (from the Greek *gnosis*, meaning a particular type of knowledge about mysteries). In the fourth chapter of his book, *The Science of Religion and the Sociology of Knowledge* (1973), Smart outlined the manner in which Berger's own approach was "subtly influenced by a particular metaphysic which he holds but which needs separate argumentation." Not knowing how the universe really is organized—not knowing if it is organized at all—the scholar of religion seeks not to establish a position in response to this question but to describe, analyze, and compare the positions taken by others.

In the sixth chapter to this same book, significantly entitled "Within and Without Religion," Smart provides an example of methodologically agnostic description where one brackets out all truth claims (using the phenomenological method). In fact, Smart has remarked that in his own lectures, where he routinely uses an overhead projector, he will often make outsider claims from one side of the projector and, from the other side, will engage in insider discourses, moving freely back and forth but *always* being sure to identify for his students the position from which he is speaking. In this particular essay, Smart uses phenomenological description followed by comparison to help understand the Buddhist doctrine of the Three Bodies of the Buddha—a doctrine that has some similarities to, yet many differences from, the Christian notion of the Trinity. Smart's interest is not to explain this belief system as a product of social or economic forces but to take it as a given and to understand it from within, all the while suspending critical judgments concerning whether it is true or false, right or wrong.

What does It Mean to be Neutral?

After looking at Smart's example of a neutral, comparative study of a religious doctrine, it may help to do some thinking about just what it means to be neutral. Peter Donovan's essay, "Neutrality in Religious Studies," poses the simple question: What sense does it make to declare one's neutrality in advance of studying an actual case? Could not such a blanket declaration, made before one has an indication of what this neutrality might involve and just what one might have to bracket out, simply be a "piece of methodological rhetoric rather than a coherent position?" Donovan proposes that the issue of neutrality is a complex one and that there are in fact a variety of types of neutrality, each appropriate to particular situations. He not only helps to clarify just what we might mean to say that scholars of religion must be impartial and disinterested, but also sketches some of the possible limitations of such claims. In doing so, he implicitly introduces readers to the two authors who follow him in our collection: Peter Byrne and Donald Wiebe.

The Problems of Unity, Uniqueness, and Naturalism

As was seen in two prior parts, where some scholars have solved the insider/outsider problem by trying to reproduce the insider's position, others have opted to develop nonreligious, outsider categories of analysis. In the case of the former, religion is presumed to be unique and one of a kind (i.e., it is *sui generis*); in the case of the latter it is presumed to be no different from other aspects of human institutions (i.e., it is reduced). And in both cases all instances of religion are generally presumed to arise from one common origin, whether it is an experience of the numinous (Otto), an experience of the sacred (Eliade), fears and anxiety (Hume), or a sense of alienation (Marx).

Given the viewpoint of a methodologically agnostic scholar, we would question exactly *how* it is that these scholars *know* that all religious practices, narratives, beliefs, and institutions share a common core or basis—whether that basis is religious *or* nonreligious. Can we defend attempts to find in all religious expressions a common origin? Can we defend the attempt to reduce or not reduce? Precisely what is entailed in such attempts? Do they venture over the line of neutrality?

In his paper, Peter Byrne brings just these questions to light. Byrne critiques reductionists who presume the need for naturalistic explanations. He argues that in order for it truly to be neutral, the study of religion must avoid claiming that religion *ought* to be reduced. If anything, Byrne writes, the "notion that religions are masking institutions [i.e., institutions that disguise other more fundamental issues] is to be proved ... on a case to case basis" rather than, as the reductionists suggest, presumed from the outset of one's work. Such a presumption is based on a stance that supposedly neutral scholars might not be capable of defending.

The Failure of Nerve

Because Byrne critiques the stance of such scholars as Donald Wiebe, it is only natural that an example of Wiebe's work will follow Byrne's essay. Wiebe is well known to those who are interested in debating the relationship between the study of religion and theology (most often understood as Christian theology). Where some scholars see these two enterprises as complementing each other, Wiebe represents a group that finds in theology the data that scholars of religion try to explain by using one or more theoretical frameworks derived from such fields as psychology, sociology, or economics. Therefore, unlike Mircea Eliade, and like Robert Segal, Wiebe is a good example of a social scientific, reductionist scholar of religion. Given that Wiebe's doctoral supervisor at Lancaster University in England was Ninian Smart, this might strike some as odd. However, perceptive readers will have seen in Smart's essay that despite his obvious commitment to developing a fair and descriptively accurate understanding of religion on its own terms, there is also an interest in developing explanations of religious phenomena. It is in his efforts to argue that such explanations also have a place in the field that Wiebe has made his contribution to the study of religion.

In what promises to become a classic essay in the field, Wiebe examined the ways in which the academic study of religion, which originally developed from a theologically motivated study of "other" religions, sometimes reverts back to a form of insider scholarship. The very title of that essay, "The Failure of Nerve in the Academic Study of Religion" (*Studies in Religion* 13/4 [1984]: 401–422), should make it more than clear that Wiebe sees attempts to recover this complementary relationship as a "failure of nerve." Scholars, he argues, have sometimes failed to recognize the significance of the early gains made by such nineteenth-century scholars as F. Max Müller (1823–1900) and Cornelius P. Tiele (1830–1902) who founded the *science* of religion that could be distinguished from the *practice* of religion. Besides arguing for the development of a nonreligious study of religion, Wiebe's essay is an exhaustive analysis of the developments and literature which comprise the history of the field.

In his subsequent commentary on the debate Wiebe's paper sparked in the Canadian journal *Studies in Religion*, the Dartmouth scholar Hans Penner has suggested that methodological agnostics, on the one hand, and scientists of religion, on the other, are actually talking on very different levels: much like Smart, the former begins with religious experience as a given and attempts to study its expressions or manifestations; the latter represents an effort to develop a theory as to *why* it is that people even talk about religious experiences in the first place. "All I am claiming," writes Penner, "is that if we wish to establish a science of religion, then we must begin by acknowledging that such experiences do not provide their own explanation." Accordingly, when comparing theologians and scholars of religion, Penner concludes, they "are simply not talking about the same thing, that's all." However, in his agreement with Wiebe's position, Penner actually pushes beyond Wiebe's critique in "Failure of Nerve": there never has been a failure of nerve, Penner maintains, for there never was any nerve to begin with! The very use of the *epoché* (the methodological device used by many scholars of religion to "bracket out" questions of truth) confirms that a theological intention has always been disguised within the science of religion ever since its origins in the nineteenth century. What we have in Penner's commentary, then, is a resounding criticism of methodological agnosticism.

The essay reproduced here is one of Wiebe's earlier papers which is a direct response to Alasdair MacIntyre's essay that appeared in the first part. As readers will recall, MacIntyre thought that there was an insurmountable gap between sceptics and believers. If one has an interest in developing theories and explanations of religious behaviors and beliefs, then clearly MacIntyre's conclusion would be troubling, for it would prevent studying religion and would simply promote either practicing it or not understanding it whatsoever. Much as Joachim Wach suggested, one would have to be it to understand it. However, given his understanding of the contributions Immanuel Kant made to such issues, Wiebe argues that MacIntyre's essay fails to present an accurate picture of what it means for a sceptic to "understand" the claims and actions of a believer. Contrary to MacIntyre and Wach, then, Wiebe argues that one does not have to have religious understanding to understand—and eventually to explain—religion.

The Scholar of "Religion" in the Classroom

Martin Jaffee ends this chapter with his frank, engaging, and sophisticated look at the religious studies classroom. Despite the importance of the scholarly debates already discussed in this volume, the strength of the field is directly related to what goes on in our classrooms—something not lost on Jaffee. Often, religious studies classrooms are sites where so-called exotic facts and details of "other" human cultures are listed in a show-and-tell manner, as if everyone involved knew these facts to be self-evidently meaningful and important. Such classes often fulfill general education or world culture requirements of the undergraduate curriculum. Jaffee's understanding of our job as teachers and the role of the religious studies class in a university education far surpasses this simple show-and-tell model; despite constantly confronting the insider/outsider problem in his classes, he goes beyond it to suggest that religion is actually a theoretical category or tool that we as scholars and teachers have developed for specific purposes. In many ways, then, his essay as well as his classes are concerned with "religion" rather than religion, suggesting that in the midst of studying so-called alien religious facts, a study that rightly prompts us to make a decision on the insider/outsider problem, there lie a number of sophisticated and often overlooked theoretical questions that must be brought to the student's attention. As Wiebe phrases it at the close of his essay, "'religion' is a primitive [or, better put, indigenous] concept"; it is an insider category used by populations whose languages are indebted to Latin (e.g., English, French or German). However, it is hardly a concept shared by all groups we study. Accordingly, students need to realize that both the concept and that to which it generally refers in the social world (most often simply understood as belief in god[s]) should not be taken for granted. The religious studies classroom, then, is one of the central sites where students can begin to understand the role played by theories in all academic pursuits.

15

NINIAN SMART, *Within and Without Religion*

৵৵

Although, hitherto I have been treating phenomenology chiefly in terms of description—that is, as a method of eliciting and evoking the meaning of religious beliefs and practices from the point of those who take part in them—this does not imply that the scientific study of religion should neglect explanations. Indeed, one main point of describing matters accurately and sensitively is that they can then be explained, or can help to explain other matters without doing so at too cheap a price. For only a small price is paid by those explanations which already are half-contained in descriptions of the data that they are supposed to explain. But if we are to contemplate explanations in religion, we must immediately consider how far it is possible to talk of *religious* explanations.

By "religious explanations" I do not mean theological or buddhological ones. If someone ascribes an event in his life to the operation of Providence, he is offering theological explanation. Again, if someone ascribes his progress in the life of holiness to the inspiration of the Buddha, he is offering a buddhological explanation. There is a sense in which the theological or buddhological explanation might turn into a phenomenological one, for we might hold that, in looking at it from the point of view of the believer, there is actual descriptive truth in the dynamic effect of the Focus upon his life. So there may be often a match between a phenomenological and a theological explanation. However, in speaking of *religious* explanations, I refer rather to the way in which particular or general features of religion explain other features both of religion, itself and/or of something contained within another aspect of human existence. This idea is bound up with the notion of the autonomy of religion, a notion which has tended to animate and legitimate the practice of *Religionswissenschaft* as a separate and independent discipline. This idea of autonomy was, for example, prominent in the thinking of Joachim Wach, and I would expect that most practitioners of the phenomenology of religion would adopt a similar stance. Those who believe in religion as a discipline are, perhaps, inclined to think that there is a religious logic as it were, just as students of politics look to a logic of politics, or perhaps to many logics, that is different patterns through which political action works itself out, political institutions change, political calculations reflect games theory, and so on. I am not here using the word "logic" with any precision at all. I am thinking of the patterns by which forces interact. How are we to describe such patterns of interaction, if they indeed exist in the required way so that we can talk of religious explanations? In particular, let us attempt to see if we can speak of intra-religious explanations, where one factor explains another. We also need to think of the possibility of extra-religious explanations, ones where there is a religious explanation of something not *prima facie* a religious state of affairs.

The idea of religious explanations is entangled with the question of the definition of religion, which as we have seen cannot be utterly precise. There is no sharp boundary between religion and non-religion. The definition of religion which I expressed in the first chapter is shot through with key terms, which themselves are vague in application.[1] But I do not see that this fact need cause serious disquiet. We do not abandon the project of studying cities on the grounds that you can't really tell where a city ends, and where the countryside begins. Nor do we abandon French studies, though parts of Switzerland and Alsace are ambiguously French in culture. Nor do we reject political science because there are aspects of human behavior, such as belonging to a club, that may be ambiguously political. So we should not be depressed by the impossibility of providing an absolutely sharp and clear-cut definition of religion. But note that in all these cases, despite the vagueness of the concepts, their shadiness on the edges, it is possible to find the unambiguous example. Nobody would say that Manhattan is rural, or that Ben Nevis is urban. Likewise, no one would say that a priest's saying mass is a secular activity, or that the Empire State Building is a sacred edifice.

(I hasten to add, since someone is bound to make the point, that there is a possible utterance that the Empire State Building is sacred to "the forces of American capitalism" which does appear to ascribe sacredness to the skyscraper. But this is sacredness in a secondary or metaphorical sense....)

As an example of an intra-religious explanation I offer an instance drawn from the field of Buddhism, but I shall add rather briefly some remarks about the Trinity doctrine in Christianity in order to provide some Western balance. The doctrine of Three Bodies of the Buddha, known as the *trikāya*, has not received a full and historical treatment, so far as I know, and some of the history of its evaluation needs to be worked out in detail. This lack of a full treatment is itself an indication of the large areas of investigation that remain only partially explored in the field of Buddhist studies. Partly for this reason I shall present the doctrine somewhat unhistorically. I do not think that this matters over-much, because in trying to give a religious explanation I shall be drawing attention to certain forces (so to speak) operative in the system which work themselves out historically and yet also structurally.

Briefly, the Three Body doctrine amounts to the following ideas. First, the Buddha is considered on three levels (I use the locution "the Buddha" though, as will be seen, this can land us in inaccuracies owing to the plurality of Buddhas at two of the levels represented by the doctrine). The most earthly of these levels is that of the "Transformation-Body" (*nirmānakāya*)—namely the form in which the historical (or any other Buddha) appears on earth (the notion that other Buddhas too appear on earth is of great significance for various purposes but perhaps can be neglected in the present discussion). At the next level, the Buddhas possess a type of body known as the *sambhogakāya*. In this form they appear as, gods, that is as celestial beings, who are worshiped and who have limited creative functions (through their capacity to emanate Buddha-fields). Finally, all Buddhas are united in the *dharmakāya*, which is in effect identical with the Absolute, variously described as Tathatā (suchness) and as the Void (*śunyatā*). In the *dharmakāya*, all Buddhas, are united. In addition to the above arrangements of Buddhahood at different levels, an important role is played by celestial Bodhisattvas, such as Avalokiteśvara. I shall on the whole treat these on a par with celestial Buddhas, such as Amitābha. We should also note that a two-decker theory of truth characterizes the systematic theology (or systematic buddhology) of which the Three Body doctrine is a part. Thus, the Void is at one level, the higher, and here all conventional distinctions of language disappear, while the lower level of truth covers both earthly and celestial realms. This in brief is the ambience and structure of the doctrine.

Despite the fact that its history remains incomplete, the doctrine is clearly the result of an attempt to synthesize and systemize some important elements in Mahāyāna Buddhism. I want to consider how it can be explained by reference to religious experience, practice, and ritual. In other words, one element or one group of elements in a structure is here being explained by other elements in the structure. To some extent my account follows the sketch given in my paper "The Work of the Buddha and the Work of Christ" in S. G. F. Brandon (ed.), *The Savior God*.

One problem about the Three Body doctrine is that it is not present in Theravāda Buddhism. So it enters into that perennial debate about the nature of original Buddhism. But I think it is reasonable to hold that the worship of celestial Buddhas does represent the culmination of a development out of early Buddhism and to some extent other forces. I do not in general consider it necessary to point to outside influences to explain the growth of Buddhist *bhakti* [ritual devotion to a deity also practiced in Hinduism] although such influences do exist—for example in Romano-Greek iconography in North West India and Zoroastrianism, not to mention the continued and developing Hindu environment in which Buddhism had its Indian being. But we must note one very significant fact: it is primarily to the celestial Buddhas, and Bodhisattvas, that the sentiment of *bhakti* is directed, ritually expressed as *puja*. Though the idea of *bhakti* is not entirely absent from the Pāli Canon, it nevertheless is not possible to speak in any strong sense of devotion to the Buddha involving worship. This is because of the inappropriateness of speaking of the Buddha as existing out there or anywhere to be a recipient of *bhakti* and so enter into relationship with the worshiper. Thus, the growth of celestial Buddhas and Bodhisattvas parallels a growth in the importance of the attitude of *bhakti* in the Māhāyana tradition. In a word, the Māhāyana is so far Therāvada Buddhism plus *bhakti*.

Let us turn now to examine the *dharmakāya*. Note that the *dharma* [the teaching, truth, or power of the Buddha's teachings] is made to have a sort of substantive existence. It is more like an entity than, say, a set of teachings. One of the reasons for this has to do with the doctrine of meaning (*artha*): that the meaning of a term is tied to what it refers. The *dharma*, as a set of teachings, that is as a set of propositions both descriptive and normative, points to something transcendental which can be called also the *dharma*. Thus in that well-known Eastern image, the finger points at the moon, and people should look at the moon rather than at the finger. The true *dharma* is, so to say, something concrete and not just the words of the Buddha. By extension, the same principle can be applied to the Lotus Sutra, so that in understanding a verse of it one can grasp the reality to which the Sutra is pointing. There is, incidentally, a similarity in structure with the Christian notion of the Word: in much modern theology the Word is what the words point to, and preaching the Word is more than preaching words—it is presenting, recreating as it were, the reality, Christ, and making him real to the hearer. Anyway, the *dharma* is concretized in a sense. It is what the words of the Buddha point to. It is thus in some way liberation, for the Buddha's message is a liberating one. It is identical with nirvana. Note that a difference has come over the latter concept, compared with its usage in the Pāli Canon. For in the latter it is not sensible to speak of nirvana as a single entity. On the other hand, in the Māhāyana texts, it increasingly comes, to look like the Absolute—indeed to become identified with it.

This is part, at least, of the secret of the mysterious identification of nirvana with *samsāra*—the identification of transcendent liberation with the stream of everyday existence. From one point of view, this identification justifies and expresses a lay ideology. For if liberation and immersion in the world are somehow not to be kept apart, then the layman can find liberation in the midst of his daily activity and without leaving the world in order to become a monk. We swim in a sea of nirvana and our trouble is merely that we do not recognize this. But the fact that the identification expresses a lay ideology is only one part of the secret. A middle term helps to explain the nirvana-*samsāra* identity. That middle term is the Void, the Absolute itself. This Emptiness pervades everything, being the shadowy and unsubstantial essence of everything. It expresses the phantasmagorical and shifting nature of the world and of living beings; it undermines substances, hollowing them out, leaving them in a state of ontological collapse. Thus we may put concretely what can also be put at the level of language. For, according to Māhāyana doctrine, our ordinary language is merely conventional and does not express the higher truth, so that, from the higher point of view, it is misleading and destroying. We are tricked by the illusions of language into ascribing permanence to things and substance to ourselves. The reality of the world is a magical web spun by concepts, but the concepts themselves are vitiated. So one function of the Void is to show the true nature of things, namely their being empty and hollow. But the Void expresses something else as well (and this aspect of it is indeed present in Theravāda Buddhism also). This second function is to express the blankness ... of the ultimate experience which liberates us or at least is central to the higher religion of the contemplative life. In saying that the experience is blank I am not implying that it is boring or worthless or even that it has no content whatsoever. A slight excursion on this point is worthwhile.

The higher sort of contemplative experience is unusual and refined in that it does not involve discursive thoughts and images. It does not involve my thinking of the battle of Gettysburg or of the Matterhorn. It does not involve working out a problem in mathematics or thinking about what should be done tomorrow. It does not even involve my thinking of celestial Buddhas in all their heavenly glory. The usual way of delineating inner experiences does not apply. But to say that negative thing is also to say something positive, for, in the experience, one is awake, and yet there is the absence of the usual workings of the mind. In addition the experience has considerable effects and can be contrasted in retrospect with the ordinary states of consciousness. I have here tended to speak of "the" experience, which is a way of simplifying the issue, for there are various stages of transcendental contemplation, such as the *dhyānas*.

I have said that one function of the idea of the Void is to express the dazzling blankness of the experience. This experience is also looked at as being non-dual (*advaya*). Thus it works on two fronts, and, like a number of other concepts in religious systems, it is a synthesizing force. Because nirvana is identified with the Void, for it is the experience of the Void that brings one to see the true nature of things and to attain liberation, there is also a sense in which nirvana is the hollowness itself which pervades empirical objects. It is, so to say, the same as *samsāra*, for *samsāra* is the flux in which we find ourselves. Because the Void is everything, it is the true nature of *samsāra*. Because nirvana is the Void, nirvana is *samsāra*. The chain of identities has a certain logic.

The Void is important in another way, and matches something important in Buddhas. All schools of Buddhism would agree that there is some transcendent aspect of the Buddha. This is why indeed he is compared to the rhinoceros, for that beast leaves no tracks as it wallows through the muddy water. Likewise birds are trackless, and Buddhas are so by analogy for there is something elusive about them. This elusiveness is clearly connected with Enlightenment, a state of consciousness which lifts the Buddha beyond ordinary mortals and so beyond their understanding. And somehow in his Enlightenment he gains a transcendental wisdom which enables him to preach and renew the *dharma*. When this idea of Enlightenment is placed in the context of the doctrine of the Void, then clearly this higher state of the Buddha will be interpreted as being the non-dual experience of the Absolute. In this non-duality the Buddha participates in the Void. To explain this, let me digress for the moment.

To say that the experience is non-dual might be just a way of saying that, in it, one has no consciousness of a distinction between oneself and the object of the experience. There is subject-object distinction. Thus the experience is not like seeing the dahlia [a type of plant], where one distinguishes between the dahlia and oneself, nor is it like imagining the Matterhorn, where again the object, namely the Matterhorn, is conceived as distinct from oneself. But something more significant is being implied in speaking of the experience as non-dual, as is also the case in the use of the term *advaita* in Śankara's system.[2] It is implied that there is an other which is yet no other. There is something to be identical with, to be non-dual with. The experience of *nibbāna* in the Pāli Canon is not described as non-dual; there is no call to do so for there is no Absolute to be united with, or to perceive one's union with. Thus *advaita* has a double force. The fact that there is no subject-object relationship perceived in the experience, the first aspect of its meaning, is one ground for affirming a kind of union or identification that is the second aspect of its meaning.

It may be complained that I am falling into the trap of reifying the Absolute. Surely, it will be said, the whole force of talking about Emptiness is to bring out the non-substantiality, the un-thing-ness of the so-called Absolute, and yet here am I speaking of the non-dual experience of the Absolute as though it is there somehow to be a state of non-duality with. On the other hand, the function of Suchness and the Void corresponds to that of the Absolute in Śankara's system and has analogies elsewhere. More decisively, the fact that it is identified with the Truth Body of the Buddha gives it some degree of reification in the Buddhist tradition itself. Also, if it is thought of as something which transcends substances, it retains the flavor thereof—or in other words, it is more appropriate to look upon the Void as a substance which is not a substance than to look upon it as a relation which is not a relation or a property which is not a property.

We may now see the way in which the Buddha participates in the Void. The Buddha in his Enlightenment achieves the realization of his identity with the Absolute, and this remark applies not merely to Gautama and to other earthly Buddhas but indeed to all Buddhas, of whom there are clouds in the later Mahā yāna tradition. This being so, in essence all Buddhas are identical. Buddha A is identical with the Void, Buddha B is identical with the Void. Hence Buddha A is identical with Buddha B. Or to put it another way, there is only one Truth Body or aspect for all the Buddhas, even though they be innumerable. Thus the Body, though he may phenomenalize himself as the Tathāgata [the title that Gautama, the Buddha, is reported to have given himself, meaning: Thus gone one, Thus come one], and so be a person at the lower level of his existence, in his transcendental aspect is non-personal, the Void. This fact must modify the emphasis on *bhakti* noted earlier in relation to the celestial Buddhas, and it also, as we shall see, makes some difference to moral actions and attitudes.

That the Buddha is not personal in his highest essence obviously places some restriction upon the ultimate significance of devotion. If the Tathāgata in his secret inner essence is not a person, then there cannot be a transaction between him and the devotee. I do not claim that all Mahāyāna schools take up this position: clearly the highly devotional Pure Land schools, especially in Japan, look upon personhood and compassion as being at the heart of Buddhahood, so that a Buddha in his form as Amida is a gracious, living, and powerful object of devotion. So much so is this the case that the theology of the Pure Land has analogies to that of Reformation Christianity, in stressing the whole idea of salvation by faith rather than by works and in offering a critique of monasticism on this very basis. I am thinking, then, in this analysis of the Three Body doctrine not of the highly devotional developments in the Mahāyāna, but rather of the classical doctrine as propounded in the milieu in which the Mādhyamika philosophy had its rise.[3] Incidentally, this philosophy was not just analytic and intellectual, though it was those things, but it was in addition a dialectic exercise in the service of spiritual progress. The dialectic which destroys all theories of existence as being incoherent, to pave the way for the doctrine of the Void, is existential. One is reminded of the story about Wittgenstein: when asked by Russell, on an occasion when Wittgenstein was sitting thinking in a depressed and gloomy way, "Are you thinking about your sins or about logic?" he replied "Both."

So then, in the classical phase of Mahāyāna doctrine, a restriction is placed upon the ultimate importance of *bhakti*. *Bhakti* does not penetrate to the heart of Buddhahood. What then does? The attainment of Buddhahood, so that the path which gets one to this is the path of the Bodhisattva, of the Buddha-to-be. Everyone can be a Buddha-to-be. No wonder the Buddhas abound as numerously as the grains of sand along the Ganges. Ultimately the Buddha's path takes him through the higher stages of contemplation, and in this Buddhism remains true to its essence, for both the classical Mahāyāna and the Theravāda emphasize centrally the contemplative life through which one gains mystical knowledge of the nature of reality together with serenity and so ultimately liberation. To put it crudely and briefly: contemplation rates above *bhakti*. *Bhakti* stops short of the highest priority. This arrangement of values of religious experience and practice is also expressed through the two-level theory of truth, to which reference has already been made. For at the conventional and lower level, men take the world for practical purposes as real, and so likewise they look upon the celestial Buddhas as in effect substantial deities who may assist them in their progress. But, at the higher level, even they disappear in the dazzling blankness of the experience of the Void. Nirvana is set beyond and above heaven. Of course, not surprisingly, the heavenly realm could come to displace nirvana in the hopes and affections of the majority of folk, so that the Pure Land becomes the real goal of salvation, even if in theory it is only a propitious location for the attainment of nirvana and so for ultimate disappearance from even the most refined celestial abode. There remains, then, a symmetry between the Mahāyāna and the Theravāda. For both these religions there is, in the last resort, no worship of the Buddha. If in the case of the Theravāda there is strictly speaking no *bhakti* toward the Buddha, in the Mahāyāna there is devotion to the celestial ones. For the one tradition, *bhakti* has had only indirect effects, such as influencing it to adopt the cult of images; for the other tradition, *bhakti* has been of profound, though not of ultimate, significance.

Finally, let us look at the Transformation Body of the earthly Buddha. This is the historical anchorage of the faith, though ultimately it shares in the non-substantial and even illusory nature of all things. That there has to be some body of the Buddha at the lower level is unproblematic, but what is surprising is the degree to which the celestial Buddhas come to replace the historical Gautama and his predecessors "in the religious" imagination. This means a change in the concept of salvation. On the one hand, for the Theravāda, the Buddha is savior centrally through his teaching; he is a preceptor who leads men by his example and by his words, rather than directly by saving action. For this reason it is claimed in a famous passage (possibly later and in reply to esoteric tendencies at the beginning of the development of Mahāyāna Buddhism) that the Tathāgata does not have the closed fist of the teacher, who holds some things back in order to retain his superiority and even possibly his job. This means that the Buddha displays to men the truth and the means of attaining liberation, and it is for them to follow this teaching by their own efforts. This is very different from the classical idea of heaven in Christianity, for here Christ saves men by his self-sacrifice upon the Cross. Likewise for the classical Mahāyāna the sacrifices of Bodhisattvas in their immensely long path to Buddhahood become the agency of saving, for the merit acquired by these compassionate works can be transferred to the faithful, if they but call on the name of the Buddha in faith. This is only a sort of salvation, for it takes place only in the Pure Land of the West, which remains ontologically inferior to the final goal of nirvana. We may note how neatly this locks together the moral life and the devotion. The loving adoration recognizes the mercy and compassion of the Buddhas and of the Bodhisattvas, who put off their own salvation for the sake of all those who suffer in *samsāra*. The faithful are thus encouraged in the imitation of this heroic compassion. But lo, in the imitation of the Buddha, one is setting oneself on the path to becoming a Buddha, one takes the vows of the Bodhisattva. And even more amazingly apt, in worshiping the Buddhas above, one is worshiping what is in essence one's own future state. There ultimately worship is overcome, for one cannot worship oneself (despite the unkind definition of the Englishman as a self-made man who worships his maker). The whole system therefore integrates morality into the two-decker universe of piety and contemplation. There is thus the remarkable beauty in the logic of the classical Mahāyāna, a logic which comes into existence on the basis of an infusion of *bhakti* religion into the Buddhist system.

I shall now consider the religious factors which have been used in the explanation of the Three Body doctrine. We are not yet concerned with why Mahāyāna Buddhism should have been attractive—why it spread as well as it did into Chinese, Korean, and Japanese cultures. First, I have used the distinction between the contemplative experience and the contrasted *bhakti* experience. Thus the Buddhas who suffuse the world with their celestial dazzling light are numinous and other, and, as we have seen, they disappear or sometimes indeed never appear in the consciousness of the contemplative. This distinction can be attested in a large number of religious contexts, but this does not mean that there are no religious movements, practices, and beliefs which combine the two types and let the other as it were interpret the other. For example, in the life of the medieval monastic orders worship and devotion, not to mention sacramental ritual, were combined with meditation in such a way that the highest object of contemplation was considered to be God. I do not wish here to establish in detail the distinction, and to this extent it needs to be taken on trust. There is little evidence that these types of experience are projections in the sense required by Berger and other social theorists. Rather it looks as though up to a point they can be regarded as facts of human existence. I say "up to a point," for it does appear that some social traditions and some historical epoch are more to their appearance than others. Thus mysticism flourished more in medieval Christendom than it did in the nineteenth century, and more in the 1970s than in the 1930s. So, I have tried to explain Mahāyāna doctrine in terms of the interplay between and the relative values of these two types of experience, arguing that in the classical Mahāyāna contemplation ultimately rates higher than *bhakti*, even if *bhakti* contributes a strong development to the buddhology.

Second, in doing this, I have appealed to the respective internal structures of the two kinds, of experience and attitude, namely to the undifferentiated quality of the contemplative experience and the polarity of the numinous and of devotion. The subject-object character of *bhakti* means that the Buddhas as gods are "over there" or "up there," but there is no such quasi-spatial contrast in the experience of the Void. I have, however, suggested that the very idea of non-duality implies the idea of something to be identified or united with. This means that, in describing the highest experience as *advaya*, the Mahāyāna builds in some interpretation. Hence, I have used the phenomenological structures as the basis for explaining some features of doctrine.

Third, I have attempted to indicate the way in which the central ethical value of Buddhism—compassion—is integrated into the scheme and indeed may be thought to encourage it, since the scheme is so effective in tying together the moral and religious values which could all too easily fall apart. It is thus significant that a major criticism of Theravāda and more generally Lesser Vehicle Buddhism was the split between the need for compassion and the theory of liberation through a kind of cool self-sufficiency.

Fourth, I have implied that the reason for the elevation of the Truth Body over the other two, and the related idea of two levels of truth, is a consequence of the desire to safeguard the position of the contemplative life as the commanding height of the Buddhist system, both in the Theravāda and in the Mahāyāna. I am not denying that there are explanations and that the order of priority sometimes become reversed, so that one gets a structure not at all dissimilar to that encountered in the *Bhagavadgītā*, where devotion and a personal Lord are the dominant themes, and ultimately the contemplative life is treated as subordinate.

So, then, I have made appeal to religious experience and practice. In this manner one feature of the system is explained in terms of other features of it, and in a way which could be made more general. One can apply a similar analysis to other schemes of belief. Still, some questions remain unanswered.

First of all, why does Buddhism take the contemplative life to be the commanding height of the tradition? The answer is doubtless in a rather brute way historical, namely that Buddhism rose out of a milieu which stressed yoga and contemplative techniques. One can supplement this by pointing to the tension existing between Brahmanism and the various mendicant groups which served as a background to the rise of early Buddhism. One can also remember that the region in which Buddhism rose and flourished was experiencing something of a social and economic revolution in a context where the culture was but imperfectly Sanskritized. Also of some importance historically was a modified opposition to the system of classes (*varnas*).

Next, why is it that, if the dominant theme of Buddhism was from its early days that through contemplative techniques and certain forms of moral behavior one could attain an understanding of the world that would bring about liberation, *bhakti* should have entered into the system so resolutely? Why does *bhakti* arise anywhere? Why did it flourish so well in the Tamil country before and during the time of Ramanuja? Why was devotion and a religion of grace so strong in the Reformation? Why did it flourish in medieval Japan? These are hard questions. I suppose one can hint at an answer, such as that *bhakti* is in an important way egalitarian, or at least perceived to be by the devotees, because all men are equally low when confronted by the adored god.

This would partly explain the appeal of *bhakti*, and one would suppose that, like certain germs, *bhakti* is in a small way latent everywhere where you find religion.

The third question is why Mahāyāna Buddhism sees the Absolute in a quasi-substantive, and yet impersonal, manner. That is, why should the injection of *bhakti* into the system have favored the doctrine of a higher reality, to the heart of which, nevertheless, *bhakti* could not penetrate? One can hazard a theory here (a theory of which I have made use both in *Reasons and Faiths* and in *The Yogi and the Devotee*). We should consider first of all what kind of theology we might expect where bhakti and devotion are the dominant spiritual motifs. We naturally look to the *Gītā*, Rāmānuja, and to Śaiva Siddhānta. In all these systems the supreme entity is treated in a very personal manner. God is a person who responds to men's faith and devotion. The stronger the devotional sentiment, the more exalted is the divine being and the more he operates by grace and favor. The more this is so, the more likely it is that the devotee will praise God for his love and compassion in bestowing grace upon those who are unworthy and unholy. However, the main point is that, in devotional religion, ultimate reality becomes highly personal. It should also be noted that there is a drift toward a unified conception of the Godhead where there is more than one god to be worshiped, as can be seen in classical Hinduism and in the synthetic coming-together of the religions of Visnu and Śiva. Consider the opposite of this situation, where *bhakti* devotionalism is virtually absent, as in early Jainism among the Ājīvikas and in the Buddhism of the Pāli Canon. There is no denial of the gods in these systems, but they are relatively unimportant, and in Buddhism they are bent and hollowed out to serve Buddhist purposes. But there is no recommendation in the Canon of devotion toward gods, and they cannot bring salvation. Moreover, the rituals of sacrifice are useless spiritually. There is not in such a system of belief a united divine being to be worshiped. The closest that one comes to an Absolute is the *dharma*. Suppose at this juncture that there is a drive to incorporate *bhakti* into a faith which is essentially oriented to the contemplative life and liberation. Then the theology becomes one where a non-personal Absolute takes on personhood at the interface with the worshiper, but not in its own inner being. Why is there belief in such a non-personal Absolute? First, the dazzling blankness of the mystical experience does not contain a personal object. Second, since a personal God who is to be worshiped in the spirit of devotion is represented as a being rather than as an event or state, what transcends the personal God is also represented in the same way, as a sort of substance. Third, strong devotionalism, as we have seen, is liable to lead to a unification of the gods through the elevation of one divine being to the supreme position and the assimilation of the other divine beings to him, so that they appear as lower manifestations of him or even sometimes disappear altogether. It is interesting to note, in this connection, that where two such movements have occurred leading to two great gods, they themselves become identified with one another as alternative manifestations of the same personal reality as has occurred in the Indian tradition in relation to Visnu and Śiva. We may therefore hypothesize that a strong injection of devotion into a religion, even when that religion is dominated by the contemplative life, will result in some doctrine of a unified but impersonal Absolute transcending and lying beyond the God of *bhakti*. The Absolute transcends the God, reflecting the higher evaluation placed on mystical liberation over against devotional reliance. Naturally this hypothesis is here crudely and simply put, and the pattern which it describes is in practice embroidered with many other particular, historical factors and complication—for example, sacramental ritual may itself favor the impersonal aspect, as happened in the Upanishads, insofar as the ritual power *brahman* came to be seen as the force which sustains and develops the universe.

Thus most of the account I have given of the Three Body doctrine is an attempt to explain religious elements by other deeper structures, themselves religious. It is thus that what I have sketched can be counted an intra-religious explanation. But I have also drawn attention to historical explanations which may depend upon factors other than those of religion itself. Thus it is that Buddhism may have spread partly because it is critical of Brahmanism, and opposition to Brahmanism may have been attractive to various social forces, of the time. Again, the fact that there was no pre-existing belief in reincarnation in Chinese culture may have influenced the ways in which certain schools of Buddhism developed there, and, though this would seem to be a religious explanation, it also needs to be geared to a consideration of the social strata of Chinese society and the role of "official" religion among the literati. The Pure Land was a heaven for many Chinese, perhaps because of its strong contrast to the hopes and ideals of the ideology of the ruling classes. In other words, intra-religious explanations become entangled, through historical particularities, with non-religious factors.

The Three Body doctrine, despite its triple character, is not to be compared facilely with the Trinity. If one were to try to explain the latter mysterious doctrine, one would surely have to note the way in which practical and experimental facts about the development of Christianity required something like the doctrine. Thus early Christianity, especially in the form in which it was preached by Paul, rejected a great deal of the legalism of the Jewish tradition out of which Christianity arose, but took up aspects of Jewish pietism. Indeed Jesus' own religion appears to have gone beyond that of contemporary Jews in its very strong personalistic emphasis and the sense of close relationship to God as Father (or, to translate *Abba* more precisely, Dad). Yet, at the same time, early Christianity focused its faith very strongly upon Christ, and insofar as it was a practice of the early church to worship Christ as Lord, then in terms of the Jewish tradition there was a problem to be faced, namely how the worship of the one God was to be reconciled with the apparent worship of Christ as distinct from the Father. The two strands of piety—the latter incidentally strongly influenced by the sacramental character of Christianity, especially in regard to the Lord's Supper—needed to be woven together and brought into harmonious relationship, and this was one of the jobs performed by the doctrine of the Trinity (it also of course attempted to weave in a third strand, to do with the Spirit and the event of Pentecost). In asserting that there are three entities in one substance, the doctrine tried to indicate that there was a sort of identity-in-difference between the Father and Christ and that the worship of Christ did not mean the worship of some god other than the God of Israel. It is in some such way that one would relate Christian practice to Christian theory.

In my attempt at an explanation of the Three Body doctrine, I have from time to time made comparative reference. It gives plausibility to an account if some of its features can be somewhat generalized, so that one looks for and finds similar patterns of thinking and development elsewhere, best of all where the cultures are not historically related. This does not mean that we can formulate universal laws, but it does mean that we can pick out recurring motifs with some degree of confidence. This is somewhat like the explanations we give to human actions by reference to character traits. Thus when we say that it was pride that drove George to commit suicide, we do not imply that all cases of pride or even all cases of the particular sort of pride displayed by George would lead to suicide, but rather that there are some typical sequences and typical recurrences, and that, in terms of these, George's suicide becomes intelligible.

Thus it appears that an implicit cross-cultural appeal is typically being made in any explanation of the sort that I have been contemplating. Similarly where one attempts to explain "secular" developments by religious ones, as has happened most notably in Max Weber's work on the Protestant ethic and the rise of capitalism, there is also in principle a comparative claim; thus should we seek similar factors in Japanese society to explain the successful industrialization of the country and adaptation to a world hitherto dominated by Western technology and capitalism? I am not here denying that one cannot, at some level, simply give historical and narrative explanations from within the confines of a given cultural tradition, but to penetrate deeper into the structure of religious experience, doctrine, and so forth, the checks which are available are cross-cultural ones....

The structural account I have attempted to give concerning the Three Body doctrine is, as I have hinted, relevant to Hindu theology, and for that matter to the theology of Eckhart. This is one of the ways in which the science of religion can hope to be illuminating in its attempts to give religious explanations as well as to categorize religious phenomena and religious entities.....

Notes

1. Ed. note. In the first chapter, Smart defined religion as follows: "A religion, or the religion of a group, is a set of institutionalized rituals identified with a tradition and expressing and/or invoking sacral elements directed at a divine or trans-divine focus seen in the context of the human phenomenological environment and at least partially described by myths or by myths and doctrine" (*The Scientific Study of Religion and the Sociology of Knowledge*, 15).
2. Ed. note. Śankara, born in southern India, remains a highly influential philosopher who lived from the mid to the late eighth century CE. He taught that liberation (*moksha*) from the seemingly endless cycle of rebirths (*samsāra*) was to be achieved through knowing that one's seemingly individual self (*atman*) was none other than the changeless eternal (*brahman*). Such knowledge removes ignorance (*avidya*).
3. Ed. note. Mādhyamika, meaning "The middle," is a school of Mahāyāna philosophy that is traced to Nagarjuna (*c.* 2nd or 3rd CE).

16

PETER DONOVAN, *Neutrality in Religious Studies*

❧❧

"Open-minded," "detached," "objective," "disinterested," "impartial," "non-partisan" and "independent" are terms typically used when Religious Studies seeks to present itself as an academic discipline. Phrases like "methodological agnosticism," "suspension of judgement," and "procedural neutrality" are also found, in attempts to formulate an appropriate methodology. Seldom are those terms and phrases precisely defined, or the differences between them examined. Yet a moment's reflection reveals that they are far from clear or unambiguous, and that if they are to be used at all effectively in this context, more work must be done by way of preliminary analysis and clarification.

In this paper I shall focus on just one of those notions, *neutrality*. I shall seek to clarify it as a concept, and then consider its actual or possible application to our field of study. I shall first propose a definition of neutrality, as follows:

> To be neutral is to stand in relation to two or more parties which are themselves in tension, in such a way that the respective interests of those parties are not thereby materially affected.[1]

When defined in that way, neutrality can be seen to be a relational concept, presupposing a particular kind of context. It does not exist per se or "at large."

Yet surely, it might be observed, it makes sense for a scholar or institution to announce a policy of neutrality in advance of actual cases. Can one not simply declare an intention to be neutral "wherever appropriate"? But where no indication is offered of what will count as being neutral in appropriate cases, and where no criteria for success or failure are given, such promised neutrality runs the risk of being empty of content, a piece of methodological rhetoric rather than a coherent position.

What counts as neutrality, whether neutrality can be achieved, and by what means it may be pursued, are matters to be considered in actual or conceivable contexts, not in general or in the abstract. How the parties stand in relation to one another will largely determine the issue. It follows that a failure by others to achieve neutrality with respect to a particular dispute may have at least as much to do with the character of the dispute in question, as with any limitations on their part (their "not trying hard enough," "having hidden biases," and the like).

Neutrality in areas like the study of religions may be pursued in three distinguishable modes.

Observer-Neutrality

First, there is what I shall call observer-neutrality. This is the position reflected in phrases like "standing on the side-line," "remaining an on-looker," or "being in a position of detachment." Observer-neutrality, it is assumed, represents the stance of the non-involved, who merely describe what they see. No explanation is offered, no evaluation made. The observer contributes nothing to the situation, simply making an accurate record of the facts.

It is widely accepted nowadays (particularly within the human sciences) that such observer-neutrality is in practice impossible for at least the following reasons.

(i)   Any onlooker is limited by his/her own location or point of view, and by his/her own frame of mind. As it is impossible to hold all details of any situation in one's mind together, so to speak, an observer will inevitably make his/her own selection and impose his/her own thought-structures. (We may call this *observer-bias*.)

(ii) An observer, unaware of the significance of the way things are for the parties themselves, may entirely miss the point, however carefully his/her observations are recorded. (This is *observer-incomprehension*.)

(iii) The presence of an onlooker, however neutral his/her intention, may itself alter or distort the facts, by becoming a concern of one or more of the parties and thereby modifying his/her behavior. (This is known as *observer-effect*.)

For those reasons, pure observer-neutrality exists as an ideal only. As a methodological principle, whether in the academic study of religions or anywhere else, it is simply unrealizable.

Participant-Neutrality

The second form of neutrality, which I shall call participant-neutrality, attempts to avoid the limitations of observer-neutrality by taking greater account of the complexities of actual situations. Since there is no question of completely avoiding involvement, the would-be neutral here seeks to balance and adjust his/her participation in such a way as to avoid any material alteration of the balance of interests between the positions in question. Such controlled participation may be informally spoken of as "acting even-handedly," "being all things to all people," or "trying to not unduly affect the outcome one way or the other."

Once again, achieving such an aim, if it is possible, will turn not so much on the intention or efforts of the would-be neutral participant, as on the interests of the parties and the nature of the issues between them. What may seem like impartiality or even-handedness from the participant's point of view may not have anything like a neutral effect for the parties themselves, given their different relative strengths, needs or interests. A practical example makes this clear:

Suppose a number of religious organizations exist on a university campus. One or more of them approach the Religious Studies department seeking permission to place posters on the department's notice-board advertising their various activities. Given that the department has a policy of neutrality in such matters, what are the possible responses it may make?

(i) The department may decide to allow no posters at all unless all organizations are represented. That might be thought to be a form of even-handedness in dealing with the issue.

Will such a response achieve neutrality? That depends on what the parties themselves desire. For some, to be treated equally with other groups will give them the recognition they are seeking. They will consider their interests well served by the policy. For others, however, to be treated as just one religion among many will be the very opposite of what they would want. They will prefer not to display their posters at all, thereby (on this policy) depriving the others of any chance to do so.

(ii) The department may see the limitations of any attempt to offer equal treatment, and adopt instead a policy of equal opportunity, giving each group the chance to display its posters if they so desire, or to refrain if they so choose. Does that achieve neutrality? Knowing, as the department must, that some groups will be more keen than others to take up that offer, it can hardly be a neutral decision simply to allow those groups a free hand. What about the scruples of the others? Achieving neutrality in the sense of equal opportunity, seems to require finding a way to ensure not equal but *equivalent* outcomes. But who can be sure such equivalence is possible, for parties with dissimilar needs or wants?

(iii) Suppose the department calls a meeting of all religious organizations, asking them to agree among themselves as to a policy to govern the use of the notice-board. Again, the department may be presumed to know the likely outcome, the relative numbers and organizational effectiveness of the groups. Is a resort to such "democracy" any guarantee of neutrality, or is it no more than a hand-washing device?

There is a further complication. By whom is the neutrality to be assessed? Is the department's duty simply to satisfy its own assessment of what counts as even-handed participation? Is it the various parties, with their conflicting opinions, who must decide? Or is it somehow the community at large which must make the judgement? A further extension of the example will make this point clearer.

(iv) Suppose the department displays one religion's posters exclusively on its notice-board, and this offends not only rival religious organizations but also the university's Humanist Society, which suspects a breach of the university's official secularity. The department may argue that the posters are displayed simply as examples of that particular religion's iconography; there is no intention to advertise or promote one religion at the expense of others, or indeed to promote religion at all. Such a justification will be unlikely to reassure either the Humanists or the other religious groups. For they are concerned about the wider community's perception of the matter, not simply the department's intentions. University departments, they believe, must be *seen to be neutral*.

We may conclude, then, that participant-neutrality is extraordinarily difficult to achieve, even in quite simple cases. There are no clear criteria for success which can be spelt out in advance. Like purely neutral observation, the idea of neutral participation seems unsuitable for adoption as a methodological principle in Religious Studies, at least without a great deal more work being done to give it content and precision.

Role-Neutrality

If we ask ourselves where clear instances of neutrality in human affairs can be found, a few familiar examples come to mind; the neutrality of a committee chairperson, for instance, a judge or arbitrator in a court or tribunal, or the neutrality of umpires and referees in sporting contests. Neutrality of this kind I shall call role-neutrality. Here we find what seems to be a special kind of participation, in a situation where there is a structure of rules and procedures. Within that structure, would-be neutrals have a defined contribution to make, a role to play. The procedures they are obliged to follow in fulfilment of that role constitute criteria as to their success or failure.

Far from such role-neutrality being merely a special case of neutrality in general, it may indeed turn out to be the paradigm case of neutrality in human affairs. It is here we see what neutrality can amount to in practice, how it becomes possible, by what criteria it is assessed, and so on. Other attempts to achieve neutrality become less clear, less decidable, the further removed they are from the role-neutral paradigm. And as for "neutrality in general," we can see now why it is of doubtful value as a principle. It lacks the apparatus of prior agreement as to procedures for pursuing an acceptable outcome, and indications of what will count as having achieved it.

With cases of role-neutrality like those mentioned, the concept of neutrality remains as in our initial definition. But criteria are provided for the successful application of that concept in particular cases, through the existence of accepted rules and procedures, a recognized role in specific types of situation.

Can we describe anything like a neutral role or roles for academic religious studies and its practitioners? If we can, we will have some indication of what a commitment to neutrality, in the methodology of this discipline, might amount to in fact.

In all familiar cases of role-neutrality we can identify sets of internal standards, codes of conduct, and procedures by which those who exercise the roles monitor and assess their own performance. For judges there are the rules of procedure, evidence and court practice. Arbitrators have their techniques for dispute resolution and conciliation. Umpires have their rule-books, disciplinary measures, appeal bodies, and so on. Those codes and standards, explicit and implicit, represent conditions which all parties expect to be observed. It is on that understanding that the participation of the neutral party is deemed by the contesting parties to be neutral, i.e., not materially to affect their respective interests in the on-going process and its eventual outcome.

Are there recognized codes and standards governing the actions and attitudes of scholars and institutions engaged in Religious Studies? There is no doubt that lists of widely-accepted internal standards could be drawn up. Jacob Neusner, for instance, has written recently:

> We should identify a body of ideas, texts, knowledge that we concur matters. We should specify those analytical skills we teach that people can carry into other fields. Above all, our field should have reached the level of appropriate institutionalization that lends recognition to people who meet high standards, who present important ideas and provide knowledge of lasting significance.[2]

While admitting, with Neusner, that those "shoulds" await full implementation, few within the discipline would dispute that there exists a core of internal standards and recognized practices aimed at ensuring a neutral role for Religious Studies. Three areas, in particular, are worthy of further discussion.

Non-prejudicial Language

For the classic theorists of phenomenology of religion, the "assigning of names" was a basic step towards comprehension. In the everyday practice of

239

Religious Studies, likewise, nothing is more important than the choice of adequate, appropriate, and non-prejudicial names and terms by which to describe and mark off from one another the endlessly varied yet remarkably comparable phenomena of the world's religions.

Writing in the early 1970s, Michael Pye described the issue of nomenclature for categorizing religious phenomena as "a pressing methodological problem" deserving of "careful international discussion."[3] Since that time, sensitivity to this issue has increased to the extent that the subject has had a noticeable influence on language-use within wider academic circles and beyond.

Words carrying long-established prejudicial overtones are gradually being replaced by more acceptable alternatives. "Islam" has ousted "Mohammedanism"; "non-Christian religions" have become "world faiths"; "Common Era" replaces *"anno domini"*; "primal" is used for "primitive," "image" for "idol," and "specialist of the sacred" for "medium" or "witch-doctor." Precise and legitimate senses have been provided for words which previously had (and often still have) offensive or misleading associations: sect, cult, myth, mystic, pagan, magic, sorcery, and so on.

Of course, sensitivity to bias in terminology is not the exclusive preserve of Religious Studies. The social sciences as a whole have found themselves forging new value-free nomenclature in many areas. But our discipline, perhaps more than any other, is bound to take note of the fact that even "neutral" terminology cannot simply be imposed. There is often required something like a negotiated acceptance, a willing compromise, on the part of those being spoken about. In other words, settling on an acceptable common terminology, with recognition of the interests of parties especially involved, requires the exercise of a mediating, conciliatory role.

That this task has become a conscious professional commitment for Religious Studies is well illustrated from the introduction to the new *Encyclopedia of Religion*. There the senior project editor, Claude Conyers, discusses matters of editorial policy, including recognition of the acute problem of having to use technical terms in translation when making cross-cultural comparisons.

> ... we endeavored to be constantly attuned to the nuances of meaning, and to the limits of meaning, of the terms we chose to employ.... [I]n all instances where genuine doubts about the suitability of our entry term could legitimately be raised with respect to a particular religious tradition, we planned to present a separate discussion under the idiom employed by the tradition itself. In all articles on cross-cultural topics, we encouraged contributors to speculate on the usefulness of the entry term as an organizing principle in the study of religion.[4]

Sensitivity to bias in the names and terms used to discuss religion is, then, clear evidence of a role-neutral intention on the part of practitioners of

Religious Studies. (A further test of the genuineness of that intention, no doubt, will be the recognition that the study of religion itself has until very recently been conducted almost entirely in gender-exclusive language.)[5]

Suspension of Belief and Disbelief

Just as the assigning of names and terms forms part of the classic phenomenological approach, so too does the idea of *epoché* or suspension of belief and disbelief. So-called "bracketing" of issues of truth and validity has come to be thought of as particularly characteristic of the methodology of modern Religious Studies, as compared with confessional and theological discussions of religion on the one hand, and naturalistic explanations and interpretations of it on the other. The effect of this strategy is to turn attention away from the contentious or dubious, so as to concentrate on matters open to investigation by agreed procedures; in particular, the careful, sensitive description of the subject-matter itself.

Like neutrality, the idea of suspending belief and disbelief calls for more preliminary clarification than it has yet received, if it is to play a fundamental part in Religious Studies methodology. As with neutrality, the merits of such "bracketing" would need to be demonstrated in actual cases. A mere declaration that one is suspending belief and disbelief in general is far from sufficient to ensure that the discussion will thereafter be unaffected by the questions which have supposedly been put to one side. Things are not so easily disentangled from their conceptual networks, and it will only be in actual instances that criteria will emerge for assessing success or failure in that enterprise.

For our purposes, however, it is the pragmatic employment of the bracketing procedure that counts, not its theoretical justification. In the practice of Religious Studies, we find judgement on certain issues being customarily suspended, so that more agreed-upon matters can be pursued without prejudice to the various parties' interests. It is recognized that religion, whatever else it may involve, does have a substantial this-worldly component, inviting scholarly study from a number of angles. As Joseph Kitagawa puts it, in his foreword to the *Encyclopedia*:

> We have assumed that there is no such thing as a purely religious phenomenon. A religious phenomenon is a human phenomenon and thus is not only religious but also social, cultural, psychological, biological, and so on.[6]

Given that the parties are prepared to see the subject-matter in the disputed area of religion as to some extent open to investigation by the normal procedures of the humanities and social sciences, role-neutral positions in accordance with those procedures clearly become possible for the study of religion.

Professional Neutrality and Personal Bias

While the study of religion may be, ideally speaking, a strictly scholarly pursuit, the people engaged in it are not only scholars. They are members of races, communities and families; they marry, educate their children, bury their dead; they attend or stay away from places of worship, observe or ignore festivals, support or oppose causes, associate with others or keep themselves to themselves. In all such activities of everyday life, professional scholars are inevitably aligning themselves, one way or another, in relation to religious issues and institutions. How is professional neutrality to escape the effects of personal bias?

In *Neutrality and Commitment*, Basil Mitchell sees this as a special case of the problem which confronts any academic who "has to reconcile the demands of scholarly caution and detachment with the need to develop and maintain a consistent 'philosophy of life'."[7] The difficulty, however, lies in the general lack of rational principles, throughout this discipline, for evaluating the effect of "personal bias" on scholarly performance.

We would be deceiving ourselves if we supposed that it made no difference to scholars' appreciation of one another's arguments, to discover that their authors had certain religious affiliations; to learn, for instance, that Schmidt, Evans-Pritchard, and Zaehner were Catholics, Tylor a Quaker, Durkheim an atheist, or William James the son of a Swedenborgian.

It might be thought that so long as scholars were prepared to "declare their interests," so to speak, neutrality could be assured, since it would then remain simply for others to make appropriate allowances in judging the merits of their views. Thus F. C. Happold, in his book on *Mysticism*, writes "If one sincerely believes anything, it is not possible to be coldly objective. Nor is it necessary to be so, provided any bias is frankly acknowledged."[8]

But that makes it sound far too easy. The difficulty lies in determining just what "biases" in fact go with the holding of any particular position with regard to religious beliefs. Clearly, common knowledge is no guide in this matter. For even if it were common knowledge how, say, typical Catholics, Muslims, or Humanists were likely to be prejudiced with regard to religious matters, Catholics, Muslims or Humanists engaged in the academic study of religions will probably be far from typical.

Deliberate misrepresentation or blatant unfairness are no doubt relatively straight-forward. Such overt bias will be so conspicuously inappropriate in modern Religious Studies as to be avoided out of academic self-interest if for no higher motive. Unconscious bias is more problematic; the suspicion that scholars' thought-patterns and sensitivities will be so shaped by their personal religious attachments or aversions that the categories they use in dealing with other positions will inevitably distort them.

But do we know that to be so? Must one-time theologians inevitably have hidden agendas? Does atheism necessarily inhibit sensitivity to spirituality? Are converts incurably one-eyed? And what about the possibility of self-aware scholars compensating for their personal biases; or over-compensating?

In the absence of rational criteria for evaluating suspicions and conjectures of those kinds, there is only one way in which judgments on these matters can avoid being utterly simplistic and arbitrary. That is for neutrality to be treated as adherence to a defined role; as the ability to comply with standards of professionalism, not simply the possession of a certain intention or frame of mind. Perhaps the strongest evidence of the academic study of religion's having attained to a stance of role-neutrality will be when it manages to embrace, within agreed standards of professionalism, the widest possible range of personal diversities in belief and practice amongst its practitioners.

Neutrality About Methodology

We are left with what is perhaps the most intriguing question of all; whether scholars of religion can find a neutral role with regard to fundamental debates within their own discipline.

In his review of articles on "theory and method" in the *Encyclopedia of Religion*, Peter Byrne regrets the lack of discussion of this central methodological question: "Can the study of religion attain to neutrality as to the truth and rationality of religion?"[9] Finding no mention of "methodological agnosticism," nor any discussion of "how we might describe the putative referents of religious beliefs without committing ourselves to their existence," Byrne continues:

> If the choice between reductionism, neutrality and religious commitment is given no proper airing, we cannot expect much of a treatment of the important question of whether the study of religion is invariably naturalistic in its working assumptions.[10]

While it may not be reflected in the *Encyclopedia*'s articles, that long-running dispute amongst methodologists of religion has been generating increasing heat in recent years. Donald Wiebe, one of the principal protagonists, argues that the distinctive character and the hard-won status of the academic study of religion are being placed in jeopardy by latter-day confusion and back-sliding. The discipline, he tells us, is suffering from a "failure of nerve," and faces a crisis of identity.

The founding fathers of *Religionswissenschaft* and their successors who sought for and achieved status for this field of study, proposed a definite, unambiguous program.

They gained the legitimation they sought—and from which we benefit— by establishing a distinct identity for their enterprise. This they achieved in clearly demarcating, in theory if not always in practice, the study of religion both from religion itself and from religiously inspired/oriented scholarship and learning. The "object" (subject-matter) and objectives of the study of religion, it was maintained, are distinctly different from the "concerns" and "interests" of religion. Religion concerns itself with transcendent reality while the study of religion focuses its attention on the (human) phenomenon; religion aims at salvation, but the study of religion merely seeks knowledge.[11]

Present-day Religious Studies, Wiebe asserts, is failing to maintain that program. It has blurred its focus by espousing hermeneutic and intuitive approaches, or by conceiving of itself as a "quest" based on some universal and humanitarian vision. As a result, Religious Studies has become increasingly vulnerable to re-theologizing pressures. Yet without a clear and uncompromisingly scientific approach and methodology (what Wiebe calls a "positive episteme") this discipline, he warns us, is in grave danger of losing its academic credibility.

The study of religion legitimated by the academic community is a study that emerges from a positive episteme. Although initially a religious exercise, the study of religion . . . has become a "naturalized citizen" of the university community. And like any other "naturalized citizen" it must live up to the obligations of neutrality and objectivity placed on it by that community.[12]

Whether or not Wiebe is entirely correct in his assessment of the situation, or completely fair to those scholars and points of view he criticizes, it is well worth our asking whether lessons learned in the foregoing analysis of neutrality can be applied to this particular dispute.

First, we are required to seek a clear specification of the respective positions, for only then can we decide what neutrality towards them may in fact entail. Again, it is desirable to avoid vague or prejudicial terms. Byrne's "reductionism" or "religious commitment" seem unsatisfactory on those grounds; as do other tempting dichotomies such as "naturalism" or "super-naturalism"; "pure" or "applied"; "positivism" or "idealism"; "social science approach" or "humanities approach."

The dispute can, however, be more precisely and neutrally formulated. Thus Eric Sharpe, for instance, speaks of it as "the debate between those who are and those who are not prepared to affirm that the comparative study of religion has some transcendental point of reference. . . ."[13]

Neutrality, I have argued, is issue-specific. A position of neutrality with respect to the issue just formulated would seem to involve leaving open the possibility of supra-empirical or transcendent realities entering into the explanation of religious phenomena. Yet what Wiebe calls "the obligations of neutrality and objectivity" employed in other academic disciplines seem to exclude that possibility in principle. The two conceptions of neutrality are clearly in conflict.

If Wiebe is right in holding that keeping faith with the intentions of the founding fathers, and with the university community's expectations, requires adhering to a positive episteme, Religious Studies is indeed faced with a methodological dilemma. Which does it value more, its academic standing, or the pursuit of a genuine neutrality, one defined specifically with reference to the questions raised by its own subject-matter?

As a warning to those who would want to reintroduce assumptions about transcendent truths or supra-empirical realities into Religious Studies, Wiebe has recently invoked the example of so-called "scientific-creationism," the attempt to re-theologize biology. "It appears," he laments,

> that the re-theologizing of the study of religion ... has achieved a place for itself in the university curriculum even though, methodologically speaking, its credibility does not exceed that of scientific-creationism.[14]

There is more to this than a mere *ad hominem*, but the comparison is a two-edged one. Scientific-creationism may indeed be something the scientific/academic establishment would wish to exclude on principle. But scientific methodology itself, these days, is expected to be open to the neutral critique of its own working assumptions. And that, as Eileen Barker has pointed out, is a role to which even scientific-creationism may have a contribution to make.

> Many Creationist scientists have a sophisticated grasp of the philosophy of science and they are by no means all living in a world of their own so far as scientific discoveries are concerned. It could be argued that *because* they work with a "rejected paradigm" they are sometimes more open to new facts than are those working within "normal science."[15]

If for "Creationist scientists" we read "theologians" (crypto- or otherwise) a parallel conclusion may be drawn. The scientific study of religion can ill afford to insulate itself from the thinking of others interested in the same subject-matter, merely because they may hold very different views about theory and method. A neutral role is desirable, to ensure an on-going critique of the discipline's own methodology. And achieving that kind of neutrality may entail remaining open to the interests and merits of widely conflicting positions, including theological, confessional, and other by no means dispassionate ones.

Commitment to a genuinely neutral methodology for Religious Studies, in other words, may require paying not less but more attention to the points of view of parties whose contributions are far removed from any "positive episteme," or the usual canons of academic respectability.

Why be Neutral?

Up to this point the discussion has assumed without question that neutrality, in some sense of the word, is not only a scholarly virtue but also a methodological prerequisite for a discipline like Religious Studies. But now we may begin to wonder whether neutrality can indeed be carried too far. Should a university-discipline bind itself to a principle which appears to absolve it from the normal academic responsibility to discard failed hypotheses and ignore less-than-reputable scholarship? A policy of permanent, obligatory open-mindedness might seem like a form of wilful obscurantism, (a strategy perhaps for protecting concealed theological suppositions).

It is difficult, however, even to frame that dilemma without begging vital questions. Suppose it could be shown that a neutralizing strategy of *epoché* or bracketing was being used for artificially keeping options open (like a judge who refuses to allow a verdict ever to be reached). Then, presumably, neutrality would be being taken too far. But where the dispute in question is about the very method for deciding such matters (what the options are, whether they are coherent, which is best supported by the evidence, and so on) then a prior decision to limit neutrality would seem entirely premature.

Once again, we find that the attempt to theorize about neutrality in general creates an unresolvable, criterialess debate just as the achievement of neutrality, then, is best assessed in relation to specific situations, so the utility or desirability of neutrality may best be evaluated in relation to specific goals or aims.

Neutrality is seldom an end in itself. Given the various aims and goals Religious Studies sets itself, there are many reasons why neutrality is worth pursuing. It helps free the subject from factional concerns or pressures. It ensures the widest possible range of relevant data, allowing world-wide comparisons and generalizations. It permits the reconsideration of established positions, the adoption of fresh points of view, the investigation of neglected or suppressed topics.

On a platform of neutrality, Religious Studies may help create opportunities for contending parties to meet and discover common ground. If accepted by the academic and religious communities as an "honest broker" it can play a valuable role in fostering scholarly collaboration and research. It can assemble accredited sources of information, draw up acceptable terminology, standardize definitions and topologies. If political institutions or the public news media give it credence, it may be able to advance the cause of human rights, speaking up for the misunderstood or under-represented. It can contribute to public education and advance multi-cultural understanding in pluralistic societies.

But even that brief list of possible aims for Religious Studies is sufficient to show that no one, across-the-board specification for a form of methodological neutrality will do. Once again, it depends on the circumstances. What some parties may treat as legitimate scholarly activities others will regard as an attack on their traditions. What looks to some like the promotion of human rights others will see as incitement to subversion. What some regard as rigorous scientific principles others will dismiss as superficial positivism. The variations are endless.

Neutrality cannot be imposed. Nor can it be achieved, in the study of religion or elsewhere, unless the circumstances permit. That, I have suggested, is most likely to be where there exist agreed practices and procedures, an accepted role or something approximating to one. Apart from that, any unilateral declaration by Religious Studies committing itself to a position of so-called "procedural neutrality" is, at very best, only a beginning.

Notes

1. In formulating that definition I have taken note of the useful but inconclusive debate between Alan Montefiore and Leszek Kolakowski in *Neutrality and Impartiality*, Alan Montefiore (ed.). London: Cambridge University Press, 1975.
2. "The Theological Enemies of Religious Studies," *Religion* 18 (1988): 31.
3. *Comparative Religion*. Newton Abbot: David & Charles, 1972: 30.
4. *Encyclopedia of Religion*, Vol. 1, ix–xx. New York: Macmillan, 1987.
5. See Ursula King, "Female Identity and the History of Religions," in *Identity Issues and World Religions*. Victor C. Hayes (ed.). Bedford Park, South Australia: Australian Association for the Study of Religions, 1986: 83–92.
6. *Encyclopedia of Religion*, Vol. 1, xv.
7. Oxford: Clarendon Press, 1968: 10.
8. Harmondsworth, Middlesex: Penguin, 1970: 16.
9. "The Theory of Religion and Method in the Study of Religion in the *Encyclopedia of Religion*," *Religious Studies* 24 (1988): 9.
10. *Ibid.*, 10.
11. "A Positive Episteme for the Study of Religion," *Scottish Journal of Religious Studies* 6 (1985): 78.
12. *Ibid.*, 90.
13. *Comparative Religion* 2nd. ed. London: Duckworth, 1986: 295.
14. "Postulations for Safeguarding Preconceptions: The Case of the Scientific Religionist," *Religion* 18 (1988): 18.
15. *On the Margins of Science*. Roy Wallis (ed.). Keele: University of Keele, 1979: 197.

17

PETER BYRNE, *The Study of Religion: Neutral, Scientific, or Neither?*

෮෮

In a penetrating survey of models of neutrality in religious studies, Peter Donovan (1990) warns of the difficulties in finding any precise, agreed understanding of what neutrality in this discipline may amount to. He defines neutrality in general in the following way: "To be neutral is to stand in relation to two or more parties which are themselves in tension, in such a way that the respective interests of those parties are not thereby materially affected" (1990: 103). In relation to the practice of the study of religion in educational institutions within the Western world, there are a number of interested parties with sharply conflicting visions of what the subject can and should mean. Can there be a way of conducting the study of religion without materially affecting the urgent religio-political interests of right wing evangelicals, of old-fashioned Church liberals, of left wing secularists, and so on? Given the contemporary revival of interest in religion as the source of political action and the renewed strength of conservative religious outlooks, this is an urgent question.

In exploring how neutrality, as defined above, can be established and maintained, Donovan presents an ideal case of the operation of neutrality and alerts us to the great gulf between the standard it embodies and what is possible in religious studies. Neutrality is paradigmatically displayed where there are established procedures for conducting a dispute or rivalry between parties (as in the law or in forms of sporting contest), procedures which in turn establish the need for some independent arbitrator or monitor of the dispute whilst also defining how that arbitrator is to act (as illustrated by the role of judge or referee) (1990: 106–107). The dispute between different religious confessions as well as between confessionalism and varieties of secularism over the meaning of religion hardly appears to be governed by such agreement on procedure and,

248

correspondingly, it seems difficult, if not impossible, for the study of religion to proceed in a neutral fashion in the face of such disagreements.

Donovan pleads, not for the abandonment of any pretense of neutrality in religious studies, but for the clear articulation and contextualization of any claim for neutrality the discipline makes. It must make clear precisely what it means by any alleged neutrality it displays and why such neutrality should be important.

Biology versus Creationism: A Model of Neutrality?

By way of illustrating the difficulties in defining and defending neutrality, let us consider the way in which the creation stories of various religions might be taught to pupils in a European or North American secondary school. A standard "religious studies approach" will treat the stories of the different faiths in the same manner, endeavoring to bring out their inner meaning for practitioners of the faiths and their literary or oral origins. It will be typical of such an approach to bracket off all questions of the truth of these stories, though the teacher might compare their contents with the latest scientific cosmological speculations. Conservative Christian parents might object that this is not neutrality. They will contend that the Jewish-Christian story is already the subject of prejudicial pre-judgment if treated on a par with all the rest. For, they will claim, it is foundational to much of the civilization which surrounds the school and its work. On its truth, they may say, depends the possibility of natural science, and/or a range of foundational beliefs about the worth of human persons. Not to teach it as something which is at least the source of truths about nature and people is to behave un-neutrally with regard to the basis of Western intellectual and moral life. At the least, they may argue for an extension of the claimed neutrality when it comes to the teaching of the origins of life and human beings in the school's biology syllabus. Why cannot the Christian account of the creation of life and humans be given equal and non-judgmental treatment when compared with the neo-Darwinist account? Here, educational practice is not neutral as between secular and confessional stories.

With regard to the last point, we can be fairly confident that the educational authorities have an answer, one that turns around the idea of the integrity and coherence of a *subject*. It has been amply demonstrated that the reason why creationism cannot be given equal time with neo-Darwinism in the teaching of biology is because one cannot do anything *in biology* with creationism (see Kitcher 1982). That is to say, creationism provides no means of unifying existing biological knowledge and no way of developing biological research programs. Only the neo-Darwinist paradigm does that at the moment, which is why, while there are debates within biology about how to develop the paradigm, there is no serious alternative to it. Giving creationism equal time in the teaching of biological theory cannot for these reasons be an exercise of neutrality in biological science.

Appeal to the integrity of a given academic discipline cannot of itself settle substantive questions of theory. Within a proper education system room will be found for debate about the truth of neo-Darwinism in comparison with literal readings of the creation myths of the Hebrew Bible. In part, these debates will be about the status of the knowledge claims of biology and about the proper orientation of that subject. These are philosophical questions, drawing upon scientific and theological issues. Biologists cannot foreclose such debates, but they can properly contend that the current practice of biological science does not depend upon them, for the subject has acquired a proper and visible momentum of its own and should proceed along its current path until some alternative paradigm for its work is produced.

Given the notion that biology has an integrity and coherence as a discipline, we can be tolerably clear what counts as neutral teaching of it. It is teaching which does not pre-judge the merits of competing, live hypotheses *within the subject*. This kind of neutrality is quite compatible with setting aside for philosophical-theological debate opinions and questions which have some bearing upon biology. Would that we could carry over this model to an understanding of the neutrality of the study of religion. Religious studies deals with a vast array of confessions, many of which have been articulated to the degree where they have views about their own origins and about their relations to other confessions. In addition, a range of secular accounts of religion compete for attention. Neutrality in the study of religion can hardly consist in giving equal weight to, or taking due account of, each and all of these perspectives on religion. At best, it can consist in establishing an integrity to the discipline which allows the core approaches to its subject matter initially to set aside debates between confessions and between them and secularism. As will be noted below, there is indeed more to neutrality in religious studies than this, but this is at least where the foundations of its neutrality lie.

Naturalism as an Option for Neutrality?

These vague prescriptions can be made somewhat clearer by considering the import of recent debates about the respective merits of methodological atheism versus methodological agnosticism in the study of religion.

Given the need in our contemporary circumstances for religious studies to retain some semblance of neutrality, it is surprising to find writers who argue that the study of religion is faced with a stark choice between a confessional and a naturalistic paradigm to govern its procedures. Such writers will go on to claim that it is only with the achieved dominance of the naturalistic paradigm that the study of religion was born as an academic subject and that its status as an academic subject can only be maintained if the naturalistic paradigm remains dominant (Preus 1987; Wiebe 1981, 1985, 1994: chapters 5, 6, 7, 10). For example, according to Preus, what was essential to the development of religious studies was the emerging possibility of understanding religion "without benefit of clergy" (1987: x). As a result of the intellectual critique of the Enlightenment, established religious ideas ceased to be the framework of thought itself, ceased to be the means of understanding, among other things, the character of history and culture, and became instead the object of critical investigation. That, in turn, enabled historians and students of society to give equal attention to other religious traditions besides the West's own. The development of the study of religion was sealed by the accompanying realization that a "science" of religion is only possible if it undertakes the explanatory as well as the descriptive task. Explanation via theological hypotheses having been excluded, the only and obvious recourse is explanation via scientifically understood mechanisms and laws of human society or the psyche (Wiebe 1985: 87). The hero of the development of a proper study of religion is then taken to be David Hume in his *Natural History of Religion*.

It is strange that this cry of "naturalism or bust" should present itself as preserving, allegedly by the only available method, the neutrality of religious studies. Yet this is what Wiebe claims in castigating those who would smuggle theological concerns into the study of religion. They would falsely exempt the subject "from the ordinary obligations of neutrality that attend our other academic/scientific activities" (1994: 127). The sense of "neutrality" in this quotation is no doubt fixed by its association with "scientific." It has associations of dispassionate, value-free, evidentially-led enquiry. But of course we know that the Preus–Wiebe naturalistic paradigm is far from being a neutral prescription for the study of religion if we bear in mind the need for neutrality to be non-prejudicial toward competing interests in the interpretation of religion. For the naturalist paradigm, as determined by exemplary figures such as Hume, assumes the falsity and/or irrationality of religious thought and practice. In particular, it assumes that such thought and practice cannot have the sense it appears to have for those whose lives are structured by it. The line of thinkers going through Hume, Feuerbach, Marx, Freud, and Durkheim agrees on the basic presupposition that how religion *appears* to those involved in the life of religion is not how it *is*, notwithstanding the attempts of some of these naturalist interpreters of religion, such as Durkheim, to represent their theories as saving the reality of religious notions (Clarke and Byrne 1993: 169). If religious studies is based on this kind of paradigm, then it is a weapon in the hands of secularism, aiding those who would expose religion as an illusion.

Religious Phenomenology and Neutrality

There is a two-fold error in the Preus–Wiebe approach: an addiction to "scientism" and a failure to see a third possibility beside what it styles "naturalism" and religious-cum-theological ways of understanding religion. Both these errors can be properly diagnosed by bringing out the nature of an alternative, cultural-symbolic program for religious studies. (We could also style this a *Verstehen* or semantic based program.)

It is common to link the cultural-symbolic program with Dilthey's ideas about *Verstehen* in the study of the human world and then with the phenomenological tradition which manifests itself in religious studies with a line of writers which includes Rudolf Otto, Mircea Eliade, Gerardus van der Leeuw, and Joachim Wach. Defined in this way, the program can be appropriately accused of making the study of religion into an adjunct of a theology of religions. For in this tradition, the notion that religious studies has as its primary task the interpretation of an inner layer of meaning in religious action becomes associated with the search for a distinct range of intellectual contents, ideas, which are at once peculiar to religion, universal across religions, and therefore hidden behind the varied ways in which they are expressed in language and behavior. The alleged discovery of such a stock of ideas sets the student of religion on a decidedly esoteric quest and gives him or her materials which appear to cry out for theological interpretation. The unique set of religious contents are then declared to be *sui generis* and thus they establish the autonomy of both religion and religious studies. That autonomy then makes a theological point, since the uniqueness of religion as a mode of awareness seems to follow from it. Before we know where we are, we are locked into viewing the *sui generis* religious contents as clear markers for the presence throughout religions of the manifestation of a relationship between human beings and a sacred, transcendent reality variously pictured by each of them.

Where the naturalist paradigm has left us with the study of religion as the academic arm of secularism, Otto and other religious phenomenologists leave us with that study as concerned with the tracing of some esoteric, continuing general revelation of the sacred to human beings. Religious studies has turned out, according to the second paradigm, to be the vehicle of a somewhat odd kind of theology, one that stands in opposition to dominant theological models in both Protestant and Catholic twentieth-century thought. It is a theology at once Christian, yet based on "evidences" allegedly drawn from many religions. No wonder the likes of Wiebe then complain that the science of religion has lost its way and suffered a failure of nerve.

Methodological Agnosticism and the Cultural-Symbolic Approach

The means of escaping the uncomfortable choices outlined so far is to return to a yet older model for understanding the claim that religious thought and action is the object of a special kind of *Verstehen*, older because I think it goes back to the work of Herder and Hegel. The alternative to avoiding naturalism by plunging into the murky waters of religious phenomenology is to see religion as but one exemplification of the general truth that human life is imbued with species of meaning, and, in particular, meaning of a symbolic, conceptual kind. The human world is a world of meaning because human thought and action is informed by concepts. These concepts are made possible by, and deposited in, the symbolic structures, particularly, but not solely, linguistic, within which human beings dwell. The first task of any human science (be it history, sociology, anthropology, or whatever) is to describe, interpret, and explain human action by bringing out its relationship to the concepts that inform it. (For modern defenses/outlines of the symbolic, semantic understanding of *Verstehen* see Clarke and Byrne 1993: chapter 2; Crick 1976; and Winch 1958.) On this symbolic approach, there is a separate discipline named religious studies only to the extent that there are distinctive religious concepts making possible distinctive forms of religious action. Since the distinctiveness claimed here is at best merely relative and not absolute, religious studies claims no absolute autonomy for itself or its subject matter. At a stroke, the claims of an Eliade for a primal religious idea manifestly reflecting contact with the sacred disappear.

On the cultural-symbolic paradigm, the aim of religious studies is to bring out the nature of the sphere of human meaning that is religion. Religious studies is important because, in the shaping of human communities, religion is one of the most vital areas of human meaning. The object of the study is not the discovery of esoteric mental contents but rather the tracing of connections between concepts embodied in symbolic structures. The discipline is scientific primarily in being critical and guided by a desire to be true to its object—the nature of meaning within human religious action. This does not entail, however, that its characteristic methods of enquiry and explanation are modeled on those dominating the natural sciences. Indeed, they cannot be, for the natural sciences investigate phenomena which have meaning only to the extent that the scientist's theories give them meaning. But the objects of the human sciences, that is, human actions and institutions, have layers of meaning prior to their investigation and characterization by the student of society, being informed by the concepts of those who participate in them. Since it is the aim of the study of religion to recover this meaning, it must *begin* by being faithful to the understanding of the religious insofar as this is revealed in the conceptual content of their beliefs and actions. Methodological agnosticism flows from this, since it is the *content* of believers' beliefs and concepts, rather than the *truth* of those beliefs or the successful *reference* of those concepts, which gives form to the meaning in which they dwell. So, matters of truth and reference can be suspended in considering these beliefs and concepts. The resulting bracketing of beliefs and concepts has nothing to do with the mysterious attempt to isolate, in the manner of phenomenology, "pure" mental contents but merely signals a desire to avoid questions of truth and reference in the business of interpretation. The reality of the gods is thus neither endorsed nor denied by the fundamentals of the study of religion, save insofar as that reality is shown in the power of human beliefs about the gods. The reality they have for religious studies is as items in the meaning-world of human actors; whether they are real or unreal as items in a transcendent world is a philosophical and theological question on which the fundamentals of the discipline need not take sides. This is the foundation of the subject's real neutrality.

Objections to the Cultural-Symbolic Approach

The Preus–Wiebe program for the study of religion will have a number of objections to offering a cultural-symbolic mode of understanding as the basis of religious studies.

1. *Religious studies becomes a purely descriptive exercise, eschewing forever the possibility of explanatory theories*

In reply we must try to separate explanation itself from the desire for explanatory theories. The cultural-symbolic approach seeks to explain religious actions by the very act of bringing out of their inner meaning. It can offer a well argued case for saying that, in the human world, describing, interpreting, and explaining flow into one another. This case builds upon the simple point that, normally, to explain an act is to bring out the agent's reasons for doing it, which is also to interpret it and to describe it more fully. The dogma to be rejected is that explanation is always and everywhere a matter of subsuming particulars under theories (Clarke and Byrne 1993: 41–48).

2. *Religious studies would be a discipline without worthwhile generalizations to make*

This does not follow from the cultural-symbolic paradigm. There are generalizations to be made when it comes to *patterns* of human meaning within the religions. Thus, when Clifford Geertz generalizes to the effect that religions serve to ground the ethos of a society in its worldview, he offers a general truth about patterns in the construction of human meaning (Geertz 1973: 127). In this respect, the student of religion goes beyond the self-understanding of the religious, without yet overturning it (and see below).

3. The cultural-symbolic paradigm prevents any links being drawn between religious and non-religious facts

Not so. First, the cultural-symbolic theorist recognizes that religious meaning is but one facet of human meaning in general. So, there are conceptual connections to be made between facets of religious meaning and facets of political and other forms of meaning. Further, the student of religion must recognize that religious meaning is constructed and continues in a context of things that happen to a people and of conditions that just obtain for them. In this way the material events and circumstances surrounding a culture provide conditions for the intelligibility of its meaning-making in general, and its religious meaning-making in particular. Though the study of religion begins and is founded upon the delineation of semantic meaning, it does not end with this. The human world of religious meaning need not be, cannot be, supposed to float free of the material circumstances of human life. All that matters is that it can be given a relative degree of autonomy, displayed in the notion that, for all their importance, material circumstances should provide no more than necessary conditions for the state of the world of meaning.

4. The cultural-symbolic approach is a species of idealism

Mention of the name of Hegel in the sources of the cultural-symbolic paradigm will cause the critic to smell a rat. The critic may generally see the tactic of eschewing naturalistic, allegedly scientific, theories while relying on conceptual and semantic content as bringing in an "unscientific" form of idealism into the foundations of an academic discipline (Wiebe 1994: 85–86, 215). Idealism may seem to be implicated insofar as it is to the ideas or concepts of the religious that we appeal to account for religious behavior. A properly scientific approach to the study of religion would rather appeal to material factors in religious explanation.

In reply to this objection, it must be pointed out that emphasis on human meaning is intended to refer to something real and "objective" about the world: the fact that human beings live in a world of meaning and are moved to action by awareness of features of that world of meaning. So this is not idealism in the sense of committing the student of human religion to the existence of an ideal realm of existence beyond the empirically manifest world. It is important to note that the very business of engaging in human (and "scientific") study commits the investigator to acknowledging the reality of this world of meaning, the world made up of awareness of reasons and the informing of belief and behavior by concepts. For to engage in the reflective study of culture involves the presentation of arguments, the marshaling of evidence, and the drawing of conclusions from assembled reasons. The student is thereby committed to the reality and power of ideas and of relations between ideas in the human world. Sadly, for the critic, human intellectual study appears to be part of the world of human, conceptual meaning itself and is unintelligible unless that world has some reality.

This last point provides part of the answer to a supplementary objection to the effect that the cultural-symbolic approach entails belief in the falsity of materialist accounts of the mind—accounts which, we know, are often advanced by philosophers on the ground that they are demanded by science. It is a well-worn objection to materialism of a radical kind that it is self-refuting as a philosophical thesis, since it is advanced on the basis of reasons while itself entailing that the operation of reason in human life is unintelligible. Whatever the final merits of this point as a reply to materialist theories of mind, it points to the necessity of at least provisionally accepting the reality of the human world of ideas until such time as the possibility and desirability of an ultimate reduction of "mentalistic" vocabulary to the physical has been proved. That time does not appear to be imminent.

Ideology Critique of Religion as "Masking Institution"

The objection based on the opposition to idealism conceals another against the notion of the study of religion as an interpretative science of a facet of human meaning. The most important objection to this understanding is that contained in the writings of the likes of Ernest Gellner and those theorists of religion influenced by Marxism who contend that no impartial investigator can rely upon actors' own understanding in explaining human institutions, since it is frequently the very nature and meaning of an institution to conceal its true function and purpose from those who participate in it (Gellner 1973; Morris 1987). In short, human institutions, especially, it may be said, religious institutions, are likely to be ideological in cause and function. They exist to cover up incoherences, conflicts, or injustices in human life. It is precisely the job of the scientific student of human religious life *not* to take religious institutions and behavior at face value, since their overall meaning may be to hide facets of personal and social life from their adherents. Religion is therefore a "masking institution" (Clarke and Byrne 1993: 53–56, 145).

The ideology objection implies that we cannot have neutrality in the study of human religion *and* take a properly objective, scientific standpoint toward the reality of religion. No one can deny that some complexes of human belief and behavior are not to be taken on their own terms and do serve to cover up the real motives and springs of human action. Though the ideology objection must thus be taken seriously, it does not yet destroy the fundamental correctness of the cultural-symbolic approach to religious studies. It could only do so if it was able to supply, as the premise for the study of religion, the hypothesis that *all* (or, the significantly major part of) human religious life was ideological in meaning, cause, and function. But I hold that the study of religion cannot know such a claim to be true as a premise for its interpretations and explanations. Such a hypothesis could be known prior to an exhaustive investigation of the meaning of religion only if it could be demonstrated as part of some philosophy of culture, for example some version of Marxist theory. Whether any such philosophy of culture has been demonstrated can reasonably be doubted, but certainly there appears to be no demonstration available to the study of religion as the basis for its work or acceptable to anything like the majority of the practitioners of this discipline.

The notion that religions are masking institutions is to be proved, if at all possible, on a case-by-case basis. That is, it would have to be shown, to the best interpretation and explanation of particular instances of human religious life, to be the interpretation that brought out most satisfactorily the meaning of those cases. Two important consequences follow from this. First, it shows that religious studies is not reliant on the ideology thesis as a discipline. It must rather retain room within itself for this thesis to be proffered, argued for, and assessed in relation to particular cases. (By the same token, it must contain similar room for theses to the effect that this or that religious phenomenon cannot be explained without appeal to theological realities—actual contact with the gods.) Second, there seems to be no easy way one could demonstrate that the ideology thesis was the best way to deal with a particular facet of religion without first uncovering its apparent human meaning, exploring it as part of the cultural-symbolic world in which human beings live. For the most obvious way in which categories of ideological explanation become attractive is when we notice gaps and incoherences between and within facets of human meaning, as when we see that what people do does not match what they say, or what they conclude does not fit how they reason.

The above concession to the ideology objection needs to be pursued further to see how far it undermines the defense of the neutrality of religious studies offered so far. The central objection to the cultural-symbolic paradigm appears to be that what, and how many, facets of the world of human religious meaning are in fact ideological is for the most part relative to the worldviews scholars bring to the study of religious phenomena. The same might appear to be true of what, and how many, facets of religion are held to require explanation by invoking actual contact with the gods.

Conclusion

The neutrality of religious studies can only be maintained in the face of these points if the following is borne in mind: a presumption must be accepted that one must *begin* with the cultural-symbolic interpretation and explanation of a religious phenomenon. This presumption obviously needs support, which comes from underlying considerations (pointed to earlier) about the

257

distinguishing features of human action and human institutions. Crudely put, the very business of identifying a human act as the act it is carries with it a presumption (albeit, rebuttable) that it is to be described, interpreted, and explained through the concepts which inform it, and of which the agent must be supposed to be at least tacitly aware. Moreover, the study of religions cannot accept, for the purposes of its own internal workings, any external claim that all or most religious phenomena or developments need explanation in naturalistic or supernaturalistic terms. It would need to be shown in relation to particular cases that gaps in the web of beliefs, ideas, actions, and institutions of a people exist which demand explanation in terms external to the meaning world of religion. Students of religion should also be wary of giving up a naturally healthy skepticism as to how anyone could know the truth of any grand naturalistic theory of human religion. Those we are familiar with, for example, Marxist, Freudian, Durkheimian theories, can easily be shown to rest more on *a priori* philosophizing about human nature and society than on empirical data (Clarke and Byrne 1993: Part II). Still less, can we know *in the study of religions* anything about the detailed character of a supernatural reality and its causal interactions with human actions and institutions. Such insights must be left to theologians. We must instead point to evident failures in the minimal coherence or rationality of the world of meaning if we are to justify invoking such external explanatory factors. Which particular body of external factors is then appropriate as an explanation, must be judged, not by reference to the demands of some "-ism," but by what would make the phenomenon in question most intelligible (Clarke and Byrne 1993: Part I).

In summary, I have argued that reflection on the ideology objection may not undermine the neutrality of the basis of the study of religion. First, such reflection leaves us with the *foundations* of religious studies as consisting in the making manifest of facets of semantic, symbolic meaning within the human world. Its *foundations* are thus neutral with respect to conflicting views about the ultimate origin, truth, or reference of religious symbol systems. Second, neutrality can be maintained if the business of exploring human meaning can develop ways of assessing claims made in any given case for going beyond or behind the meaning a human religious institution has to its participants.

The discipline of religious studies is scientific to the extent that there really is a world of human meaning with religious facets awaiting exploration and to the extent that there are means of distinguishing better and worse descriptions, interpretations, and explanations of this world, ways revealed in comparing the scholar's account with the speech, writing, art, music, architecture, and action of the religious. To be worthy of the labels "objective," "scientific," and "neutral," the study of religion need not look over its shoulder at the details of natural scientific procedures. It needs, instead, to establish that there is a publicly accessible object for it to study and publicly agreed ways, acceptable to folk holding different philosophies of life, for revealing the facets of that object.

References

Clarke, Peter B. and Peter Byrne 1993. *Religion Defined and Explained*. London and Basingstoke: Macmillan.

Crick, Malcolm 1976. *Explorations in Language and Meaning: Toward a Semantic Anthropology*. London: Malaby Press.

Donovan, Peter 1990. "Neutrality in Religious Studies." *Religious Studies* 26: 103–116.

Geertz, Clifford 1973. *The Interpretation of Cultures*. London: Hutchinson.

Gellner, Ernest 1973. *Cause and Meaning in the Social Sciences*. London: Routledge & Kegan Paul.

Kitcher, Philip 1982. *Abusing Science: The Case Against Creationism*. Cambridge, MA: MIT Press.

Morris, Brian 1987. *Anthropological Studies of Religion: An Introductory Text*. Cambridge: Cambridge University Press.

Preus, J. Samuel 1987. *Explaining Religion: Criticism and Theory from Bodin to Freud*. New Haven: Yale University Press.

Wiebe, Donald 1981. *Religion and Truth: Towards an Alternative Paradigm in the Study of Religion*. The Hague: Mouton.

—— 1985. "A Positive Episteme for the Study of Religion." *Scottish Journal of Religious Studies* 6: 78–95.

—— 1994. *Beyond Legitimation: Essays on the Problem of Religious Knowledge*. London and Basingstoke: Macmillan.

Winch, Peter (1958). *The Idea of a Social Science and its Relations to Philosophy*. London: Routledge & Kegan Paul.

18

Donald Wiebe, *Does Understanding Religion Require Religious Understanding?*

ॐॐ

I

Some years ago Professor Alasdair MacIntyre raised the philosophically and religiously interesting question as to whether understanding religion is incompatible with believing in it.[1] For the student of religion the methodological implications of his answer to that question are of sufficient critical significance to warrant wider recognition and discussion. But they have gone unnoticed, I suggest, because MacIntyre's argument is really less concerned with the stated question "Is understanding religion compatible with believing it?" than it is with the unexpressed question "Does understanding religion require religious understanding?"

MacIntyre concludes that understanding Christianity[2] is not compatible with believing in it, but he reaches this conclusion not on the basis of the vulnerability of Christian belief to sceptical objections, but rather on the ground that Christian belief is *necessarily* invulnerable to sceptical objections.[3] Where religious belief is vulnerable to sceptical objection understanding and belief, quite obviously, would not be compatible because the belief, in the light of the understanding achieved, would be seen to be a false belief. In this case, however, the understanding (i.e., the belief about the nature of religious belief) of the sceptic and the belief of the religious would be of the same order. Where religious belief is invulnerable to sceptical objection, however, no such similarity exists. To "understand" religion in this case is not to hold a belief or set of beliefs about the nature of religion but is, rather, to "inhabit" religious beliefs. MacIntyre recognizes that the sceptic's rejection of religious belief implies a common understanding of the use of religious concepts by the sceptic and the believer, but he denies that such an understanding *necessarily* involves the "religious commitment" requirement implied in the "invulnerability thesis" of the religious believer. Rather, he argues, whenever Christian beliefs are seen as necessarily invulnerable to sceptical objection one has indication of Christianity's acceptance of a "deviant" (i.e., non-scientific and therefore non-rational) set of criteria of intelligibility which, if we are really to understand (i.e., have an acceptable belief about the nature of religious belief), must be transcended. Using "anthropological understanding" as analogue of "understanding religion" MacIntyre suggests that we can both understand the religious concept (religious belief) as the religious person understands it and transcend that "understanding" in understanding the Christian's use of concepts in a way that the Christian does not. As he puts it: "For a sceptic to grasp the point of religious belief, therefore, he has to supply a social context which is now lacking and abstract a social context which is now present and he has to do this for the Medieval Christian, just as the anthropologist has to do it for the Azande or the aborigines."[4] "Religious understanding," therefore, in the sense of understanding that involves religious commitment, is not only not necessary in coming to understand religion but must, in fact, be transcended if religion is ever to be properly understood. "Religious understanding" is required only in the sense that the anthropologist needs "Azande under-standing" in coming to an anthropological understanding of the Azande. Since the latter, and MacIntyre has argued this point (although perhaps not altogether persuasively),[5] does not entail becoming or being a Zande person (even by resocialization), then neither does the understanding of religion require becoming or being a religious believer.

Disagreement with MacIntyre, especially from the religious quarter, has been significant. It is obvious, for example, that many contemporary Christians are quite at home with modern scientific thinking and the "acceptable" criteria of intelligibility who, nevertheless, find it possible to hold to many Christian beliefs with sincerity. MacIntyre *seems* cognizant of this fact for he admits that "in dialogue with contemporary Christians the sceptic is forced to recognize that they see a point in what they say and do although they lack that [i.e., the appropriate] context."[6] Furthermore he seems to admit that just as the sceptic can understand the Christian's use of concepts in a way that the Christian does not, so the Christian can understand the sceptic in a way the sceptic does not. But MacIntyre fails to see the significance of these admissions. Given such possibilities as he admits to, the claim that understanding religion does require the peculiar religious understanding of the devotee (gained only in the religious commitment that results from the religious experience) gains a great deal of plausibility. Indeed, Clarke, in responding to MacIntyre's paper, insists that "it is not possible to achieve full understanding of Christian belief save through the illumination from within that comes from the existential commitment of faith to the personality of Christ."[7] Clarke, in turn, admits that some degree of common understanding of religious concepts by sceptic and believer can be

261

achieved—at least for the purpose of intelligent discussion—but nevertheless still maintains that it is an essential part of the Christian faith "that its principal doctrines are 'mysteries' revealed as true by Christ but never philosophically explained or justified by internal evidence, nor even accessible to any adequate comprehension by the human mind in this life."[8] This latter claim, of course, places the *essential* meaning of the doctrines, and, consequently, of the Christian religion, beyond the grasp of the sceptic and beyond the grasp of the "outsider," academic student of religion.

The question "Does understanding religion require religious understanding?" can, it seems, therefore be persuasively argued either negatively or affirmatively. If MacIntyre is right in arguing the incompatibility of understanding and believing, then understanding religion necessarily implies the falsity of "religious understanding." On the other hand, if Clarke is right, then no critical (academic, scientific) study of religion is even possible, for religion (in this case, Christianity) is known to be true but its truth can only be known in a religious act of submission. The methodological implications of either of these two positions are unacceptable to the academic student of religion, for it assumes that a proper understanding of religion can be achieved only if one makes an a priori judgment as to religion's truth or falsity. I shall argue in this paper that other alternatives are possible, but that they are so on epistemological and not metaphysical grounds.

II

The problem outlined above arises, as should now be obvious, because of conflicting notions of "understanding." "Does *understanding* religion require *religious understanding*?" uses the concept in logically distinct ways. The recognition that it does so, however, does not seem to be there. The understanding of religion sought by the critical scholar concerns explanation—accounting for the religious phenomenon in terms of rules and principles already understood and accepted by the scholar in other areas of research and study which he then brings to the study of religion. It is an understanding from *without*. "Religious understanding" on the other hand, the immediate understanding of experience, is indistinguishable from the experience itself. The understanding is gained from within. Such "religious understanding" comes from "standing under" the "object" of religious devotion.[9]

The two kinds of understanding, it seems, are mutually exclusive, much in the sense that it is impossible to see the goblet and the faces in Köhler's[10] famous Goblet-and-Faces diagram simultaneously, or the duck and the rabbit of Wittgenstein's[11] Duck-Rabbit figure simultaneously. The argument between the sceptic and the believer is based, of course, on the incapacity of each to see the "figure" of the other.

Recognizing this ambiguity in the use of the concept of understanding one might be inclined to say that the original question raised for discussion in this paper is simply incoherent, for it asks, in effect, whether a naturalistic interpretation of religion requires a "supernaturalist" foundation. MacIntyre, it must be remembered, maintains, with some plausibility, that the understanding of alien concepts, whether by the anthropologist or by the critical student of religion, can only be achieved in terms of the "outsider's" criteria of intelligibility. The knowledge gained by the "outsider," that is, can never be "internal knowledge."[12] Given MacIntyre's secularist stance, therefore, the supernaturalism of religion is a problem—precisely the problem—that requires explanation, not a reality to be encountered. And to require and encounter with that "reality" for explanation to be possible is obviously absurd.

Clarke's response to MacIntyre's paper suggests the incoherence of the central question raised in this essay from the "opposite" point of view. The experience of the supernatural is, by definition, beyond naturalistic explanation. What lies beyond all words cannot, that is, be conceptually explained. Consequently to ask for an academic study of religion is absurd because such study can only distort the very "thing" it is meant to reveal (explain) for it assumes that religion can be reduced to words.[13]

Both the student of religion and the religious believer (the sceptic and the devotee), then, are insiders and outsiders. The student of religion is an outsider with respect to religious belief but an insider with respect to the belief that words, discussion and argument can provide an understanding of all reality. The opposite, of course, holds for the religious believer. Each, therefore, inhabits a different world-view; each perceives "the world" from a different, mutually exclusive and apparently incommensurable perspective. It appears, therefore, that we have here a Kuhnian paradigm conflict that cannot be settled by argument.[14] For either party in the debate to see the other's perspective requires something more akin to conversion. This point finds superb illustration in the anthropological work of Castaneda.[15] Castaneda attempts to learn "the Yaqui way of knowledge" by means of critical rationalism but is continually frustrated. At one point he draws the following remark from his Yaqui Teacher Don Juan: "You insist on explaining everything as if the whole world were composed of things that can be explained.... Has it ever occurred to you that only a few things in this world can be explained your way!"[16] Juan, and his friend Don Genaro, also "a man of knowledge," are puzzled beyond belief by Castaneda's attempt to learn how to *see* (i.e., to learn the Yaqui way of knowledge—to understand them) "by writing down notes." Castaneda ultimately comes to the conclusion that to "observe" what Juan observed is far more than a simple matter of looking; that it involves a strenuous effort of learning to see in a new way (an apprenticeship, in Castaneda's case, of some ten years). Castaneda's description of this process of resocialization, so to speak, as set out in *A Separate Reality* may be helpfully reproduced here. He writes: "Don Juan's task, as a practitioner making his system accessible to me, was to disarrange a particular certainty which I share with everyone else [i.e., with everyone else in Castaneda's scientific world or lifespace], the certainty that our 'common sense' views of the world are final. Through the use of psychotropic plants, and through well-directed contacts between the alien system and myself, he succeeded in pointing out to me that my view of the world cannot be final because it is only an interpretation."[17]

Whether Castaneda, at the end of his experience with Don Juan, is still an anthropologist is debatable. It is questionable whether Castaneda's experience, that is, is a matter of the sound anthropological procedure of participant-observation or a matter of "going native."[18] What does become clear, however, is the conversion-like character of Castaneda's coming to an understanding of "the Yaqui way of knowledge."

III

Given the difference of perception of the nature of the phenomenon to be examined one might legitimately ask how the idea of an academic study of religion ever got off the ground in the first place. Such a study surely presumes the existence of religious phenomena. It is obvious, that is, that no objective study of religion could ever have emerged unless religion involved something more than internal religious experience. Pure religious experience, wholly internal, if ever it exists, is, so to speak, silent. Such experiences, however, would be unknown except by the "experiencer" for whom, by definition, it remains inexpressible. And the silence of religion is really indistinguishable from silence *simpliciter*.[19]

Religion it is admitted, therefore, even by the most ardent defender of its subjective character, is more than just inner experience. If there were no outward expressions of any kind connected with religious experience no discussion, not even the present one, would be possible.[20] This does not, however, mean that the idea or concept of a critical study of religion is trouble free. Although various forms of expression are considered to be religious, so many of these appear to be of secondary significance only—indeed, they are often seen to be insignificant compared to the experience from which they flow. This would seem, consequently, to make the study of those expressions equally insignificant. A brief look at W. C. Smith's argument in this regard will help to clarify the issue.[21]

Smith, as is well known, claims that "religion" does not exist as a systematic entity characterizing a distinct community; that is the result of man's tendency to reify concepts.[22] In talking of the religious life of a people, he argues, one ought rather to talk of their faith and the accumulated tradition associated with it. And it is the accumulated tradition only that, according to Smith, is the subject matter of the critical study of religion. Thus he writes: "The observable part of man's religious history, it must be admitted, is an open question so far as scholarship is concerned."[23]

This admission one might expect would entail the conclusion that the critical student of religion can provide some understanding of religion without having to "experience" the "reality" of which he speaks and certainly, without commitment of any sort to that religious "reality." The expectation, however, is short-lived and Smith's admission is seen to have been grudging at best. The main contention of Smith's work, that is, is that "the whole path and substance of religious life lies in its relation to what cannot be observed."[24] He maintains, therefore, that "the student's first responsibility is to recognize that there is always and in principle more in any man's faith than any other man can see."[25] As he puts it elsewhere, "one's faith is given by God, one's beliefs by one's century."[26] Consequently a basic principle in the academic study of religion he insists "is an ability to see the divine which I call faith."[27] The study of religion, therefore, if it consists *merely* of an analysis of the various expressions of religious people is wholly inadequate for understanding religion because, given the radical distinction between faith and tradition (expression), "a preliminary insistence in the academic study of religion must be that when any of these things is an expression of religious faith, then it cannot be fully understood except as an expression of religious faith."[28]

The recognition of the dual character of religion then—its esoteric/doxoteric structure—makes a kind of academic study of religion possible, and yet, the kind of emphasis given the esoteric aspect by Smith virtually rules out its significance, if not, in fact, making the enterprise altogether impossible. If Smith is right, faith cannot be known objectively and its expressions can only be properly understood from within the faith experience. Consequently, the scholarly study of religion in terms of a detached examination of the tradition is an objectification of what is essentially subjective and therefore a distortion of what it is the scholar really wishes to understand. An understanding of religion, according to Smith then, is impossible without "religious understanding."

There are numerous problems in Smith's proposal which cannot be pursued here,[29] though it must be pointed out that his faith/tradition distinction with the implied "superiority" of faith presumes foreknowledge of the Truth of religion. And insofar as it does so, it is itself a kind of religious or theological position. A study of religion based upon that distinction, therefore, becomes a kind of religious exercise. As such it becomes an object of study like any other religious phenomenon. Its results and conclusions compete in the "theological fray" as does any other religious belief or theological stance. Smith, that is, enters the metaphysical debate between the sceptic and believer on the side of the believer.[30] But it is precisely this "metaphysical condition" that the critical or academic study of religion was, in its origins, intent upon avoiding. It was the hope of the founders[31] of the academic study of religion to provide a knowledge about religion without entering into the debate between and amongst the various theological positions and religious traditions. This does not mean that the student of religion has no concern for the value of religion (and any religious reality that might in fact exist) for human history and in the lives of believers. It is simply to recognize, as one student of the subject puts it, that "if . . . we are to justify the science of religion [critical study of religion] it is centrally upon intellectual grounds, not on the ground of its utility or of its capacity to improve people."[32]

The break with the theological or religious perspective was a deliberate attempt to move towards an intellectual impartiality towards religious traditions other than one's own and to be objective in a detached and scientific manner. The academic study of religion, then, is not a rejection of the religious ideal in life; it is rather an attempt to reflect upon that ideal.

Given Smith's position it is hard to know what of intellectual-cognitive value, if anything, the academic study of religion could uncover that is not already "known" through experience, and "known" much more thoroughly and perfectly in the experience. Why such study, when the essence of religion is "known" intuitively in the experience of faith, would be undertaken at all is a mystery. If Smith is right, the independent and critical study of religion (as an academic exercise) is impossible because the real study of religion is "reduced" to a religious exercise. In "Comparative Religion: Whither and Why?" Smith leaves no doubt about the religious character of the study of religion: "The practitioner of religion, then, I am suggesting, may become no longer an observer *vis-à-vis* the history of the diverse religions of distinct or even closed communities, but rather a participant in the multiform religious history of the only community there is, humanity. Comparative religion may become the discipline's self-consciousness of man's variegated and developing religious life."[33]

IV

If the critics of the scholarly study of religion are to be believed, the critical study of religion is either impossible or absurdly insignificant. If religious experience and the truth revealed in it are ultimately inexpressible then, of course, no detached and objective examination of religion is at all possible. An absolute silence is academically insurmountable. But if silence is the only adequate response to the religious experience one should not know religion at all—at least not "true religion." But those who do enjoy religious experience do not all remain silent; many "speak out" and "act out" their experience and so "embody" it in a diversity of observable, intellectual, practical and social expressions. And it is this "embodied" experience that is the object of examination by the academic student of religion. While the devotee's talk is about the experience of God, the student's talk is about the devotee's talk. This presumes that knowing something about the devotee's talk admits of conclusions that bear on the devotee's experience and the intentionality of that experience. If Smith's claim is true that such expressions can only be understood from within the devotee's circle of religious experience then again the study of religion is a spectator's absurdity. Professor Neusner, arguing in a similar vein but with specific reference to the study of Judaism, captures the absurdity well: "In the study of religion, accordingly, deep calleth unto deep, the religious intellectuals, laying down the norms and meanings of their worlds in words, speak to the intellectuals who describe religions. By definition, the one is deprived of the power of speech, the other of the power of hearing. In the academic study of religions, the dumb address the deaf."[34] Neusner's comment, though, only makes sense if the question "Does understanding religion require religious understanding?" is considered metaphysically, and if "the world" is properly understood "supernaturalistically." Taken metaphysically "the world" must be considered in either naturalistic or supernaturalistic terms. To the metaphysically-minded, denial of the need for "religious understanding" assumes the wholly naturalistic character of the religious phenomenon; it presumes, that is, that the "gods" do not exist—that the belief in the gods is the sum and substance of the reality of the gods. On the other hand, the student of religion sees the argument for "religious understanding" as a necessary prerequisite to the study of religion as presuming the existence of the "gods" and implying thereby the need for a supernaturalistic view of "the world." The methodological helpfulness of the question "Does understanding religion require religious understanding?", therefore, can only emerge if the metaphysical issue is transcended.

That the critical and scholarly study of religion is a fact admitted even by the religiously-minded scholar is of great significance because it reveals at least some common ground shared by the religious believer and the academic "outsider." Both agree that religious experience commonly finds expression in concepts, community and action. And both admit that it is here that the methods of the scholar are appropriate.[35] But this, as I have pointed out above, is as far as the agreement goes. Each side in the discussion views the nature of the relationship between the esoteric experience and the public expressions or embodiments of that experience differently. The behavioristic reductionism of the naturalist places no significance on the interior, subjective element of religion. The relationship of faith to tradition here is one of necessity because it is in fact one of identity; the faith is simply what the tradition happens to be. It is this kind of identity thesis that makes so much of Smith's argument salutary. The supernaturalist, providing he allows for some expression of the faith, takes the relationship of tradition to the faith experience to be "contingent." The revelatory character of the faith experience so far transcends the capacity to embody it in verbal expression or ritual action that such embodiments must never be taken too seriously. Such an analysis, however, is tantamount to a "reduction" of religion solely to a faith element, as if it could exist entirely independently of conceptual and practical expression. Both of these reductionisms, I suggest, are premature. At present we have no way of knowing whether or not either of these metaphysical positions is true or false. Yet an adequate grounding of the academic study of religion seems to require a resolution of this debate which, however, does not seem to be resolvable.

V

The metaphysical question as to the existence or non-existence of the gods is obviously one of great importance in coming to a theoretical understanding of the nature of religion (religious phenomena).[36] But to admit this is not to capitulate to the wholly different claim that the very study of religion requires a conclusive (positive) answer to that question before it can properly be embarked upon. Such a claim builds upon very shaky foundations given the fundamental philosophical dispute in which that question is held. Further, a methodological position which assumes either the truth or falsity of religion presumes, in part at least, what the study of religion is concerned to find out. In attempting to characterize the nature of the study of religion without surrendering the philosophical neutrality of that study requires, I suggest, an evasion, at least temporarily, of the metaphysical question. And this can be done, as I shall argue here, by adopting as a model for our talk about religion Kant's talk about our knowledge of the physical world.

Kant's critical philosophy, as is well known, is inspired by two fears[37]— namely the fear that the mechanical vision of the universe does not hold and the fear that it does. If the first fear is justified then science is endangered because genuine explanations become impossible. If the second is justified, morality seems to be undermined. The central problem under discussion here is also beset by two fears—the fear that religion is not at all an observable phenomenon and the fear that it is. If the first is justified no study of religion is possible; if the second is true then religion, including the values it embodies, seems to be endangered. Gellner's comment that Kant "never stooped to the silly supposition that accepting either of the two disasters would evade the other [but rather] he attempted to prevent both,"[38] is particularly relevant here.

Kant's solution to his problem lies not in metaphysical claims about the nature of the world; but in a critique of human understanding itself, of *how one must think* in order to make sense of the natural world. Unless one assumes, for example, that causality must exist (without, of course, knowing in an *a priori* fashion any specific causal generalizations) one could not know the world. It is not a matter of knowing the external world first and then "deciding" whether or not to assume that it obeys causal laws, but rather that in the very seeing of that world such causal orderliness is being assumed. The world may in fact be a chaos and nothing Kant says about our knowledge of the world can guarantee that it is not. What Kant shows, rather, is that there are constraints on our thought to force the assumption of order. But it also appears that such order as makes knowledge possible also rules out the freedom necessary to morality. Nevertheless, Kant argues that the threat to the moral order is not real. The irrevocable order "in the world" is not really in the world but rather imposed on the world by us. Since we impose it, we have no necessity to suffer under it. Gellner summarizes Kant's position very perceptively: "This is a desperate remedy, and Kant does not use it lightly. It is only because, without such an assumption, and without such an exemption, all morality and freedom would disappear, that we must in his view assume, in the interest of preserving this absolute minimum which gives meaning to our lives, that we are indeed exempt from the vision we have ourselves imposed. Only such great need justifies this step; and only the previous discovery that causal necessity was man-made also makes it permissible. Without this, it would be impermissible, *however* great the need might be.[39]

The point then is this. Kant is a materialist (mechanist) in his natural philosophy but not in the sense of assuming that such a vision gives us the last word on the ultimate nature of things. It is well known that Kant placed practical reason in supremacy over theoretical reason, thus making theoretical knowledge subservient, so to speak, to experience. Nevertheless, he was, epistemologically one might say, a materialist: "... in the sense of supposing that the machine tradition tells us what the world is like in as far as it is available for understanding, for cognitive exploration *by us*. The kind of explanatory structures that we can work with, can only operate on the assumption of a certain kind of material."[40]

As Kant struggled to bring both freedom and mechanism into a coherent unity so we need to bring into one coherent view faith and tradition. Tradition as discussed above, it has been suggested, is inimical to faith in the same way that mechanism precludes freedom. In order to know religion, that is, one must restrict oneself to tradition. This is equivalent to Kant's epistemological mechanism. If religion is indeed faith and tradition, then faith can only be known through the tradition. This is admittedly reductionistic, but it is not metaphysical reductionism. This approach is reductionistic, to paraphrase Gellner, "in the sense of supposing that the tradition tells us what faith (real religion) is like in so far as it is available for cognitive exploration." The kind of descriptive and explanatory structures that the scholar requires can only operate on the assumption that religion is objectively available—that is, as tradition.

This reductionism in the scholarly exploration of religion, however, need not rule out the reality and value of religion as faith. Theoretical knowledge about religion may well be subservient to religious experience in the same sense that

Kant's theoretical reason bows to practical reason. Perhaps this is what Smart means in his rather cryptic comment to the effect that being a saint—a religious devotee—is far more important than studying religion: "I am far from claiming that the study of religion is the most important thing to be undertaken in connection with religion. Being a saint is more important."[41] And this despite the fact that he insists the academic study of religion be based upon intellectual grounds and not on grounds of religious utility.

The critical turn in philosophy, I conclude therefore, allows us to answer the question "Does understanding religion require religious understanding?" without entering the metaphysical debate. Epistemologically we can conclude that knowledge about religion does not require religious understanding or religious experience. "Religion" is a primitive concept and cannot be reduced to elements called "faith" and "tradition" as is suggested by Smith. The only faith that can be known theoretically is "embodied faith," which is tradition. Analytically we can distinguish between the esoteric experience we name "faith" and the expressions of that faith which become the "tradition." But we must avoid the temptation here to reify faith. Religious expression and hence tradition, therefore, at least for "theoretical reason"—i.e., for the academic student of religion—is inseparably connected to faith. In general, what is true about "the tradition" is the truth about "the faith" from which that tradition emerges. As far as the academic student of religion is concerned, then, the question of whether "religious understanding" in the sense of "empathetic insight" (i.e., the believer's apprehension of religion) is a prerequisite of scholarly understanding of religion, can be answered with an unequivocal "No!"[42]

Notes

1. Alasdair MacIntyre, "Is Understanding Religion Compatible with Believing?" *Faith and the Philosophers*. John Hick (ed.). London: Macmillan, 1964.
2. MacIntyre's "test case" in this article is the Christian religion but it is obvious that he assumes his argument valid with regard to other religious traditions.
3. This necessity is not, however, logical necessity. He distinguishes the invulnerability here from the logical invulnerability to falsification of religious belief which he discusses in his "The Logical Status of Religious Beliefs," *Metaphysical Beliefs: Three Essays*. A. MacIntyre (ed.). London: SCM, 1957.
4. MacIntyre 1964: 132.
5. MacIntyre's discussion of the nature of anthropological knowledge is necessarily brief and, consequently, does not do justice to the variety of opinion and argument on this issue. His critique of Winch and relativism in particular are less than persuasive but time does not permit analysis of that problem here.
6. MacIntyre 1964: 132.
7. Norris Clarke, "It is Compatible," *Faith and the Philosophers*. John Hick (ed.).

London: Macmillan, 1964: 150.

8. *Ibid.*, 150.

9. That is, "in submission to it." This kind of argument is set out at great length by T. F. Torrance, for example, in his *Theological Science*. Oxford: Oxford University Press, 1969 and especially in his *God and Rationality*. Oxford: Oxford University Press, 1971. I have subjected his argument to criticism in my *Science, Religion and Rationality: Questions of Method in Science and Theology*, Unpublished Doctoral Dissertation, University of Lancaster, 1974: 55–66.

10. See W. Köhler, *Gestalt Psychology* (1929), quoted by N. R. Hanson, *Patterns of Discovery*. Cambridge: Cambridge University Press, 1965: 12.

11. See L. Wittgenstein, *Philosophical Investigations*. Oxford: Basil Blackwell, 1968: 194.

12. See here, especially, F. Allen Hanson, "Understanding in Philosophical Anthropology," *Journal of the Anthropological Society of Oxford* 1970: 67, and F. Allen Hanson and Rex Martin, "The Problem of Other Cultures," *Philosophy of the Social Sciences* 1973. This, of course, raises important questions about the value of phenomenological studies which have been of critical significance for the academic study of religion. These cannot, however, be dealt with here.

13. This has been a common argument against the academic study of religion which has generally been seen to be reductionistic. Rudolph Otto's comments in this respect, in his *The Idea of the Holy* (Oxford: Oxford University Press, 1931), have been taken up by many scholars. A particularly "virulent" form of this argument can be found in Jacob Neusner's "'Being Jewish' and Studying About Judaism," *Address and Response at the Inauguration of the Joy and Leslie Cohen Chair of Judaic Studies*, Emory University, 1977. See also his "The Study of Religions as the Study of Tradition: Judaism," *History of Religions* 1975. This line of argument is central to W. C. Smith's discussions of the nature of the study of religion which I shall submit to criticism below.

14. See T. S. Kuhn, *The Structure of Scientific Revolutions*. Chicago: University of Chicago Press, 1962 (expanded edition, 1970).

15. There are some, of course, who would question whether Castaneda's work is anthropology; see for example, R. DeMille, *Castaneda's Journey: The Power and the Allegory*. Santa Barbara, CA: Capra Press, 1976. See also, however, Stephen Reno's review of DeMille in *Religion* 7 (1977), as well as his earlier "Castaneda and Don Juan: Some preliminary Observations," *Religious Studies* 11 (1975).

16. Carlos Castaneda, *A Separate Reality*. Harmondsworth: Penguin Books, 1971: 132.

17. *Ibid.*, 16.

18. There are, I think, logical problems with the notion of "the participant-observer" akin to the problems of the "concept" of squaring the circle. Time does not allow a discussion of that notion here. However the problem related to that of relativism is raised in note 5 above.

19. It is interesting to notice here that eastern religions, such as Zen, so concerned with silence have produced an extensive literature and elaborate religious practice. T. R. Miles, in *Religion and the Scientific Outlook* (London: George Allen & Unwin, 1959) similarly suggests that the only appropriate religious response is silence. However, Miles, inevitably, proceeds to suggest that such silence must be "parabolically" qualified. Qualified silence, I suggest however, is *not* silence.

20. See here A. N. Prior's interesting article "Can Religion be Discussed?" *New Essays in Philosophical Theology.* A. Flew and A. MacIntyre (eds.). London: Macmillan, 1955.

21. This chiefly in his *The Meaning and End of Religion: A New Approach to the Religious Traditions of Mankind.* London: Macmillan, 1962. However, see also his *The Faith of Other Men.* New York: Harper & Row, 1962; *Questions of Religious Truth.* London: Victor Gollancz, 1967; and *Belief and History.* Charlottesville: University of Virginia Press, 1977.

22. W. C. Smith, *The Meaning and End of Religion,* 119.

23. *Ibid.,* 155.

24. *Ibid.,* 136.

25. *Ibid.,* 141.

26. W. C. Smith, *Belief and History,* 95–96.

27. W. C. Smith, *The Faith of Other Men,* 46.

28. W. C. Smith, *The Meaning and End of Religion,* 171.

29. I have attempted such an analysis of his work elsewhere, chiefly in my "The Role of 'Belief' in the Study of Religion: A Response to W. C. Smith," *Numen* 26 (1979): 231–249. [Ed. note. See also Wiebe's later essay, "On the Transformation of 'Belief' and the Domestication of Faith in the Academic Study of Religion," *Method & Theory in the Study of Religion* 4/1–2 (1992): 47–67.]

30. This becomes especially obvious in his most recent work *Faith and Belief* (Princeton: Princeton University Press, 1979), that aspires, as he puts it, "to make a contribution towards a new planetary self-consciousness of faith" (10), so as to "reclaim," it appears, our "pitiably dehumanized society" engendered by the modern western notion "that society can be organized on the assumption that faith does not really matter" (139).

31. The founders of the academic study of religion include Max Müller, Cornelius Tiele, Chantepie de la Saussaye, Gerardus van der Leeuw, W. B. Christensen, *et al.* One might profitably consult Jacques Waardenburg's *Classical Approaches to the Study of Religion: Aims Methods and Theories of Research,* Vol. 1. The Hague: Mouton, 1973. I have discussed the aims of the founders briefly in my "Is a Science of Religion Possible?" *Studies in Religion* 7 (1978): 5–17.

32. N. Smart, *The Science of Religion and the Sociology of Knowledge: Some Methodological Questions.* Princeton: Princeton University Press, 1973: 8.

33. W. C. Smith, "Comparative Religion: Whither—and Why?" *The History of Religions: Essays in Methodology.* Mircea Eliade and Joseph Kitagawa (eds.). Chicago: University of Chicago Press, 1959: 55. The increasing emphasis upon the concept of story as hermeneutical tool in the study of religion reflects this sentiment that man's study of religion is, or perhaps *ought* to be, a religious exercise. See in this regard, especially M. Novak's *Ascent of the Mountain, Flight of the Dove: An Invitation to Religious Studies.* New York: Harper & Row, 1971. See also the essays gathered by J. B. Wiggins, *Religion as Story.* New York: Harper & Row, 1975.

   A very similar position is set out by L. Dupré in his *The Other Dimension.* New York: Doubleday, 1972; "without at least some previous experience of faith the full meaning of the religious act must remain closed to the analyst. An adequate description undoubtedly requires more than an extrinsic acquaintance with the religious act." (110). Dupré, like Smith, recognizes that faith cannot dispense with "tradition" (62) but still insists that a study of the "tradition" can never reveal the essential character of religion (108).

34. J. Neusner, 1977: 12. L. Dupré (1972) also makes use of paradox when discussing this issue of the study of that which can't be studied. He writes: "The paradox of the act of faith is that it throws a bridge by declaring the gap unbridgeable" (108).

35. For a further discussion of the price paid by the religious believer in refusing to grant this matter see T. Penelhum, *Problem of Religious Knowledge*. London: Macmillan, 1971: 122 ff.

36. I have argued this at some length in my "Truth and the Study of Religion," *Philosophical Studies* 25 (1977): 7–47.

37. My account here rests on E. Gellner's discussion of Kant in his *Legitimation of Belief*. Cambridge: Cambridge University Press, 1974.

38. *Ibid.*, 185.

39. *Ibid.*, 187.

40. *Ibid.*

41. N. Smart, 7.

42. I wish to acknowledge here the assistance of my colleague Dr T. Day for a thorough and critical reading of this paper which has helped to clarify its intention and argument.

19

MARTIN S. JAFFEE, *Fessing Up in Theory: On Professing and Confessing in the Religious Studies Classroom*

ॐ॰ॐ॰

Introduction

My awakening, in college, to the pleasures of intellectual life, occurred in the setting of the academic study of religion. I have regarded myself as a practitioner of such study ever since. All my degrees were earned in departments of "Religion" (Syracuse, BA, 1972; Florida State, MA, 1974) or "Religious Studies" (Brown, PhD, 1980). For the first seven years of my professional life I taught in a "Religious Studies" department at the University of Virginia. Since 1987, I have held an appointment in and now chair a program in "Comparative Religion" at the University of Washington. By whatever name my bureaucratic cubby-hole in the university has been called, it has always represented the study of religion as a distinct area of Humanistic inquiry— disciplined interpretation of the historical, social, and symbolic dimensions of religion as a cultural form. I have been privileged to pursue this charge by engaging the particular traditions of Judaism.

I am, then, by socialization and self-interest, disposed to accept the notion that the academic study of religion is best pursued in the context of a special unit of the university distinct from other departments in the Humanities or Social Sciences. It is not clear to me why a unit composed of "religionists" exploring "religious structures" need be more controversial than a unit of "economists" exploring "economic structures." While I have profited immensely from studies of religion emerging from various departments of the university, I am convinced that the richest study of religion is possible only in the inter-disciplinary "clearing house" of perspectives which the department or program of the study of religion provides. More importantly, we play a crucial role in the intellectual interchange of the university. It is not simply that our units house highly-trained specialists in traditions much discussed (and often misconstrued) by sociologists, historians, anthropologists, and political scientists. The "religion unit" is also the sole faculty with a fundamental commitment to place empirical and theoretical pressure upon the disciplinary blindspots of models of religion developed by our Humanistic and Social Scientific colleagues.

The present essay, however, is not an exercise in "theory of religion" or "theory of the study of religion." Nor does it defend the cogency of religious studies as an academic field, although it touches on these matters at various points. Rather, it reflects upon the distinctive pedagogical environment that the departmental or programmatic context fosters (or, I argue, *ought* to foster). It addresses three related matters: (i) an explanation of why theorizing about religion and its study is, in principle, crucial to our pedagogy; (ii) an account of my own attempts to integrate a certain range of theoretical reflection into my pedagogy; and (iii) a reflection on how the personal religiosity of the teacher (or lack thereof) can emerge as a legitimate topic for theorizing in the classroom. Overall, I hope to suggest how a general theory of what we do as teachers implies the legitimacy of contextualizing the entire person of the teacher in the discourse of comparison, analysis, and interpretation of religion as a cultural form.[1]

Theory and Pedagogy in the Study of Religion

At the risk of asserting a proposition which only a metaphysician could properly defend, let me nevertheless go out on a limb: there is no theory-free study of anything, no pure description of any object—from geological formations, to sub-atomic particles and graphic markings on hard surfaces—which is not already enabled by a point of view or set of assumptions. There are, however, descriptions which are aware of their prior interpretive commitments and those which are not. I assume that the one indispensable imperative that distinguishes thinking in university classrooms from thinking on bar stools or in living rooms is precisely the obligation to become aware of the interpretive commitments which shape the way we understand whatever it is we deem worth knowing.

The study of religion in the university setting, therefore, has little choice but to engage in the systematic cultivation of the intellectual self-consciousness that theorizing represents. Indeed, I have long ago accepted Jonathan Z. Smith's argument that the very object of our study—"religion"—is itself a theoretical construction, an intellectual invention serving a broader cultural taxonomy (see in particular the programmatic introduction in J. Z. Smith 1982: xi–xiii). The traits that make various cultural projects—most long dead, many still living in various forms—evidence of something called "religion" are not self-evident (as the sad history of definitions of religion testifies). Nor is it clear that "religion" is a necessarily more viable concept than "discipline" to describe the thing which, say, Buddhists and Muslims exemplify by virtue of their commitment to historically distinct—but typologically comparable—bodily, cultural, and intellectual praxes. Obviously, "religion" is a concept that emerged out of the distinctive Greco-Roman cultural tradition, played a significant role in the development of European popular and learned culture within Christendom, and thus continues to serve as a convenient way for Western Christendom's cultural descendants ("us" by virtue of "our" academic vocation) to organize otherwise diverse kinds of information about human thought and action. We are, I believe, more or less stuck with "religion" as a piece of mental furniture. Indeed, an effort to abandon the concept because of its rootedness in a specific cultural tradition would simply render our discourse unintelligible to most of the thinking people—in and beyond the academic circle—whom we hope to interest in our work. Our task, rather, is continually to renew and reconstruct the concept so that it can enrich not only our own research but that of colleagues throughout the university.

Is not the inventedness of "religion," after all, a trait shared with all of the more traditional objects of the Humanities? The objects of study labeled "art," "literature," and even "history" are all constructed by traditions of theoretical discourse, as the succession of their various conceptualizations in the modern European university attests.[2] All are entities which exist not as found objects or natural formations, but as objects of reflection. They are categorical frameworks or historical traditions of conceptualization that enable certain comparative or constructive intellectual tasks.

But to recognize that "religion" shares with, say, "literature" the character of a theoretical abstraction, does not necessarily place the academic study of religion on the same rhetorical playing field as the study of literature. The fact is that "literature" has been a recognized object of Humanistic learning since the Renaissance discovered it as a theoretical framework for exploring human imagination ("imagination"—yet another theoretical invention of the Humanities). Not long after, "religion" surfaced as the symbol of the enslavement of that imagination to priestcraft, superstition, and folly. The course of the ensuing debate about whether and how the origins and persistence of "religion" ought to be explained has been brilliantly traced by Sam Preus, and need not concern us here (Preus 1987). The point is simply that rhetorically, at least, we "religionists" have a certain amount of negative tradition to overcome; theorizing our subject matter is a pressing concern for us in a way that it has not been for other more traditional Humanistic fields.[3]

This is why "theory" must lie at the center of what we do as teachers. Theoretical reflection about "religion" is not something for our future leisure, after all our research results are encyclopedically cataloged. Rather, it should be a continuous constructive enterprise, present at all points in the curriculum—from the introductory course to the most advanced undergraduate majors seminar. No majors should be released from our clutches without working knowledge of specific theories of religion, a grasp of the cultural inheritance which problematizes religion as an object of reflection, and, most crucially, experience in constructively bringing "theory" and "data" together into a mutually illuminating conversation.

Such theorizing, in my judgment, may begin with general reflection on the nature of religion as an object of study—the question of definition. But it cannot remain there. Students ought to be made aware of what is gained and lost by any particular path of approach to the landscape of the religious field. They should learn to care whether or how the study of religious "ideas" differs in method and goal from the study of "myth" or "ritual." They should be able to demarcate some rough and ready boundaries between, for example, "religion," on the one hand and "law," "culture," or "ethnicity," on the other—and then recognize the permeability of those boundaries. Finally, it should be impossible to imagine an undergraduate major in our field who cannot adduce cogent grounds for distinguishing "academic" knowledge of religion from the "experiential" knowledge of participants in religious traditions.

In fact, this final consideration—the status of knowledge produced by academic research in religion and its relation to the knowledge of the religious participant—is the most crucial one, for through it others may be approached. Let me illustrate how I have tried to bring my students into conversation with me about it and where that conversation often leads. I draw upon experiences in two large introductory lecture courses which I routinely teach—Introduction to Western Religions and Introduction to Judaism[4]—as well as innumerable advising sessions in my office, primarily with majors in our Comparative Religion program.

Understanding Religion and Doing Religion

A fact of life (at least this has been my experience at two major state universities) is that many students routinely confuse a bystander's *interpretation* of "religion" (what we offer in class) with the *active pursuit* of "a religion" (which, as we claim, people do in multiform ways in countless societies, but only in perverse cases for a grade). Simply put, students are not clear that teaching people how to embody religion is not the same as teaching them to reflect upon its structures or history.

This disentanglement of "the study of religion" from "being religious," is, of course part of the venerable rhetorical strategy for defending the study of religion in publicly funded universities.[5] Apart from its political significance in fostering the growth of our field, I find the distinction pedagogically crucial. Accordingly, I weave the theme throughout my lectures, from the introductory comments on the syllabus through the specific historical or comparative discussions which make up the body of the course.

But it only begs the question to stipulate baldly that "in class we *study* religion, in the world people *do* it." The reason, of course, is that a thoughtful student will respond: "Well, if I want to *understand* religion, would it not be better to *do* it? What do I need *you* for?" Years of academic socialization have conditioned most of us to sniff at the *naiveté* of this question. Nevertheless, it must be seriously entertained, for at stake in the answer is the cogency of our claim to constitute an independent focus of Humanistic learning. What, indeed, do we know that the most sophisticated "believer" does not and, except through our disciplines, *cannot* know? Is it *worth* knowing? Our courses are appropriate places to attempt an answer.

While I attempt to make all of my introductory students theorists on this issue, the question is usually most urgently raised by prospective majors. Many, in fact, do not choose to major in Comparative Religion because they are interested in "religion." Rather, they are interested in "*a* religion" (theirs or some other which they admire and would perhaps wish to emulate). Not a few are frustrated by the Major curriculum, which forces them to do substantial comparative study and engage theoretical questions in a focused way. They wonder: if there are innumerable "religions" out there (including extinct ancestors of existing species), how will knowing, say, two of them get anyone much further along in the project of understanding "religion"? And how well, anyway, could one get to understand any of these religions as an undergraduate major in Comparative Religion (out of politeness, perhaps, they do not add: or as a specialist in the rabbinic texts of third to sixth-century Palestine and Mesopotamia)?

So I have come to say: "It all depends upon what you mean by *understanding*." Here is something to sink a theoretical tooth into, for it returns us to the fundamental issue which, as Gadamer taught us, undergirds everything that happens in the name of the Humanities. What do humans grasp, by virtue of their possession of language, that non-human beings do not? I find myself convinced by those who answer this question rather simply as follows: "It is through language that humans understand themselves as beings with a world." Human acts of understanding bear an ontological weight sustainable only by those who come to know themselves in the midst of a meaning-laden (i.e., linguistic) universe. This is why understanding the division of labor in a human society is a far more open-ended exercise than, say, the analysis of task divisions in a bee-hive or ant-hill.

This recognition of the linguisticality of human beings, foundational to the Humanities as a whole, is also the bridge to the distinctive enterprise of interpreting religion as a specific formation of human meaning. I conceive the academic study of religion, therefore, in a rather Geertzian mode. On the one hand, our classrooms offer space to explore the most comprehensive symbol-systems by which diverse human cultures have encoded their grasp of the world. On the other, they provide an opportunity to reflect upon the multiple connections and gaps between such systems and the societies which deploy them. Between these two hands, moreover, lies a connecting torso in the form of a question—what implications do such socially deployed symbol-systems have for the individuals whose lives are ineluctably shaped by enmeshment within them?

The object of our study, then, is neither a psycho-social "experience" nor an historical or phenomenological "essence" which can be isolated or analyzed in terms of its intrinsic nature. "Religion," rather, is a potentiality of cultural formation that may be activated in numerous institutional settings through the synergy of a wide variety of historical and social factors.[6] Our theories about its fundamental structures will help us recognize it in unusual forms; our recognition of it in unsuspected forms will tutor our reflections about its fundamental structures across cultural and historical boundaries. In the face of this protean theoretical object, what we offer in our teaching and research is a certain sharpening of perception or education of taste. The goal is to enable our students and other interested parties to interpret the impact and discern the resonances of "religion" within the larger discourses of historical cultures and in the patterns of individual lives.

It is precisely because we educate taste and judgment that we must engage in the identification and interpretation of objects for comparison. Taste is sharpened in the act of discerning distinctions and judgment gains acuteness through discrimination and synthesis. With regard to the precise definition of our comparative perspectives—and what may be compared within them—however, I remain open-minded. Both our data and the theoretical ranges for interpreting them are too rich to bear confinement within a narrow canon of theories of comparative inquiry. Here I can only speak for myself and the role I relish in my own work as an historian of Judaism in particular, with strong comparative interests in the histories of Christianity and Islam.

My way of teaching about "religion" within the conventional boundaries of Judaism, Christianity, and Islam is to focus attention on the complex means by which cultures transmit their fundamental pictures of reality—what William Paden has called their "religious worlds" (Paden 1993). How, I routinely ask, do Judaic, Christian, or Islamic cultures create people who are either capable of drawing nourishment from specific conceptions of the world or committed to struggling against such conceptions? For answers, I turn to the "religions" of such cultures—by which I mean primarily the ritual formations, narrative traditions, and symbolic languages which model or delimit comprehensive conceptions of that "whole" within which their members find themselves. This "whole," naturally, includes the social world and its diverse relations and hierarchies. But the distinctive focus of my concern with "religion" is upon worlds conceived as before and after, above, below, and parallel to the one human society inhabits. It includes as well all the diverse personal beings (fearsome, loving, or both) and abstract forces which humans may encounter in those other worlds (e.g., angels and demons, gods or Fate). I am not yet sure what, in principle, the "religious world" as such *cannot* include.

The point of my comparative exercises in the teaching of religion, therefore, is to broaden my students' appreciation of what is at stake in having a world of any kind whatsoever and to clarify the distinctiveness of their own. This exercise in appreciation has—or ought to have—an unsettling intellectual consequence. The ability to grasp the coherence of diverse world pictures, and to see when, where, and how they begin to loose their coherence for those who live within them, presuppose on the student's part a certain state of ironic detachment from Truth. By reflecting upon the most comprehensive constructions of the world's order, one cannot escape an impression of the historically contingent character of all worlds, including one's own.

To conclude the present turn of thought: I conceive the Comparative Religions classroom as a place to model a theoretically articulate pluralism regarding the cultural definition of Truth.[7] But I also see it as a place in which the study of those who have certainty of Truth (or who seek to live richly with its loss) draws attention to a crucial issue: namely, the moral consequences and rhetorical dimensions of the very theoretical positions which enable our perspective. Obedience to the morality of the classroom's intellectual project, it seems to me, institutionalizes and privileges ironic distance as the normative standpoint for interpreting the world. This is what our students usually mean by "objectivity," until we remind them that "objectivity" is itself a point of view grounded in a commitment to a cultural form of Truth.

And here is the problem: it may be possible to theorize from within irony and even to theologize about irony; but it is less possible to bring ironic distance—the simple-minded sense of "objectivity"—into the center of one's existence. Whatever one *thinks*, one still wants to *live* in a world that is rooted in the real, even if that reality is as thoroughly disenchanted as any Weberian model of Modernity might imply. It is not a thoroughly rude thing, therefore, for students to ask us what world *we* live in when we are not theorizing about, or analytically de- or re-constructing the religious worlds of others. Should not *that* world be part of our theorizing as well?

Does the Professor Confess a Religion and does it Matter?

This last observation opens directly into the question of the role of religious commitment or its opposite, personal detachment from religious commitment, in the pedagogy of the study of religion. I cannot help but observe that this very way of framing the matter hardly makes sense within the context of the academic study of religion. Does membership in a late-twentieth-century confessional tradition exhaust the possibilities of "being religious"? Are the "unchurched" by that fact alone "irreligious"? Better, in my view, to redirect the question: How may teachers use their experience as insiders or outsiders to inherited religious traditions as a resource to engage students in theoretically self-conscious studies of religion?

The most important point I have to make in this regard is this (let me emphasize it so as to approximate the volume of its announcement in class): *No matter what religion or irreligion we personally pursue, and no matter what religious tradition we study, we are as scholars outsiders to the thing we are trying to grasp. We are, therefore, potentially equal in our capacity to make informed judgments about it based upon disciplined study.* To return to a modulated voice: Our achievement in this task of informed judgment is never a function of our religion or irreligion alone. It depends primarily on the disciplined exercise of curiosity.

Let me expand on this. It is at times argued that the surest interpretations of religious traditions are offered by those who live within them. All the better, of course, if they have historical and textual training and can speak from the perspective of broad research experience. Crucial, however, for this point of view is an inner commitment to the Truth of the religious thing one attempts to understand. Wilfred Cantwell Smith, perhaps the most influential exponent of this view, has put it quite sharply:

> No statement about Islamic faith is true that Muslims cannot accept. No personalist statement about Hindu religious life is legitimate in which Hindus cannot recognise themselves. No interpretation of Buddhist doctrine is valid unless Buddhists can respond, "Yes! That is what we hold." (W. C. Smith 1981: 97)

Even taking account of Smith's own clarification that this statement applies to "faith" rather than "historical tradition" (of which outsiders, apparently, can have accurate knowledge), the point is hardly convincing.

Trapped as we are in our own time, place, culture, and gender, our attempts to understand anything beyond our own immediate framework require delving either into the historical past or into contemporary cultural "otherness." Neither of these domains is knowable through unmediated apprehension. We know the past only through the prism of imaginative reconstruction, while the contemporary cultures of others are, as ethnographers so well know, continually filtered through our own interpretive frameworks (see especially Boon 1982). We are, that is, inescapably complicit in the construction of whatever knowledge we transmit.

Let us focus for the moment solely on the problem of knowing past forms of surviving religious traditions. Even those to which we have connections through the traditions of family and ethnicity, rather than through the more circumscribed traditions of the academy, are known through tutored imagination rather than direct personal knowledge. W. C. Smith himself—who represents religious faith as "what the universe means to [the faithful], in the light of ... tradition" (W. C. Smith 1981: 47)—would concede that the "faith" he regards as a hermeneutical touchstone is itself wholly an historical product. It is something that engages this person, here and now, in light of the specific ways in which selected forms of tradition are communally preserved and interpreted here and now. For this very reason, the possession of "faith" alone places one in no privileged position regarding the knowledge of the "faith" of those long dead. For the traces of that "faith" can only be laboriously reconstructed from surviving texts and other artifacts of cultural tradition—many of which have long ago fallen out of the stream of living "faith."

It is of crucial importance, in my view, to expose students to these considerations. It helps them to grasp why the "religious" professor who mediates knowledge of bygone forms of her own contemporary "faith" finds herself sharing a boat with the "irreligious" professor, or the professor of a different "faith," who studies and teaches the same subject. Let me illustrate this point further by inserting my own personal situation into the picture I am trying to draw.

When I walk into class on the first day of the quarter, my students perceive a figure who appears something like a rabbi, complete with unruly beard, covered head, and a "back East" accent. They note on the syllabus cancellations of class on Jewish holy days. Here, they assume, is an "authentic" interpreter of Judaism. It is, unfortunately, part of my obligation as a teacher of the academic study of religion to disappoint them. I can best do so by selectively submitting my own life to the intellectual business of the classroom.

True, I appear to them, in light of their own cultural baggage, as an embodiment of a classical form of Judaism. Nevertheless, they can understand no "Judaism" without coming to grasp that the Judaism I actually live is a contemporary form that finds its cultural coherence not in ancient Babylonia or nineteenth-century Poland, but among other traditions of contemporary Judaic culture in North America and Israel. I may as a scholar of Judaism, nevertheless, develop a rich and supple knowledge—mostly textual—of many earlier forms of Judaism. These traditions may, in fact, nourish my own Judaic embodiment in ever more complex ways. Moreover, my own engagement with Judaic discipline may alert me to interpretive cruxes in earlier forms of Judaism that may stimulate the thinking of scholars of Judaism or other religions. Yet, the most I can say is that my embodiment of Judaism remains, if it is successful, a more or less rich contemporary embodiment.

For that very reason, my students must realize that I am evidence, first of all, only of myself—not of what "Judaism" *is* as a modern religion or *was* as an historically contingent tradition at some specific moment in the vanished past. Accordingly, the cogency of my interpretations of historical forms of Judaism will have to be judged by their persuasiveness to others who are as well or better informed than I. Some of these people will themselves have chosen to become personal embodiments of Judaic "faith," others will embody another "faith," and yet others none at all. But only the simple-minded will evaluate the cogency of my scholarly propositions on the grounds of my "faith."

There is a corollary to this position which I also seek to spell out to my students. That is, just as my participation in contemporary Jewish religion places me at little advantage over "irreligious" scholars in the interpretation of the history of Judaism, my "irreligion" as regards other religious traditions does not disable my capacity to develop insights which might escape the faithful of those traditions. My training as an historian of religion, I claim, provides me surer historical knowledge of Christianity and Islam, and surely more penetrating insight into what is at stake in their vanished forms, than "believers" without comparable training.

There is in principle, then, no inherent advantage to being "religious" or "irreligious" in the academic study of religion. Each point of view permits and obscures insight; the point of our common activity is to narrow our blindspots through the sharing of our work on the thing which fascinates us all. This is why the fact of a teacher's religiosity or lack of it is pedagogically salient. Foregrounding one's own position, and subjecting it to theoretical articulation, clarifies why, at bottom, our common intellectual life is a thing distinct from the cultural forms in which the "faithful" pursue their projects (even if some of us are the "faithful" as well).

The point is that, in our official role as teachers, we simultaneously know more and less than the "faithful." The comparative or historical student is usually correct to claim a broader knowledge of the tradition than that possessed by those who embody it in some contemporary form. Yet the "faithful" are surely correct in claiming that the outsider's knowledge is not the knowledge that matters at all. As I like to put it in class: I may know far more about the history and forms of Christian piety than most untutored Christians. But none of that knowledge will allow me to find salvation in Christ. That salvation is a thing I may *understand* with greater nuance and historical appreciation than many Christians; but, barring unforeseen circumstances, it is something I will never *have*.

Conclusion

In his 1989 Presidential Address to the American Academy of Religion, Robert L. Wilken suggested, in a post-Enlightenment mood, that the future of religious studies and the future of religious traditions are somehow bound up with each other. Attempting to deconstruct the traditional antagonism between the Academy and religious traditions, he echoed an earlier predecessor, Wendy Doniger O'Flaherty, in urging us to "care for" religion; to recall in our teaching and research that religions have not only a past but a future, and that "what has a future has life and can become part of *our* future" (Wilken 1989: 703). Throughout the crafting of the present essay I have often wondered whether I agree with him or not. Reviewing what I have written, I think I must.

But not without reservation. Wilken properly chastises those in our profession who bludgeon religions with blunt instruments of theoretical caricature. But to criticize hostile caricature entails no obligation to grant the religious insights of the scholar any epistemological privilege in our common interpretive enterprise. Wilken, in my view, leaves himself open to misinterpretation on this point. Obviously, "there is no reason for the scholar as scholar to shed her or his convictions to exercise the vocation of scholar" (Wilken 1989: 712). But, as I have argued, scholars who speak for their own tradition so as to privilege its claim to truth in competition with other such claims have moved from "professing religion" to "religious confession." Those of us who pursue what conventionally passes for "faith," are not privileged to obscure the difference between confessing the meaning of that pursuit in our own lives and our professional concern to articulate in publicly accessible terms what is at stake in the worlds constructed by the "faithful."

What we should be "caring for," perhaps, is not "religion" but our students.[8] The most alert of them, after all, will be fully susceptible to the vertiginous perspective afforded by conceptual travel through the worlds of others. We best express our caring for them by cultivating their awareness of the contingency of all perspectives—including that of "religion." But just as surely we must cultivate an awareness of the contingency of the discursive practices which enable those of us with university training to remain untouched by the spectacle of worlds of meaning lying dissected into patches of tissue and organ on our tables. In this delicate pedagogical project much depends upon the teacher's intellectual honesty and the cultivation of the student's capacity for informed disagreement. It is a task which demands all the resources not only of our academic training, but of our whole selves.

Notes

1. Wendy Doniger O'Flaherty (1986) and Judith A. Berling (1993) have both provided some important reflections on this issue in their Presidential Addresses to the American Academy of Religion.
2. For remarkable discussions of the nature of the university disciplines as traditions under construction, see Shils 1981: 120–161.

3. Thus, historical studies, for example, are enriched these days by theoretical dissensus regarding the nature of historiography, its methods, and its sources. But few historians, I suspect, question the need for departments of history.

4. "Large" in our setting means from sixty to one hundred students. Our program does indeed require majors to take a "theory and methods" course on the comparative study of religion. I have on occasion taught it. I prefer, however, to focus on the large "service" course in which majors are far outnumbered by students who, at least on the first day of class, assume that this will be their first and last "religion" course.

5. In a provocative article, Jonathan Z. Smith has recently wondered whether the political utility of this distinction, from which our profession has benefited immensely, enjoys any genuine theoretical coherence (J. Z. Smith 1988). The bulk of this paper, I hope, amplifies why the distinction must remain firm.

6. In insisting upon the "inessentiality" of religion and the unpredictable relationships between symbolic and social systems, I am instructed by Talal Asad's stimulating critique of Clifford Geertz (Asad 1993: 27–54). For two views from within the guild of "religious studies," see Paden 1992 and Cannon 1996.

7. Here I cannot resist reporting that a fine way of getting students to appreciate the problem is to get them reading Paul Veyne's *Did the Greeks Believe in Their Myths?* (1988). I rarely miss a chance to shoe-horn it into more advanced courses.

8. For a brilliant elaboration of this theme in the specific context of the teaching of rabbinic texts, see Handelman 1994.

References

Asad, Talal 1993. *Genealogies of Religion: Discipline and Reasons of Power in Christianity and Islam*. Baltimore: Johns Hopkins University Press.

Berling, Judith A. 1993. "Is Conversation About Religion Possible (And What Can Religionists Do to Promote it)?" *Journal of the American Academy of Religion* 61: 1–22.

Boon, James A. 1982. *Other Tribes, Other Scribes: Symbolic Anthropology in the Comparative Study of Cultures, Histories, Religions, and Texts*. Cambridge: Cambridge University Press.

Cannon, Dale 1996. *Six Ways of Being Religious: A Framework for Comparative Studies of Religion*. Belmont, CA: Wadsworth Publishing.

Handelman, Susan 1994. "The 'Torah' of Criticism and the Criticism of Torah: Recuperating the Pedagogical Moment. *Journal of Religion* 74: 356–371.

O'Flaherty, Wendy Doniger 1986. "The Uses and Abuses of Other People's Myths." *Journal of the American Academy of Religion* 54: 231–235.

Paden, William E. 1992. *Interpreting the Sacred: Ways of Viewing Religion*. Boston: Beacon Press.

—— 1993. *Religious Worlds: The Comparative Study of Religion*. Boston: Beacon Press.

Preus, J. Samuel 1987. *Explaining Religion: Criticism and Theory from Bodin to Freud*. New Haven: Yale University Press.

Shils, Edward 1981. *Tradition*. Chicago: University of Chicago Press.

Smith, Jonathan Z. 1982. *Imagining Religion: From Babylon to Jonestown*. Chicago: University of Chicago Press.

—1988. "'Religion' and 'Religious Studies': No Difference at All." *Soundings* 71: 231–244.

Smith, Wilfred Cantwell 1981. *Towards a World Theology: Faith and the Comparative History of Religion*. Maryknoll, NY: Orbis Books.

Veyne, Paul 1988. *Did the Greeks Believe in Their Myths? An Essay on the Constitutive Imagination*. Chicago: University of Chicago Press.

Wilken, Robert L. 1989. "Who will Speak for the Religious Traditions?" *Journal of the American Academy of Religion* 57: 699–717.

Part V

REFLEXIVITY AND THE ROLE OF THE RESEARCHER

INTRODUCTION

❧❧

The Observer as Subject

In recent years there has been a virtual revolution in the way in which scholars conceive of themselves in relation to the people they write about. This revolution has entailed rethinking the very opposition between insiders and outsiders, between subjects and objects, that has so far been simply presumed by many of those we have studied to this point. What some writers have begun questioning—writers varying from literary critics to philosophers and cultural anthropologists—are the limits of the subject, the limits of the object, and whether anyone can ever attain neutrality when it comes to studying human behavior. In other words, where does the detached observer begin and the observed subject end? Is the gap between the two as apparent as many have assumed, or is it merely an illusion, constructed and maintained by writers in an effort to generate authority through supposed objectivity? If it is the latter, as some writers now maintain, we might no longer even talk about *solving* the insider/outsider problem as much as *deconstructing* it.

"Reflexivity" is the term that has come to represent this position, one which recognizes the ability of language and symbols—in fact, any and all systems that re-present—continually to turn back on themselves. Although we should not mistake Clifford Geertz for such a reflexive scholar, if one recalls his stand on the relativity of experience-near and experience-distant viewpoints (that they are separated by degree and not kind), then we can see one early version of the reflexive response to so-called objectivity.

The Case of Orientalism

Before discussing the essays in this part, a few words must be said about Edward Said's landmark work, *Orientalism* (1978). Said, who is a literary critic, examines the history of European scholarship on the "other"—

specifically, the Muslim other. In European writings on the Muslim world, or what was once termed the Orient, Said finds a fairly stable series of stereotypes and assumptions, all of which consistently portray the Oriental as inferior to the European. For Said, then, orientalism denotes a complex series of associations, assumptions, texts, political policies, representations, etc., that maintain and legitimize the superiority of the European world.

Said's thesis is all the more convincing if one recalls that today the term "Orient" has little to do with the Muslim or Arabic-speaking world. Instead, the term has been pushed further East: most people using the term today would probably be referring to China, Japan, Korea, etc. Therefore, what is most intriguing is the elasticity of the term; in its history, "Orient" seems to have been perfectly capable of representing anyone not considered like "us." It is a powerful category that organizes and portrays complex and diverse cultures and histories as if they were simple, uniform, and completely understandable to the outsider. According to Said, it is a term that is intimately linked to economic, political, and cultural imperialism. Accordingly, "to orientalize" has come to mean the manner in which people (scholars included) take what is dynamic, routine, and heterogeneous and represent it as static, exotic, and homogeneous.

This brief discussion of Said opens this part on reflexivity because, according to him, the work of orientalism has more to do with "us" than it does with "them." In other words, to orientalize is to define oneself by means of stereotyped portraits of the other. In the final analysis, then, his book, *Orientalism*, is not so much about the Muslim world as it is about the way in which European writers and scholars traditionally attempted to distinguish and define their own cultural and national histories. That much scholarship on "them" and their so-called exotic or primitive customs is actually about "us" and our search for identity is an insight that, for many people now writing in this tradition, can be traced in part to the work of such writers as Said.

Scholarly and Personal Voices

David Hufford provides us with an opening exploration of just what we might mean when we employ the term reflexive. Arguing that disinterest, or neutrality, is impossible in the study of belief systems (including religion), he maintains that when it comes to studying something in which everyone has an interest or a stake, such calls for neutrality actually betray the effort on the part of one group to construct and justify their own power over another group, i.e., the powerful, uninvolved observer versus the powerless, passive subject. Hufford sees the reflexive turn as applied to the study of religion as enabling scholars not only to identify those moments when they have over-stepped their self-created authority, but also to distinguish between their scholarly and their personal voices.

Mama Lola and Writing About the "Other"

Perhaps no one scholar of religion has been as associated with this turn toward reflexivity in the study of religion than Karen McCarthy Brown, the author of the widely read *Mama Lola: A Vodou Priestess in Brooklyn* (1991). On one level one could say that the book is simply a study of the role played by Vodou (what Brown characterizes as a healing tradition) in an immigrant Haitian community living in New York. To do so, the book focuses in part on one Vodou priestess named Alourdes or Mama Lola. However, after even a brief look at the book it becomes very apparent that it is also about Brown herself, her growing relationship with Alourdes, as well as her developing relation with Vodou itself. Brown's reasoning is rather straightforward: "If I persisted in studying Vodou objectively," she writes in her Introduction, "the heart of the system, its ability to heal, would remain closed to me. The only way I could hope to understand the psychodrama of Vodou was to open my life to the ministrations of Alourdes."

A fitting entry into her work is a chapter entitled "Plenty Confidence," which is one of the "fictional" chapters from the book: the chapters in *Mama Lola* alternate between more traditional ethnographic reporting and fictional stories that narrate aspects of her experiences over twelve years of being involved with the Vodou community. "Plenty Confidence" is particularly significant for it tells the story of Karen Brown's own initiation. Brown's story is written in the third person, thereby making the author herself one of the subjects of her own story. This part of the anthology provides a brief essay written by Brown in which she discusses the issue of "objectivity" in research and what is at stake in making the people we study merely objects rather than recognizing and representing them as subjects, peers, and even friends. One thing that is at stake is perpetuating what Said has recently termed the "imperialist dynamic"—the constant impulse to objectify, simplify, and decontextualize people in the service of political and economic power.

Recovering Lived Experiences

In the reflexive scholar's interest to communicate and recover the "lived experiences" that comprise the beliefs, practices, and institutions that scholars study, a common theme has been to critique the manner in which the very categories we use to describe and compare human behaviors can often obscure the very thing we might be looking to find. In a way, it is precisely at this point where we can see the influence of Marx and Engels on reflexive scholars: this is not to say that, for example, reflexive postmodernists or feminists are Marxists, but that they show their debt to Marx and Engels in their emphasis on recovering not abstract ideas but the manner in which these ideas, beliefs, and concepts are the products of actual human beings living complex lives.

Just such a recovery effort is central to Michael Jackson's essay, "The Witch as a Category and as a Person." The events he narrates at the outset of the essay immediately challenge one to address the insider/outsider problem: a woman in village in northern Sierra Leone is accused of killing her brother by witchcraft. She soon falls ill and then confesses (as was predicted by the witch-hunters); as her punishment she is buried alive just outside the village. Is her death, as Jackson confesses to have thought himself, a murder? How can we understand the fact that after her death, the witch's "shade" terrorized people in the village—was it a product of their guilt for having murdered her? Is her death even something we can describe by means of the category "murder"? If her death was not a murder, then is "guilt" even an appropriate category? Because she confessed on her own, could her death possibly be described as "suicide"? Examining these very issues, Jackson concludes that it is not up to us "to decide whether witchcraft is a social pathology or the individual witch a victim of some delusional psychosis, for our task is to throw light on the lived experience that lies behind the masks and facades of category words—even those used by the self-confessed witch herself."

Using Other People's Myths

It is in the reflexive scholar's interest to see in the stories and practices of others instances of their own experiences that we can see some overlap with the scholarship associated with the names of Schleiermacher, Otto, and Eliade. As we saw earlier, the efforts of such scholars to determine the essence of religion was rather problematic for it entailed importing a number of categories which often had little to do with what insiders might have meant (e.g., what religious insider claims to be worshiping the sacred?). Reflexive scholars, however, are not as interested in discerning the essence of religious behavior as they are interested in establishing the fundamental unity of the observer and the subject under study—a unity all too often overlooked, they might maintain, by reductionists *and* nonreductionists alike.

In Wendy Doniger O'Flaherty's well-known essay, "The Uses and Misuses of Other People's Myths," we find a position that bridges two different stands on the insider/outsider problem: the attempt truly to understand the other which at the same time entails understanding ourselves. Like Eliade, she bases much of her position on the study of myths. She writes: "their myths have always been our myths, though we may not have known it; we recognize ourselves in those myths more vividly than we have ever recognized ourselves in the myths of our culture." Although this position shares much with Eliade's scholarship—enough so that one could argue that this essay could have been placed much earlier in the collection—the fact that it is so explicitly based on O'Flaherty's own experiences suggests that the reflexive tradition has influenced her considerably. Noting the manner in which her own myths (those of Judaism and Christianity) failed to comfort her upon the death of her father, she elaborates how, in "other people's myths," we can sometimes find solace. Perhaps it makes sense, then, that she is able to maintain that "on some deep level ... all truly creative scholarship ... is autobiographical."

Experience is a Messy Thing

In the concluding chapter to her book, *A Thrice-Told Tale: Feminism, Postmodernism, and Ethnographic Responsibility* (1992), Margery Wolf quotes the anthropologist Renato Rosaldo who writes: "If classic ethnography's vice was the slippage from the ideal of detachment to actual indifference, that of present-day reflexivity is the tendency for the self-absorbed Self to lose sight altogether of the culturally different Other." In other words, where scholars such as Brown and Doniger work to make the apparently exotic more familiar, others warn that such efforts can actually be caught up with constructing yet a new dominant, intellectual elite. Simply put, is the other lost in these attempts to rebuild oneself? Is Doniger spinning her own myth or reporting on the various myths she discusses? Is Brown telling us about Vodou practices or merely writing autobiography?

Much as reductionists have been accused of obscuring the participant's own interpretation through importing their own theories, and much as nonreductionists replace insider language with universal categories of their own making, so too the reflexive scholar may be involved in appropriating the other's myths, practices, and experiences in their own autobiographical quest. As much as scholars may wish to recover the untainted experiences of these others, "experience is messy"—Wolf is highly aware of this and, as a conclusion to this part, brings this important point to the forefront.

References

Brown, Karen McCarthy 1991. *Mama Lola: A Vodou Priestess in Brooklyn*. Berkeley: University of California Press.

Said, Edward 1979. *Orientalism*. New York: Vintage Books.

Wolf, Margery 1992. *A Thrice-Told Tale: Feminism, Postmodernism, and Ethnographic Responsibility*. Stanford: Stanford University Press.

20

DAVID J. HUFFORD, *The Scholarly Voice and the Personal Voice: Reflexivity in Belief Studies*

৵৵

Reflexivity is a metaphor from grammar indicating a relationship of identity between subject and object, thus meaning the inclusion of the actor (scholar, author, observer) in the account of the act and/or its outcomes. In this sense reflexivity shows that all knowledge is "subjective."

Reflexivity is a popular and potentially powerful concept in the interpretation of epistemological activities. In grammar *reflexive* refers to a verb that has the same "thing" as both subject and direct object. My dictionary illustrates with the sentence, "She dresses herself" (DeVinne 1991). In metaphorical use, the concept of reflexivity can indicate that scholarship is not only done *by* scholars, but that it can also be done to scholars. Scholars can study themselves. Scholarship can be an *object* of scholarship, as in "the history of folklore studies." But still more important, because scholars are human beings, the study of human life is always and inescapably reflexive. Humans study humans.

Furthermore, the scholar is always the *subject* of scholarship in the grammatical sense, that is, "the doer of the action" (DeVinne 1991: 1211), and those we study are the *objects* of our scholarship. If we speak of finding things out, the finder is the subject and the found is the object. This underlines the central point of reflexivity: all knowing is subjective; that is, *knowing* is an experience that is had by someone. Acknowledging the subjectivity of knowledge grants that points of view, perspectives, are inevitably a part of knowing. Observations are all made from somewhere. This recognition may either lead to a pessimistic debunking of all knowledge, or it may help to rehabilitate and broaden our appreciation of the subjective. The pejorative connotations of the term *subjective* (imaginary, illusory, unverifiable) arise from an old-fashioned objectivism that merely denies the egocentric predicament.

All knowing is subjective, and the "objective world" is what knowers claim to know about. Reflexivity in knowledge-making involves bringing the subject, the "doer" of the knowledge-making activity, back into the account of knowledge. As Edward M. Bruner puts it in his Introduction to *The Anthropology of Experience*, in inquiring into knowledge "we take expressions as objects of study and we become 'conscious of our self-consciousness' of these objects. We become aware of our awareness; we reflect on our reflections. Anthropologists of experience take others' experiences, as well as their own, as an object. Our activity is inherently reflexive ..." (1986: 23). Here the metaphors of the mirror and of the reflexive sentence combine, showing us ourselves in our images and our sentences.

Reflexivity completes our sentences, requiring that our accounts should include subjects as well as predicates. Without reference to ourselves as subjects, our knowledge claims sound too much like the locutions that our children and our politicians use when they want to leave themselves out of the account: "My milk got spilled," or "Mistakes were made," or "It has been shown.... " Oddly passive. Or they suggest facts that simply exist with no history: "The lamp is broken," "The money is gone," or "The Xande believe...." Unfortunately, this is what *objective* has come to mean, descriptions and analyses in which reference to the subject, the describer or the analyst, is omitted. This makes of *objectivity* merely the name of a rhetorical style.[1] If we obtain the appearance of objectivity by leaving ourselves out of our accounts, we simply leave the subjective realities of our work uncontrolled. If we manage to make our facts speak for themselves, those "facts" cease to be evidence in an argument, and we become ventriloquists instead of scholars.

Reflexivity is a response to the egocentric predicament, and it parallels responses to awareness of the ethnocentric predicament. Both risk mere self-justification, but both have the potential to reveal the culturally-situated, human quality of all knowledge.

The widespread academic use of the term *reflexivity* is a postmodern development. But the concept has a very enlightening prepostmodern foundation. In classical Greek philosophy, skepticism, Protagorean relativism ("man is the measure of all things"), and nihilism used reflexivity to destroy certainty about knowledge. And as personal reflexivity acknowledges the *ego*centric predicament, the age of exploration ushered in a gradual awareness of the *ethno*centric predicament, its social counterpart. But recognizing that interpretations of other cultures involve comparison with one's own did not lead directly to cultural relativism. European culture was inserted in the account of other cultures within an evolutionary theory that served both to justify European belief and practice and to stigmatize all others. Self-congratulation seems to be the natural first response to finding oneself thrust into an account with others, especially if one is more powerful than those others.

Exactly the same thing happened when academic disciplines, beginning with science, started to make themselves an object of study. The first serious, modern effort at a philosophy of science was developed by mathematicians and scientists, and it gave rise to logical positivism. Similarly, the history of medicine was for a long time a chronicle of the remarkable accomplishments of physicians. But when professional philosophers and historians became involved, these fields began to change dramatically. The topics became rather less fun for members of the groups under study. But this was not just because the actors and stories were not all noble. More fundamentally, it was because reflexivity led to assertions about method and about interpretations. These assertions did not just show the humanity of scientists and physicians, they showed the humanity of scientific and medical knowledge.

Reflexivity, then, can be triumphal. It can also be defeatist, lapsing into the infinite regress of reflections of reflections. This kind of reflexivity leads to extreme subjectivism, *nihilism* of the kind promulgated by the Greek philosopher Gorgias, "No thing can be said to exist.... If anything did exist, we would not be able to know it, and if we were able to know it we would not be able to communicate it" (Angeles 1992: 278).

The revelations of reflexivity can also lead to a struggle to escape from the limitations of perspective by the creation of elaborate rules for knowledge-making. The goal is to transcend perspective, to achieve what Thomas Nagel calls "the view from nowhere" (1986). This urge to have confident knowledge without reference to its subject results in a kind of neo-positivism, a worship of right method that Robert Rubinstein calls "methodolatry" (Rubinstein 1991). It is this slavish adoration of particular methods, and the resulting assault on other epistemological traditions, that Feyerabend criticizes in *Against Method* (1988). He summarizes the brutal possibilities of methodolatry when he says, "I am against ideologies that use the name of science for cultural murder" (1988: 4).

But the response to reflexivity can also be realistic and pragmatic. We must learn to tolerate uncertainty and ambiguity, while holding the reduction of uncertainty and ambiguity in our knowledge as primary goals (always sought, never completely achieved). That is not a contradiction or a paradox. It is a fact of life. Certainty is a direction, not a goal. Uncertainty, and the political importance of knowledge, require reflexivity as a check on the natural tendency for tacit interests to exploit ambiguity; that is, reflexivity helps to control hidden bias. Reflexivity and the strong light that it shines on the importance of viewpoint and perspective urges on us a multiplication of perspectives. We can never have a set of observations made from *every*where anymore than we can have a view from nowhere, but the more views we consider, the more reason we have to be hopeful about our conclusions. As Feyerabend put it, "The only principle that does not inhibit progress is: *anything goes*" (1988: 14).

Disinterest is urged on scholars of religion, but disinterest is impossible in religious issues.

Common academic definitions of religion designate it as people's "ultimate concerns," that is, the most important things in their world. At the same time, the general demand for impartiality in scholarship is applied with special stringency to the study of spiritual matters.[2] So much so that it is often assumed that believers cannot be competent scholars of belief traditions. For example, in an article on fieldwork among "folk Baptists and Pentecostals," Jeff Todd Titon (1985) notes ironically that the spiritually conservative worldview of such people is "in direct opposition to the folklorist's scientific gospel.... No ethnomusicologist could maintain a scholarly reputation if he attributed the cause of the religious music and behavior he observed in the field to God. Instead, scholarly reputations have been built on insisting the opposite" (1985: 22). What Titon observes about the study of these groups is a scholarly commonplace with regard to any group of committed believers, and I shall give additional examples of this below. But, is this prevalent position a proper corollary to the scholarly value placed on impartiality? Does holding a "scientific gospel" or arguments in direct opposition to a Divine role in the world constitute impartiality? Could we, in fact, imagine any world-view that was impartial concerning matters of "ultimate concern"? Is *disbelief* in the study of spiritual belief a view from nowhere? I would answer "no" to each question, on the basis of a reflexive analysis of belief scholarship.

Spiritual beliefs lie at the heart of many central human questions, as in the following, intentionally provocative, examples: What does it mean to be human? (BELIEFS: Fetuses have souls and are persons from conception, vs. Babies become babies, separate human persons, only at birth); What is the basis of morality? (BELIEFS: What is good is determined by God's law, vs. Social contracts among humans determine what is good); What is the ultimate fate of persons? (BELIEFS: You have an immortal soul, vs. When you're dead, you're dead). These polar illustrations are not dichotomous, and they are only a few of the many beliefs that people hold on each topic. I use these examples to illustrate that spiritual beliefs are strongly felt and can have socially important consequences. It is for this reason that I consider impartiality in spiritual matters an impossibility. That being the case, the tendency to count disbelief as the "objective" stance is a serious, systematic bias that runs through most academic studies of spiritual belief.[3]

If impartiality in belief studies cannot consist of having no personal beliefs, then impartiality must be a methodological stance in which one acknowledges one's personal beliefs but sets them aside for scholarly purposes. Recognizing that each of us has a personal voice, for research purposes we choose to speak instead with our scholarly voice. This is but one of many forms of multivoicedness (Mikhail Bakhtin's *heteroglossia*) in culture and the study of culture (See Clifford 1983; Quantz and O'Connor 1988). But I believe that it is one that has been generally neglected by scholars of belief.

The requirement of disinterest as a qualification for the study of matters in which all persons have an interest is a paradox that reflects the tensions produced when one (powerful) group studies another (less powerful) group.

The paradoxical academic insistence on an impossible disinterest in the study of spiritual matters reflects the tensions present whenever one, or one's group, is to be studied by another. To appreciate this, most scholars need only think of how it feels to approach the published results of their course evaluations, or their tenure and promotion proceedings, or their department's most recent outside evaluation. The greater the differences in the political interests of the two parties, the greater the tensions. Those being studied generally feel that they can be most accurately appraised by those who know them best—those closest to them. That is why we are usually more comfortable with *internal* reviews. What is increased objectivity to the outsider (and the administrator who *also* has distinct interests) is increased risk to the insider.

In the study of spiritual beliefs, the political interests of the scholarly community and those of believers are substantially different, and in some respects antagonistic. The historical struggle for cultural authority—that is, permission to define reality for others (Starr 1982: 13; also called "epistemic authority" by DeGeorge 1985)—between religious institutions and secular academic institutions guarantees this clash of interests. This tension is not negated by the presence of individual believers within the academic community and academics within many religious groups. The cultural authority of scholars, the complex language used in scholarly discourse, and the esoteric nature of academic channels of communication render academic interpretations of the beliefs of ordinary people generally inaccessible to those being studied. Nonetheless, those interpretations, in concert with other congruent scholarly interpretations of the culture of nonscholars, have very significant impacts on both official culture and general thought. Many of those impacts have important social consequences, ranging from the allocation of stigma (e.g., mystical experience as hallucination) and legitimacy (e.g., the valorization of charitable social action above proselytization or contemplation) to legal decisions utilizing expert testimony (e.g., separation [of church] and state or decisions about which groups really are religions and which are "cults"). The result is an asymmetrical political relationship between scholars and those they study, a relationship that is typical of experts in modern society. This relationship is exemplified by that of physicians and their patients.

Doctors are a prototype of the asymmetrical political relationship of experts and lay people, a relationship that is characterized by tacit conflicting interests and thus requires reflexive analysis.

Physicians are the prototypical professional experts and cultural authorities in our society, and they are the most visible focus of a skepticism and anger about experts and authorities that has been growing at least since the 1950s (see, for example, Illich 1976 and Burnham 1982). This is a social change that seems likely to affect all of us in the academic world. In medicine this phenomenon has produced a struggle toward a reflexive account of doctoring. This developing account recognizes that the interests of physicians and patients are neither identical nor always harmonious. This recognition is contrary to the long-held image of doctors and patients sharing a single agenda, the struggle against sickness and toward health.

While doctoring, physicians are at work, and this fact creates interests regarding fee setting, reasonable hours, distribution of prestige and status within the profession, and so forth. These interests are generally tacit and are indirectly addressed within an occupational ideology. These interests of the physician are largely either irrelevant to the patient or in conflict with patient's desire to receive care when it is needed, for care to be of high quality and low cost, etc. Furthermore, doctor and patient engage in a social interaction in which personal needs for reassurance, validation, and so forth are salient, but in which the physician has a situational monopoly on power, allowing personal differences to be medicalized, as when a reasonable complaint is converted to a symptom. A reflexive account of doctoring recognizes that medical knowledge and practice develop in response to many different forces and are always culturally situated (Gerson 1976). While this account may diminish the idealization of doctors as selfless heroes, it also counters the "medical nemesis" view (Illich 1976) in which doctors are heartless and motivated solely by greed.

The scholar–informant relationship is similarly fraught with implicit conflicting interests but explicitly shared goals, and thus also requires a reflexive reformulation.

The reformist observations made about the doctor–patient relationship also apply to scholars studying the spiritual beliefs of others (as well as many other academic situations). Scholarship is our work, and in addition to the pursuit of truth we are in pursuit of tenure, promotion, prestige, reassurance, personal affirmation, empowerment, and so forth. Many of our goals are irrelevant to our informants. We do share with them an interest in "the truth," but we also seem to share a general disagreement about what the truth is. These differences arise from both personal and social characteristics of scholars, and they frequently produce interests that conflict with the interests of those we study.

The truth claims of folk religion and the basic thrust of scholarly hermeneutics of a religion constitute a primary, fundamental conflict of interest between the scholar and those studied.

Now to return to the differences of interest between folk religion scholars and our informants. There are *many* such differences, but I shall illustrate with the most central and pervasive one. Since people hold their beliefs to be true, by definition of belief, and since their spiritual and religious beliefs are by definition their most important beliefs, their interests include a portrayal of those beliefs as credible. This applies equally to the beliefs of scholars and of those they study. Therefore, to the extent that "folk" and scholarly beliefs diverge, group interests diverge in the description and interpretation of belief. An analysis of differences between scholarly beliefs about spirituality and the beliefs of those whom they study is an important topic, but it is also very complex and beyond the scope of this article. For the present purpose, it is enough that the reader grant that such differences exist and are substantial. And to the extent that scholarly knowledge claims any practical significance, those divergent interests are likely to have important consequences.

Because the personal religious beliefs of scholars are diverse, scholars of religion must recognize that they have at least two sets of rules for discourse and problem solving: rules manifested in their personal voices and their scholarly voices.

It is at this point that my distinction between the personal voice and the scholarly voice becomes crucial. The scholarly community is not monolithic, and the personal beliefs of scholars variously conflict or harmonize with beliefs being studied and even with the alleged academic consensus. Many folklorists (as other scholars) share religious beliefs with many of our informants. There are some folklorists with religious commitments within each of the religious traditions that folklorists study. These commitments may have little relevance to many folkloristic studies, but their relevance to the study of belief is obvious. Except in schools of theology, we reject scholarly positions that assume the truth of a particular religious tradition. If I developed a Byzantine Catholic approach to the study of folk belief or if Bert Wilson developed a Mormon approach, we would be correctly challenged. Nonetheless, I remain a Byzantine Catholic who studies spiritual beliefs. And when Bert or I study and write about beliefs that we personally share we can do so as scholars and still gain some insight from our intimate familiarity with the tradition and what it is like to be within it—just as non-believers can gain insight from their "outsider" perspective. We can also speak personally about our beliefs, and at times that may be useful to our students or colleagues—but only if we are aware and clearly state that we are now using our personal voice. The difference is analogous to that between what a physician does when describing the standard practice in a serious medical situation, and what happens if that same doctor says, "Here is what I think I would do in your situation." We must distinguish our personal voices from our scholarly voices.

To confuse the personal and the scholarly voices will evoke sanctions, either scholarly or personal.

It would be as foolish for me to stand up in my home parish and offer a functionalist interpretation of our traditional beliefs as it would be for me to argue here against a functionalist interpretation on the basis of scripture. (In saying this, I do *not* accept the common belief that such interpretations necessarily conflict with one another.) The academic world and any particular religious tradition constitute different universes of discourse, and I must recognize and competently negotiate those differences or I will be discredited.

But the hearer as well as the speaker must master the personal–scholarly voice distinction. When a scholar presents findings that are congenial to her or his own personal views, there is the *possibility* that those views have unduly influenced the inquiry. However, to *assume* that rational conclusions can only be reached by those who do not find them congenial would be ludicrous. Hidden bias is controlled by having many points of view and many kinds of interest within the inquiring community, not by forbidding a particular set of views and interests. But this seems to be exactly what is done in the study of spiritual beliefs: those who hold them are heard as speaking personally (giving "testimony" rather than doing ethnography) whenever their findings appear congenial to their beliefs. If believers should be reflexive and careful about the distinction between their personal and scholarly voices, and they should, so should their audience.

The boundaries of scholarly discourse on religion are supposed to be ones that can accommodate the diversity of belief among scholars, but they have in fact come to reflect the commitments of a particular religious tradition.

One good reason that scholarly consensus must differ from the belief position of any particular tradition is precisely because the scholarly community is made up of scholars with different beliefs. That condition requires a negotiated agreement to limit our scholarly assumptions to those that people from many different traditions can share, avoiding those that are limited to a single tradition. The benefit is a pluralism of views and a reduction of unexamined assumptions. However, despite a commonly held explicit commitment to the accommodation of a diversity of beliefs, the boundaries of scholarly discourse on spiritual matters in particular have come to reflect the institutional and secular, as characterized in the following statement by Norman Malcolm:

In our Western academic philosophy, religious belief is commonly regarded as unreasonable and is viewed with condescension or even contempt. It is said that religion is a refuge for those who, because of weakness of intellect or character, are unable to confront the stern realities of the world. The objective, mature, *strong* attitude is to hold beliefs solely on the basis of *evidence*. (1977: 621)

As sociologist Peter Berger has recently put it, using northern European cultural developments as a benchmark, Western intellectuals "fulfill the predictions of secularization theory. One could call them 'elective Swedes'" (1992: 32).

Such developments in scholarship derive from a convergence of the historical scholarly need to capture cultural authority from the church and the personal interests of a variety of scholars whose religious beliefs have supported similar goals.

Why have such positions become so prevalent in modern scholarship, when "the rest of the world is as furiously religious as ever, and possibly more so"? (Berger 1992:32). As already noted, the reasons are to be sought in the historical development of the academic world as a community of professional experts who had first to wrest cultural authority from the Church. Even today religious authority represents one of the major challenges to other kinds of authority, despite whatever secularization may have occurred. Therefore, it has been in the group interests of scholars to undermine the grounds of religious authority, and those grounds are the truth claims of the various traditions. Those group interests have created some ambivalence for people who are both scholars and religious believers, but those same interests have been identical to those of scholars with either personal commitments to atheistic beliefs or personal opposition to the power of particular religious institutions. A variety of very different religious and ideological positions have proven harmonious with scholarly goals in the fight against religious authority: Protestant versus Catholic, Marxist versus religious, New Age religion versus Christianity, and Judaism, and so on.

The result of these historical developments is a conflict that can be illuminated by reflexively including both the community of scholars and the personal commitments of scholars in our account. Consider the following questions: "What do you believe?" "What does the literature suggest?" and "What do the data show?" Each refers to a radically different kind of discourse, accessing different sets of reason and evidence, and the same person may well be obliged (if truthful) to give completely different answers to each, on the same subject, and speaking in a different voice. But in the study of supernatural belief in general, given the elevation of disbeliefs to the position of self-evident truths, the distinction between the personal and the scholarly voice has been submerged and suppressed. The question "What do you believe?" has become an academic test of faith to which there is only one appropriate answer.

The narrowing of academic views on spirituality is illustrated by the shift of the meaning of skepticism *from suspended judgment to a commitment to the belief that certain kinds of traditional religious ideas are false.*

The domination of belief scholarship by a particular religious tradition is illustrated by the meaning that has come to be attached to "skepticism" as a value in belief studies. *Skepticism* may convey a range of meanings from a generally pessimistic view of the possibility of genuine knowledge, to "suspension of judgment ... a tentative doubt in a process of reaching certainty" (Angeles 1992: 276). In most academic settings *skepticism* has come to have the latter meaning, a suspension of judgment while gathering data. But with regard to the study of spiritual issues, the beliefs of lay people especially, this meaning has been replaced by a firm disbelief. In most fields, for practical purposes of scholarship and communication, the extremes of skepticism have been relegated to the status of intellectual curiosities, and attention has turned to the means of intersubjective validation. However, for religious claims, the standard scholarly view embraces the nihilism of Gorgias (quoted above) which we might paraphrase as "No supernatural thing can be said to exist, if it did we could not know it, and if we did know it we could not communicate it." This is not the effort to avoid questions of truth, but rather the insistence on particular truth claims, although these claims have not been directly debated and established.

Sometimes this disbelief has been explicitly urged on methodological grounds. For example, Christina Larner, in *Witchcraft and Religion: The Politics of Popular Belief*, states:

> Perhaps because of the personal commitments of some modern scholars the question of methodological atheism is overtly discussed rather than taken for granted. In methodological atheism, religion is to be viewed as a human projection. It is possible to believe and yet to set that belief aside for purposes of research. Absence of partisanship makes comparison more possible. It makes the latent functions of a belief more easily detectable.... I see methodological atheism as a necessary starting point for any sociological exploration of the concept of God. (1984: 111)

The argument for "methodological atheism" naively advances one culturally loaded belief as dispassionate neutrality, while unfairly asking scholars not sharing the belief to reflexively confess to bias.

Larner apparently does not view with favor the existence of scholars of religion with personal religious commitments, but she offers no serious justification for her position beyond her own personal commitment to atheist belief. Certainly, the assertion that atheism constitutes an absence of partisanship fails altogether to grant atheism its due as a religious position. This eliminates partisanship the old-fashioned way, by legislating that only one party may exist. There are useful forms of balanced scholarly skepticism that can easily be urged on believers as a research stance. As Ninian Smart put it in calling for "methodological neutralism" (1973: 94) or "methodological agnosticism" (1973: 108), avoiding the *assumption* that a belief under investigation is false "is important so that we keep options of interpretation open and so that we can actually use data to test theory" (1973:148). That is setting belief *and* disbelief aside for purposes of research. But Larner's claim is rather like me calling for methodological Catholicism. It is a requirement to *adopt* a particular religious belief for purposes of research. But the common view illustrated by Larner is especially unfair, because while it pretends to be a value-neutral position with no reflexive component, it calls on scholars with all other beliefs to display personal reflexivity in *a social context that guarantees such reflexivity will result in charges of bias unless one's scholarly work discredits one's personal beliefs*. The alleged methodological requirement serves ideological purposes of social control. Deep reflexivity is demanded of believers, and their personal beliefs (if they have the nerve to own them in public) are given the appearance of deviance within the scholarly consensus.

A fine example of this implicit function of reflexive references to scholars is offered in a recent book by religion scholar Carol Zaleski. Writing a sophisticated explanation of why visionary experiences are evidential to the naive but make no cognitive claim on scholars, Zaleski says:

> Such incapacity for wholehearted participation is the intellectual's occupational disease; among scholars [of] comparative religion it can produce a sense of nostalgia for the days of innocence or for some idealized form of archaic or traditional religiosity. When we try to evaluate the near-death experience we are stymied by our own sophistication. (1987: 204)

In other words, we (that is, *serious* scholars) wish we could share religious belief, but we know too much. What does this account imply about a scholar who may actually possess traditional religiosity, or whose near-death experience has convinced her of the immortality of her own soul? Not an intellectual? Not sophisticated? Full of archaic innocence?

The rules of scholarly belief talk are enforced by implication through accounts that reflexively probe personal reasons for the beliefs of believers, while leaving out the scholar's own background. These rules serve two important functions: first, they suppress explicit academic dissent very effectively; and second, they do so while giving the impression that there aren't any dissenters to be suppressed. This is the height of effective social control.

Ethnographers of religion are uncomfortable with informants' natural desire to convert them, because the central conflict of belief is tacit, being a product of scholarly socialization rather than scholarly research and education.

The pervasive influence of skepticism as fixed disbelief is further illustrated by the unease many fieldworkers describe about their informants' attempts to convert them. I frequently hear this in discussions among ethnographic students of religion. Elaine Lawless has put the matter as concisely as anyone in print. She calls the issue "troublesome and painful" in her study of Pentecostals (1988: xvi), and in her latest book she states plainly, "I intensely dislike proselytizing and religious argumentation intended for conversion" (1993: xii). But why wouldn't believers try to convert us if they believe they know the truth. The only plausible reasons for not wanting to convert us would be if they hated us or if they believed us ineligible for the truth, as in some racist religious frames. And why should we not want them to try to convert us? What better way to find out what someone believes? Do *we* want to *convert them* to the belief that one religious position is as good as another, and that all proselytizing is wrong? That view follows from a relativization of spiritual truth as locally helpful metaphor, and that is as much a religious position as any other—a position that directly conflicts with what most of our informants believe to be true. This does not suggest that everyone should enjoy or approve of proselytization. But this personal preference should not be confused with a position grounded in scholarly knowledge (not that Lawless suggests it is). After all, scholars as a tribe are as avid proselytizers as any group I know.

I believe that one reason proselytization makes scholars uncomfortable is that our informants' efforts to share their truth with us illuminate too starkly the contradictions and inconsistencies in the scholarly world view, wherein occupational ideologies and personal commitments have been confused with justified knowledge. We know that scholars just aren't supposed to believe things *like that*, but we have never been taught exactly why. This is the same discomfort and sense of threat many Catholics feel when a Jehovah's Witness argues, complete with scriptural citations, against prayers to the saints as spiritualism or the presence of statues in churches as idolatry—the Catholic often know *what* to believe without knowing *why*. Many scholars of religion are in the same position, and a vulnerable position it is. This is because academic disbelief attitudes are largely acquired, in the absence of counter arguments, through the socialization process of becoming a scholar—a process that parallels the education of a scholar but should not be confused with it.

A reflexive analysis of our scholarship enables us to distinguish among the beliefs of our informants, our scholarly knowledge, our personal beliefs and our occupational ideology. This permits coherent discourse and variously warranted moral actions.

It is fairly common for the kind of argument I am advancing, an argument for radical and symmetrical skepticism, to be equated with an all-out relativism that paralyzes moral action. Larner, for example, complains of a "concentration on neutral issues of rationality at the expense of emotional issues of morality" (1984: 161). More recently Jacqueline Simpson, characterizing my own position as "neutralism" (Hufford 1982, 1987) in the study of belief, suggested that such neutrality might prevent scholars from using "their reasoned disbeliefs in a socially responsible way, to combat false beliefs" (Simpson 1988: 13). But it is not unbridled relativism that I favor. Instead, I call for reflexivity and its accompanying shift to an epistemological discussion. And reflexivity and epistemological restraint do not require the acceptance of all beliefs. Rather, they require a reasoned skepticism about our own beliefs, a recognition that even scholars have multiple reasons for holding beliefs, and that this entails an obligation to give our reasons. Such self-examination is what counts as "reasoned beliefs," not merely the fact that they are held by a class of people with a reputation for doing a lot of reasoning. As Martin Hollis puts it, with reflexivity "the social destruction of reality is off the agenda," and this rescues the possibility of warranted social action (1982: 85).

A reflexive analysis that disentangles scholarly beliefs from our occupational ideologies and from our personal beliefs permits a move away from unrestrained relativism without surrender to an ethnocentric reliance founded on a "growing body of irreversible knowledge" (Larner 1984: 158 ff.). Larner's notion of irreversibility derives from a foundationalist theory of rationality which asserts that modern valid knowledge is secured by a "bridgehead" of facts with no history. This is what Feyerabend described as the idea that "we can cut the way from the result without losing the result," which he calls "the separability assumption" (1988: 262). This is the futile but endless effort to arrive at ontological statements that do not depend on epistemological conditions—achieving the view from nowhere. But reflexivity refuses to accept statements of knowledge that do not include the knower; ontological assertions cannot be made independent of epistemology.

Reflexive analysis also can show where many different kinds of beliefs and supporting reasons converge, as in the case of religious justifications offered for racist beliefs and practices.

A stubbornly reflexive stance can both enrich our ethnographic work and rescue the possibility of warranted moral action. Not only can I frame questions that reflect a particular theoretical orientation, but I can also say to my informant, "Here is what I believe about this, what about you?"[4] At the same time that it prevents us from groundlessly assuming our informants' beliefs to be false, reflexivity frees us to pursue belief issues as truth claims rather than exclusively as artistic metaphors—if and when that is appropriate. And in our analysis, it frees us to explicitly argue that some of those beliefs are false or even that some are true, instead of claiming either that we are not interested in the truth (it takes a lot of training to be able to say that with a straight face) or, equivocating like mad, that all beliefs are "in some sense" true. But that freedom is at the cost of knowing and showing which of our grounds for belief and disbelief are scholarly and which are personal. I believe in latent functions but not in classic psychoanalysis for academic reasons; I believe in souls but not in reincarnation for personal (including religious) reasons. Further, there are many beliefs and actions that can be supported by both scholarly and personal reasons simultaneously. For example, we can show that the religious arguments for racism advanced by South African Afrikaners are false on the basis of numerous well-accepted academic criteria. We are under no obligation to hold that just because this is part of their religion we cannot be justified in saying that it is false. I also believe that racism is unChristian (which is not to say that no one claiming to be a Christian is a racist), and that is another reason that I oppose it, but that is not a scholarly reason. Both kinds of reasons are good, but different, grounds for my belief and action. Scholarship can inform moral action and everyday life in general, but it cannot be the sole source of justified action and thought. Reflexivity destroys the silly idea that academic grounds for belief and action are the only valid grounds, at least for legitimate academics. If we actually believed that, we would never get the groceries bought, the lawn mowed, or the children raised. I am still waiting for sound scientific evidence on what toothpaste is best, but I continue to brush my teeth in the meantime.

Moral action based on the study of belief has been held back by the confusion among the various grounds for action.

The utilization of scholarly reasons for moral action is paralyzed by an unwillingness to confront conflict and disagreement, not by the insistence that both the disagreement and the action should be reflexively explicated and justified. The notion that scholarship is made objective by transcending culture entails at least one of two highly questionable consequences. A scholarship that transcends culture must either eliminate the moral dimension, because moral values are cultural facts, or it must make the metaphysical claim of having located moral values that have a basis independent of the human context. This latter is a common claim of religious traditions, but it does not square well with explicit academic values. To demonstrate and justify the moral implications of scholarship it is necessary to recognize scholarship as itself a culturally situated activity.

The cultural authority of scholars can only be legitimate when it is limited to scholarly positions that are explicitly justified in scholarly terms. The confusion of personal and guild interests, valid in themselves, with scholarly knowledge invalidates cultural authority and risks revocation of the social contract that granted cultural authority.

I do not mean to suggest that we can make truth claims or advance moral arguments on scholarly grounds only when a consensus has been reached among scholars. We know that waiting for a consensus among scholars on most important issues will be as disastrous as waiting for the perfect toothpaste. The point is that we must advance our scholarly positions on *explicit* scholarly grounds and justify those positions in scholarly ways. We may, and often should, also voice our personal convictions and views. *What we must not do* is to claim that a position is scholarly merely because it is held by a scholar, or even by all or most scholars. That is like telling a patient who has asked for an explanation of medical treatment, "Because it's doctor's orders," and, when the orders are questioned, telling the patient "You wouldn't understand." Cultural authority assumes that behind authoritative statements there are reasons that can be persuasively advanced. Without such reasons kept in good repair, cultural authority ceases to be legitimate (see DeGeorge 1985: 34–42). And since cultural authority is based on a social contract, illegitimate authority risks being revoked. That is what is going on in the revolution of non-experts in our society today, from consumers to patients to the poor. This also characterizes the relationship between academic experts in religion, from theologians to comparative religion scholars, and the religious public.

The natural tendency of groups that have been granted both cultural authority and self-policing (peer review) is to overextend their authority. Reflexivity is an essential ingredient in redressing that overextension.

Every group that achieves authority and then the privilege of internal policing of that authority (peer review, tenure, etc.) is in danger of extending the boundaries of its authority beyond the limits of its legitimate expertise because of the personal interests of its members, and because of the inherent interest of the group in maintaining and expanding its authority. A reflexive account of our knowledge making work can give us a more accurate sense of where we are, because it will always require us to tell how we got there. Reflexivity should also free us from the stultifying fiction that our every belief and action can and should derive from our scholarly training, or else be suspect. And most importantly, it should help it to relieve some of the awful asymmetry that currently exists in our field as we apply to our informants and their institutions culturally and psychologically based interpretations from which we exempt ourselves.

Notes

1. Paul Feyerabend provides an excellent discussion of this false rhetorical "objectivity" (1988: 238–239).
2. Because I am speaking of a broad range of belief topics, not all of which are considered religious (e.g., belief in ghosts), and because *supernatural* is such a problematic term, I will use *spiritual* in its narrow sense of referring to "spirits" or "souls," not just mind and emotion, throughout this article.
3. I do recognize that some have specifically argued that disbelief is impartial. For example, Antony Flew argues that the presumption of atheism is a neutral position (1984). Christina Larner's view, discussed below, is another instance of this claim being made explicitly. I disagree with both this explicit claim and the more common tacit assumption about what constitutes skepticism in spiritual matters. However, it is not possible to explore this complex philosophical issue in depth in this article.
4. For an excellent use of this possibility in fieldwork see Edith Turner's *Experiencing Ritual* (1992).

References

Angeles, Peter A. 1992. *Dictionary of Philosophy*. New York: Barnes & Noble Books.

Berger, Peter L. 1992. *A Far Glory*. New York: Free Press.

Bruner, Edward M. 1986. "Introduction: Experience and Its Expressions," *The Anthropology of Experience*, 3–30. Victor W. Turner and Edward M. Bruner (eds.). Urbana: University of Illinois Press.

Burnham, John C. 1982. "American Medicine's Golden Age: What Happened to It?" *Science* 215: 1474–1479.

Clifford, James. 1983. "On Ethnographic Authority." *Representations* 1/2: 118–146.

DeGeorge, Richard T. 1985. *The Nature and Limits of Authority*. Lawrence: University Press of Kansas.

DeVinne, Pamela B. (ed.) 1991. *The American Heritage Dictionary of the English Language*. 2nd ed. Boston: Houghton Mifflin.

Feyerabend, Paul 1988. *Against Method*. Rev. ed. London: Verso.

Flew, Anthony 1984. *God, Freedom, and Immortality: A Critical Analysis*. Buffalo: Prometheus Books.

Gerson, Elihu 1976. "The Social Character of Illness: Deviance or Politics?" *Social Science & Medicine* 10: 219–224.

Hollis, Martin 1982. "The Social Destruction of Reality," *Rationality and Relativism*, 67–86. Martin Hollis and Steven Lukes (eds.). Cambridge: MIT Press.

Hufford, David J. 1982. "Traditions of Disbelief," *New York Folklore Quarterly* 8/3–4: 47–56. Reprinted in *Talking Folklore* 1/3 (1987): 19–29.

—— 1987. "Afterword to Traditions of Disbelief," *Talking Folklore* 1/3: 29–31.

Illich, Ivan 1976. *Medical Nemesis: The Expropriation of Health*. New York: Pantheon Books.

Larner, Christina 1984. *Witchcraft and Religion: The Politics of Popular Belief*. Oxford: Basil Blackwell.

Lawless, Elaine J. 1988. *God's Peculiar People: Women's Voices & Folk Tradition in a Pentecostal Church*. Lexington: University of Kentucky Press.

—— 1993. *Holy Women, Wholly Women: Sharing Ministries of Wholeness Through Life Stories and Reciprocal Ethnography*. Philadelphia: University of Pennsylvania Press.

Malcolm, Norman 1977. *Thought and Knowledge*. Ithaca: Cornell University Press.

Nagel, Thomas 1986. *The View from Nowhere*. New York: Oxford University Press.

Quantz, Richard A., and Terence W. O'Connor 1988. "Writing Critical Ethnography: Dialogue, Multivoicedness, and Carnival in Cultural Texts," *Educational Theory* 38/1: 95–109.

Rubinstein, Robert (ed.) 1991. *The Fieldwork: The Correspondence of Robert Redfield and Sol Tax*. Boulder: Westview Press.

Simpson, Jacqueline 1988. "Is Neutralism Possible in the Study of Belief?" *Talking Folklore* 1/4: 12–16.

Smart, Ninian 1973. *The Science of Religion & the Knowledge: Some Methodological Questions*. Princeton: Princeton University Press.

Starr, Paul 1982. *The Social Transformation of American Medicine*. New York: Basic Books.

Titon, Jeff Todd 1985. "Stance, Role, and Identity in Fieldwork Among Folk Baptists and Pentecostals," *American Music* 3: 16–24.

Turner, Edith, with William Blodgett, Singleton Kahona, and Fideli Benwa 1992. *Experiencing Ritual: A New Interpretation of African Healing*. Philadelphia: University of Pennsylvania.

Zaleski, Carol 1987. *Otherworld Journeys: Accounts of Near-Death Experience in Medieval and Modern Times*. New York: Oxford University Press.

21

MICHAEL JACKSON, *The Witch as a Category and as a Person*

❧ ❧

In February 1970 an epidemic of insect-borne encephalitis swept through the village of Kamadugu Sukurela in northern Sierra Leone. There were many deaths. The village was under a pall. In due course, the chief and elders summoned a male witch-hunting cult known as *Gbangbane* from Farandugu, four miles away. At night, as we huddled indoors, the "devil" moved among the houses. Its ominous, muffled voice, the shuffle of feet in the darkness, the staccato of wooden clappers *gban gban, gban gban*, infected us all with deep disquiet.

My field assistant, Noah Marah, and I spent several days in the village, thinking we might be of some use, but there was little we could do, so we left. A couple of weeks later we returned and sought out a friend of Noah's, Morowa Marah, whom I'd met on our initial visit. We sat on the porch of Morowa's house. His wife served us a meal of rice and groundnut stew. I asked Morowa to tell us what had happened in our absence.

The witch-hunters had diagnosed the cause of one man's illness as witchcraft and promised to deal with the witch before returning to Farandugu. According to Morowa, *Gbangbane* had told the chief and elders that the offending witch would fall ill with chest, neck, and head pains and shit herself or himself before dying. The following day the sick man succumbed and died, as *Gbangbane* had predicted. Eight days later his sister fell gravely ill. In her pain and distress, she confessed she had killed her brother by witchcraft. "I was hunting him for a year," she said. "The first time I tried to kill him was when he went to brush his farm, but I missed him. The branch only knocked out some of his teeth [such an accident had occurred]. But this year we [her coven] lay in wait for him on the path to his palmwine trees. We beat him up and injured him. Then he fell ill." The woman also explained her motive for wanting to kill her brother: she had once asked him for some rice and he had refused her. But why she had used witchcraft against her brother rather than cursing him, as is a sister's right, was left unexplained. Then, as the woman lay ill inside her house, *Gbangbane* came again and ordered that she be buried at once. Men bound her hands and feet and dragged her to the outskirts of the village. There they dug a shallow grave and buried her alive. Banana leaves and stones were thrown in on top of her. During the entire episode, all the women of the village remained indoors.

When Morowa had finished his account I found it impossible not to accuse him of being accessory to a murder. My outrage astonished him, and he tried to help me understand.

"If it had been my choice," he said grimly, "I would have had her thrown into the bush without burial. But we buried her in the grassland beyond the Mabumbuli [stream] so that when the grass is dry we can set fire to it and turn her face into hell. A witch deserves no respect. A witch is not a person."

I knew Morowa and his wife had lost children as a result of witchcraft; I also knew what appalling tension the community was under. But the image of a woman being buried alive poisoned my feelings toward Morowa and, for a time, toward all Kuranko who shared his view. My only consolation came from Morowa's report that shortly after the murder (for I could not think of it otherwise), the witch's shade or *pulan* invaded the village and Morowa had been the first to be haunted.[1] As he slept, it settled on his head. He opened his eyes but could not cry out. He lay in terror as though an immense weight were pressing down on him. Other men in Kamadugu Sukurela were also afflicted. The *pulan* terrorized the village. Finally, the chief and elders summoned a *pulan*-catcher (*pulan brale*) from Bambunkura, a village twelve miles away. This man, Musa, bagged the *pulan* in the form of a lizard in the dead woman's house. However, her son, distressed by the awful circumstances of his mother's death, refused to accept that the lizard was his mother's shade. Piqued, Musa went back to Bambunkura. But the *pulan*-haunting continued, and the dead woman's son was now afflicted by it. Once more the *pulan*-catcher was summoned from Bambunkura, and the son was ordered by the chief and elders to pay the fee as well as apologize to Musa for doubting his skills. Musa then caught the *pulan* (again in the form of a lizard) and killed it.

These events introduce the ethical and epistemological issues I want to address in this chapter. The most obvious question is whether the Kuranko word *suwage* corresponds to the English word "witch" and whether there is any justification for calling Morowa's haunting "guilt" or the killing of the woman "murder." This is not just a matter of semantics and "accurate translation"; we have to work out whether it is possible to gain access to ideas and experiences designated *suwa'ye* ("witchcraft") in Kuranko and understand them in terms of ideas and experiences familiar to us in our own culture. A critical issue here is elucidating the relationship between conventional notions of witchcraft and the experiences of women who actually confess to being witches—the relationship between episteme and experience, knowledge and event. But underlying all these questions, I shall argue, is a problem that affects

Kuranko villagers as well as anthropologists: the way our discursive categories distort our perception of persons. Thus, the pathology of conventional Kuranko thought, which denies personhood to a woman who in extreme distress confesses herself a "witch," is uncannily like the pathology of much anthropological discourse which buries the experience of the individual subject in the categories of totalizing explanation.[2]

Images of the Witch

To understand what the Kuranko mean when they say a witch is not a person, it is necessary to clarify the indigenous concept of *morgoye* ("personhood"). *Morgoye* implies respect for and mindfulness of others, an abstract attitude in which personal purposes are consonant with collective goals. Ideally, a person is magnanimous, open, and straightforward in his or her dealings with others. A sociable person is "sweet" (*morgo di*), he or she likes the company of others. Or a person is "open" (*morgo gbe*; literally, person clear/white) and "straight" (*morgo telne*). An unsociable person is "bent" and "devious" (*morgo dugune*) like a crooked path. Or a person is "broken-down" (*kore*), on an analogy with a dilapidated house (*bon kore*), a broken calabash, worn-out clothes, an abandoned farm, and similar "useless" things. Sometimes an antisocial person is referred to as a "bush person" (*fira morgo*) or an "unwell person" (*morgo kende ma*), *kende* meaning physically "healthy" as well as socially or morally "proper." Anyone who sets himself or herself apart from others is quite simply "not a person" (*morgo ma*).

The stereotype of a witch includes all these notions of deviance, resentment, wildness, and sickness; essentially, it is a dialectical negation of the moral concept of *morgoye*. As the Kuranko word *suwage*[3] (literally, "night owner") suggests, a witch acts surreptitiously, under cover of darkness, using powers which are invisible to ordinary eyes: witch weapons, witch medicines, witch gowns, witch animals, even witch airplanes. These are the things the witch-hunting cults attempt to track down, for *Gbangbane* cannot directly destroy a witch, only disarm her. Witchcraft (*suwa'ye*) is not inherited; it is an inborn proclivity—which is why, though witches are criminals, a witch's kin are never tainted by or held accountable for her actions. Witches have "bad *yugi*," something that cannot be resisted or willed away.

A witch's "life" (*nie*) supposedly leaves her sleeping body at night and moves abroad, often in the body of an animal familiar. As her "life goes out" (*a nie ara ta*), her body may be shaken by convulsions and her breathing cease. In this state of suspended animation, the body is vulnerable; if it is turned around, then the witch's *nie* will not be able to reenter it and she will die.[4] A witch will also perish if the dawn finds her out of her body. The animals most commonly associated with witches sum up the traits of witchcraft: predatory (leopard), scavenging (hyena, vulture), underground (snakes), nocturnal (bats, owls); indeed, the owl (*gbingbinyaga*) is sometimes called the "witch bird" "because it is seldom seen and flies by night."

Witches are predatory and cannibalistic. But they do not attack a victim's "life" (*nie*) directly; they "consume" some vital organ (usually the liver, heart, or intestines) or drain away the victim's blood or break the victim's backbone by tapping him on the nape of the neck. It is said that witches work in covens and that the greatest threat of witchcraft attack lies within the extended family (*kebile*), i.e., "from those who share a common inheritance."[5] As one man put it, "Witchcraft is eating yourself" (meaning that a witch usually "eats" her own child, her co-wife's child, her grandchild, or her brother's child) but "sorcery is destroying others."[6]

Witchcraft operates through blackmail and indebtedness. A witch will somehow "open the door" of her own house by nullifying the protective medicines which the household head has placed over the lintel. Then a witch from her coven steals into the house and "eats" one of its occupants—usually a child, because children are less likely to be protected by personal medicines. The aggressor is obliged to discharge her debt at some later time by making it possible for her co-witch to claim a victim from her house. One informant told me that "only someone close to you could betray you to the witches by telling them where you sleep in the house and by opening the door to them." A Kuranko adage is often used in support of this reasoning: *sundan wa dugu koro worla bor duguranu de I sonti i ye* (if a stranger [guest] uncovers something hidden, someone living in that place [the host] must have told him where it was).

These popular stereotypes of witches and witchcraft are logically derived through a systematic inversion of what is regarded as ideal social behavior (Beidelman 1986: chapter 9; Middleton 1971: 238–250): day/night, open (*kenema*)/underhanded (*duworon*), villagers/bush creatures, sociability/self-ishness, generalized reciprocity/negative reciprocity.

So far I have summarized what Kuranko men told me about witchcraft when I broached the subject with them. But directed interviews and leading questions bring into relief only one dimension of the phenomenon. Consider, for instance, that many men were loath to discuss witchcraft with me in public lest their conversancy with the subject be taken as evidence that they themselves were witches. This immediately suggests that the definition of a witch as a nefarious and self-seeking woman does not exhaust the semantic range of the term *suwa'ye*. In fact the polysemic character of the term can be readily established. Thus, Kuranko acknowledge that the notoriously unstable and jealous relationship between nonuterine brothers (known as *fadenye*) is a potential source of witchcraft. It is also frequently pointed out that a farmer who produces a surplus above his subsistence needs, a man of wealth and position, and a child who excels at school or is well favored are all likely to be envied and resented—fertile grounds for witchcraft attack. The illicit use of destructive medicines, independent of a medicine-master, to bring shame, adversity, or death to an enemy is also spoken of as witchcraft. So too is the use of poisons (*dabere*) such as *munke* ("gunpowder") and *gbenkan*,[7] which malevolent old women allegedly sprinkle in children's food or water.

Clearly, witches are not invariably women. Nor do they just use psychic powers, at the mercy of evil instincts. Nor is witchcraft unequivocally antisocial; *suwa'ye* is a common metaphor for extraordinary powers. Thus, white men may be likened to witches because of their technological wizardry and remarkable mobility (in ships and aircraft), and legendary figures such as Mande Sunjata and Yilkanani are sometimes said to have been witches because their powers were beyond ordinary comprehension. Even more significant is the fact that *Gbangbane* (or *Gbangbe*), the witch-hunter, is spoken of as a witch. This is how Saran Salia Sano of Firawa described *Gbangbe* to me:

> It is like the other *sumafannu* ["secret things"]. When you are a boy, you try to imagine what it is. You are told it kills people. You are afraid. But you also feel it is something extraordinary, and want to see it. Then, when you are initiated, you see that it is a person—not an ordinary person, but a witch. Its witchcraft is greater than that of a host of people [*a suwa'ya morgo sigama n ko*]. *Gbangbe* is a *subingban* ["ruler of the night"]. He is immune to all evil, and has the power to rob men of their shape-shifting abilities. *Gbangbe* forces people to confess. He seizes their possessions. The person cries out, "He's taken my things!" and the kinsmen plead with *Gbangbe* not to destroy them lest the person die.

I asked Saran Salia to clarify what he meant by "seizure" of a witch's "possessions," since the word *miran* can denote both material things and psychological "self-possession." Were people "seized" by terror when *Gbangbe* was out, or did *Gbangbe* actually take their property and physically force them to confess? To the Western mind, always keen to discriminate between "psychic" and "physical" realities, the question is crucial. To Saran Salia it seemed somewhat beside the point, but he gave me a specific example of what he meant.

The incident he described took place at Bandakarafaia six years earlier. It was night, and *Gbangbe* was abroad in the village. *Gbangbe* stopped outside a house:

> It seized this woman's headtie, shirt, and shoes. Inside the house, the woman started struggling and shouting, "*Gbangbe* has got me! *Gbangbe* has got me!" [*m'bi Gbangbe bolo*, "I am Gbangbe's hand in"]. Her kinsmen gave *Gbangbe*, two mats, and ten kola nuts. *Gbangbe* said, "I have heard." He gave back the headtie and shirt, but not the shoes. The

woman cried, "Give me the shoes." *Gbangbe* gave them to her. Then she shouted, "*Soburi* [hooray], I've got them!" She became normal again.

"But were the clothes real?" I asked.
"They were like real ones, but they were witch's clothes."
Seeing my perplexity, Saran Salia recounted another case. It was the first I'd ever heard in which a man confessed to witchcraft.

It happened in Firawa twelve years earlier. A man called Yimba Koroma became agitated and collapsed in his house one night while *Gbangbe* was out. On this occasion, *Gbangbe* seized the man in his witch's clothes and also seized his witch's things (*suwa'ya mirannu*).

The man's clothes tightened around his neck; he felt strangled. He cried out to *Gbangbe*, "Leave me alone, give me back my things!" He confessed to having eaten people's children. "I ate Yira, I ate Karifa and Yira. I ate them. Please give me back my things [*mirannu*.]." Gbangbe told him to name his other victims. "No," he said, "I won't name anyone else." That is why he was not forgiven. He was a member of a night *kere*.

A *kere* is a labor cooperative (Jackson 1977: 8–11); it epitomizes the spirit of conviviality and mutual aid in a community. Were witches in their night *kere* or coven bound by the same ties of reciprocity as bound men in a farming *kere*?

"Yes," Saran Salia said, "except witches join forces to take life, not make it."

In the company of women and children, men cultivate the fiction that *Gbangbane* is a bush spirit, not a person. But *Gbangbane* is a person, as Saran Salia observes, though not an ordinary person; he is a witch. Underlying this view is the notion that the same wild powers that can destroy people can also protect them. In short, *suwa'ye* is not just semantically ambiguous; it denotes an indeterminate power or faculty. And though this power of *suwa'ye* is in essence "wild" or extrasocial, whether it becomes good or bad *depends entirely on how it is harnessed or used*.

This pragmatist emphasis on contexts of use brings me to a consideration of the analysis by Hallen and Sodipo of the Yoruba word *àjé*, commonly translated "witch." On the basis of detailed comparative research, they argue that it is impossible to define a universal category "witchcraft" that can cover without distortion all the phenomena commonly brought under this rubric (Hallen and Sodipo 1986: chapter 3; Prince 1970: 915). Thus, while the Yoruba *àjé*, the Kuranko *suwage*, the Zande *mangu*, and the English *witch* all share some family resemblances, they also connote quite divergent phenomena and personality types. This point is vitally important. However, I do not go along with Hallen and Sodipo in construing this problem as basically semantic, a problem of accurate translation. True, the difference between Kuranko informants' stereotypes of witches and particular accounts (like those of Saran

Salia) correspond to the distinction Quine makes between standing sentences"
and "observation sentences," the first being abstracted from immediate sensory
experience, the second issuing from specific situations (Hallen and Sodipo 1986:
17).[8] And it is imperative that we do not overlook the indeterminate
relationship (the "empirical slack," the "evidential gap") between episteme
and experience, knowledge and event (17, 41–42). But I do not see why we
should want to overcome these discrepancies by defining our terms more
precisely, trying to make words and world coalesce and correspond. My own
interpretive preference is to consider not what words mean *in essence*, but what
they are *made* to mean in the contexts of everyday life. It isn't words we want
to compare when we try to understand the phenomenon we provisionally call
"witchcraft," but the exigencies of life, the events and experiences which the
words are brought to bear upon.

I now propose to shift my focus to the level of event—actual confessions to
witchcraft—and explore the interplay of stereotypical ideas about witches and
the experiences of Kuranko women who confess to witchcraft.

The Evidence of Confession

Within Africa, one can make a rough-and-ready distinction between
accusation-oriented and confession-oriented societies, though in each society
accusation and confession may be emphasized differently in different contexts
(Douglas 1970: xxxiv; Ruel 1970: 333; Wyllie 1973: 74–75).

Of the Azande, Evans-Pritchard reported: "I have never known a Zande
admit his witchcraft" (1972: 125) and "I have only received cases of confession
from one Zande ... perhaps the least reliable of my informants" (118). By
contrast, other societies, most notably in West Africa, are characterized by a
rarity or absence of direct accusation and the presence of confession: Effutu
(Wyllie 1973), Banyang (Ruel 1970), Ashanti (Ward 1956; Field 1960). Yet other
African societies are notable for the rarity of both direct accusation and
confession: Dinka (Lienhardt 1951), Mbugwe (Gray 1969). And some, such as
the Korongo, "have no witchcraft beliefs at all" (Nadel 1952).

Among the Kuranko, confession, not accusation, is the norm.[9] But the rare
and elusive character of these confessions, coupled with the fact that women
usually confess during terminal illness or are killed on account of what they
confess, makes it very difficult to gain direct knowledge of the experiences of
the Kuranko women who own to being witches. The ethnographer is obliged to
rely on hearsay accounts of events that have often been half-forgotten, if not
actively suppressed. Particularly problematic are the manifest prejudices of
Kuranko men when speaking of women witches. Witchcraft epitomizes the
worst in women, and men make witches the scapegoats for their own anxieties
about their vaunted autonomy and strength. Indeed, their stereotypes of

women as weak-willed, impulsive, and inclined toward hysteria are sadly similar to those still current in the discourse of many Western men.[10]

To understand the witch as a subject (*pour-soi*), to rehabilitate her as a person in a society which reduces her to a negative category, is not unlike the task contemporary historians face writing about the consciousness of the colonized—their "culture of silence" (Freire 1972). Nevertheless, as Ranajit Guha so brilliantly shows in his study of peasant insurgency in colonial India, it is possible to glean, from the distorted discourse of the oppressor, fragmentary clues "to the antonymies which speak for a rival consciousness" (1983: 17). This is also our task.

Here, in summary form, are details of thirteen cases of witchcraft confession, giving first the relationship of the victim to the witch and then the background and confessed reason for the witchcraft:

1. No relationship. Man confessed to *Gbangbe* that he had "eaten" several children (all male). He died after confessing. (Case of Yimba Koroma of Firawa.) Informant: Saran Salia Sano, elderly man, Firawa, 1979.
2. No victim. Woman "succumbed" to *Gbangbe* but did not confess to witchcraft. Her kinsmen "begged" and paid *Gbangbe*; the woman recovered her senses. (Case of woman from Bandakarafaia.) Informant: Saran Salia Sano, Firawa, 1979.
3. No relationship. A man, Fore Kande of Bandakarafaia, tested his witchcraft against Saran Salia. Dying, he confessed: "I went abroad as a witch; I went and saw his *Kome*; it killed me" (*m'bora suwa'ye ro; n'tara a ma felen n'ya I Komeye; wo le m'faga*); i.e., Saran Salia was immune to witchcraft attack, so the witchcraft was turned back on Fore, who died. He'd never before shown animosity toward Saran Salia. Informant: Saran Salia Sano, Firawa, 1979.
4. Brother's daughter's son. Informant's grandson died suddenly. A local woman was said to have confessed to killing him, but her kin hushed up her confession. Informant: Bundo Mansaray, middle-aged man, Kamadugu Sukurela, 1972.
5. Brother. Eight days after her brother's sudden death, a woman fell ill and confessed she'd once asked her brother for rice and he'd refused her. After one unsuccessful attempt on his life, she and other witches beat him up and killed him. She was buried alive. Informant: Morowa Marah, young man, Kamadugu Sukurela, 1970.
6. Husband. Woman fell ill with chest and head pains; on her deathbed she confessed that her husband had never liked her. Indeed, her husband blamed her for the awful tropical ulcers on his foot. A diviner had told him "evil people" (*morgo yugunu*) were getting at him; he formerly cursed the evil-doer who, he suspected, was his own wife. Her first husband had divorced her because of her "bad behavior" (*son yugi*). There were no

children by the second marriage (four years). After she died, her *pulan* came out and had to be caught and dispatched. Informant: husband, Ali Koroma, middle-aged man, Kamadugu Sukurela, 1972.

7. Husband; brother's son's wife. A child died suddenly. A few days later the child's father's sister fell seriously ill and confessed that she was responsible for the child's death. She owed her coven a child, but being childless, gave them the life of her brother's grandson. She said she had "got her destiny through that child," i.e., her sickness was a punishment for having killed him. When she entered her brother's house to get the child, the house had been surrounded by fire from the antiwitchcraft fetish *sase*; she'd been badly burned when leaving. She also confessed that when, many years earlier, her husband had accompanied a white man into the Loma mountains to hunt elephants she had transformed herself into an elephant and tried to kill him. She'd also prevented him from becoming chief. Finally, she told how, when *Gbangbe* was abroad, she would assume the form of a vulture or fly by plane and sit near the moon to evade detection. She would take her co-witches with her in a back hamper, but one night *Gbangbe* came unexpectedly and "seized" her hamper. Her co-witches, left stranded, cried out to her: "*Mama Yeri, sole wara mintan de me tala minto?*" ("Grandmother Yeri, the hamper is burned, where are we going to go?") When her confession had been heard, she was taken from the house and left in the backyard to die. Informant: woman's brother's grandson, Noah Marah, young man, Kabala, 1970.

8. Husband. Woman confessed to feeling resentful when her husband gave more rice and meat from a sacrifice to her co-wives than to her. During terminal illness, she confessed to trying to kill him by witchcraft, but his protective fetishes turned the witchcraft back against her. After her death, her *pulan* came out, turning food and water bad. Informant: woman's co-wife's son, Steven Marah, schoolboy, Kabala, 1970.

9. Husband; co-wife's son. Woman confessed on her deathbed to killing her husband by witchcraft and eating her co-wife's son. My informant believed the confession to have been mistaken; the woman never showed animosity to anyone. Informant: woman's co-wife's son, town chief at Fasewoia, 1970.

10. Husband. During severe illness, a woman confessed that her husband had refused to have sex with her during her pregnancy. Humiliated, she hired a night *kere* to beat him up; when the coven failed to find him it fell on her instead. She delivered stillborn twins and died.

11. Not specified. A woman confessed on her deathbed that she was a witch and named four associates. *Gbangbane* brought the four women before the chief's court; they were ordered to demonstrate their powers and prove they were witches. They asked that some pawpaws and a lizard be brought; they were then locked in a room. When they were let out of the room they

told the elders to cut open the pawpaws; they were seedless. They told the elders to examine the lizard; it was dead. Each woman was fined a cow. Two of the cows were sacrificed and a curse was put on the livers; the women were then obliged to eat the livers together with raw rice flour (*dege*) from the sacrifice. Within a few weeks three of the women died; the fourth, it was said, wasn't a real witch: "she wasn't guilty of actually eating anyone; she was a witch but did not practice witchcraft." Informant: Keti Ferenke Koroma, Kondembaia, 1970.

12. Brother's son. When a small boy died suddenly, a diviner was consulted; witchcraft was diagnosed as the cause of death. The witch was cursed. Ten days later the boy's father's sister fell ill and confessed to having killed the child because her brother refused to give her rice. The woman was buried alive.

13. Co-wife's son's son. A woman quarreled with her co-wife's son's wife over the sharing of some locust-seed cakes. Shortly afterward, her co-wife's son's son became ill and died. When the woman also fell ill she confessed to having killed the child to get even with its mother. She died after confessing.

What is arresting about most of these cases is that there are so few allusions to the stereotypical imagery of witchcraft. Covens and cannibalism are mentioned in only four cases (witches usually "kill" or "beat up" their victims); animal familiars and out-of-body travel in only one (case 7). Clearly, general *beliefs* about witchcraft and the particular *experiences* of self-confessed witches are seldom congruent.[11] Like the Azande, the Kuranko "normally think of witchcraft quite impersonally and apart from any particular witch or witches" (Evans-Pritchard 1972: 37).

The stereotype of the witch is, as I've already observed, a logical inversion of the stereotype of moral personhood. It encapsulates what Monica Wilson so aptly called "the standardized nightmares of the group." For the Kuranko, these collective anxieties center on self-containment and protection. However, the use of various objects or medicines, *kandan li fannu* ("enclosing/protecting things"), to magically seal off self, house, village, farm, and chiefdom reflects more than a history of actual invasions; it is an index of a quotidian problem: accommodating strangers who may also be enemies. To divine the thoughts of a stranger/guest (*sundan*) through the techniques of the *Due* cult or to disarm a visitor with gifts is thus a counterpart to the use of protective medicines (Jackson 1977: 57–60). But perhaps the central focus of men's fears is the figure of the in-marrying woman.

The notion of a witch as someone within the household yet in league with enemies without (her night *kere*) is grounded in the ambiguous social position of young married women, legally bound to their husbands yet emotionally attached to their natal families and "sisters." Something of this ambiguity is suggested by the phrases a man uses when giving his daughter in marriage to her husband's group: "Now we have come with your wife. She is your thief, your witch, your daughter, your all. We have brought her to you alive, but even in death she will remain your wife." It is also worth pointing out that the animals most commonly associated with witches—palmbirds, lizards, toads, snakes, cats, vultures, owls—are also structurally ambiguous: they are of the wild, yet often enter and live within the village.

Witchcraft and Kinship Stress

To properly understand the sociogenesis of witchcraft confessions it is not enough to speak of women solely as wives. Here is how Keti Ferenke Koroma explained the sources of antagonism between men and women in everyday life:

> You know, if you see women showing treachery (*monkekoe*) toward men it is because, in this world, all men are in the hands of women. We say we are in the hands of women because women gave us birth. In the beginning it might have been a good idea had *Altala* declared that women lead and men follow. But women follow, because *Altala* gave the power of leadership to men. We had nothing to do with that....
>
> Now, to know why we say women are not equals. It is because when a baby girl is born, it is a man who goes and pays bridewealth for her. She becomes his wife, subordinate to him. But when women think of how they gave birth to us and raised us, yet we pay bridewealth for them, they get angry. They use all manner of treachery to ruin us. For instance, if you have four wives and you call one to be with you for three days, the other three will spend all their time thinking of ways to get even. Women are treacherous because they want to control men. But this isn't possible because we pay bridewealth for them. And because they ate the forbidden fruit. (Jackson 1977: 88–89)

Apart from the light these remarks throw on Keti Ferenke's personal opinion of women, they bring into relief two distinct ways of explaining women's inferiority. The first is mythological; it invokes the disobedience of Mama Hawa (Eve), the first woman, to explain why women are *innately* weak-willed. The second is sociological and stresses the complementarity of a woman's role as wife and her roles as mother and sister. The key to understanding this complementarity is bridewealth. As a wife, a woman is subordinate to her husband and, if she is a junior wife, to his senior wife as well. Sinkari Yegbe, a middle-aged woman from Kamadugu Sukurela, summed up this situation of double disadvantage as follows:

Men pay too much bridewealth for us.... It gives them control over us and the right to order us about. You cannot cook unless your husband gives you rice. You cannot go to market unless he tells you to go, and gives you money to spend. If you are a junior wife, whatever you get first goes to the senior wife. You cannot even wear clothes without them first going through her hands.

As a mother, however, a woman enjoys real control and influence because the fortunes of her children are entirely in her hands. "You are in your mother's hands" (*i i na le bolo*), goes a popular song. Proverbial wisdom points out that "A man has many children; a woman raises them; his children are in her hands" (*Ke l dan sia; muse don den; ke l den wo bolo*). More ominously: "If a child flourishes or if a child perishes, ask the mother the reason why." As a sister, a woman also enjoys some degree of control because her brother marries with bridewealth received from her marriage. In theory, this indebtedness entitles her to claim material and emotional support from her brother and curse him if he denies it.

Ordinarily, a woman's autonomy as sister or mother compensates her for her lack of autonomy as a wife, especially a junior wife. The resentments that nurture witchcraft stem from a loss of this balance, either through gross unfairness on the part of a husband or senior co-wife or neglect on the part of a brother. In four of the cases cited, unjust apportionment of food was the cause of resentment; in two cases, conjugal neglect. Understandably, the focus of witchcraft attack is either a husband (five cases) or brother (one case) or someone vulnerable and closely related to them: a co-wife's child (one case) or grandchild (one case) or a brother's child (one case) or grandchild (two cases).

But while witchcraft can be seen as a stratagem for regaining a sense of autonomy and control, it must also be seen as masochistic and suicidal. Why, one may ask, don't women explore less destructive ways of redressing injustices, appealing to a senior woman (the *dimusukuntigi*) with powers to represent cases of male injustices in the chief's court, enlisting the help of the women's cult, *Segere*, or, in the case of a brother's neglect, using the sister's power to curse? Or, if they feel hard done by, why don't women do as Sinkari Yegbe advocates: voice their grievances in stories that mock men, connive with their "sisters" to make trysts with other men, or refuse to work and slave for their husbands? (Jackson 1977: 102).

To answer these questions, an analysis of kinship stress and women's roles is not enough. Such factors condition women's experience but do not wholly explain it. It is therefore necessary to consider the psychology of witchcraft confession in more detail.

The Compulsion to Confess

Kuranko people endure the tribulations of life with a fortitude that many Westerners, conditioned to expect medical science to guarantee them long lives without excessive suffering, might find unsettling. In the course of my fieldwork I helped sick people as much as my medical knowledge and supplies permitted. At first, however, it was usually I who sought people out, giving electrolyte solution to infants with dysentery and chloromycetin to people suffering from conjunctivitis, supervising courses of antibiotics. Even when distressed by the worsening condition of a child, parents showed no great interest in my medical resources. Afflicted by painful and debilitating diseases such as elephantiasis, encephalitis, malaria, and leprosy, men and women assented to my help rather than sought it. As for their attitude toward sick kinsmen or friends, it was often, to my mind, apathetic and perfunctory. *In toro*, you suffer, they would say in commiseration, then turn away.[12]

But what I saw as stoicism and fatalism is less a form of self-denial than self-mastery. And self-mastery is nowhere more deliberately cultivated than in the rites of initiation.

Initiation involves a whole battery of ordeals calculated to test the mettle of neophytes. To stay awake in a smoke-filled room, lashed with switches, upbraided and bullied by elders, to be tormented by tales of bush spirits and lethal medicines, to have one's genitals cut and not wince or cry out, to undergo traumatic separation from one's parents—all this to learn the sternest and most important lesson in life: to endure pain, show forbearance, be masterful in the face of every adversity. "To resist is hard ('not sweet')," the saying goes, "but freedom (from trouble) come of it" (*in sa ro, a fo ma di, koni lafere hayi la*). Despite men's view that women control their feelings and withstand hardship less well than they do, this theme pervades both men's and women's initiations.

It is therefore understandable why Kuranko were indifferent to my medical intervention. To place themselves in my hands meant isolation from kin and from the tried and tested world of their own medicines, most of which, it must be remembered, have a protective and insulating function. It would entail forfeiting their autonomy. A Kuranko adage sums up the dilemma: *Morgo ben ta nyenne bolo komo ko* (Better to be in the hands of a *nyenne* than in the hands of *Kome*). Both *nyenne* and *Kome* are bush spirits, but *Kome* is especially awesome and capricious. Thus, the known is always preferable to the unknown, the familiar to the foreign—better the devil you know than the devil you don't.

It isn't only Kuranko who adopt this view. One encounters it often in our own society when a seriously ill individual prefers to decide his or her own treatment rather than submit to the impersonal and mystifying regimes of the medical system. Sometimes the risk of death is to be preferred to the sacrifice of one's autonomy and dignity.

The seemingly fatalistic attitude of Kuranko in the face of misfortune reflects not a blind acceptance of suffering but an active recognition that it is an inevitable part of life. Pain and sickness are not seen as aberrations from which one might be saved. The insane and sick are never sequestered. Death is not denied. Nor do people react to suffering with the outrage and impatience so familiar in our own society—the tormented sense that one has been hard done by, that one deserves better, that permanent health, unalloyed happiness, even immortality, might one day be guaranteed as a civil right. In my experience, Kuranko people show little interest in an afterlife where one might escape the tribulations of this world and yet retain one's mundane identity. To die alone, to be refused decent burial, to have one's lineage die out: such things are terrible, not one's own extinction.

The focus, then, is on the *field* of relationships of which one is a part, not one's self per se. Accordingly, illness is seen as a disturbance in the field of social relationships (which include ancestors, God, bush spirits, and witches), not a result of disease *entities* such as germs or viruses. Thus, if you behave badly or even harbor ill will toward another person *who is innocent or protected by medicines*, then the malice will react against you and make you ill. It will be said that the other person's *hake* has "got out" on you (*a hake ara bo*) or that his *hake* "goes against you" (*a hake si bo i ro*). To "set things straight" or "clear things up" (the Kuranko images are the same as ours), you will have to beg forgiveness (*ka madiyale ke*) of the person you have wronged or confess (*ka porondo*) your ill will.

So pervasive is this notion of agentless, retributive justice (*hake*) that diviners commonly advise confession as a way of making things well or "cool," of clearing or straightening the path between people. Indeed, it has the same redressive effect as offering a sacrifice to one's ancestors. And people often spontaneously confess animosity to neighbors and friends in everyday life, speaking of the "pain" (*koe dime*) oppressing them. Or women wishing to forestall possible punishment for adultery sometimes sit down with their husbands and unburden themselves with such words as "*M'buin, ma be Fore lon; i hake ka na n'to*" ("My husband, we and Fore are [having an affair]; may your *hake* not get out on me").

But why is the onus usually on women to confess? Why, when illness strikes and diviners are consulted, are women blamed? And why, when *Gbangbane* is abroad, do women fall prey to secret fears far more than men? The answer to these questions lies in the contrast between the confined life of women and the public life of men.

For the Kuranko it is a contrast between the house (*bon*) and backyard (*sundu kunye ma*), the domain of women, and the courtyard (*luiye*) which opens onto the village, the domain of men. Women, they say, are encompassed by men as a house is encompassed by *luiye* (Jackson 1986: 130). As a consequence, men go out, women turn in upon themselves. While men seek the causes of discord in the world around them, women search for the causes within. Men apportion blame, women take the blame; men accuse, women confess.

But the pressures that bring a woman to find the cause of a child's death, a husband's bad luck, barrenness, or family discord *in her own thoughts and deeds* are not only social. Certainly the advice of a diviner, the carping of a husband or senior co-wife, kinship stress, village gossip, and the terrifying sound of *Gbangbane* moving about in the night all work to erode a woman's confidence (*miran*). But the precipitating cause of confession to witchcraft in over half the cases I collected was severe illness, illness seen as punishment for unconfided sins.

It is this existential crisis, in which both social and personal autonomy is momentarily lost, that I now want to consider.

"The Last Freedom"

It may appear that Kuranko women are so conditioned to bear responsibility for the misfortunes around them that they readily assent, when pressure is put upon them, to serve as men's scapegoats. The self-confessed witch would seem to embody this self-abnegation to an extreme degree: a victim of a world which denies her any legitimate outlet for her frustrations and grievances. But such a conclusion only recapitulates the prejudices of those Kuranko men who see women solely as a category—for "witch," "scapegoat," and "victim" are all category words, and negative ones at that.

For this reason it is important to recognize that witchcraft confession is also a desperate stratagem for reclaiming autonomy in a hopeless situation.[13] This is borne out by the allusions to witch-possessions (*suwa'ya mirannu*) in several cases (*miran* also means self-possession), and, in other cases (7, 11), by the defiant attitudes of the women in the face of death. But even when such defiance is not evident, witchcraft confession can still be seen as a powerful form of self-expression in which words and images substitute for acts (Reik 1966: 194, 199). Confession to witchcraft exemplifies what Victor Frankl calls "the last freedom"—that which remains to us when external circumstances rob us of the power to act: the choice of determining how we will construe our plight, the freedom to live it as though it were our will. It is the freedom Genet discovered as a child (Sartre 1963). Accused of being a thief, he suddenly saw himself reduced to an object for others, a projection of their fears, a scapegoat for their anxieties. His escape was into neither suicide nor insanity; it was a decision to become his fate, to live it as though he himself had conceived it: "*J'ai décidé d'être ce que le crime à fait de moi—un voleur.*"

As our evidence shows, the self-confessed witch does more than passively submit to the succession of misfortunes that have overwhelmed her. Nor does she blindly recapitulate the stereotypes men promulgate; rather, she actively uses them to give voice to long-suppressed grievances and to cope with her suffering by declaring herself the author of it.[14] Thus, she determines how she will play out the role which circumstance has thrust upon her. She dies deciding her own identity, sealing her own fate.[15]

It is not enough for us to decide whether witchcraft is a social pathology or the individual witch a victim of some delusional psychosis, for our task is to throw light on the lived experience that lies behind the masks and facades of category words—even those used by the self-confessed witch herself. Such an approach demands to know not whether a witch's death is "suicide" or "murder" but how that death is lived. It seeks not to know whether *hake* is best translated as "guilt" or "shame" or whether *suwage* is semantically equivalent to "witch," but what experiences find expression in these words and how we might recover them. It is for this reason that I have no sympathy with those anthropologists and philosophers who debate endlessly over the rationality or irrationality of witchcraft beliefs. Beliefs have no reality apart from the people who make use of them, and to try to see how beliefs *correspond* to some allegedly "objective" reality or how they cohere as a so-called "system" seems to me far less edifying than trying to see what people do with beliefs in *coping* with the exigencies of life. At this level, the bizarre appearance of Kuranko witchcraft images is less significant than the realities of human distress that find expression through them—realities with which we can readily identify.[16]

Notes

1. When a confessed witch dies, his or her shade is known as *pulan*. The *pulan* haunts, oppresses, and terrorizes people, especially small children. It is often said that the pulan resembles a lizard or assumes the form of a lizard, and a *pulan*-catcher may show people a lizard wriggling inside the bag with which he has allegedly caught a witch's shade. A *pulan*'s power enables it to lift country-pots or oppress people in their sleep. So terrified do some people become that they are physically immobilized and have to be straightened out in the morning. Theoretically, a *pulan* will not enter a house that has white cotton over the doorway. If it does enter an unprotected house it counts off people in pairs, declaring "this and this are all right, this and this are all right" until it comes to a single and therefore vulnerable person when it says, "this and myself are all right" and proceeds to oppress him or her. Since a *pulan* cannot attack two people at once, one may take precautions against *pulan*-haunting by sleeping in pairs.

2. Niels Bohr referred to this "principle of destruction" as the *Abtötungsprinzip* [literally, destruction principle]. Explanations, when pushed too far, destroy ("explain away") the phenomenon one seeks to understand (Devereux 1978: 9–13).

3. See Mandinka (Gambia) *suubaga* ("night person") (Innes 1974: 313).

4. If anyone disturbs the sleeping body of a suspected witch or is witness to such an

event he will not make this publicly known lest the kinsmen of the alleged witch accuse him of murder. The Kuranko point out that in such cases there is no real evidence of witchcraft. Furthermore, to accuse a person of witchcraft is a serious matter. Of all cases heard in the Native Court in Sengbe chiefdom between 1946 and 1967 only two cases of witchcraft accusation are recorded (the defendants were fined and ordered to "beg," i.e., apologize to the plaintiffs). The sole case of witchcraft accusation which came to my attention during fieldwork occurred in Kamadugu Sukurela in 1966. Two women, weeding a farm, quarreled. One said, "Now look, you are a witch!" The other rejoined, "Yes, I used to sit on your house." The case came before the chief's court and the accuser was ordered to withdraw her accusation and apologize; the women were not related. In another case (also from Kamadugu Sukurela) a woman was rumored to have confessed to killing her brother's daughter's son by witchcraft, but the confession was made within her family, and her husband was a "big man"; no one dared accuse her publicly of witchcraft. Even *Gbangbane* does not make direct or specific accusations; the cult masters, like ordinary diviners, simply ascertain whether or not witchcraft is the cause of a person's illness or death. When I asked one informant to give me evidence that witchcraft really did exist he said that his knowledge came from three sources: "it has a name and we have heard of it"; "we have seen people die because of witches"; "witches confess."

5. See LoDagaa (Goody 1969: 71). The Kuranko admit that the father's sister could be a witch but the mother's brother never; "he belongs to another *kebile*."

6. Although "sorcery" (the use of powerful magical medicines, *besekoli*) may be distinguished from witchcraft in terms of externally controlled and internally controlled powers (Douglas 1970: 119; Leach 1961: 22–25), in practice the distinction is not always clear. According to Saran Salia Sano, a medicine-master (*besetigi*) usually specializes in one of three branches of medicine: curative and prophylactic (deals with afflictions "caused by God," *altala kiraiye*, and with antidotes for afflictions "caused by persons," *morgo kiraiye*); destructive (involving the use of harmful medicines); and destructive (involving the use of curses, *gborle*). Many Kuranko adopt a fatalistic attitude to diseases "caused by Allah" but take active steps to prevent and cure afflictions caused by human agency, i.e., witchcraft and sorcery.

As Saran Salia observed on a number of occasions, witchcraft and the use of magical medicines were quite different things; he himself knew nothing of witchcraft. He could only protect people from witches—and in fact young boys often stayed in his house when their parents felt they were vulnerable to witchcraft attack. The second and third categories of medicine might be labeled "sorcery," but a *besetigi* usually works on behalf of a client and is not culpable for what happens to the victim of his medicines. If a person has a legitimate grievance against someone else and all other avenues of legal redress are closed, then he may enlist the services of a *besetigi*. Checks against the abuse of harmful medicines and curses do, however, exist. If a grievance is entirely a matter of personal malice, then the medicines will be ineffective against the victim and they will return to harm the person on whose behalf they are being "sent out." Before a *besetigi* will curse a man, his client must also take an oath, declaring "If I am unjust/wrong in my accusation against X then may I suffer; if I am just/right in my accusation against X then may he suffer." However, a person can sometimes circumvent these checks by purchasing powerful medicines from a foreign sorcerer or from a *mori* (Muslim medicine-master) and then using them independently. The curse, on the other hand, can never be purchased; it must always be uttered by a *besetigi*. Moreover, the curse must always be made public. Not only is it an extension of secular legal controls; its efficacy depends upon the victim knowing he has been cursed. The curse is only lifted when the offender confesses or, if he dies, when representatives of his family pay the *besetigi* to do so. The curse (*gborle*) used by medicine-masters is, of course, quite different from the curse (*danka*) associated with certain kinship roles (sister, mother, father).

7. *Gbenkan* is said to be pounded in a mortar at midnight by a person standing on his or her head and using his or her feet to grasp the pestle; the pestle makes the sound *gbenkan gbenkan*.

8. See Marwick: "Informants may ... make very different statements about the same phenomenon when they are speaking generally and when they are referring to a series of specific instances" (1970: 284).

9. Accusation and confession under duress are reported from other areas of Sierra Leone: Limba (Finnegan 1965), Mende (Harris and Sawyerr 1968), Temne (Littlejohn 1967), Kono (Parsons 1964: 51–52).

10. Consider, for example, the views of Freud on the "psychology of women":

   It must be admitted that women have but little sense of justice, and this is no doubt connected with the preponderance of envy in their mental life; for the demands of justice are a modification of envy; they lay down the conditions under which one is willing to part with it. We also say of women that their social interests are weaker than those of men, and that their capacity for the sublimation of their instincts is less. (Freud 1932: 183)

   Thomas Szasz cites this as just one example of "scapegoating in the phenomena called witch-craft, hysteria, and mental illness" (1972: 197).

11. This discrepancy has been noted by other Africanists: Gray (1969: 171), Levine (1969: 239), Ruel (1970: 338). Ruel's hypothesis that "introspective" witchcraft and rigid stereotypes tend to be mutually incompatible is confirmed by the Kuranko data (Ruel 1970: 334–335).

12. During his fieldwork among the Jelgobe Fulani, Paul Riesman noted that feelings of hurt or pain were rarely indulged or expressed to solicit sympathy. "It was the same with all pain, physical and mental: people talked about it freely and objectively, so to speak, but they did not express it by that language of intonation and gesture which is familiar to us" (Riesman 1977: 147). According to Riesman, this equanimity was the result of neither repression nor stoicism, but of control. "To name pain and suffering in a neutral tone is to master them, *because the words do not escape thoughtlessly but are spoken consciously* ..." (148, my emphasis).

13. See Kluckholm (1967: 83-84) and Brain (1970: 170) on witchcraft confession as an "attention-seeking device" among "deprived" individuals. Keith Thomas (1973) advances a similar argument in his work on European witchcraft: the role of witch offered downtrodden and outcast women a means, albeit illusory, of protest and vengeance.

14. In his study of Mohave suicide, Devereux observes that witches often persuade themselves "by a retroactive self-deception of the 'opportune confabulation' type" that they actually bewitched someone who just happened to die at a time when they were experiencing strong suicidal impulses (1969: 387). Witchcraft confession is thus a kind of "vicarious suicide," an impulse, Devereux notes, that "is a human, rather than a specifically Mohave impulse."

15. See Oliver Sacks (1986: 4): "it must be said at the outset that a disease is *never a mere loss or excess* that there is always a reaction, on the part of the affected organism or individual, to restore, to replace, to compensate for and to preserve its identity, however strange the means may be" (emphasis added).

16. Some Kuranko men can identify with the situation of self-confessed witches as a result of their experiences as migrant workers in the diamond districts of Kono. It seems that one reason why Kuranko men are so readily hired for positions of trust in the Security Police Force is that they are honest to a fault, often confessing to crimes they have not committed simply to "clear the air." Kuranko men like to vaunt their openness and integrity, but does their marginality and powerlessness make them "like women" and therefore predisposed to assume responsibility for some of the resentments and tensions that pervade the diamond fields?

References

Beidelman, T. O. 1986. *Moral Imagination in Kaguru Modes of Thought.* Bloomington: Indiana University Press.

Brain, R. 1970. "Child-Witches," *Witchcraft Confessions and Accusations.* M. Douglas (ed.). A.S.A. Monograph 9. London: Tavistock Press.

Devereux, G. 1969. *Mohave Ethnopsychiatry and Suicide: The Psychiatric Knowledge and the Psychic Disturbances of an Indian Tribe.* Smithsonian Institution Bureau of American Ethnology Bulletin 175. Washington, DC: US Government Printing Office.

—— 1978. *Ethnopsychoanalysis: Psychoanalysis and Anthropology as Complementary Frames of Reference.* Berkeley: University of California Press.

Douglas, M. 1970. "Introduction," *Witchcraft Confessions and Accusations.* M. Douglas (ed.). A.S.A. Monograph 9. London: Tavistock Press.

Evans-Pritchard, E. E. 1972. *Witchcraft, Oracles, and Magic Among the Azande.* Oxford: Clarendon Press.

Field, M. J. 1960. *Search for Security.* London: Faber & Faber.

Finnegan, R. 1965. *Survey of the Limba People of Northern Sierra Leone.* London: Her Majesty's Stationery Office.

Freire, P. 1972. *Cultural Action for Freedom.* Harmondworth: Penguin.

Freud, S. 1932. *New Introductory Lectures on Psycho-Analysis.* New York: Norton.

Goody, J. 1969. *Comparative Studies in Kinship.* London: Routledge & Kegan Paul.

Gray, R. F. 1969. "Some Structural Aspects of Mbugwe Witchcraft," *Witchcraft and Sorcery in East Africa.* J. Middleton and E. H. Winter (eds.). London: Routledge & Kegan Paul.

Guha, R. 1983. *Elementary Aspects of Peasant Insurgency in Colonial India.* Delhi: Oxford University Press.

Hallen, B. and J. O. Sodipo 1986. *Knowledge, Belief, and Witchcraft: Analytic Experiments in African Philosophy*. London: Ethnographica.

Harris, W. T. and H. Sawyerr 1968. *The Springs of Mende Belief and Conduct*. Freetown: Sierra Leone University Press.

Innes, G. 1974. *Sunjata: Three Mandinka Versions*. School of Oriental and African Studies. London: University of London.

Jackson, M. 1977. *The Kuranko: Dimensions of Social Reality in a West African Society*. London: C. Hurst.

—— 1986. *Barawa, and the Ways Birds Fly in the Sky*. Washington, DC: Smithsonian Institution Press.

Kluckholm, C. 1967. *Navaho Witchcraft*. Boston: Beacon Press.

Leach, E. 1961. *Rethinking Anthropology*. London: Athlone Press.

Levine, R. A. 1969. "Witchcraft and Sorcery in a Gusii Community," *Witchcraft and Sorcery in East Africa*. J. Middleton and E. H. Winter (eds.). London: Routledge & Kegan Paul.

Lienhardt, G. 1951. "Some Notions of Witchcraft Among the Dinka," *Africa* 21: 303–318.

Littlejohn, J. 1967. "The Temne House," *Cosmos and History*. J. Middleton (ed.). American Sourcebook in Anthropology. New York: Natural History Press.

Marwick, M. 1970. "Witchcraft as a Social Strain-Gauge," *Witchcraft and Sorcery*. M. Marwick (ed.). Harmondsworth: Penguin.

Middleton, J. 1971. *Lugbara Religion: Ritual and Authority Among an East African People*. London: Oxford University Press.

Nadel, S. F. 1952. "Witchcraft in Four African Societies," *American Anthropologist* 54: 18–29.

Parsons, R. T. 1964. *Religion in an African Society*. Leiden: E. J. Brill.

Prince, R. 1970. Review of L. Mair, *Witchcraft*, *American Anthropologist* 72/4: 915–917.

Reik, T. 1966. *The Compulsion to Confess: On the Psychoanalysis of Crime and Punishment*. New York: Wiley.

Riesman, P. 1977. *Freedom in Fulani Social Life*. Chicago: University of Chicago Press.

Ruel, M. 1970 "Were-Animals and the Introverted Witch," *Witchcraft Confessions and Accusations*. M. Douglas (ed.). A.S.A. Monograph 9. London: Tavistock Press.

Sacks, O. 1986. *The Man Who Mistook His Wife for a Hat*. London: Pan.

Sartre, J. P. 1963. *Saint-Genet*. B. Frechtman (trans.). New York: George Braziller.

Szasz, T. 1972. *The Myth of Mental Illness*. St. Albans: Paladin.

Thomas, K. 1973. *Religion and the Decline of Magic*. Harmondsworth: Penguin.

Ward, B. 1956. "Some Observations on Religious Cults in Ashanti," *Africa* 26: 47–61.

Wyllie, R. W. 1973. "Introspective Witchcraft Among the Effutu of Southern Ghana," *Man* 8: 74–79.

22

WENDY DONIGER O'FLAHERTY, *The Uses and Misuses of Other People's Myths*

ॐ॰ॐ

The Hunter and the Sage

A metaphor that we often use to describe complete empathy with or understanding of someone else is "getting inside someone else's head." This metaphor might be expected to have a more literal interpretation in India, where mental constructs are regarded as in some way publicly accessible (O'Flaherty 1984). The theme of entering someone else's body is a popular one in Indian literature; any respectable yogi can do this trick, which may lead to embarrassing or amusing situations (as when the mind of a yogi enters the body of a whore, and her mind enters his body in return) (Bloomfield 1917).[1] But the most striking dramatization of the metaphor of "getting inside someone else's head" that I know is a myth that occurs in an Indian text. This text is the *Yogavasistha*, a Sanskrit philosophical treatise composed in Kashmir sometime between the 6th and the 12th centuries AD. The myth is the story of a hunter who meets a sage who has entered another man's body and lodged in his head:

> There was once a gigantic, proud demon, who harassed the hermitage of a sage. The sage cursed him to die and become a mosquito. The fire of that curse burnt the demon to ashes in a moment, and he was reborn as a mosquito. A mosquito's life lasts only two days; then he was trampled under the foot of an antelope, and because he died while looking at an antelope, he was reborn as an antelope. The antelope was killed by a hunter, and was reborn as a hunter. The hunter wandered in the woods until he came to the home of a sage, who became his teacher. One day the sage told him this story:
> In the old days I became an ascetic and lived alone in a forest hermitage.

I studied magic. I entered someone else's body and saw all his organs; I entered his head and then I saw a universe, with a sun and an ocean and mountains, and gods and demons and human beings. This universe was his dream, and I saw his dream. Inside his head, I saw his city and his wife and servants and his son.

When darkness fell, he went to bed and slept, and I slept too. Then his world was overwhelmed by a flood at doomsday; I, too, was swept away in the flood, and though I managed to obtain a foothold on a rock, a great wave knocked me into the water again. When I saw that world destroyed at doomsday, I wept. I still saw, in my own dream, a whole universe, for I had picked up his karmic memories along with his dream. I had become involved in that world and I forgot my former life; I thought, "This is my father, my mother, my village, my house, my family."

Once again I saw doomsday. This time, however, even while I was being burnt up by the flames, I did not suffer, for I realized, "This is just a dream." Then I forgot my own experiences. Time passed. A sage came to my house, and slept and ate, and as we were talking after dinner he said, "Don't you know that all of this is a dream? I am a man in your dream, and you are a man in someone else's dream."

Then I awakened, and remembered my own nature; I remembered that I was an ascetic. And I said to the sage, "I will go to see that body of mine (that was an ascetic)," for I wanted to see my own body as well as the body which I had set out to explore. But he smiled and said, "Where do you think those two bodies of yours are?" I could find no body, nor could I get out of the head of the person I had entered, and so I asked him, "Well, where are the two bodies?" The sage replied, "While you were in the other person's body, a great fire arose, that destroyed your body as well as the body of the other person. Now you are a householder, not an ascetic."

When the sage had said this, I was full of amazement. He lay back on his bed in silence in the night. I did not let him go away; he stayed with me until he died.

The hunter said, "If this is so, then you and I and all of us are people in one another's dreams." The sage continued to teach the hunter and told him what would happen to him in the future. But the hunter left him and went on to new rebirths. Finally, the hunter became an ascetic and found release. (Pansikar 1918: 6.2. 136–157)[2]

This remarkable story has many meanings that we may use for our own purposes, but first let us try to understand it in its own terms. An ascetic sage tells the tale of entering the body of a dreamer who is a married man—entering his breath, his head, and his consciousness. The sage inside the dreamer dreams of the same village that the dreamer was dreaming of, and becomes a householder like him. His "outer" or original body does not simply decay in the absence of the conscious soul (as it does in many tales of this type) (O'Flaherty 1984: 231–234); it is destroyed by a fire that burns the hermitage in which the outer body was lodged. This is a strange fire: it came from the doomsday flames that the sage dreamt about when he was lying asleep in that hermitage (and inside the body of the sleeping man that he had entered).[3] Moreover, whereas the first doomsday fire seemed real to him, so that he wept to see it destroy the inner world, this second doomsday fire seemed to him to be nothing but a dream, and *déjà vu* dream at that, so that he did not feel any pain when it burnt him. Yet the first fire *did* not burn his outer body, because he merely saw it in another man's dream, while the second fire did burn his outer body, because he saw it in what had become his own dream, too. Since he had dreamt his outer body into non-existence, he was physically trapped inside his dream world.

Inside the dream village, the new householder (*né* sage) meets another sage, who enlightens him and wakes him up. Yet, though he is explicitly said to awaken, he stays where he is inside the dream; the only difference is that now he knows he is inside the dream. Now he becomes a sage again, but a different sort of a sage, a householder sage, inside the dreamer's dream. While he is in this state, he meets the hunter and attempts to instruct him. But the hunter misses the point of the sage's saga: "If this is so, . . ." he mutters, and he goes off to get a whole series of bodies before he finally figures it out. The hunter has to experience everything for himself, dying and being reborn;[4] he cannot learn merely by dreaming, as the sage does. Where the sage moves through imaginary doomsday fires without dying, the hunter is "burnt" by a curse that destroys his body and forces him to enter another.

If we return at last to the metaphor that is enacted in this parable, the hunter is the person who cannot get inside other people's heads and so is driven by his emotions to go on being reborn himself over and over again, in order to have the series of experiences that are the necessary prerequisites for enlightenment. But the sage, who can go inside other people mentally, mentally experiences countless lives without ever having to be reborn.

Scholars and People

Hunters and sages can be taken as two types of people, the sort who leave to experience everything physically in order to understand it, and the sort who can understand things merely by imagining them. Hunters are ordinary, unenlightened people, householders, *hoi polloi*; sages are intellectuals, the elite. To be a hunter one need not necessarily believe literally in the doctrine of transmigration; one might be able to live several lives within a single rebirth, living a life in one career and then in another, in one country and then in another, with one person and then with another. So too, to be a sage one might literally enter another person's head, as a yogi does, or simply enter other people's consciousness through some other, milder means perhaps by entering their myths. I will use the image of the sage to denote the person who mentally enters the non-physical essence of other people, in contrast with the hunter who physically, through his body, experiences many lives.

Anyone can be reborn in the bodies of other people, but not everyone can enter their minds; we are all hunters, whether we know it or not, but the hunters who know what it means to be a hunter are sages. Since sages *know* that they are experiencing many lives, they can do it on purpose; hunters live their multiple lives unknowingly, helplessly. The sage is always part hunter because he is a human being and therefore an emotional, experiential creature; but because he is a sage, he is always trying to be what be cannot be, entirely free from the hunter inside him. That is, the sage has a hunter in him in addition to a sage, just as Dr. Jekyll had in him both the evil Mr. Hyde and the good Dr. Jekyll; but the hunter may not have a sage in him, just as Mr. Hyde did not have Dr. Jekyll in him (Stevenson 1886). (It is interesting to note the names that Stevenson gives to these two characters: Jekyll is a *Dr.*, a sage; Hyde *hides*, like a hunter, lying wait for his prey.) Good hunters *do* have sages in them, sages who bring some degree of self-awareness to the hunting; bad hunters do not. Hunters are carnivorous killers; they must destroy one body (their last) in order to cannibalize it as fuel for their next body. That is, hunters reject the past and do not learn from it. Sages are vegetarians; they can milk another living body of what they need without destroying it; they are historians. The lives and myths of hunters are violent; those of sages are gentle.

The sage in our story enters what in Sanskrit is called *manas* (translated as both heart and mind), the organ (located in the head) which is responsible for both reason and emotion, the place where one does algebra but also the place where one falls in love. This term provides a good example of the way in which Indian thought fails to distinguish some of the categories that we tend to think of as inherently polarized,[5] for, as we shall see, we tend to demarcate rather sharply people who are ruled by the heart and people who are ruled by the head. Indians do not do this; the Indian sage experiences life through both the head and the heart, though he tries not to experience it with his body. Indian aesthetic theory calls the sympathetic reader or member of the audience the one "whose heart is with [the poet or actor]" the *sa-hrdaya*, whose heart melts in response to poetry or art (Parab 1891: 2.9, cited in Masson and Patwardhan 1970: 21). But the narrow-minded scholar's heart is hardened and encrusted by his reading of dry metaphysical texts. The accomplished sage becomes literally *sa-hrdaya* when he literally shares the heart of the person with whom he empathizes. The narrow-minded scholar is the sage who wants to live entirely in the head and never in the heart; he is the sage who attempts utterly to deny his inevitable hunter component. The empathetic scholar is the sage who acknowledges his need to live both in the head and in the heart; he accepts his hunter component, attempting to deal with that aspect of his nature with greater understanding than that of the hunter who lives only in the heart and never in the head. Just as there are mere hunters and sage hunters, there are mere sages and hunting sages.

Getting Inside Other People's Myths

In India, sages are enlightened wise men, gurus or priests. In the West, sages are another sort of professionals or specialists: scholars, such as classicists and anthropologists. Classicists (by which I mean not just people who read Greek and Latin but, more broadly, all those historians, philologists, and other humanists and social scientists who deal with the past) attempt to enter a world that is perhaps as foreign and unattainable as any world can be—the lost world of people who are dead, but who may once have lived where we live now, or have spoken ancient forms of languages related to our own. Though anthropologists do not usually travel in time, they make all the greater effort to travel far in space, to the farthest reaches of Otherness. But although anthropologists pride themselves on entering other people's heads (that is, their thoughts), they also pride themselves on *not* entering other people's hearts (that is, their emotions and their lives).[6] Malinowski (1967: 167) once remarked, "I see the life of natives ... as remote from me as the life of a dog."[7] Nevertheless, sometimes anthropologists *do* enter the hearts of the people that they study, just as non-professionals (hunters) do.

People who study myths constitute a sub-caste of historians of religion, more precisely a half-caste formed through an illicit liaison between anthropologists and classicists. Mythologists, too, are Western sages, and like other sages they are also hunters. To the extent that they are sages, mythologists may enter into other people's heads (that is, understand other people's myths). But to the extent to which they are hunters, mythologists, like other sages, may also enter into other people's hearts and bodies (that is, enter other people's emotions and lives). Like other sages, they do absorb, if only, sometimes, unconsciously, myths that become personally meaningful to them, that become *their* myths.

It may be recalled that after a while Mr. Hyde took over Dr. Jekyll's life; Dr. Jekyll could not *help* being Mr. Hyde, and could not get back to his existence as Dr. Jekyll. In our Indian text, the life of the man whose mind the sage entered became the sage's life. In that story, the sage who began his scientific experiment in cold blood became drawn helplessly into the life of the man whose head he had entered (a householder, whom we may call a hunter in the broad sense in which we are using that metaphor). Once he made the dreamer's dream his own dream, *he forgot that he was a sage*—he became a hunter. Yet, eventually, still within that dream, he awakened to become another sort of sage, a sage inside a hunter.

Once we enter other people's heads through their myths, we may find that we cannot get out again; we enter their hearts and their lives too. Their myths become our myths whether we like it or not, particularly when, as often happens, we discover that their myths have always been our myths, though we may not have known it; we recognize ourselves in those myths more vividly than we have ever recognized ourselves in the myths of our own culture. This can happen to any of us, no matter whether we think such an experience good or bad.

The Rabbi from Cracow

On some deep level, I think, all truly creative scholarship in the humanities is autobiographical, but it is particularly true that people who traffic in myths are caught up in them, *volens nolens*. In 1971, I was struggling to come to terms with the death of my father (my first major experience of inexplicable and unjust evil), I failed to draw any comfort from Jewish or Christian approaches to the problem, not through any inherent inadequacy in them but simply because they were not *my* myth. As the child of relentlessly assimilated, secularized, and Enlightened Jewish refugees from Poland and Vienna, I had grown up with the Christian and Jewish stories as myths, but without the supporting context of any shared ritual. My father, whose father had been a Talmudic scholar, worked his way through NYU [New York University] as a "stringer" for the *New York Times*, going around to all the churches every Sunday and summarizing the sermons; he was paid by the inch. Eventually it dawned on him that it might be profitable to serve as a kind of matchmaker (*yente*, in Yiddish) between those ministers who yearned to see their sermons in print and those ministers who were eager to have at their disposal each week the sermons of the first sort of ministers. Thus he founded in the late 1930s and published throughout his life two magazines for the Protestant clergy, *Pulpit Digest* and *Pastoral Psychology*.

Perhaps I was unable to live the Jewish or Christian myths because I had already unconsciously replaced them with the Hindu myths in which I had been steeped since entering college, at the age of 17 (though still without any supporting shared ritual); perhaps I simply had an innate affinity for the Hindu myths, an immediate individual response. In any case, I found that I could in fact make some sense of my father's death in terms of the Hindu mythology of death and evil—the subject of the book that I was working on at that time, and had begun some years before the onset of my father's illness.[8] In a certain sense, I had been experiencing, like a hunter, the same events that were narrated in the myth that I had been reading and writing about as a sage, though at first I did not realize that this was the myth that I was in.

The tendency to make use of other people's myths has long been a habit of the Jews, wandering or dispersed as they are.[9] Jews have always lived among Others—have always *been* the Others wherever they lived. The great Indologist, Heinrich Zimmer, retold the well-known Hasidic tale told by Martin Buber, about a Rabbi who lived in a ghetto in Cracow (a town not far from the village where my father was born). The Rabbi dreamt that he should go to Prague, where he would discover a hidden treasure buried beneath the principal bridge leading to the castle of the Bohemian kings. He went to Prague and waited by the bridge for many days, until one night he was questioned by the Christian captain of the guard on the bridge, and the Rabbi told the captain about the dream that had sent him there. The captain laughed and said that it was foolish to trust a dream, since he himself had been commanded in a dream to go to Cracow and to search for a great treasure buried in a dirty corner behind the stove of a Jewish Rabbi named Eisik son of Yekel—clearly a ludicrous proposal, since half the men in the ghetto were called Eisik and the other half Yekel. The Rabbi, who was Eisik son of Yekel, said nothing, but hurried home and found in his house, behind the stove, the treasure. As Zimmer comments on this myth, "Now the real treasure . . . is never far away; it is not to be sought in any distant region; it lies buried in the innermost recess of our own home, that is to say, our own being. . . . But there is the odd and persistent fact . . . that the one who reveals to us the meaning of our cryptic inner message must be a stranger, of another creed and a foreign race" (Zimmer 1946: 219–221, citing Buber 1928: 532–533 [1948: 245]).[10]

I continued to wrestle with my own manifestation of this archetypal problem, and twelve years after my father died I had a dream about it. I dreamt that I was at a meal in the Commons Room of the Divinity School at the University of Chicago, sitting at one of the long tables as I have so often done at formal and informal dinners, with friends on either side and across from me. And suddenly I looked up and realized that I was inside the Leonardo da Vinci painting of the Last Supper, that Jesus and the disciples had come forward in time to join us now at the table in Chicago. As I realized this, the person sitting beside me said to me, "But Wendy, what is *your* religion?" and I replied, "My myths are Hindu, but my rituals are Christian."

This dream puzzled me when I awoke; why did I not say, "My rituals are Jewish"? Instead, like the Rabbi from Cracow, I had borrowed from Christianity to make the collage or *bricolage* of my dream image.[11] More than that: I had had to read a book about India by Zimmer (a Lutheran) to find a parable from my own, Jewish tradition. Through this indirect path, my dream also incorporated the ceremony of the sharing of the leftovers (or *prasāda*) of the Hindu gods, the food distributed to the worshipers after the god has tasted them in the temple. For the myth of the communal meal served me simultaneously as a Passover seder, a Christian eucharist, a Hindu *prasāda*, and a University of Chicago dinner; my dream incorporated my four rituals (three religious and a non-transcendent fourth): Jewish, Christian, Hindu, and academic.

If I were a Fish

It is possible for us to assimilate the myths of other cultures, both professionally and personally, through the sort of distancing that the Rabbi experienced. Claude Lévi-Strauss has pointed out that the myths of other cultures are good to think with; and we can learn to think with them. More than that: we can learn to *feel* with them

Thinking and feeling with other people's myths has serious implications. There are several things that it does not mean. It does *not* mean that a scholar of religion should become an apologist for another tradition, let alone convert to it; though conversions of this type do in fact occur from time to time, they are not the usual course of events, and they are hedged with problems that are beyond our present inquiry.[12] Nor does it mean that the mythologist should proselytize for the texts that he or she studies, using them in an attempt to cure the ills of a demythologized age; people other than mythologists certainly do take up foreign myths (just as they do convert to foreign religions), but they do not take them up in the same way that the historian of religions takes them up, and in any case it is not the task of the historian of religions to facilitate such conversions. Nor does it imply that the way to study other people's myths is to take them into our own lives; the way to study them is to study them, learning the languages in which they are composed, finding all the other myths in the constellation of which they are a part, setting them in the context of the culture in which they occur—in short, trying to find out what they mean to the people who have created and sustained them, not what they mean to us.

But sometimes, as we have seen, something happens to us when we study other people's myths; sometimes they enter our hearts as well as our heads. Some scholars have come to think with other people's myths, an enterprise that always affects the construction of the scholar's personal world view (his life as a hunter) and may also affect his professional scholarship (his life as a sage). We have seen some of the hunter aspects of the personal adventures of the Rabbi from Cracow. But Rabbis are sages, too. How did his dream affect his intellectual life as a scholar (let alone his religious life as a Jew)? The myth does not tell us, but we may ask: What happens to the scholarship of sages who take seriously the myths that they study?

We might begin by asking whether the myths are the same once they have made the perilous journey from the heads of the people who have always thought with them to the heads (and the hearts) of the scholars who have learned to think and feel with them. Evans-Pritchard (1965: 43) once remarked that it was futile to try to imagine how one would think or feel, "If I were a horse." It is, however, the pious belief of many horsemen that they can think like horses.[13] And maybe they can. But we can never know if they have done it or not. There is a Taoist parable to this effect:

> Chuang Tzu and Hui Tzu had strolled on to the bridge over the Hao, when the former observed, "See how the minnows are darting about! That is the pleasure of fishes." "You not being a fish yourself," said Hui Tzu, "how can you possibly know in what consists the pleasure of fishes?" "And you not being I," retorted Chuang Tzu, "how can you know that I do not know?" "If I, not being you, cannot know what you know," urged Hui Tzu, "it follows that you, not being a fish, cannot know in what consists the pleasure of fishes." "Let us go back," said Chuang Tzu, "to your original question. You asked me how I knew in what consists the pleasure of fishes. Your very question shows that you knew I knew. I knew it from my own feelings on this bridge." (Giles 1926: 218–219).[14]

Let us take this story as a metaphor for the problems faced by scholars (Chinese philosophers) trying to understand people from other religious traditions (fish)—and, indeed, to understand other scholars (other Chinese philosophers).[15] How *can* we tell which of us can understand the fish and which of us cannot? More precisely, do we understand fish better if we *do* take their myths into our lives (that is, if we find their myths "good to feel with") or if we do *not* take their myths into our lives?

Fire and Ice

It has been well argued that to study marine biology one does not need to become a fish; indeed, that one had better *not* be a fish (or even "committed to fish"). As Ernest Nagel (1956: 365) put it, "Must a psychiatrist be at least partially demented to study successfully the mentally ill?"[16] Some have phrased the assertion even more strongly, pointing out that a bacteriologist does not have to *like* bacteria.[17] Indeed, many scholars who have written great studies of religion have been motivated not by love of religion (*piscophilia*) but by hatred of religion (*piscophobia*), or at least by anger directed against religion. Freud and Marx are the most outstanding examples of brilliant *piscophobes*, but there are others.[18] Hate is, like love, fueled by the heart rather than the head, and emotional fuel has great staying power.[19] Hunters *must* love and hate; ideally, sages do neither, if they remain in the cool realm of the head. But, as we have seen, they do not always remain in the realm of the head; they, too, hunt in the heart, and so they, too, may love and hate what they study in the head.

Robert Frost (1949: 268) wrote of the power of hate compared with the power of love:

Some say the world will end in fire;
Some say in ice.
From what I've tasted of desire
I hold with those who favor fire.
But if it had to perish twice,
I think I've known enough of hate
To say that for destruction ice
Is also great,
And would suffice.

So hate, like desire, can destroy; and I think that, like desire, hate can create.

But hate may have been a more appropriate motivation in the salad days of the academic study of religion, when we were green in judgment, and trying to be cold in blood (Shakespeare 1954: 1.5.74–75). Nowadays, when we can, and must, be more subtle, hate has its limits. The attempt to empathize is always interesting, perhaps because it is ultimately impossible; but the enterprise of killing is ultimately boring. It doesn't take very long to kill something academically—that is, to demonstrate how wrong or bad a religion, or a colleague in the study of religion, may be—but then you're finished; there is nothing left to do. Killing may be amusing while it lasts, but it never lasts very long, and then you are back where you started from; there is nowhere to go on to.[20] Hunters have to kill; sages do not. Sages have their opinions, of course, but they have learnt to move with a subtle tolerance in strange waters. Hate is creative but not generative; the scholar who studies what he hates goes round and round, obsessively, *ad infinitum*, like an *ouroboros*, biting its *own* tail forever—or until it burns out.

I suspect that the scholars who come closest to the unreachable goal of knowing how fish think are those who are fond of fish, who are interested (like the Chinese sage) in whether fish are happy, not whether fish are sad or mad or bad. And I think that some scholars may well know how happy the fish are. They understand fish not because they hate fish (as many ex-fish do) but because they love fish (as another sort of ex-fish does). A few—I think of Mircea Eliade, and Evans-Pritchard himself—have been able to use their own religious experience as a touchstone through which to understand the religious experience of others; they have had some experience of fish-hood, though not always experience of the particular species that they have studied. Such a scholar is like a sighted person who becomes temporarily blind and then sighted again; not only will he have an unusual understanding of blindness, but he will also have an unusual understanding of what it means to see (Duerr 1985: 133).[21]

But not all scholars can walk the razor's edge between detachment and empathy as they do. Some fail to become true fish and merely become fishy, sitting like mugwumps on the boundary fence between us and the others. An anthropologist who attempts to live such a double life was described by Evans-

Pritchard (1973: 4) as being, at least during the period of his field work, "a sort of double outsider initiated from both worlds." And some people believe that this alienation may in fact become permanent; one may be caught not only between one's own culture and the other culture, but between the world of fish (or the world of hunters) and the academic world (the world of Chinese philosophers and sages); one may be "forever excluded from the world of talking animals and from the world of talking anthropologists as well" (Duerr 1985: 133).[22]

Academic Hardware and Religious Software

The issue of the legitimacy of affect (the heart) in the academic study of religion (a discipline of the head) thus involves us once more in the question of the relative validity of two different sorts of affect, love and hate. Hate seems to provide an answer to the embarrassing problem of *caring* about what one teaches when what one teaches is religion. For though it is deemed wrong to care for religion, it is not wrong to care *against* religion. Criticism is more *wissenschaftlich* than praise in all academic disciplines, but particularly in religious studies. Since the Enlightenment, hatred of religion has been a more respectable scholarly emotion than love, particularly hatred of one's own religion. (Bigots, who hate other people's religions, are not a major problem *within* the academy; bigots are usually primarily hunters, not sages.)

For the problem of affect is thornier when one is studying not the myths of others but one's own myths, a delicate enterprise that has been much discussed. If we teach what we believe in, our subconscious commitment may skew our supposedly innocent approach to the data; the heart may pollute the head. Hunters lead dangerous lives; there are many traps that lie in wait for scholars who bring their lives into their work, who allow too many liberties to the hunters in them.

Many of these traps were laid for us long ago in the jungles of our unconscious assumptions. E. M. Forster describes a shrine in India that was created when, according to legend, a beheaded warrior contrived somehow to continue to run, in the form of a headless torso, from the top of a hill, where he left his head, to the bottom of the hill, where his body finally collapsed; at the top of the hill is now The Shrine of the Head, and at the bottom, The Shrine of the Body (Forster 1979 [1924]: 287). This seems to me to be a useful parable for much of Western civilization, certainly for that fraction of it that studies religion. Woody Allen (1976: 193) once described a mythical beast called the Great Roe, who had the head of a lion and the body of a lion, but not the same lion. Scholars of religion tend to regard themselves as Great Roes, not realizing that they have the head and the heart (the *manas*, in Sanskrit) of the same lion.

The simultaneous use of the heart and the head seems to violate many of the unspoken canons of scholarship, particularly the rather nervous scholarship of those of us who study religion (Laney 1985: 23–24). Scholars of religion tend to be particularly gun-shy when it comes to admitting to any sort of personal investment in the subject that they teach, and with good reason: the battle between those who believe that religion has a place in the academic curriculum and those who believe that it does not has a long and ugly history. Americans have generally assumed that one could not be both pious and educated; this formulation was challenged long ago by William Rainey Harper, the founder of the University of Chicago, but his challenge was never truly accepted, least of all at Chicago. The battle still rages today; die-hard Creationists still rouse passions with their objections to Darwin, and Fundamentalists with their demands for prayers in schools. Religion remains the academic Scarlet Woman, pilloried primarily by those who react against the Reaction of the Moral Majority, but also by those who have always been, rightly, frightened by the power that religion has (like alcohol, drugs, sex, and nuclear energy) to do evil as well as good.

Scholars of religion are not unique in caring about the personal implications of what they teach, but their commitment is usually more vulnerable than that of many of their colleagues. For though the personal commitment of scholars engaged in the teaching of Marxism, women's studies, black studies, and even regional studies (Chinese, Near Eastern) is often just as intense and just as potentially disruptive of academic objectivity, scholars of religion have made the most self-conscious effort to be more objective than the chemists, *plus royaliste que le roi*. This is all well and good; if one is going to teach a highly charged subject like religion, one needs to be more aware, not less aware, of the impossible goal of pure objectivity. It behoves us, even more, perhaps, than it behoves anthropologists or classicists, to play by the rules of the game of scholarship—to learn languages, read commentaries, examine first-hand reports, take into consideration the various biases of the many people in the chain of transmission that ends with us. The fact that one must admit that it is impossible to produce a perfectly sterile environment is no excuse to perform surgery in a sewer.

We tell ourselves (and others, particularly our colleagues in "harder" disciplines) that we study our texts from the outside, in the approved manner of the head, like sages—cool and objective—while we deal with the religious affairs of the heart, if we deal with them at all, from the inside, like hunters, with passion and commitment. We maintain an objective interest in one sort of religion and a subjective faith in another. For historians of religions, the "objective" religion may be obviously other—Hinduism or Islam—but even if we are dealing with our "own" tradition we are prey to a kind of schizophrenia in artificially defining it as "other" for the duration of the period in which we have it under the academic microscope. That our stock in trade is ideas about gods rather than ideas about electrons or phonemes is not supposed to bother anyone. The same basic rules should apply; the mental computer follows the same synapses, and we merely change the software to *very* soft software.

But in making such assertions, in attempting to play the game of objectivity with the Big Boys on the playing fields of the harder sciences, we often tend to play down the more subtle but equally genuine sort of objectivity that good scholars of religion can and do bring to their discipline, a critical judgment that allows them to be critical even of their own faith claims. And leaning over backwards is not always the best posture in which to conduct a class; it is a posture in which one can easily be knocked over by any well-aimed blow from the opposition. Moreover, this pressure often makes scholars of religion deny that they care about religion, which is untrue; we do care, which is why we have chosen this profession, instead of becoming lawyers and making lots of money.

Orthopraxy and Heterodoxy

Some scholars—think of Paul Ricoeur, David Tracy—do manage to accomplish the rapprochement from the heart to the head, using their own religious commitment in their academic study; but others take the safer path, using their academic study of other people's religions in their private religious understanding (the approach from the head to the heart). (The tension between the heart and the head in the writings of Paul Ricoeur is captured in a French aphorism: *Ricoeur a ses raisons, que la raison ne connaît pas* [Ricoeur has his reasons, that reason does not know].) This latter approach, the way of the empathetic sage, is, as we have seen, more easily achieved, though it is less often discussed. To write about what one cares about is academically unfashionable; but to let what one reads and writes affect one's life is academically irrelevant. The assertion that a critical objectivity makes it possible for a scholar to deal even with his own faith claims in an academic forum demands a far more delicate defense than the assertion that a scholar may derive new faith claims from the subject matter that he or she begins by studying with critical objectivity.

A cynic might view this second process as merely a disguised form of the first, achieving the same end through a means less susceptible to criticism. I am reminded of the Jesuit who was informed that he was not permitted to smoke while he meditated. Quite right, the Jesuit replied; but surely no one would object if he meditated while he was smoking. In fact, I think the two procedures that I have outlined are truly distinct, though my justification for both admittedly rests upon my conviction that it is not necessary for the head and the heart of the scholar of religion to answer two different masters, that the head and the heart can nourish rather than sabotage one another. It sometimes seems to me that we arrange our talents and weaknesses like the blind man and the lame man in the old story: they agreed to team up, but the lame man carried the blind man on his shoulders. If the blind but physically whole man is the hunter, the experiencer, surely we should let him be led about by the lame sage, the seer, the scholar. As we have seen, though the hunter is basically limited to one side of experience (the physical and emotional), a sage is not necessarily limited to only the other side of experience (the intellectual). In any case, since it is ultimately impossible for the sage to deny the hunter within him, it is best for him to come to terms with his hunter. But more than that; the sage who acknowledges his hunter aspect is a better sage, the sage whose heart melts (in the Indian example) rather than the one whose heart is dried up by his books.

Though the love of religion is never considered as academically legitimate as the hatred of religion, the love of *other* people's religions is at least less illegitimate than the love of one's own. (This may account for the fact that some historians of religion who have *piscophiliac* leanings let down their guard to such a point that they may be accused of committing the deadly academic sin of cryptotheology. I name no names.) Yet it might be argued that people who take into their hearts (rather than merely into their heads) the myths that they pick up promiscuously in Oriental bazaars risk a crisis of faith when these myths infect the myths of their own traditions—or, in the case of academics, a crisis of atheism when the myth of objectivity is challenged. I think that this false argument is based upon a confusion between myths and rituals. For most people are more orthoprax than orthodox: they define themselves by their rituals, by what they do as hunters, not by their myths, by what they think as sages. This is particularly true of Hindus and Jews, who are often able to embrace a seemingly infinite range of heterodox views while remaining, at heart, firmly anchored to surprisingly orthoprax behavior.[23] As long as the rituals remain intact, the faith remains intact, however much the myths may change.

We are usually, though not always, tied for life to the rituals that we are born with, the rituals that we grow up with, the rituals of our own religion. But we are not necessarily tied exclusively to the myths of our own culture. The rituals are deeply ensconced in our hearts. The myths may enter through the head—and, ultimately, come to lodge in the heart. A person who continues to live with his or her given rituals in the orthopraxy of the heart can still absorb other myths in the heterodoxy of the head. Such a person is yet another incarnation of the Great Roe who is in fact a whole lion.

Eclecticism in personal cosmologies may be too elusive and idiosyncratic to be subjected to the structures of a public, communal, academic discourse; it is dangerous for the sage to be controlled by the hunter inside him, for scholars to use their personal religion in their work. But eclecticism does have a legitimate place in the evolution of private universes; sages who enter the dreams of hunters and awaken become hunters with sages inside them. Such people are better hunters, people who use their academic discoveries to enrich their personal world-views; they embody Socrates' famous dictum that the life that is unexamined is not worth living. And I think that they are better sages, too, scholars whose empathy gives them greater understanding of the subject that they teach; for it is also true that the life that is not lived is not worth examining.[24]

Eclecticism may be too arrogant a word for this process, implying that we decide what myths are true, or make up gods that suit our moods. Perhaps we should find some more modest, passive word, to describe what we do in receiving and accepting the myths from other people's religions. Perhaps our myths, like greatness in Shakespeare's formulation (1968: 2.5.159), are not something that we are born with, or achieve, but something that we have thrust upon us, to confront not only with our heads but with our hearts.

Notes

1. See also the *Bhagavadajjuka* of Baudhāyana.
2. I have greatly summarized this story, which occupies 21 chapters (not 21 verses) of the Sanskrit text. In some ways, this condensation makes the story more confusing than it is when one reads it at length; in some ways, it oversimplifies it.
3. A similar process is described by Paul Scott (47). The servant, Ibrahim, thinks about Mrs. Smalley: "Memsahib upright against her piled-up pillows, under that cascade of cob-webbed net playing in her dreams, perhaps, Miss Havisham in *Great Expectations*, still waiting for her groom. At 5 a.m. he kicked out the last spark of the wood fire in case at dawn there was a mysterious association of ideas and The Lodge burnt down because she had dreamed it."
4. See the story of the hundred Rudras and the wild goose in chapter 5 of O'Flaherty (1984).
5. O'Flaherty (1984, introduction and chapter 1). It is significant that for a long time we defined the moment when death occurred as the moment when the heart stopped working. We now define it as the moment when the brain stops working. I use "head" and "heart" as metaphors as they have often been used in the West, indicating rational, objective, scientific, methodological mental processes on the one hand—the thoughts of sages—and irrational, subjective, artistic, and inspirational mental processes on the other—the emotions of hunters. This is, of course, not merely anatomically incorrect; it is a logically inconsistent way of dividing up reason and emotion.
6. An epidemic of self-conscious discussions of this problem was set off by Claude Lévi-Strauss in *Tristes Tropiques*.
7. Clifford Geertz's essay on this topic begins with a response to Malinowski's diary.
8. O'Flaherty (1976, especially Chapter 6, "The Birth of Death"). It was my husband, Dennis O'Flaherty, who pointed out to me the relevance of my work on death to my experience of death.
9. This talent (or weakness, if you will) of a particular sort of Jew must be understood in the context of Judaism as a whole. An overwhelming majority of Jews are of a

very different sort. They live and die in the religion of their birth and find it entirely sufficient to their religious needs. Let me say again that I am not talking about religious conversion, let alone the anti-Semitic proselytizing of such groups as the Jews for Jesus. I am thinking of the ways in which Jews have been forced, for their very survival, to *learn* other people's religions, and in some cases to learn *from* them as well.

10. The moral of the story according to Rabbi Simha Bunam of Pzhysha (the original author of the story, according to Buber) is somewhat different from the moral drawn by Zimmer: "There is something you cannot find anywhere in the world, not even at the zaddik's, and there is, nevertheless, a place where you can find it."

    And yet another moral is pointed in the version "retold" by Woody Allen (1972: 52–56): "Rabbi Yekel of Zans ... dreamed three nights running that if he would only journey to Vorki he would find a great treasure there. Bidding his wife and children goodbye, he set out on a trip, saying he would return in ten days. Two years later, he was found wandering the Urals and emotionally involved with a panda. Cold and starving, the Rev was taken back to his house, where he was revived with steaming soup and flanken.... After telling the story, the Rabbi rose and went into his bedroom to sleep, and behold, under his pillow was the treasure that he originally sought. Ecstatic, he got down and thanked God. Three days later, he was back wandering in the Urals again, this time in a rabbit suit.... The above small masterpiece amply illustrates the absurdity of mysticism."

    I must apologize for using Heinrich Zimmer's version of this story here, when I have cited it before in several other contexts (O'Flaherty 1973, 1980). This recycling is characteristic of such adopted myths.

11. Ed. note. *Bricolage* is a French term meaning to tinker about, or to do odd jobs. Hence, a *bricoleur* is a do-it-yourselfer or possibly a handyman, even a jack-of-all-trades.

12. Hindus, for instance, do not proselytize, nor do orthodox Hindus consider it possible for anyone who is not born a Hindu to become a Hindu; what, then, is the status of the Americans who regard themselves as followers of Hindu gurus?

13. Anna Sewell's *Black Beauty, His Groom and Companions: The "Uncle Tom's Cabin" of the Horse* and Rudyard Kipling's "The Maltese Cat" are narrated by horses. See also Smythe.

14. Chuang chou, *chuang-tzu*, book 17, paragraph 13. I am indebted to Paul Wheatley for this reference.

15. It was only after delivering this speech in Anaheim that I learned, from Roger Corless, that my predecessor in the AAR [American Academy of Religion] Presidency, Wilfred Cantwell Smith, had already used the fish metaphor in a similar context; he had compared methodologists to flies crawling on a goldfish bowl trying to guess what it might be like to be a fish.

16. To which Hans-Peter Duerr (127) replied: "Under no circumstances should one turn into a werewolf just to understand what being a werewolf is like. Under no circumstances must the werewolf's experiences ever be comprehended."

17. This is what one famous scholar of Turkish studies told another in answer to the surprise expressed by the latter when the former stated that he did not care for the Turks.

18. One striking example of a scholar who hated what he wrote about was Julius

Eggeling, who devoted his life to the massive Sanskrit text of the *Śatapatha Brāhmana*, his translation of which was published in Oxford in 1882, in five volumes. In his introduction, Eggeling (ix, cited by O'Flaherty 1985a: 4) complained that "For wearisome prolixity of exposition, characterized by a dogmatic assertion and a flimsy symbolism rather than by serious reasoning, these works are perhaps not equaled anywhere...."

19. The peculiar Hass-Lieb relationship that has bound many important historians of religion to their subject matter (particularly, but not only, when those historians of religion have been Indologists, more particularly when they have been Jewish Indologists) has long been apparent to scholars working in the field. I do not make bold to explain this phenomenon, except by citing (with reference to the last of these three categories) the law of physics that like repels like. On the other hand, Jewish scholars not entirely at home in their own home may move not into a general *piscophobia* but into a general *piscophilia*: such was the case with Emile Durkheim, Claude Lévi-Strauss, and David Shulman—the tradition within which I would locate myself.

20. Wendy Doniger O'Flaherty, cited (*à propos* of J. L. Masson, a Jewish Indologist who has written about Freud) by Malcolm (163–164).

21. A wonderful play that describes what happens when a pair of blind people became sighted is John Millington Synge's *The Well of the Saints*. In this play, an ugly man and woman, blind from birth, have been happily married for years, each believing the other to be beautiful; when they are given sight, through a miracle, they are appalled by what they see and are mercifully made blind once again. This, too, may be read as a metaphor.

22. Such a fate may await both scholars and witches (Duerr 370); it was also the destiny of Kipling's Mowgli, who understood the language of the animals. For a further discussion of this problem, see O'Flaherty (1985b).

23. There is a telling anecdote about Jewish orthopraxy: The Jews in a small town in East Europe were forced to convert to Catholicism. When they persisted in eating meat on Fridays and were upbraided for this lapse, they insisted that they were not eating meat; before putting the roast into the oven, they made the sign of the cross over it and said, "Roast, you're a fish." This seems to me to say a lot about the futility of attempts to convert to new rituals. There are also certain sorts of Hindus (those who embrace the post-classical devotional cults) who regard themselves as orthodox and who, unlike classical Hindus, proselytize. I still think that the distinction between heterodoxy and orthopraxy is applicable to most people, and particularly applicable to Hindus and Jews.

24. David Tracy pointed this out in a speech at the University of Chicago on November 6, 1985. And Malcolm (26), in discussing the resistance against the Freudian approach to the unconscious, remarked that "The unexamined life may not be worth living, but the examined life is impossible to live for more than a few moments at a time."

References

Allen, Woody 1972. "Hassidic Tales, with a Guide to their Interpretation by the Noted Scholar," *Getting Even* 48–53. New York: Vintage Books.

—1976. "Fabulous Tales and Mythical Beasts," *Without Feathers*, 191–195. New York: Warner Books.

Bloomfield, Maurice 1917. "On the Art of Entering Another's Body: A Hindu Fiction Motif," *Proceedings of the American Philosophical Society* 41: 1–43.

Buber, Martin 1928. *Die Chassidisclien Bucher*. Hallerau: I. J. Hegner.

—1948. *Tales of the Hasidim: II, Later Masters*. Olga Marx (trans.). New York: Schocken Books.

Duerr, Hans-Peter, 1985. *Dreamtime: Concerning the Boundary Between Wilderness and Civilization*. Felicitas Goodman (trans.). New York: Basil Blackwell.

Eggeling, Julius (ed. and trans.) 1882. *Śatapatha Brāhmana*. Oxford: Clarendon Press.

Evans-Pritchard, E. E. 1965. Theories of Primitive Religion. Oxford: Clarendon Press.

—1973. "Some Reminiscences and Reflections on Fieldwork," *Journal of the Anthropological Society of Oxford* 4: 1–14.

Forster, E. M. 1979 [1924]. *A Passage to India*. Oliver Stallybrass (ed.). Abinger Edition, Vol. 6. New York: Meier.

Frost, Robert 1949. "Fire and Ice," *The Complete Poems of Robert Frost*, 268. New York: H. Holt.

Geertz, Clifford 1983. "'From the Native's Point of View': On the Nature of Anthropological Understanding," *Local Knowledge: Further Essays in Interpretive Anthropology*, 55–70. New York: Basic Books.

Giles, Herbert A. (trans.) 1926. *Chuang Tzu: Mystic, Moralist, and Social Reformer*. London: Bernard Quaritch.

Kipling, Rudyard 1898. "The Maltese Cat," *The Day's Work*. London: Macmillan.

Laney, James T. 1985. "The Education of the Heart," *Harvard Magazine* 88/1: 23–24.

Lévi-Strauss, Claude 1955. *Tristes Tropiques*. Paris: Plon.

Malcolm, Janet 1984. *In the Freud Archives*. New York: Knopf.

Malinowski, Bronislow 1967. *A Diary in the Strict Sense of the Term*. Norbert Guterman (trans.). London: Routledge & Kegan Paul.

Masson, J. L. and M. V. Patwardhan 1970. *Aesthetic Rapture: The Rasādhyāya of the Nátyāśāstra*. Poona: Bhandarkar Oriental Research Institute.

Nagel, Ernest 1956. *Logic Without Metaphysics*. Glencoe, IL: Free Press.

O'Flaherty, Wendy Doniger 1973. *Asceticism and Eroticism in the Mythology of Siva*. London: Oxford University Press.

—— 1976. *The Origins of Evil in Hindu Mythology*. Berkeley: University of California Press.

—— 1980. "Inside and Outside the Mouth of God: The Boundary Between Myth and Reality," *Daedalus* 109/2: 93–125.

—— 1984. *Dreams, Illusion, and Other Realities*. Chicago: University of Chicago Press.

—— 1985a. *Tales of Sex and Violence: Folklore, Sacrifice, and Danger in the Jaiminiya Brahmana*. Chicago: University of Chicago Press.

—— 1985b. Review of Hans-Peter Duerr, *Dreamtime*, *New York Times Book Review*, September 8: 10–12.

Pansikar, W. L. S. (ed.) 1918. *Yogāvasisthamahārāmāyana*, attributed to Vālmīki. Bombay: Nirnaya Sagara Press.

Parab, D. Pandurang and K. Pandurang Parab (eds.) 1891. *Dhvanyāloka* of Ānandavardhana, with the *Dhvanyalokalocana* of Abhinavagupta. Bombay: Nirnaya Sagara Press.

Scott, Paul 1977. *Staying On*. London: Heinemann.

Sewell, Anna 1877. *Black Beauty, His Groom and Companions: The "Uncle Tom's Cabin" of the Horse*. New York: G. Munro's Sons.

Shakespeare, William 1954. *Antony and Cleopatra*. M. R. Ridley (ed.). London: Methuen.

—— 1968. *Twelfth Night, Or What You Will*. Sir Arthur Quiller-Couch and John Dover Wilson (eds.). Cambridge: Cambridge University Press.

Smith, W. C. 1950. "The Comparative Study of Religion," *Inaugural Lectures*. Montreal: McGill University Press.

Smythe, R. H. 1965. *The Mind of the Horse*. London: J. A. Allen.

Stevenson, Robert Louis 1886. *The Strange Case of Dr. Jekyll and Mr. Hyde*. London: Longman, Green.

Synge, John M. 1982. *The Well of the Saints*. Nicholas Grene (ed.). Washington, D.C.: Catholic University of America Press.

Zimmer, Heinrich, 1946. *Myths and Symbols in Indian Art and Civilization*. Joseph Campbell (ed.). New York: Pantheon Books.

23

KAREN MCCARTHY BROWN,
Writing About "the Other"

ক্রু ক্রু

I see now, more clearly than I did during the 12 years of labor on it, that my book, *Mama Lola: A Vodou Priestess in Brooklyn*, is the product of unconventional methods of anthropological research and writing. Published by the University of California Press last year [1991], the book weaves stories of Mama Lola's ancestors together with ethnographic narratives that are woven, in turn, from my own scholarly and personal voices and from several of Mama Lola's voices, including those of six Vodou spirits who routinely possess her.

I did not set out to do experimental fieldwork, nor, when I was writing, did I see myself as jumping into the middle of a postmodernist debate on ethnography. Yet now that the book is done and I can afford the luxury of sticking my head up and surveying the wider terrain, I see that I did flout some of the conventions of anthropological fieldwork. I also have become involved, willy-nilly, in the current spirited debate about what we anthropologists— mostly white Euro-Americans—are doing when we write about those whom scholars sometimes call "the Other."

Contemporary critics argue that the greater social power of the researcher overwhelms the subject and that ethnographic texts are, by default, little more than fictions, revealing more about the culture and the preoccupations of the writer than about those of the people being studied. *Mama Lola* enters this debate in two ways: first, by deliberate attention to the power issues between Mama Lola and me; and second, by an implicit claim that more extended, intimate, and committed contacts between researcher and subject can undercut the colonial mindset of much anthropological writing.

I met Alourdes (the name that I usually use to address Mama Lola) in the summer of 1978. She was then in her mid-40s and had immigrated from Haiti in 1963. I was ten years younger and the great-granddaughter of European immigrants. On the surface we were very different. By the time I reached my mid-20s, I had my first college teaching job: at the same age, Alourdes was living in the squalor of Port-au-Prince, raising two children on her own, and, when there was no other way to feed them, resorting to prostitution. Yet, ironically, when we met, we shared a sense of upward mobility. A member of the first college-educated generation of my family, I had recently received my Ph.D. and had taken a position on the faculty of Drew University. Alourdes by that time owned her own home and was firmly ensconced as the head of a lively, three generational-household.

She also was working full-time as a Vodou priestess, a vocation requiring the combined skills of priest, social worker, herbalist, and psychotherapist. Three generations of healers in her family had preceded her, but she was the first family member to muster the financial resources needed to pay for the elaborate initial rituals that make the role official.

When we were introduced, I was living in a loft in SoHo, an artists' district in lower Manhattan. Alourdes' home, where she also held regular Vodou ceremonies and consulted daily with individual clients, was a small row house in the Fort Greene section of Brooklyn. The social distance between us was great, but the geographic distance was small. Her house and the Vodou world she inhabited were a mere 20 minutes by car from my front door.

Something clicked between Alourdes and me, although I cannot say that we liked or trusted one another right away. Perhaps it was just that each of us sensed in the other someone who could extend and challenge our world. She seemed a formidable person, strong and moody. One moment she was electric, filled with charm: the next, dour and withdrawn. I, no doubt, appeared overly polite and overly white.

For a while, we engaged in a formal little dance. I stopped by her house to visit frequently and brought her small gifts; she usually offered me coffee and took the time to sit and talk with me. Sometimes she invited me to ceremonies. I was utterly fascinated by her charismatic priestcraft and by the intimate and familial style of ritualizing that was so different from what I had seen during the years I worked on Vodou in large, urban temples in Haiti. Despite my fascination, I mostly hovered on the edge of the crowd at Alourdes' "birthday parties" for the spirits. Sometimes she went into a trance, the Vodou spirit "riding" her would seek me out and give me advice or blessing. Later I found out that one or two regulars at these events objected to my presence and suggested that I was a spy from the immigration office. Alourdes reportedly answered that no one could tell her how to choose her friends.

After a few months, I offered to help Alourdes with ritual preparations. I ran errands, helped to cook the ritual meal, and lent a hand constructing the altar that is the focal point of each Vodou ceremony. Our friendship grew through intimacies shared in the midst of routine work as well as through stronger bonds forged in the midst of life crises. Her son got in trouble with the law, and she turned to me for help; I went through a divorce and felt grateful for her support, which often took the form of offers of ritual healing. Soon a friendship developed that blurred and confused our previous roles of academic researcher and representative Vodou priestess. These days she calls me her "daughter," and, when I am not able to spend holidays with my biological family, I am more likely to celebrate them at her house than anywhere else.

As our friendship grew, participating in her religion felt like a natural step. I did not tumble into it in reaction to a life crisis; I chose to participate in Vodou for a mix of professional and personal reasons that I will never untangle. The single clear feeling was a powerful need to understand what Vodou was about, what it had to offer those who turned to it in times of trouble. My own attitude was very much like Alourdes's when she offered to let me *kouche* (literally, lie down or sleep)—in other words, to participate in healing ceremonies that also function as rights of initiation in Vodou. "Try it," she said. "See if it works for you."

And it did work. Vodou gave me a rich, unblinkingly honest view of life that has been one of several resources that I have drawn on in the last decade or so to sort out life's problems. Participating in rituals and deciding to offer myself as a candidate for healing have given me valuable insights into how Vodou works, insights that strengthened my book considerably.

Yet my academic colleagues have raised questions. Have I lost my objectivity? Has my friendship with Alourdes biased my account of her family history, her daily life, and her spirituality? Has my participation in Vodou colored the way in which I present the religion? The answer to all these questions is a qualified Yes, although that doesn't disturb me as much as some of my colleagues wish it did.

The analogy commonly drawn between anthropology and the natural sciences has ceased to be helpful to me. While I still care about factuality and freedom from bias, those standards are no longer the most demanding ones for my work. Over the years I have come to understand anthropological fieldwork as something closer to a social art form than a social science. It involves a particular type of relationship, yet one that is subject to all the complexities and ambiguities of any other kind of human interaction. This conception of fieldwork does not mean that no standards are applicable; they simply are different from the traditional ones. Truth telling and justice, for example, seem to be more fitting criteria than the canons of scientific research.

In relation to *Mama Lola*, truth telling not only required enough care and persistence to get the facts straight, but also enough self-awareness and self-disclosure to allow readers to see my point of view (another term for bias) and make their judgments about it. Because I believe that a writer's perspective is more than a collection of facts that can be listed in an introduction and then forgotten, I chose to present myself as a character in the story, interacting with Alourdes. The challenge was to do this enough to reveal the way in which I relate to her without turning the book into a story about me.

A standard of truthfulness also demanded that I tell as complete a story as possible, including all the complexities, without boring or confusing readers. In other words, telling the truth required me to perform an intellectual–aesthetic balancing act in which the order and clarity of abstractions were placed in tension with the dense tangle of lived experience.

Justice, which like truth telling can never be fully achieved, was an even more challenging criterion of scholarship in this case. I felt compelled to do justice to Alourdes and to her world in my writing. Both moral and aesthetic judgments came into play, for example, in choosing the telling detail or the revelatory incident designed to capture definitive aspects of her life.

Justice as a goal in my relationship with Alourdes has meant, among other things, that I could not exploit her, misrepresent my intentions, or turn away from her once I had what I needed. Financial obligations, like those of time and energy, could not be limited to what was necessary to grease the flow of information for the book. A true friendship is not over just because a writing project is done. So she will share the profits from the book with me, and, when she cannot meet a mortgage payment or raise the money for a trip to Haiti, I expect to continue to contribute.

It has not always been easy for me to negotiate the responsibilities that I have accepted as a result of Alourdes' gift of friendship, but I would not have it any other way. Despite her limited reading and writing skills, Alourdes helped to keep me truthful and not just while writing *Mama Lola*. When I was tempted to soft-pedal information that I feared might embarrass her (for example, her prostitution), she pushed me: "You got to put that in the book. Because that's the truth. Right? Woman got to do all kinda thing. Right? I do that to feed my children. I'm not ashamed." The nature of anthropological fieldwork changes in situations of cultural mixing where the subject has her own vision of the project and her own views on the standards to which it should be held accountable.

I could not have written *Mama Lola* if Alourdes had not challenged me, trusted me, and become my friend. Through our friendship, we have served scholarship's end of deepened understanding, in this case by showing Vodou at work in the intimate details of one person's life. We both hope that our risk taking will help to counter the distorted image of this ancient religion.

24

MARGERY WOLF, *Writing Ethnography: The Poetics and Politics of Culture*

❧ ❧

The title of this chapter is, obviously, a play on the title of Clifford and Marcus's celebrated collection of essays, *Writing Culture: The Poetics and Politics of Ethnography* (1986). I use it not out of disrespect for that important set of papers, but because it captures how different my perspective on ethnography is from that of Clifford and Marcus. We are not in the business of anthropology, as Clifford Geertz so nicely states it, "to capture primitive facts in faraway places and carry them home like a mask," but rather "to reduce the puzzlement," to discover "the informal logic of actual life" (1973: 16–17). Some of us hope to uncover the cross-cultural commonalities that underlie our diversity; more of us hope only to reduce the puzzlement about one or two unfamiliar places.

The means by which we acquire the experience that starts us on the path to understanding—our field methods—have always been eclectic and, as a result, slightly troubling to our colleagues and to us. We do not sit around in our villages and atolls absorbing culture like sunshine, as some of our postmodernist critics appear to think. In fact, most of us exhaust ourselves mentally and physically in our attempts to see, hear, and experience as much as we can in the too brief period academic schedules allow for fieldwork. We *do* research. It is not something that simply happens to us as a result of being in an exotic place. Our willingness to speak and write about that experience results from our serious engagement in discovering what we can about how life is lived in another social/cultural setting.

The first field trip is a stunning roller coaster of self-doubt, boredom, excitement, disorientation, uncertainty, exhaustion, bullying, being bullied, cajoling, being cajoled—in the course of which we somehow accumulate "data," precious notebooks packed with disorganized thoughts, detailed observations of minutiae, descriptions of rituals, transcripts of conversations, diagrams, and detritus. Doing fieldwork is a matter of being in the right place at the right time (not necessarily the time your informants told you would be the right time) and asking the right questions of a wide variety of people. Unfortunately, we rarely know the right place, right time, right question, or right people until we have nearly finished the job, or *have* finished it and are three thousand miles away. We are dependent upon our ability to match up clues, our luck in following hunches, a couple of chance encounters, an observation jotted down that only makes sense days or even years later. Some of us do systematic and well-organized interviews and observations in the field, but in the end, when the stack of filled notebooks is much higher than the stack of blank and waiting notebooks, when we ask ourselves if we have the material to "reduce the puzzlement," we as often as not have no answer and leave the field site because we must, not because we feel we have finished the work.[1]

The experience of fieldwork does not produce a mysterious empowerment, but without it, the ethnographer would not encounter the context—the smells, sounds, sights, emotional tensions, feel—of the culture she will attempt to evoke in a written text. Before I lived in Taiwan, I had seen beautiful *National Geographic* pictures of rice paddies inhabited by water buffalo and peasants in quaint hats. This did not prepare me for the intense stench of "night soil" (human feces mixed with water and allowed to stew in the sun for a few weeks before being poured into the flooded paddy) or for the despair with which an unemployed middle school graduate turns over the putrid muck of his father's land. There was nothing mystical or even pleasant about most of these experiences, but without them, my ability to convey any part of their meaning would have been seriously compromised.

Experience is messy. Searching for patterns in behavior, a consistency in attitudes, the meaning of a casual conversation, is what anthropologists do, and they are nearly always dependent on a ragtag collection of facts and fantasies of an often small sample of a population from a fragment of historical time. When human behavior is the data, a tolerance for ambiguity, multiplicity, contradiction, and instability is essential. When we at last sit down at a clean desk in a quiet study and begin to assemble the vivid images and cryptic notes, searching for a coherency, we must constantly remind ourselves that life *is* "unstable, complex, and disorderly" (Flax 1987: 643), everywhere. As ethnographers, our job is not simply to pass on the disorderly complexity of culture, but also to try to hypothesize about apparent consistencies, to lay out our best guesses, without hiding the contradictions and the instability.

How in heaven's name do we do that? As Clifford asks for us:

If ethnography produces cultural interpretations through intense research experiences, how is unruly experience transformed into an authoritative written account? How, precisely, is a garrulous, over-determined cross-cultural encounter shot through with power relations and personal cross-purposes circumscribed as an adequate version of a more or less discrete "other world" composed by an individual author? (1988b: 25)

Clifford in particular, and the postmodernists in general, not only object to the way anthropologists have attempted to answer these questions in the past, but question the ethnographic enterprise itself—our ability to understand what we see if we are not of that culture, and the ethics of presenting such understandings as fact. They assert that the self of the ethnographer should be decentered in terms of the authority of voice, but at the same time should be front and center in the text so that the reader is constantly aware of how biased, incomplete, and selective are the materials being presented.

And yet, as Clifford himself points out, if the ethnographer can construct culture in her writings, she can also construct a self.... Clifford assumes in "On Ethnographic Self-Fashioning: Conrad and Malinowski" (1988c: 97) that the "real" Malinowski is not the Malinowski of the *Argonauts* but the one of the *Diary*. I don't see one self as any more real than the other: they simply show different aspects of Malinowski's personality. Moreover, their literary construction occurred at different times. The ethnographic self I am constructing here is very different from the one I created in "The Hot Spell" or for that matter in my 1968 book, *The House of Lim*. Which of these constructions is my "real" self?

How, then, is a fully reflexive experimental ethnography going to be an improvement over "realist" accounts, where the rules are at least fairly well known? In a sense, Clifford comments on this himself when he says:

> Thus the discipline of fieldwork-based anthropology, in constituting its authority, constructs and reconstructs coherent cultural others and interpreting selves. If this ethnographic self-fashioning presupposes lies of omission and of rhetoric, it also makes possible the telling of powerful truths. But ... the truths of cultural descriptions are meaningful to specific interpretive communities in limiting historical circumstances. (1988c: 112)

The "telling of powerful truths" is possible but perhaps confined to specific communities that share the rules? Surely this kind of known authoritative voice is safer than the artifice of the fictionizer, who has no obligations beyond making the text plausible, interesting, and faithful to whatever aesthetic integrity is peculiar to the period's genre?

Renato Rosaldo, in a book that is wonderfully accessible and gently reflexive, warns: "If classical ethnography's vice was the slippage from the ideal of detachment to actual indifference, that of present day reflexivity is the tendency for the self-absorbed Self to lose sight altogether of the culturally different Other" (1989: 7). Although Rosaldo agrees with those who have declared a crisis in the production of ethnography (38), he is not content with solutions that mystify the ethnographic process further, such as leaving the work of making sense of the text to the reader. Rosaldo explains:

> Alien cultures, however, can appear so exotic to outsiders that everyday life seems to be floating in a bizarre primitive mentality. Social descriptions about cultures distant from both the writer and the reader require a relative emphasis on familiarization, so they will appear—as they also in fact are—sharply distinct in their differences, yet recognizably human in their resemblances. (1989: 39–40)

Rosaldo also points out that the reverse is true when the culture being subjected to analysis is one's own. "Social descriptions by, of, and for members of a particular culture require a relative emphasis on defamiliarization, so that they will appear—as in fact they are—humanly made, and not given in nature" (39).

"Defamiliarization" is not a term feminists have used, but ever since second-wave feminism empowered feminist social scientists in the late 1960s, we have employed the technique. In order to make gender a proper subject of study, we first had to locate women in culture and society, and then get our colleagues to recognize that their location is no more natural than that of the male half of humanity. As Pat Caplan indicates, the latter task has been absurdly difficult: in England, research on women—whether done by feminists or not—has been dismissed as just another specialization, ignoring the feminist critique that addresses issues of *gender* and should concern the discipline as a whole (Caplan 1988: 14). In the United States, the opposition for a long time came from those who viewed our openly revisionist agenda as merely political, therefore not objective scholarship, hence discountable. Now that the postmodernists have themselves problematized the concept of objectivity, feminists might expect serious attention to the work they have already done on the very issue that was formerly used to condemn them (Harding 1990). Reflexivity, it seems, does not begin at home: postmodernists who criticize social science with a terminology that requires learning a new vocabulary seem unable (unwilling?) to "read" the feminist work unless feminists who speak postmodernism make the translation for them.[2]

Before reflexivity was a trendy term, feminists were examining "process" in our dealings with one another—questioning the use of power and powerlessness to manipulate interactions in meetings, examining closely the politics of seemingly apolitical situations, evaluating the responsibilities we bore toward one another, and so on. The awareness developed in these small "consciousness-raising" sessions quickly spilled over into the work world of social scientists who recognized their double responsibility as feminists doing research on women. I do not mean to imply that *all* feminist social scientists are reflexive in their research and writing, but it is much more common to find a serious questioning of methodology and creative involvement of both researched and researchers among feminists than in the work of mainstream social science (e.g., Haraway 1985; Harding 1987; Shostak 1981; Stacey 1988).

Whether we are talking about nonexploitative methodology in field research or authority in writing ethnography, we are talking about power—who has it, how it is used, for what purposes. This is what study of gender, class, and race is really about: subordinated sectors accommodate to and resist the power of privileged sectors, how privilege (like resistance) is camouflaged, how power is earned, learned, and occasionally spurned. Just as the reality of male privilege affects the lives of every woman, whether she is conscious of it or not, the concept of power is by definition a factor in every feminist's research. Feminist standpoint theorists claim that those who occupy a subordinate position will have a more complete and less distorted knowledge of the system under which they live, and that only through struggle against the oppressing group can a researcher acquire knowledge of the social reality she wishes to study (Harding 1987; Hartsock 1983; Nash 1976). This is a very appealing theory, intellectually and politically, but it creates problems for feminists who do not work in their own society. (Marilyn Strathern points out some of these problems, but at the same time she makes the error of assuming that *all* feminist anthropologists are standpoint theorists—which we are not.) According to standpoint theory, it would be almost impossible for me to understand the oppression of Chinese women or to understand my own potential for being an oppressor in a postcolonial research project.

When the Western anthropologist first strolls into a third-world village, she is a walking symbol of her native country's power, assuming (as is usually the case) that she is white and accompanied by boxes bristling with modern technology. If the anthropologist is male, his panoply of power is further enhanced. After the first pratfall, the anthropologist's aura of power may be tempered, but it is still taken seriously. Within a few months, specific situations become factors in the influence of the still obvious differential power relations. In a Chinese village, the anthropologist, if she is to be one, learns quickly to be deferential to people older than herself, to males, and to those who have taken on the role of teacher. She does not lose the power associated with being a "guest" from a rich and powerful country, but as she tries to negotiate her way through the complexities of village life, her observers become more aware of her dependency on them and less conscious of her power over them.

In our concern over our colonial luggage, we tend to forget the complex power negotiations that also go on among individuals. Even the most arrogant neocolonialist soon discovers that one cannot order rural people to reveal important thoughts about their culture. For at least the first few months, most fieldworkers are dependent on their informants to help them figure out what the questions are (and in some environments, how to stay alive). Those who carry the culture and those who desperately want to understand it may participate in a minuet of unspoken negotiations that totally reverses the apparent balance of power. An extreme example of this is E. E. Evans-Pritchard, who strode into Nuerland with the confidence of his race and education—and was led around by the nose by the unwilling subjects of his study (1969). Wu Chieh, our field assistant in Taiwan, was all too conscious of our privilege as Americans, but the longer she was in our employ, the more power she had over the success of our project—a fact she was quite aware of and on occasion put to good use.

The inequalities of power that exist when first-world anthropologists work in third-world countries must be recognized as playing a major role in our research results, but they are not the only factors, and they may in some circumstances be higher in the consciousness of the anthropologists than in the informant's. For example, when Margaret Rodman became seriously ill while doing fieldwork with her husband on the island of Ambae, it soon became clear that heroic measures would be required if her life was to be saved. The headman of the village, who was their host, prime informant, and good friend, made one set of plans, and her husband made another, conflicting set. Both men were shocked and profoundly surprised when the other did not, in this serious emergency, automatically submit to his obvious authority (Rodman and Rodman 1990). In this case, and in other examples each of us could draw from our own fieldwork, the locus of power/authority is not so obvious as it might seem from the distance of the first world. In our desire to avoid objectifying our informants, we run the risk of patronizing them.

The feminist's sensitivity to power as a factor in all our research, and our enhanced understanding (through political struggle) of both the ubiquity of gender asymmetry and the deep roots of male privilege, should make us even more cautious about postmodernist "reforms" than other social scientists. The male-dominated traditions of the sciences, social sciences, and the humanities have been the accepted reservoirs of knowledge (and the source of power) for centuries, and their guardians can now afford to modestly reconsider the partialness of their truths and the ambiguities in the construction of their knowing.[3] Feminist work has always been under suspicion, often for the same things the postmodernists' critiques now celebrate—like questioning objectivity, rejecting detachment, and accepting contradictory readings. Feminists who have only recently gained some academic security might think carefully about whether intense reflexivity in their research and writing will be evaluated as being in the new postmodernist mode or as simply tentative and self-doubting. Feminists would also do well to consider whether following a postmodern Pied Piper might not lead them away from a commitment to the research and struggle that is hard because it is feminist. How many women, feminist or not, are defining the issues around the postmodernist seminar tables?[4]

Anthropologists always have searched and, I trust, always will search for ways to improve their research and make the results of that research more accessible to their various audiences. James Clifford, George Marcus, *et al.*, as part of the postmodernist fascination with style and rhetoric, suggest that we are in crisis (Clifford 1988a; Clifford and Marcus 1986; Marcus and Fischer 1986) because we have claimed an authority that does not exist, told truths that are only partial, and (mis)represented an Other that conceals the construction of the Other by an invisible anthropological Self. Their solutions to these problems, however, do not include better ways of doing fieldwork, but different (better?) ways of writing ethnographies. Paul Roth suggests of the postmodernists, "Authority is taken to accrue not, as before, from the role of field scientist but rather from that of author" (1989: 555). Indeed, any authority the field scientist attempts to assert as a result of her research can be held against her.

Nonetheless, the postmodernist critique has encouraged a lot more reflection (reflexivity?) in recent years about ethnography as both process and product than many of us recognize. If we are not all becoming more reflexive, some of us are at least becoming more self-conscious.[5] Anthropology has a politics and has always had a politics, one aim of which is to help Western society recognize itself as but one community among many human communities (Mascia-Lees *et al.* 1989: 8). Although of different theoretical persuasions, most anthropologists would probably accept that basic goal if translated into their particular vocabulary. But this period of intensified reflexivity has made a good many of us take stock of who is now in our audience and of how ragged the line between our community and the communities we study has become.

To my thinking, if there is any crisis in ethnography, it is a growing uncertainty about our dual responsibility to our audiences and our informants. If there is a conflict, which should be privileged? At first glance, that seems obvious—of course, we must protect our informants above all else. Those are the ethics of our profession. But how far does this go? Judith Stacey found herself forced "to collude with the homophobic silencing of lesbian experience" because she had agreed to give her informants a pre-publication veto over a manuscript (1988: 24). Others have found themselves in similar politically compromised situations. And some of us have found ourselves making paternalistic decisions to avoid potential harm to informants. More and more often now our informants are also of the community for whom we write. Then what? And what of conflicting interests among our informants? These are not new problems, but they have become more complex problems because we can no longer assume that our analyses will not be read by our informants (or their enemies). We can no longer assume that an isolated village will not within an amazingly short period of time move into the circuit of rapid social and economic change. A barefoot village kid who used to trail along after you *will* one day show up on your doorstep with an Oxford degree and your book in hand.

The growing presence of third-world scholars among our readership and in the discipline itself certainly increases the pressure on us to think carefully about what we publish, and it also gives us another kind of understanding of the societies we study. We have all recognized at one time or another in our research that each field experience allows us to peel back yet one more layer of meaning—those who were raised in the culture have more immediate access. However, as those who have done research in their own culture are aware, there are also disadvantages to studying "at home." To do it successfully requires a great deal of reflexivity, and that may be even more difficult for third-world anthropologists competing in first-world academia, where there are those who doubt their competence because they *are* third-world and those who resent their competence for the same reason. Openly discussing one's problems with rapport in the field or one's bouts of irritability during fieldwork or similar reflections might be good methodology to one group and good ammunition to another whose members do not wish one well.

The blurring line between readers and informants carries one set of responsibilities, but there is a new set of responsibilities to our audiences that seems to have eluded the postmodernist critics, although I am not the first to mention it (e.g., Caplan 1988; Mascia-Lees *et al.* 1989; Sangren 1988). Experimental ethnography so obscure that native speakers of English with a Ph.D. in anthropology find it difficult to understand is written for a small elite made up primarily of first-world academics with literary inclinations. The message of exclusion that attaches to some of these texts contradicts the ostensible purpose of experimental ethnography, to find better ways of conveying some aspect of the experiences of another community. The message to nonacademics who simply want to know what the foreigner has to say about them is confusing at best.

So what will come of all this? Some of our colleagues will not notice that "an experimental moment in the human sciences" (Marcus and Fischer 1986) has come and gone; others have already dismissed it; some of us will find ourselves more self-conscious about what we do in the field and how we write about what we did when we return home; some of us will not be aware of how much we have changed until some fearless graduate student draws it to our attention in a term paper; some of us will gradually drift off into writing fiction. I suspect that in no time at all the alarming banners of a new generation of crusaders for prefuturist studies will unfurl, provoking outrage among the old postmodernist graybeards.

Notes

1. Indeed, as Mac Marshall pointed out to me, one *never* finishes the job, because each time we return to the field, the people we study have changed, and each new insight brings new questions. If we ever did fully remove the puzzlement, either the culture would have disappeared from the face of the earth or we would be wrong.

2. The essays by Deborah Gordon (1988) and Frances Mascia-Lees *et al.* (1989) speak directly to the writing of ethnography. A broader spectrum of the feminist translators can be found in Linda Nicholson's excellent collection, *Feminist/ Postmodernism* (1990).
3. For an intelligent summary of these positions, see Linda Nicholson's "Introduction" to *Feminism/Postmodernism* (1990: 1–16), and for a more thorough exploration, see the other essays in the collection.
4. Steven Sangren (1988) raises some of these same issues, although not necessarily as a caution to feminists.
5. This may, alas, be similar to the "affirmative action" rhetoric of university administrators who insist on having a woman and a person of color on every committee, preferably chairing it, without troubling to change their ideology one whit. It is simply another bureaucratic requirement to be met or explained away. The "reason" for the requirement is irrelevant.

References

Caplan, Pat 1988/1989. "Engendering Knowledge: The Politics of Ethnography," *Anthropology Today* 4/4: 8–12; 4/6: 14–17.

Clifford, James 1988a. *The Predicament of Culture: Twentieth-Century Ethnography, Literature, and Art*. Cambridge, MA: Harvard University Press.

—— 1988b. "On Ethnographic Authority," *The Predicament of Culture* (Clifford 1988a), 21–54.

—— 1988c. "On Enthnographic Self-Fashioning: Conrad and Malinowski," *The Predicament of Culture* (Clifford 1988a), 92–113.

Clifford, James and George E. Marcus 1986. *Writing Culture: The Poetics and Politics of Ethnography*. Berkeley: University of California Press.

Evans-Pritchard, E. E. 1969. *The Neur*. Oxford: Oxford University Press.

Flax, Jane 1987. "Postmodernism and Gender Relations in Feminist Theory," *Signs* 12/ 4: 621–643.

Geertz, Clifford 1973. "Thick Descriptions: Toward an Interpretive Theory of Culture," *The Interpretation of Cultures*. New York: Basic Books.

Gordon, Deborah 1988. "Writing Culture: Writing Feminism: The Poetics and Politics of Experimental Ethnography," *Inscriptions* 3/4: 7–24.

Haraway, Donna 1985. "A Manifesto for Cyborgs: Science, Technology, and Socialist Feminism in the 1980s," *Socialist Review* 15/80: 65-107.

Harding, Sandra 1987. *Feminism and Methodology*. Bloomington: Indiana University Press.

—— 1990. Feminism, Science, and the Anti-Enlightenment Critiques," *Feminism/ Postmodernism*, 83–106. Linda J. Nicholson (ed.). New York: Routledge.

Hartsock, Nancy 1983. *Money, Sex, and Power: Toward a Feminist Historical Materialism*. Boston: Northeastern University Press.

Marcus, George E. and Michael M. J. Fischer 1986. *Anthropology as Cultural Critique: An Experimental Moment in the Human Sciences*. Chicago: University of Chicago Press.

Mascia-Lees, Frances E., Patricia Sharpe, and Colleen Ballerino Cohen 1989. "The Postmodernism Turn in Anthropology: Cautions from a Feminist Perspective," *Signs* 15/11: 7–33.

Nash, June 1976. "A Critique of Social Science in Latin America," *Sex and Class in Latin America*, 1–24. June Nash and Helen Safa (eds.). New York: J. F. Bergin.

Nicholson, Linda 1990. *Feminism/Postmodernism*. New York: Routledge.

Rodman, William L. and Margaret C. Rodman 1990. "To Die on Ambae: On the Possibility of Doing Fieldwork Forever," *The Humbled Anthropologist: Tales from the Pacific*, 101–120. Philip R. DeVita (ed.). Belmont, CA: Wadsworth Publishing.

Rosaldo, Renato 1989. *Culture and Truth: The Remaking of Social Analysis*. Boston: Beacon Press.

Roth, Paul 1989. "Ethnography Without Tears," *Current Anthropology* 30/5: 555–569.

Sangren, Steven 1988. "Rhetoric and the Authority of Ethnography: 'Postmodernism' and the Social Reproduction of Texts," *Current Anthropology* 29/3: 405–435.

Shostak, Marjorie 1981. *Nisa: The Life and Words of a !Kung Woman*. Cambridge, MA: Harvard University Press.

Stacey, Judith 1988. "Can There be a Feminist Historiography?" *Women's Studies International Forum* 11/1: 21–27.

Wolf, Margery 1968. *The House of Lim: A Study of a Chinese Farm Family*. Englewood Cliffs: Prentice-Hall.

Part VI

Conclusion

INTRODUCTION

❧❧

So where does all this lead us? With all of these options before us, how is it that we can come to know something about the complexity of human behaviors? Can we even know anything at all about other people's behaviors, let alone our own? I happen to think that we can. Having tried to introduce each of the previous parts accurately, identifying each option's various strengths and weaknesses, I have left it to the end to provide readers with my own stand on these issues. However, placing these readings last is not meant to privilege them—in other words, readers should not think that the previous readings have led us to this point where the secrets will finally be revealed. Instead, following some insights of the reflexive tradition, this last part is my attempt, as the editor of this volume, to put some of my cards on the table. Although I have selected just these twenty-seven readings from countless possible essays, and even though I have framed each reading in light of my own questions, many readers will not have seen my ever-present editorial hand; instead, many will have read these essays as if they naturally were organized as they are in this volume. This last part makes a more concerted effort to place the often free-floating editor in the midst of the discussion.

In an effort to provide readers with a concrete example of just how perplexing human behavior can be, as well as the role that can be played by the scholar of religion in helping us to understand and explain this behavior, this part provides examples of scholars grappling with two recent events that have interested, perplexed, or even disturbed many people: the 1978 deaths at Jonestown in Guyana and, almost two decades later, the 1997 deaths of the Heaven's Gate members just outside San Diego, USA. I have selected just these essays, addressing just these topics, because many solutions to the insider/outsider problem are developed in light of, and applied to, cases that are not all that different from the worlds and experiences of the researcher or student. The deaths associated with both Jim Jones' Peoples Temple and Heaven's Gate strike many as utterly mysterious, as something that defies rationality and understanding. No wonder many commentators refer to these events as "cult deaths," a term that tells us nothing and which simply represents *our* failure to understand *them*. In his essay, Mark Muesse goes so far as to suggest that "a cult is any religion more bizarre than your own."

The first two readings presented in this concluding part—by Jonathan Z. Smith, who is by far the most influential and creative scholar of religion now working in the field, and Mark Muesse—suggest that we fail to live up to the challenges and responsibilities of scholarship on human behavior if we see ourselves *either* as having unimpeded access to the people we study *or* as being so utterly isolated from them that we cannot come to know them at all. Smith's essay is an extremely useful example of the way scholars who have acquired accurate descriptive knowledge of the phenomenon they study can try to understand the seemingly puzzling material they study by applying models with which they are familiar. Although the overlap will likely never be complete, such a use of the comparative method will surely bring to light interesting and unanticipated similarities and differences between the model and that to which it is applied. The benefits of the comparative method are also central to Muesse's essay on Heaven's Gate; if, as Muesse and others have suggested, one of the goals of the study of religion is "to make the strange familiar and the familiar strange," then comparing well-known and acceptable behaviors to those that are judged to be foreign or puzzling may provide some surprising results.

Muesse's essay nicely demonstrates that the comparative religionist who is able to contextualize human behavior has much to contribute to the study of culture. However, simply describing the similarities and differences between assorted behaviors is hardly enough; another goal of scholarship on human behavior must be to understand, explain, and account for various behaviors. Because Smith attempts to do all this in his essay, it provides a useful model for our own scholarship; the challenge will be to use the insights gained from Muesse's description and comparison as the basis for developing theories as to why virtually all religions house small numbers of individuals who practice one or another form of renunciation or world/self-denying behaviors. Although such behavior strikes many as grotesque, stories abound concerning how such religious founders as Gautama, Jesus and Muhammad practiced forms of fasting and extended periods of meditation and prayer; ritual specialists in virtually all of the traditions continue to practice any number of such behaviors. They own little or nothing and go without sleep, food, clothes, talking, marriage, sex, and, sometimes, they die in the process. Why is this? Are they always revered for doing this, or are they sometimes dismissed as crazy by their peers? Why is it that not all members of these social formations practice such behaviors? Why have injunctions against practicing such behaviors been put in place in many religions (e.g., rules against suicide)? What function does a renunciant play in a social community? All of these questions circulate in the case of Heaven's Gate, a movement whose basic belief system regarding a soul—or as they called it, a seed—that outlives the physical body seems to be rather similar to those systems taken for granted by countless human beings. If one understands Muesse's essay as the starting point, there remain many questions in need of study.

The volume closes with a short essay, the brevity of which might lead the reader to overlook its sophistication and importance. This reading, from the contemporary scholar of religion Bruce Lincoln, is entitled "Theses on Method" and is modeled on Karl Marx's well-known "Theses on Feuerbach" (1845) where Marx critiqued the manner in which Ludwig Feuerbach's (1804–1872) own criticism of religion was simply concerned with ideas and mentalities as opposed to social and economic conditions. In his own thirteen theses, Lincoln makes it entirely clear that, in the end, the responsibility of the researcher and teacher is not to sympathize with, promote, or protect religion, for, in his words, "reverence is a religious, and not a scholarly virtue." Instead, Lincoln proposes that professors of religion hold a responsibility to probe "beneath the surface" of appearances (including the insider's own perceptions of the situation). Presuming that human perceptions can sometimes be fundamentally mistaken, misled, or mystified, Lincoln recommends that students of religion strive to engage in critical *inquiry* rather than *advocacy*. When we fail to do this, when "one permits those whom one studies to define the terms in which they will be understood," Lincoln believes that we have "ceased to function as historian or scholar." In his words, one then becomes a collector, advocate, cheerleader or even voyeur—all of which are interesting roles but none of which "should be confused with scholarship."

Having come this far in studying the insider/outsider problem, it should be clear that the following essays are not the last word on the topic. For instance, readers sympathetic to some of the approaches represented in previous parts will undoubtedly find in this part's selections things with which they might disagree. Such disagreements, however, are not a bad thing so long as they can be stated in such a way that a debate can begin; if nothing else, the university classroom ought to be one of the main sites of engaged debate. Given the particular topics of the three concluding essays, they will hopefully prompt instructors to have their classes investigate so-called "cults" or marginalized social formations in an effort to learn not only how to describe accurately their behavior and belief systems but also how to use this information as the basis for investigating the utter complexity of all human behavior.

25

JONATHAN Z. SMITH, *The Devil in Mr. Jones*[1]

❧ ❧

I

My starting point in this essay will be three curious titles that are attached by my university to my name: "religion and the human sciences," "religion and the humanities," "history of religions." What might these terms mean? All three set religion within a context. All three suggest limiting perspectives on religion: that it is human and that it is historical (two propositions that I understand to be all but synonymous). All three suggest academic conversation partners for the enterprise of the study of religion: anthropology (in its broadest sense), humanities, and history. These terms locate the *study* of religion. Religion, to the degree that it is usefully conceived as an historical, human endeavor, is to be set within the larger academic frameworks provided by anthropology, the humanities, and history.

All three titles are, as well, highly polemical. Although their daring has been obscured by time, none would have been understood in academic circles a little more than a century ago. Indeed, if understood at all, they would have been thought to embody a contradiction. Although we tend to use the word "humanities" (or the human sciences) as synonymous with liberal learning, with Cicero's *humanitas* and the older Greek *paideia*, and tend to identify its scope primarily with the study of the classical culture of our own past and the more recent works dependent on it, this is not its primary academic sense. When it was revived by the Italian humanists of the fifteenth century, it had a more pointed and argumentative meaning. As first used by Coluccio Salutati, a Florentine chancellor, "humane studies," the "human sciences" were to be contrasted with the "divine sciences"—that is to say, the humanities with theology. Thus, if the study of religion was anything, it was the study of that which was utterly different from the human sciences. The two were perceived to be mutually exclusive.

This was all changed when, on 1 October 1877, the Dutch Universities Act separated the theological faculties at the four state universities (Amsterdam, Groningen, Leiden, and Utrecht) from the Dutch Reformed Church. For the first time in Western academic history, there were established two, parallel possibilities for the study of religion: a humanistic mode within the secular academy and a theological course of study within the denominational seminary. The original draft of the legislation had used a term coined four years earlier, proposing to call the new university department a "Faculty of Religious Sciences," but, after much compromise, the older title, "Faculty of Theology," was retained. Nevertheless, dogmatics and practical theology, the central core of theological education, were removed from the curriculum, to be taught only in the seminaries. Their place in the academy was taken by a new program in history of religions which was assumed to be more "neutral and scientific."

France followed soon after. In 1884, the French Ministry of Education abolished the state Catholic Theological Faculties and a year later replaced them (in the very same building) by the "Fifth Section of Religious Sciences" as part of the École Pratique des Hautes Études. Religious study was added alongside the other four "sections": mathematics, physics and chemistry, natural history and physiology, and the historical and philological sciences. The minister of public instruction charged the new faculty: "We do not wish to see the cultivation of polemics, but of critical research. We wish to see the examination of texts, not the discussion of dogmas."

In 1904, the University of Manchester, which was rare among British universities in being nondenominational and in applying no confessional tests to either students or faculty, established its new Theological Faculty which taught theological subjects and comparative religions but excluded courses in systematic theology and the history of Christian doctrine. All theological students were required to take work in comparative religions. What was intended may be gleaned from the fact that James George Frazer was invited to join the faculty and teach comparative religions. As stated at the inauguration of this new program, this was "the first occasion in this country on which theology, unfettered by [denominational] tests, has been accepted as an integral part of the University organization and has been treated like any other subject."[2] Rarely did any other European country until today follow this pattern. In most of Europe, religious studies were part of the divine sciences.

In the United States, until some twenty years ago, when religious studies were recognized, a sequential pattern prevailed. A doctoral degree in religious studies at a university had as its prerequisite a bachelor of divinity degree from a seminary. It was not until the rise of programs in state universities, a development which followed the 1963 US Supreme Court decision on the *School District of Abington* v. *Schempp*, in which Mr. Justice Goldberg observed, "it seems clear to me ... that the Court would recognize the propriety of the teaching *about* religion as distinguished from the teaching *of* religion in the public schools," that the parallel course of religious studies in the academy, instituted a century ago in Holland, became possible in this country.

This political and legislative history, as important as it has been, should not be allowed to obscure a more fundamental base. Simply put, the *academic study of religion is a child of the Enlightenment*. This intellectual heritage is revealed in the notion of generic religion as opposed to historical, believing communities. But it is not this element, as significant as it was, on which I wish to dwell. Rather it is the mood, the exemplary Enlightenment attitude toward religion that concerns me.

To put the matter succinctly, religion was domesticated; it was transformed from *pathos* to *ethos*. At no little cost, religion was brought within the realm of common sense, of civil discourse and commerce. Rediscovering the old tag, "Nothing human is foreign to me," the Enlightenment impulse was one of tolerance and, as a necessary concomitant, one which refused to leave any human datum, including religion, beyond the pale of understanding, beyond the realm of reason.

It was this impulse, this domestication, that made possible the entrance of religious studies into the secular academy. But the price of this entry, to reverse the Steppenwolf formula, is the use of our mind. As students of religion, we have become stubbornly committed to making the attempt (even if we fail) at achieving intelligibility. We must accept the burden of the long, hard road of understanding. To do less is to forfeit our license to practice in the academy, to leave the study of religion open to the charge of incivility and intolerance.

Against this background, I have deliberately chosen for my topic an event which is a scandal in the original sense of the word. Such scandals erupt from time to time and perturb the assumptions of civility. For the Enlightenment faith in intelligibility, it was the shock over the utter devastation of the Lisbon earthquake on 1 November 1755—reread Voltaire's *Candide!*[3] For those of us committed to the academic study of religion, a comparable scandal is that series of events which began at approximately 5.00 p.m., on 18 November 1978 in Jonestown, Guyana. From one point of view, one might claim that Jonestown was the most important single event in the history of religions, for if we continue, as a profession, to leave it ununderstandable, then we will have surrendered our rights to the academy. The daring and difficult experiment in parallel courses of religious study begun in Holland a century ago will have concluded in failure.

One final, preliminary matter. To interpret, to venture to understand, is not necessarily to approve or to advocate. There is a vast difference between what I have described as "tolerance" and what is now known as "relativism." The former does not necessarily lead to the latter. In the sixteenth century, that great precursor of the Enlightenment, Montaigne, argued in his essay "Of Cannibals":

Everyone terms barbarity, whatever is not of his own customs; in truth it seems that we have no view of what is true and reasonable, except the example and idea of the customs and practices of the country in which we live. We may call them barbarians, then, if we are judging by the rules of reason, but not if we are judging by comparison with ourselves, who surpass them in every sort of barbarity.[4]

He was stating a principle of toleration, but he was also making a normative claim: we cannot judge another culture by reference to ourselves; we may judge (both another and ourselves), if our criteria are universal "rules of reason." The anthropology of the last century, the study of religions in the academy, has contributed to making more difficult a naive, ethnocentric formulation of the "rules of reason," but this does not require that such "rules" be denied, or suggest that we should slacken in our attempts to formulate them.

It is a far cry from the civility of Montaigne and his Enlightenment heirs to the utter conceptual relativism of D. Z. Phillips when he writes, in *Faith and Philosophical Enquiry*:

If I hear that one of my neighbors has killed another neighbor's child, given that he is sane, my condemnation is immediate.... But if I hear that some remote tribe practices child sacrifice, what then? I do not know what sacrifice means for the tribe in question. What would it mean to say I condemned it when the "it" refers to something I know nothing about? I would be condemning murder. But murder is not child sacrifice.[5]

If the *skandalon* of Jonestown requires that we make the effort of understanding, it requires as well that, as members of the academy, we side with Montaigne against Phillips. For fundamental to the latter's conceptual relativism is the claim that, "what counts as true in my language may not even be able to be described in yours. Translation becomes impossible in principle."[6] But if this be the case, the academy, the enterprise of understanding, the human sciences themselves, become, likewise, impossible in principle since they are fundamentally translation enterprises.

II

The basic facts concerning Jonestown that are matters of public record may be rapidly rehearsed.[7] James Warren Jones was born 13 May 1931 in the small town of Lynn, Indiana. Like many other towns of the region and of the time, Lynn was a seat of both Christian fundamentalism and Ku Klux Klan activity. (The Klan's national headquarters had been in Indianapolis.) There is considerable evidence that by the late forties Jones was deeply committed to the former and had decisively rejected the latter in favor of a vision of racial equality and harmony. In 1950, Jones (now married) moved to Indianapolis and, although not ordained, became a pastor at the Sommerset Southside Church and director of an integrated community center. In difficulty with the Sommerset congregation for his outspoken views on civil rights, he left and, by 1953, had founded his own, interracial Community Unity Church, largely subsidized by his efforts, including the door-to-door peddling of pet monkeys. For a while he also served as associate pastor of the Laurel Street Tabernacle, but, again, his integrationist views forced him out. In 1956, he founded the Peoples Temple, an integrated but predominantly black congregation. He also began the practice of adopting children of various races (he was to adopt a total of seven) and urging his congregants to do so as well. Moving to larger quarters, he began his visits to a variety of evangelists, the most significant being a trip to Philadelphia to talk with Father Divine. By 1960, his efforts in community work had become so well known that he was appointed director of the Indianapolis Human Rights Commission, and articles about him began to appear in the press. In 1961, the Peoples Temple Full Gospel Church became affiliated with the Christian Church (Disciples of Christ), and, in 1964, Jones was ordained a minister by that denomination. In this same period, Jones appears to have introduced more discipline into his congregation (e.g., establishing an "interrogation committee") and to have begun to practice increasingly vivid forms of faith healing; he claimed that he had resurrected a number of dead individuals (by 1972, he would claim to have resurrected more than forty) and that he was able to cure cancer. (This latter led to an investigation by the state of Indiana, but the results were inconclusive.)

In 1965, after reading an article on nuclear destruction in *Esquire Magazine*, Jones predicted the end of the world in a nuclear holocaust which would occur on 15 July 1967. Concerned for the society that would emerge after this event, he sought to find sanctuary for a small, interracial remnant. The magazine mentioned ten places as the safest from destruction, including Belo Horizente, Brazil, and Ukiah, California. Jones visited Brazil, meeting with several of the leaders of messianic cults there as well as stopping off in Guyana on his return. He then moved about 150 members of his congregation from Indianapolis to Ukiah, incorporating the Peoples Temple, Disciples of Christ Church in November 1965. He began a pattern of commuting between his Indianapolis and his California congregations, but increasingly concentrated his activities in Redwood Valley.

By 1967, Jones was an important civic institution in northern California. Several officials had joined his church. He was the chairman of the local Legal Services Society and foreman of the Mendocino Grand Jury.

By 1972, he had expanded his activities, founding churches in San Francisco and Los Angeles. He published a newspaper, *The People's Forum*, which had a press run of 60,000 copies, and had a half-hour radio program, each week, on KFAX. In 1973, he leased 27,000 acres of undeveloped land from the government of Guyana to serve as an "agricultural mission" and a "promised land."

By 1974, his combined California congregations had grown to such a degree that the *Sacramento Bee* declared, "Peoples Temple ranks as probably the largest Protestant congregation in Northern California," and Jones became an important political force. Still combining his preaching of racial equality with services of healing, Jones began to speak to, and attract, a different audience. While still predominantly a black and working class congregation, he also brought into Peoples Temple a new, white, liberal, educated, middle-class membership. In 1975, he was named one of the hundred most outstanding clergymen in the United States by *Religion in Life*. He also worked for the political campaign of San Francisco mayor, George Moscone, and entered into the center of West Coast politics. Visibly active in support of freedom of the press causes, he received, in 1976, the *Los Angeles Herald*'s Humanitarian of the Year award. He became active in the presidential campaign of Carter, turning out a huge audience for Rosalynn Carter's appearance; he was later invited by her to the inauguration and corresponded with her in the White House.

Appointed to the San Francisco Housing Authority by Moscone in 1976, he became its chairman in 1977, and received the Martin Luther King Humanitarian of the Year award in San Francisco that year.

Although there had been a few "exposés" of Peoples Temple (most notably a planned eight-part series by Lester Kinsolving in the *San Francisco Examiner* in 1972, which was suppressed after four installments had appeared), it was not until the 1 August 1977 issue of *New West Magazine* with its lurid reports of financial misdealings, beatings, intimidation, brain-washing, and hints of murder that another side of Peoples Temple came into public view. After an unsuccessful attempt to have the story quashed, Jones left for Guyana.

The mission in Guyana had been run, since its establishment, by a skeleton crew. In 1975, there were only 15 members in Jonestown. By 1976, when California's lieutenant governor visited the site, there were some 50 individuals. In May 1977, there were 70 full-time residents. Between late July and December 1977, Jones and some 900 other congregants had moved to Jonestown. A core of about 100 members was left behind to staff the California churches and provide logistical support for the community in Guyana.

Between 1 April and 7 November 1978, there was a flurry of legal actions. Former cult members entered lawsuits against Peoples Temple charging assault and fraud. There were investigations by the San Francisco district attorney's office and by the United States consul in Guyana. Relatives of citizens of Jonestown began making public statements, charging violations of human rights and mistreatment in Jonestown. In June, a former Temple official filed an affidavit to the effect that Jones had assumed "a tyrannical hold over the lives of Temple members," that he had become paranoid, and was planning "mass suicide for the glory of socialism." In the same month, James Cobb filed suit against Jones in San Francisco, charging him with planning "mass murder [that] would result in the death of minor children not old enough to make voluntary and informed decisions about serious matters of any nature, much less insane proposals of collective suicide."

On 14 November 1978, Congressman Leo Ryan, of California, left for Guyana to investigate the situation, accompanied by fourteen relatives of Jonestown citizens and representatives of the press. On the afternoon of 17 November, and the morning of the next day, Ryan visited Jonestown and interviewed a number of the Peoples Temple members. A small number indicated that they wished to leave with him, but, in the main, Ryan was positively impressed.

At 4.00 p.m. on the afternoon of 18 November, after having been threatened with a knife in Jonestown, Ryan and four members of his party were shot to death while waiting to board their chartered plane. Eleven members of his party were wounded. Their assailants were members of the Jonestown community.

About an hour later, Jones began the "White Night," an event that had been previously rehearsed, the suicide of every member of Peoples Temple in Jonestown. When it was over, 914 people had died, most by taking a fruit drink mixed with cyanide and tranquilizers; most apparently died voluntarily. (Four individuals, including Jones, died of gunshot wounds. The bodies of some 70 individuals showed puncture wounds which suggest that they were injected with poison—whether voluntarily or not cannot be determined. Two hundred and sixty infants and small children had been administered poison, most by their parents. Dogs, livestock, and fishponds had been poisoned as well.)

Some one hundred of the inhabitants of Jonestown, the majority of whom had been away from the settlement, and a small number who fled the White Night, survived.

With the exception of one Guyanese, all of the dead were American citizens. Most were family groups. The majority were black. Jonestown was a national movement. The birthplaces of the dead were in 39 states and 4 foreign countries. With the exception of one individual from Philadelphia, the last home of all the dead, before Jonestown, was in California with the largest group from the San Francisco Bay area (229), and almost equal numbers from the site of the first Temple in Ukiah-Redwood Valley (139) and Los Angeles (137).

Since the events in Jonestown, I have searched through the academic journals for some serious study, but in vain. Neither in them, nor in the hundreds of papers on the program of the American Academy of Religion (which was in session during the event in 1978 and which meets each year about the time of its anniversary) has there been any mention. For the press, the event was all too quickly overshadowed by other new horrors. For the academy, it was as if Jonestown had never happened.

The press, by and large, featured the pornography of Jonestown—the initial focus on the daily revisions of the body count, the details on the condition of the corpses. Then, as more "background" information became available, space was taken over by lurid details of beatings, sexual humiliations, and public acts of perversion. The bulk of these focused on Jones as a "wrathful, lustful giant": his bisexuality, his mistresses, his all-night sermons on the "curse of his big penis," his questionnaires to adolescent members about their sexual fantasies concerning him, his arrest on a morals charge, his sexual demands on his congregants, including a secretary whose job it was to arrange liaisons for him with male and female members of his congregation, beginning with the formula, "Father hates to do this, but he has this tremendous urge." Everything was sensational. Almost no attempt was made to gain any interpretative framework. According to the journalists Maguire and Dunn, it was an event "so bizarre that historians would have to reach back into Biblical times[!] to find a calamity big enough for comparison."

It was not surprising, I suppose, considering the fact that a major metropolitan daily, the *New York Post*, found it impossible to mention the Ayatollah Khomeini's name without prefacing it by "that madman," that it was the language of fraud and insanity that dominated the accounts. There were several options: he began sincere and went mad; he began a fraud and went mad; he was always a fraud; he was always mad—or, sometimes impossibly, a combination of all of these. Thus *Newsweek* could, in one article, call Jones: "self-proclaimed messiah," "a man who played god," "full of hokum ... and carnival stuff," "one who mesmerized," "fanatical," "a foul paranoid," "one vulnerable to forces in his own mind," "gifted with a strange power," "victim of darker forces," "a wrathful, lustful giant," "nightmarish," "bizarre." This is the usual language of religious polemics: read the Western biographies of Muhammad! There is neither anything new nor perceptive in this all-but-standard list. There is certainly nothing that will aid understanding. A few journalists of modest literary bent played on his name and made reference to "The Emperor Jones," but little light was shed by that.

More troubling, the newspapers gave a substantial amount of space to other religious leaders and their gyrations in distancing themselves from Jonestown. Perhaps the greatest single scandal in this regard occurred in the *New York Times*, one of whose longer analytical pieces on Jones was an article on the "Op-Ed" page entitled, "Billy Graham on Satan and Jonestown," in which the evangelist fulminated against "false prophets and messiahs," "satanically inspired people," and "the wholesale deception of false messiahs like Jim Jones," concluding:

> One may speak of the Jones situation as that of a cult, but it would be a sad mistake to identify it in any way with Christianity. It is true that he came from a religious background but what he did and how he thought can have no relationship to the views and teachings of any legitimate form

of historic Christianity. We have witnessed a false messiah who used the cloak of religion to cover a confused mind filled with a mixture of pseudo-religion, political ambition, sensual lust, financial dishonesty and, apparently, even murder.... Apparently Mr. Jones was *a slave of a diabolical supernatural power* from which he refused to be set free.[8]

This is to give way to the forces of unreason. I find Billy Graham's presence on the editorial pages of the *New York Times* a more stunning indication that the faith of the Enlightenment upon which the academy depends is in danger than the events in Jonestown!

The profession of religious studies, when it would talk, privately, within its boundaries, had a different perspective. For many, Jones's declarations that he was a Marxist, a communist, one who rejected the "opiate" of religion, were greeted with relief. He was not, after all, religious. Hence there was no professional obligation to interpret him. Never mind the fact that one of the most important religious phenomena of this century has been the combination of revolutionary Marxism and Roman Catholicism in Latin America, Marxism and Buddhism in southeast Asia, Marxism and Islam in the Middle East.

For others, it was not to be talked about because it revealed what had been concealed from public, academic discussion for a century—that religion has rarely been a positive, liberal force. Religion is not nice; it has been responsible for more death and suffering than any other human activity. Jonestown (and many of the other so-called cults) signaled the shallowness of the amalgamation between religion and liberalism which was, among other things, a major argument for the presence of religious studies in the state and secular universities. Religion was not civil. And so a new term had to be created, that of "cult," to segregate these uncivil phenomena from religion.

But civility is not to be reduced to "nice" behavior. A concomitant of the Enlightenment "domestication" of religion was the refusal to leave any human datum beyond the pale of reason and understanding. If the events of Jonestown are a behavioral *skandalon* to the Enlightenment faith, then the refusal of the academy to interpret Jonestown is, at least, an equivalent *skandalon* to the same faith.

It is remarkable to me that in all the literature on Jonestown that I have read the closest expression of the fundamental mood of the Enlightenment should have come in a sermon preached by a minister to the First United Methodist Church in Reno, Nevada—a minister who lost two daughters and a grandson in the White Night of Jonestown:

> Jonestown people were human beings. Except for your caring relationship with us, Jonestown would be names, "cultists," "fanatics," "kooks." Our children are real to you, because you knew [us]. [My wife] and I could describe for you many of the dead. You would think that we were describing people whom you know, members of our church."[9]

This recognition of the ordinary humanness of the participants in Jonestown's White Night must certainly be the starting point of interpretation. For, "nothing human is foreign to me."

Our task is not to reach closure. Indeed, at present this is factually impossible, for we lack the majority of the necessary data. We know the pornography of Jonestown; we do not know its mythology, its ideology, its soteriology, its sociology—we do not know almost everything we would need to know in order to venture a secure argument. We know, for example, that Jones characteristically held all-night meetings at which he spoke for hours. We know almost nothing of what he said. But we do know enough, as a matter of principle, to refuse to accept prematurely the option of declaring that it is unintelligible and, hence, in some profound sense inhuman. In a situation like this, it is not irresponsible to guess, to imagine Jonestown, for the risk of a model, however tentative, will suggest the kinds of data we might require. And, as enough of the participants are still living and accessible, as enough documentation, including "hundreds of reel-to-reel tapes and cassettes," has been gathered by legal agencies that are incompetent to interpret them, we might hope, in time, to have the data that we need.[10]

How, then, shall we begin to think about Jonestown as students of religion, as members of the academy? How might we use the resources available for thinking about human religious activity within the context of the corporate endeavor of the human sciences? A basic strategy, one that is a prerequisite for intelligibility, is to remove from Jonestown the aspect of the unique, of its being utterly exotic. We must be able to declare that Jonestown on 18 November 1978 was an instance of something known, of something we have seen before. We must perform an act of reduction. We must reduce Jonestown to the category of the known and the knowable.

In a primitive form, this initial move was made in the press which provided lists of suicides for religious and/or political reasons that have occurred in the past. From Masada, a first-century event which has become a foundation myth for the contemporary state of Israel (and which featured the same combination of isolation, homicide, and suicide) to the self-immolation of Buddhist monks and American pacifists during the Vietnam War, we have seen it and heard about it before. Works such as Foxe's *Book of Martyrs* (1563)—one of the most popular books in the English language—supplied vivid portraits of those who would rather accept death, whether by their own hand or from another's, than renounce their religion. And works by J. Wisse (1933) and the psychiatrist Gregory Zilboorg (1939) supplied lengthy catalogs of corporate suicide among tribal peoples. Then, too, we have not lacked attempts to make such acts comprehensible, to make them less exotic. In studies by a distinguished series of scholars and writers, the act of self-destruction has been rescued from its legal and moral status as irrational. But none of these lists take us very far. Nor are they designed to. They do not allow us to propose an interpretation of

Jonestown in its brute specificity. But they do allow us the beginning of reduction, that first glimpse of familiarity that is the prerequisite of intelligibility.

III

In this essay I would like to suggest two models, one quite old, one relatively new, which may illuminate aspects of the White Night of Jonestown. They are necessarily partial. They are far from being final proposals. But they are a beginning at an enterprise of looking at Jonestown rather than staring or looking away. We will have to continue this enterprise. We may, in the end, be frustrated. But not to have attempted an understanding, to allow the pornography of Jonestown to be all that can be thought, is, in a fundamental sense, to have surrendered the academy. It is to deny the possibility of there being human sciences.

The first model we might attempt is exceedingly old. It has been used in Western discourse about religion for close to 2,500 years in order to interpret the uncivility of religion. It is a model for which the figure of Dionysus stands as a sign. Regardless of whether it is an adequate understanding of the complex historical development of the vast variety of Dionysiac cults (it is not), the Dionysiac *pattern*, as classically established by Euripides, elaborated by Livy and other Late Antique writers, rediscovered by Nietzsche and the early Rodhe, and, more recently, rediscovered again by René Girard in *Violence and the Sacred* (1972), has proven compelling.

The utility of this model reminds us that the prime purpose of academic inquiry, most especially in the humanities, is to provide *exempli gratia*, an arsenal of classic instances which are held to be exemplary, to provide paradigmatic events and expressions as resources from which to reason, from which to extend the possibility of intelligibility to that which first appears novel. To have discussed Euripides' *Bacchae* is, to some degree, already to have discussed Jonestown.

The *Bacchae* is a complex play. More than many others, it resists univocal interpretation. Here, we are not engaged in studying the *Bacchae*. We are using, perhaps even misusing, Euripides' play for our own, quite particular, purpose. We are using this artifact from 407 BC in order to become more familiar with Jonestown.

The play immediately attracts our attention because it takes as one of its themes the introduction of a new religion, that of Dionysus. It focuses, as well, on forms of violence. Dionysus, as he is presented to us in the drama, is one who obliterates distinctions. He is "polymorphous," able to assume any form at will: god, man, beast, male, female, old, young. He abolishes, as well, distinctions among his devotees. They are presented to us as a nameless collective band. They represent a motley mixture of ethnic origins: barbarians, Greco-Asiatics, and Hellenes that have been melded together into a religion that strives for universality, one where no one is excluded, a religion for all mankind. The cult group in the play is exclusively women—although they can act as if they were men. Their chief mode of life is, from their viewpoint, "sober ecstasy." Hence the dualities. They are the "eaters of raw flesh," and they are "devoted to peace." They are the wild "dancers," and they are under strict discipline, being agents of "Justice, principle of order, spirit of custom."

The entrance of Dionysus and his band into a city is perceived, from the point of view of the city, as an invasion, as a contagious plague. It produces civil disorder and madness. Hence its official, civil interpretation will be that it is "alien," that it is founded by a "charlatan and a fraud," one who wishes to profit financially and seduce women. The civil response to such a cult, to its "impostures and unruliness," is expulsion or death. There is *no room* for this sort of religion within *civil space*.

Yet the Messengers give us another, quite different, portrait of the Dionysiac band. Within *their own space*, apart from the city, on a mountain, they live in a paradise of their own making. Here they contravene the civic portrait. They are not "drunk with wine or wandering," but, "modest and sober"; Pentheus will see to his "surprise how chaste the Bacchae are." On both occasions when they are spied on by representatives of the city, we see the Bacchae inhabiting *utopian space*, living in gentle, free spontaneity. In each case a Messenger carries this report back to the city, a report of the positive aspects of the obliteration of distinctions: not madness, but freedom.

The first Messenger's report is of a sacred and miraculous "peaceable kingdom," where the women tame and suckle wild beasts, where rivers of water, wine, and milk burst forth from the earth, where honey spurts from the wands the women carry. "If you had been there and seen these wonders for yourself, you would have gone down on your knees and prayed to the god you now deny." The second Messenger's report is of domestic peace. "We saw the Maenads sitting, their hands busily moving at their happy tasks."

But the Messengers represent something else. They are not only reporters of Bacchic ethnography, bearing reports on the utopian civil life of the Bacchics within their own space, they are, as well, *invaders* of that space. They are "spies" and intruders. As the Bacchics disorder the city when they "invade," so too the figures from the city disorder paradise when they spy on it and intrude on it. The response in both cases is the same. The Bacchics are instantly transformed into wild figures of violence. The motif of the obliteration of distinctions continues, but now in a way that elicits civil disgust and fear rather than envy and reverence. In the first case, the women tear live, domesticated animals apart with their bare hands. More seriously, they attack civic space. "Like invaders," they swooped down on the border villages, "everything in sight they pillaged and destroyed. They snatched children from their homes"—

and they did this with supernatural power, without conventional weapons. When the men of the village fought back, the women routed them with their wands, while the weapons of the men were unable to draw blood. In the second instance, it is a man who is pulled apart by the women's bare hands, a mother who slays her son.[11]

Moving several centuries in time, we find a modulation of the Bacchic paradigm. When, in 186 BC, the Roman Senate suppressed the Bacchic cults, all of the older elements of religious propaganda were reaffirmed. It was an "invasion" and an "epidemic." It was foreign, fraudulent, characterized by violence and sexual excesses. But the speech that Livy puts in the mouth of the consul Postumius reveals another dimension of our theme. There is no longer a dichotomy between civil space and Bacchic utopian space, the cult now dwells within the city. It lives in *subversive space* where "some believe it to be a kind of worship of the gods; others suppose it a permitted sport and relaxation." Civil understanding has domesticated the Dionysiac cult, and this makes it all the more dangerous. The external utopian space of the Bacchae has become internal, subversive space within the city. The Bacchae now live in a *counterpolis*. In his speech from the Rostra, Postumius declaims:

> Unless you are on your guard, Citizens of Rome, this present meeting held in the daylight, legally summoned by a consul, can be paralleled by another meeting held at night. Now, as individuals, they [the Bacchics] are afraid of you, as you stand assembled in a united body; but presently, when you have scattered to your houses in the city or to your homes in the country, *they* will have assembled and will be making plans for their own safety and at the same time for your destruction and then you as individuals will have to fear them as a united body.[12]

But, since the Bacchics are within civil space, they may be dealt with by civil means: trials, executions, banishments, and laws for their suppression.

I suggest no simple parallels. There are profound differences between Dionysiac cults and Peoples Temple Christian Church. Yet the spatial considerations that I have advanced from the one, supply some instance of familiarity when we seek to understand the other.

The fundamental fact about Jones is that he sought to overcome distinctions. At times he termed this impulse, Christianity, at times, socialism or communism, but the effort was the same. While one can point to bisexuality and other forms of liberation and libertinism that bear some resemblance to Dionysiac praxis, these parallels are superficial. The major distinction that Jones labored to overcome was a distinctly modern American one: it was the distinction of race. This was the consistent theme as he moved from established civil and religious space (the Sommerset Southside Church, the Laurel Street Tabernacle, the Human Rights Commission, the Housing Authority) to a space of his own making. In one of the earliest official reports on Peoples Temple by the district superintendent of the United Methodist Church for Oakland and the East Bay, it is described as "a caring community of people of all races and classes. They bear the mark of compassion and justice—compassion for the hungry and jobless, lonely and disturbed, and also for the earth and her offspring."[13] In some sense, the predominance of Blacks in Peoples Temple is equivalent to the predominance of women in the Dionysiac religions.

Prior to Jonestown, Peoples Temple might be described as inhabiting subversive space. It participated in civil activities and won major forms of public recognition for these efforts. But, hidden from public view, it was also a parallel mode of government. Internally, it was a *counterpolis*. It had its own modes of leadership, its own criteria for citizenship, its own mores and laws, its own system of discipline and punishment. When this was revealed to the public, civil world by disaffected members (as was the Dionysian cult in Rome), the reaction could have been predicted from Livy. An exposé of its founder in terms of fraud and of the Temple in terms of a subversive danger to the community brought legal and legislative remedies to bear: official investigations, lawsuits, criminal charges. Seen in this light, the article in *New West Magazine* is parallel to the speech of Postumius.

Jones's reaction was one of exodus to utopian space, to Guyana. As one reads through the various reports on Jonestown prior to November 1978, the equivalents of the speeches of the Messengers in the *Bacchae*, both those from visitors and those produced by Peoples Temple, there is little doubt that one is reading the language and rhetoric of paradise. One such report, from the summer of 1978, begins by quoting Matthew 25: 35–40:

> I was hungry and you gave me food, I was thirsty and you gave me drink, I was a stranger and you welcomed me, I was naked and you clothed me.... Truly I say to you, as you did to one of the least of my brethren, you did it to me.

and continues:

> What a miracle it is! Over eight hundred acres of jungle have been cleared since 1974, most of it within the last year.... What we found at the cooperative was a loving community in the true New Testament sense.... Jonestown offers a rare opportunity for deep relationships between men and women, young and old, who come from diverse racial and cultural backgrounds.[14]

A pamphlet put out by the Temple to extol Jonestown was entitled, "A Feeling of Freedom," and Jones elaborated:

> We enjoy every type of organized sport and recreational games. Musical talents and arts are flourishing. We share every joy and every need. Our lives are secure and rich with variety and growth and expanding

knowledge.... Now there is peace ... there is freedom from the loneliness and the agony of racism.... We have found security and freedom in collectivism and we can help build a peaceful agricultural nation.[15]

There is little doubt that whatever the "reality," this evaluation was shared by the majority of the citizens of Jonestown. It was, to use the title of the Peoples Temple home for retarded children back in Redwood Valley, truly "Happy Acres."

Into this utopian space, figures from the city came to invade and to spy. Congressman Ryan and the press disordered paradise and the result could have been predicted from the *Bacchae*—the rapid shift from peace to terror and the furious murder of the intruders. In the *Bacchae*, the Maenads, after routing the invaders, go on to attack the border villages. At Jonestown, the violence was directed inwards, the White Night, the total destruction of themselves. In part, this was a measure of realism. There was no possible military solution for Jonestown against those they perceived as the aggressors. The Temple lacked the Maenads' supernatural weapons. But, in part, this was as well a spatial reaction. Utopia had been invaded, and it was time for another exodus.

On 15 March 1979, the *New York Times* published the transcript of a tape recording of Jones, during the White Night, exhorting his followers to suicide. It is a remarkable document.[16] Jones clearly interprets the visit of Ryan as an "invasion": they "came after our children." Following the shooting at the airport, more powerful military invaders will return; they will annihilate the community. There is "no hiding place down here." No further terrestrial exodus will serve, there is no utopia, no "nowhere" where they will not be sought out. The tape reiterates: "It's too late for Russia." "There's no plane." So "Let's get gone. Let's get gone. Let's get gone."

The language for death used by Jones and other voices on the tape is consistently spatial—indeed, it suggests a communal rhetoric. "Step over," "step to that other side," "stepping over to another place," "stepping over to another plane," "you have to step across ... this world was not our home," "if you knew what's ahead of you, you'd be glad to be stepping over." But this language suggests as well the sort of additional data that we need. What was their view of afterlife? Of the "other" world? On the tape there is only a twice-repeated reference to "the green scene thing." But this reference is sufficient to establish a postmortem paradisiacal context, in a place where they will not be followed, where they would not be further intruded upon.

By reading Jonestown in light of the *Bacchae* and Euripides in light of Jonestown, we can begin to understand its utopian logic. We can begin to find Jonestown familiar. Its failure to secure subversive space was predictable, as was a violent conflict when representatives from civil space invaded utopia. By this interpretation, the most proximate responsibility for the events of White Night was Ryan's.

IV

Let me go on to suggest a second option, a second partial interpretation, a second act of making Jonestown familiar.

As I read the various, early press reports of the White Night, my eye was caught by one detail. Not only 914 human deaths, but also all the animals. In the words of the first reporter on the scene:

> I noticed that many of them had died with their arms around each other, men and women, white and black, young and old. Little babies lying on the ground too. Near their mothers and fathers. Dead. Finally, I turned back toward the main pavilion and noticed the dogs that lay dead on the sidewalk. The dogs, I thought. What had they done? Then I realized that Jones had meant to leave nothing, not even animals, to bear witness to the final horror. There were to be no survivors. Even the dogs and Mr. Muggs, Jonestown's pet chimpanzee, had their place in the long white night into which the Peoples Temple had been ordered by the mad Mr. Jones. The heat and stench were overpowering. There was nothing to drink because Jones had ordered the community water supply contaminated with poison.[17]

Leaving aside Krause's lurid prose and his editorializing, the destruction was intended to be total: men, women, children, animals, fish, and water supply—and this destruction alongside a deliberate presentation of utopian harmony—bodies lying together, "arms around each other," uniting the sexes, age groups, and races.

This, too, has a certain familiarity to the student of religion, although it is a recent model, rather than an old one that will be called on: the model of the cargo cult. Let me give one specific example from Espiritu Santo in the New Hebrides.[18]

In 1923, a native prophet, Ronovuro, announced that the ancestral dead would return to the island, after a flood, on a ship bearing rice and other foods. This would be distributed to members of his cult if they were fully paid up. (He charged fees for entrance, ranging from 5 shillings to one pound). A stone storehouse was built to hold the cargo. However, Ronovuro prophesied, the Europeans would attempt to prevent the ship from landing and distributing its gifts. Therefore, the natives must rebel. While, eventually, all Whites must be killed, for now, one European was to be singled out. He would serve as a surrogate for the others. In July 1923, a British planter named Clapcott was murdered by Ronovuro's followers. He was shot, and his body was mutilated. According to some reports, parts of it were eaten. The cult was suppressed by military means. Six of the leaders were condemned to death, others were sentenced to prison terms. In 1937, the cult was revived, but was quickly suppressed by the authorities.

In 1944, a new prophet, Tsek, arose and founded the Ronovuro school. It was likewise a cargo cult, but of a somewhat different form. His message, according to J. G. Miller, was:

> Destroy everything which you got from the Whites also all [native made] mats and basket-making tools. Burn your houses and build two large dormitories in each village: one for the men and the other for the women. . . . Stop working for the Whites. Slaughter all domestic animals: pigs, dogs, cats, etc.

New social forms were developed. The members of the cult went nude, they spoke a common language although the villages from which they came had originally belonged to different linguistic groups. Tribal friction and quarreling were eliminated in favor of cultic solidarity. A road several miles long, the result of enormous collective labor, was built to the sea, terminating at the site of Clapcott's murder, where the cargo ship would land and discharge the goods.

Again the cult was suppressed, although there are indications that it still continues in modulated forms. Ecstatic speech and hearings have been added, and there is a secret room with vines stretched between poles that serves as "wireless belong boy," a place to wait for news of the arrival of the cargo ship.

There are many striking parallels of detail between these cults and Jonestown. But there is so much that is specifically Oceanic in cargo cults that a pursuit of these would be dangerous. Yet there is much, in the general ideology, that is suggestive. In the preceding chapter, I tried to summarize the underlying logic. It need not be rehearsed here. It is sufficient to recall that the central, moral idea was one of achieving exchange reciprocity between the Whites and the natives. A variety of stratagems were employed, the most desperate, such as on Santos, involving a total destruction of everything the natives own as if, by this dramatic gesture, to awaken the white man's sense of obligation to exchange, in order to shame him into a recognition of his responsibilities. "We have now given everything away. What will you give in return?"[19]

I am not suggesting simple parallels. Peoples Temple was not a cargo cult although, if we sought to interpret the religion of Peoples Temple rather than its end, we would be helped immeasurably if we understood it in the context of messianic, nativistic, cargo cults. But Ronovuro and Tsek can help us become familiar with Jones at the moment of the White Night. (Perhaps they could help us become even more familiar with him if we knew more about his religious and political ideologies.) Indeed, Jones himself draws a parallel between White Night and native crisis cults. On the transcript, someone protests, and Jones answers:

It's never been done before you say. It's been done by every tribe in history. Every tribe facing annihilation. All the Indians of the Amazon are doing it right now.... Because they do not want to live in this kind of a world.

Alongside the spatial language for death on the last tape from Jonestown, there is another language, the language of "revolutionary suicide" (a term borrowed from the writings of Huey P. Newton). "We are not committing suicide, it's a revolutionary act." "What I'm talking about is the dispensation of judgment, this is a revolutionary—a revolutionary suicide council. I'm not talking about self-destruction." "[Let's] lay down our lives to protest." "We didn't commit suicide. We committed an act of revolutionary suicide protesting the conditions of an inhumane world." And finally, "I'm sure that they'll—they'll pay for it. This is a revolutionary suicide. This is not a self-destructive suicide. So they'll pay for this. They brought this upon us. And they'll pay for that. I leave that destiny to them." Who are these anonymous figures who will "pay"? Who are "they"? The cargo model suggests Whites.

On the tape, although Jones does refer to the congressman and other external enemies, his primary hostility seems to be directed clearly against defecting members of Peoples Temple, both those who have defected in the past and, more immediately, the small group who left for the airport with Ryan a little more than an hour before.

> That we lay down our lives in protest against what's been done. That we lay down our lives to protest what's being done. The criminality of people. The cruelty of people. Who walked out of here today? Do you know who walked out? Mostly white people. [Voices] Mostly white people.

And, more eloquently, an unidentified woman's voice:

> It broke my heart completely. All of this year the white people had been with us and they're not a part of us [now]. So we might as well end it now, because I don't see.... [Music and voices]

Jones and Peoples Temple had labored mightily, at extraordinary cost, to achieve their vision of racial equality. And they had failed. They had failed earlier, even in their internal organization—the leadership group was entirely white. And they failed, most immediately, in the defections. What was left was a gesture—a gesture designed to elicit shame, a gesture that the mixed rhetoric of Jonestown termed a "revolutionary suicide." By destroying all, by giving their all, they sought to call forth a reciprocal action. They would show the world, but most particularly, in death they would achieve a corporate picture of peace and harmony—the picture indelibly recorded by Krause and the news photographers. They failed, as the cargo cults failed; but we may catch a glimpse of the logic of their deed, aided by familiarity gained from Oceania.

I have by no means supplied a final answer to Jonestown's awesome final solution. But this preliminary attempt has kept faith with the responsibilities attendant on being a member of the academy. It is now for others to continue the task, with Jonestown, or wherever the question of understanding human activities and expression is raised. For if we do not persist in the quest for intelligibility, there can be no human sciences, let alone, any place for the study of religion within them.

Notes

1. Ed. note. This essay was originally delivered as the Woodward Court Lecture at the College of the University of Chicago in 1980.
2. For this brief historical narrative, I have drawn on the convenient account in E. J. Sharpe, *Comparative Religion: A History*. London: Duckworth, 1975: 119–143.
3. For the role of the Lisbon earthquake in the European history of ideas, see T. D. Kendrick, *The Lisbon Earthquake*. Philadelphia: Lippincott, 1957.
4. Montaigne, "Of Cannibals," in *The Complete Works of Montaigne*. D. M. Frame (trans.). Stanford: Stanford University Press, 1958: 152–153.
5. D. Z. Phillips, *Faith and Philosophical Enquiry*, New York: Schoken Books, 1970: 237, as quoted in R. Trigg, *Reason and Commitment*, Cambridge: Cambridge University Press, 1973: 22.
6. Trigg, *Reason and Commitment*, 24–25.
7. In addition to contemporary press accounts, I have used J. Maguire and M. L. Dunn, *Hold Hands and Die* (New York, 1978); M. Kilduff and R. Javers, *The Suicide Cult* (New York: Bantam Books, 1978); C. Krause, *Guyana Massacre* (New York: Berkeley, 1978); and the useful collection of source materials in S. Rose, *Jesus and Jim Jones* (New York: Pilgrim Press, 1979). I have also made use of the Report of a Staff Investigative Group to the Committee on Foreign Affairs, US House of Representatives, *The Assassination of Representative Leo J. Ryan and the Jonestown Guyana Tragedy* (Washington, DC, 1979). Despite a number of more recent works, published since 1980, I have not seen cause to alter this essay in either matters of fact or, especially, in conclusions.
8. *New York Times*, 5 December 1978.
9. *United Methodist Reporter*, December 1978, as quoted in Rose, *Jesus and Jim Jones*, 186.
10. Subsequent to the original presentation of this essay (1980), J. L. Reston, Jr., gained access to 900 hours of these tapes through a freedom-of-information suit. Reston's book, *Our Father Who Art in Hell* (New York: Times Books, 1981), makes little use of this precious material. A 90-minute selection from the tapes was played over National Public Radio in April 1981. While the editing and selection were savagely contrived, there is enough in this selection (including Jones interpreting himself by means of a full-blown gnostic myth) to indicate that a careful study of the entire collection of tapes by a trained and sensitive historian of religion would yield valuable results.
11. Euripides *Bacchae*, especially lines 672–768.

12. Livy, *History* 39.16.
13. J. Moore, as quoted in Rose, *Jesus and Jim Jones*, 132.
14. Ibid., 162.
15. J. Jones, as quoted in Rose, *Jesus and Jim Jones*, 30, 32.
16. See Appendix 2 for the full text. [Ed. note. This appendix is not reproduced here.]
17. Krause, *Guyana Massacre*, 132.
18. For factual material, I have used J. G. Miller, "Naked Cults in Central West Santos," *Journal of the Polynesian Society* 57 (1948): 330–41; J. Guiart, "'Cargo Cults' and Political Evolution in Melanesia," *South Pacific* 5 (1951): 128–29; Guiart, "Forerunners of Melanesian Nationalism," *Oceania* 22 (1951): 81–90. My interpretation of the exchange ideology of total destruction is quite different from the understanding of this radical act in M. Eliade, *The Two and the One* (London: Harvill Press, 1965): 125–128.
19. J. Z. Smith, *Map is Not Territory* (Leiden: E. J. Brill 1978): 305–307, and chapter 6, above [Ed. note. Smith is referring to his essay, "A Pearl of Great Price and a Cargo of Yams," *Imagining Religion: From Jonestown to Babylon*, Chicago: University of Chicago Press, 1982/1988: 90–101].

26

MARK W. MUESSE, *Religious Studies and "Heaven's Gate": Making the Strange Familiar and the Familiar Strange*

☙☙

With the suicides of 39 members of the Heaven's Gate sect in Rancho Santa Fe, CA, the world confronted the enigma of yet another seemingly outlandish religious group. The more we learned about it, the stranger it appeared. Stories of ritualized death, castrations, and expectations of rescue operations by alien beings in spacecraft stretched the limits of our understanding. Even by the grotesque standards of the Peoples Temple in Jonestown and the Branch Davidians, Heaven's Gate seemed bizarre. But simply characterizing the group that way, I suggest, is both too easy and potentially hazardous. Tempting though it may be, we should not make Heaven's Gate so strange, so exotic that we lose sight of the ways the group's beliefs and practices are not that far removed from those adhered to by many "mainstream" Americans. As a student of religion, I believe that, at the very least, it might enhance the level of public debate if people acknowledged that some of their own beliefs and practices could appear strange to others.

It is true that the initial reports about Heaven's Gate made it easy to use the word "bizarre." We learned of the 39 bodies, all dressed in identical black outfits, neatly arrayed on cots and bunk beds. We learned of videotaped farewells by group members, serenely explaining to loved ones the reasons for their actions. Everything they said bespoke deliberation, intention, and absolute confidence that their deaths would convey them to the "next level." These were not the panic-driven suicides of Jonestown and Waco. We saw no indication of struggle, coercion, or second thoughts. No federal authorities were threatening the group. Members of Heaven's Gate seemed to welcome their deaths with the same equanimity and determination as any patient of Dr. Kervorkian's. Indeed, the rational way in which they approached their deaths made them seem ever more irrational.

Even the sexual overtones, which we have come to expect in cases such as these, were unusual. Instead of a sex-crazed leader who abused his disciples, as Jim Jones and David Koresh did, Marshall Applewhite, or, as he preferred "Do," emphasized sexual negation rather than sexual expression. Sexuality, he taught, was merely an aspect of the bodily container that would be sloughed off as believers passed to the next level "above human." The standard dress and buzz cuts were ways of diminishing sexual differences, just as castration for some of the men was a way of diminishing sexual desires. Do himself had been castrated, perhaps as a desperate effort to cope with his own homosexual proclivities, about which he felt apparent guilt.

Strangest of all was the group's science fiction mythology, blended with elements of Christianity and astrological divination. As the Heaven's Gate page on the World Wide Web explained, the appearance of the Hale–Bopp comet signaled the advent of extraterrestrials, whose starship in the comet's wake would rescue the faithful from Planet Earth. Yet the members of Heaven's Gate saw themselves as following the same pattern established 2,000 years ago, when Jesus of Nazareth discarded his physical vessel in exchange for a spiritual one. There was surely significance in the group's decision to exit this planet during the Christian Holy Week.

How have we made sense of these events? The most common strategy, one favored by the media and many citizens, has been to relegate Heaven's Gate and similar groups to the category "cult." Many people seem to take some comfort in the idea of a cult; the word effectively distances them from the unsettling activities of groups like Heaven's Gate. But cult is a term that I and many other religious studies scholars resist. Academics who study these phenomena are well aware of the absence of precise, universally accepted definition for "cult." I jokingly say a cult is any religion more bizarre than your own.

Bizarreness is a comparative term, not an absolute standard. We judge things as bizarre according to how much they diverge from our own way of seeing things, which we usually privilege as being closer to the truth than all others. But there is a potential danger in privileging our own point of view in this way—a danger that sometimes leads precisely to events such as the Heaven's Gate suicides. When we hallow our own perspective, we seal ourselves off from critical scrutiny, effectively isolating our beliefs just as sect members do locked away in a compound.

Among the many objectives and benefits of the academic study of religion, I find two aspirations to be of particular value whenever the issue of "cults" looms large in the public imagination. One is that scholars in religious studies endeavor *to make the strange familiar.* We take ideas, beliefs, and practices that seem odd and try to show how they make sense to adherents, or at least how they operate within the framework of another construction of reality. We often do this by demonstrating how alien notions compare with more familiar beliefs and practices. For instance, it helps students to understand the caste system in India—which seems diametrically opposed to Western democratic ideals—to point out the ways our own society maintains a hierarchy of value based on a person's race, sex, or economic situation. As with any analogy, the comparison is imperfect, but it is useful.

On the other hand, scholars in religious studies endeavor *to make the familiar strange*. By comparing other beliefs and practices with our own, we shed light on the assumptions and perspectives that we take for granted but which other people do not subscribe to. Our own values and beliefs—many of them unacknowledged until they are challenged—appear to us in a new light. This may even be the discipline's chief benefit. Long after students have forgotten the particulars of a religion's beliefs and practices, they will still remember how it felt to have their own view of the world challenged. While studying traditions that practice arranged marriages, for example, students might learn that other religions look upon the American dating scene with the same horror that many American students experience when they contemplate arranged marriages. To such students, aspects of the world that once seemed given are now seen to be mutable. Having once seen the strangeness of our worldview, it is difficult to return to it with the dogmatism of the true believer.

What does making the strange familiar and the familiar strange tell us about Heaven's Gate? Take just a few elements of this sect's worldview. There is nothing particularly startling or unusual about the group's finding ominous significance in the appearance of a comet. Across the centuries and across human cultures, scanning the heavens to discern the signs of the times has been the standard rather than the exception. Further, there is really nothing strange about sacrificing one's sexuality through celibacy and even castration. Anyone aware of the history of Christianity—or the history of virtually any religious tradition—knows that these are not uncommon practices for many faithful. The Apostle Paul clearly believed in the spiritual superiority of celibacy over marriage, a view still reflected today in the vows of Roman Catholic priests and nuns. Origen, one of Christianity's early theologians, even castrated himself to become a "eunuch for the sake of the kingdom of heaven" (Matthew 19: 12). Finally, wearing identical clothing and haircuts and following a regimented life style is not a unique religious practice, either. The professional clergy and monastics in most religions do so, as do many lay people, such as the Amish.

Even the sci-fi mythology of Heaven's Gate is not as weird as it might appear at first blush. Millions of people do believe in extraterrestrials and alien visitations to Earth. These include sane, thoughtful individuals, not just readers of tabloids who seek the titillation of the eerie. Even if we find it difficult to accept the idea of alien visitations, let us at least consider whether some common religious beliefs might not seem a little strange to others. Is the idea that extraterrestrials will come to Earth to rescue believers really that much more implausible than the belief that a man who lived 2,000 years ago will return to Earth to rescue *his* followers? Tertullian, one of the great "fathers" of the early Christian church, had a firm grasp of this point. He maintained that the absurdity of Christian belief was, in fact, its virtue. *Credo quia absurdum est*, Tertullian is reported to have said: "I believe *because* it is absurd." I find it difficult to see how we can say one set of beliefs is based in reality and the other in purely cultish fantasy. Both seem to me to be equally rational or equally bizarre, depending on how one judges these matters. My point is not to challenge Christian orthodoxy, but rather to challenge the casual tendency of many people, both religious and nonreligious, to brand the beliefs of others as outlandish, absurd, and bizarre while privileging their own perspectives.

One might, of course, grant all these points but argue that the real issue with Heaven's Gate is not the group's beliefs—however sane or irrational—but the fact that they led to a fatal conclusion. "Whether my beliefs are rational or not," we might imagine someone saying, "you don't see the members of my church reaching for the phenobarbital and vodka." This, to be sure, is an important argument. But we might also consider other instances of religious beliefs leading to death. Throughout Christian history, for example, scores of martyrs have yielded their bodies to lions and gallows to serve what they believed to be a higher purpose. (When they have been unwilling to give up their own lives, they often have been all too willing to take the lives of others in the name of an ideal cause.) These dynamics are not limited, of course, to the Christian traditions. Jewish history honors Masada, where over 900 men, women, and children engaged in a mass suicide in 72 CE rather than succumb to Roman authority. In more recent decades, we have the example of Buddhist monks who immolated themselves in Vietnam during peace protests. We can easily find instances of similar events in other religious and nonreligious traditions. People throughout history have gone to war ready to sacrifice themselves to a higher ideal, such as "liberty" or "country." On what grounds do I say that *my* self-sacrifice is more rational and more noble than yours? The men and women at Rancho Santa Fe died in pursuit of the ideals of freedom and happiness.

Perhaps the lesson to be drawn is that we ought to abolish all religion. This is an age-old notion embraced by freethinkers everywhere. After all, is it not religion, as such, that drives people to mass suicides and crusades? Why not abandon all religious beliefs in favor of, say, a more enlightened, scientific perspective? The problem with this argument is that cruelty and absurd beliefs are not exclusive to religion. No realm of human culture—science and technology, law and government, education and scholarship—is immune to the destructive potential of "bizarre" notions. In the nineteenth century, modern science "proved" the intellectual inferiority of non-European races; in the 1930s and 1940s, the government of Germany acted on that belief. No, the lesson to be drawn from Heaven's Gate is not about finding the *right* belief. Our beliefs will always seem bizarre to someone, rational to ourselves. The lesson concerns what we believe about our beliefs. Can we ever afford to be so self-righteous that we cannot contemplate that our beliefs could appear strange or questionable to others; or to consider that we cling to them with perhaps too much intensity, that perhaps we love our beliefs too much?

It is important for us to resist the temptation to demonize the members of Heaven's Gate. Fascinated and repulsed at the same time, we may easily consign these events to the categories of "mystery" or "evil" or some other notion that effectively distances the group from us. Alienating "them" from "us" only serves to reinforce the smug belief in *our* rationality and *their* bizarreness. The members of the Heaven's Gate were human beings; they *were* us.

27

Bruce Lincoln, *Theses on Method*[1]

❧❧

1

The conjunction "of" that joins the two nouns in the disciplinary ethnonym "History of Religions" is not a neutral filler. Rather, it announces a proprietary claim and a relation of encompassment: History is the method and Religion the object of study.

2

The relation between the two nouns is also tense, as becomes clear if one takes the trouble to specify their meaning. Religion, I submit, is that discourse whose defining characteristic is its desire to speak of things eternal and transcendent with an authority equally transcendent and eternal. History, in the sharpest possible contrast, is that discourse which speaks of things temporal and terrestrial in a human and fallible voice, while staking its claim to authority on rigorous critical practice.

3

History of religions is thus a discourse that resists and reverses the orientation of that discourse with which it concerns itself. To practice history of religions in a fashion consistent with the discipline's claim of title is to insist on discussing the temporal, contextual, situated, interested, human, and material dimensions of those discourses, practices, and institutions that characteristically represent themselves as eternal, transcendent, spiritual, and divine.

4

The same destabilizing and irreverent questions one might ask of any speech act ought be posed of religious discourse. The first of these is "Who speaks here?," i.e., what person, group, or institution is responsible for a text, whatever its putative or apparent author. Beyond that, "To what audience? In what immediate and broader context? Through what system of mediations? With what interests?" And further, "Of what would the speaker(s) persuade the audience? What are the consequences if this project of persuasion should happen to succeed? Who wins what, and how much? Who, conversely, loses?"

5

Reverence is a religious, and not a scholarly virtue. When good manners and good conscience cannot be reconciled, the demands of the latter ought to prevail.

6

Many who would not think of insulating their own or their parents' religion against critical inquiry still afford such protection to other people's faiths, via a stance of cultural relativism. One can appreciate their good intentions, while recognizing a certain displaced defensiveness, as well as the guilty conscience of Western imperialism.

7

Beyond the question of motives and intentions, cultural relativism is predicated on the dubious—not to say, fetishistic—construction of "cultures" as if they were stable and discrete groups of people defined by the stable and discrete values, symbols, and practices they share. Insofar as this model stresses the continuity and integration of timeless groups, whose internal tensions and conflicts, turbulence and incoherence, permeability and malleability are largely erased, it risks becoming a religious and not a historic narrative: the story of a transcendent ideal threatened by debasing forces of change.

8

Those who sustain this idealized image of culture do so, *inter alia*, by mistaking the dominant fraction (sex, age group, class, and/or caste) of a given group for the group or "culture" itself. At the same time, they mistake the ideological positions favored and propagated by the dominant fraction for those of the group as a whole (e.g., when texts authored by Brahmins define "Hinduism," or when the statements of male elders constitute "Nuer religion"). Scholarly misrecognitions of this sort replicate the misrecognitions and misrepresentations of those the scholars privilege as their informants.

9

Critical inquiry need assume neither cynicism nor dissimulation to justify probing beneath the surface, and ought to probe scholarly discourse and practice as much as any other.

10

Understanding the system of ideology that operates in one's own society is made difficult by two factors: (i) one's consciousness is itself a product of that system, and (ii) the system's very success renders its operations invisible, since one is so consistently immersed in and bombarded by its products that one comes to mistake them (and the apparatus through which they are produced and disseminated) for nothing other than "nature."

11

The ideological products and operations of other societies afford invaluable opportunities to the would-be student of ideology. Being initially unfamiliar, they do not need to be denaturalized before they can be examined. Rather, they invite and reward critical study, yielding lessons one can put to good use at home.

12

Although critical inquiry has become commonplace in other disciplines, it still offends many students of religion, who denounce it as "reductionism." This charge is meant to silence critique. The failure to treat religion "as religion"— that is, the refusal to ratify its claim of transcendent nature and sacrosanct status—may be regarded as heresy and sacrilege by those who construct themselves as religious, but it is the starting point for those who construct themselves as historians.

13

When one permits those whom one studies to define the terms in which they will be understood, suspends one's interest in the temporal and contingent, or fails to distinguish between "truths," "truth-claims," and "regimes of truth," one has ceased to function as historian or scholar. In that moment, a variety of roles are available: some perfectly respectable (amanuensis, collector, friend, and advocate), and some less appealing (cheerleader, voyeur, retailer of import goods). None, however, should be confused with scholarship.

Notes

1. The following thirteen theses were originally part of a presentation to the Comparative Studies in Religion Section at the 1995 meeting of the American Academy of Religion in Philadelphia.

SOURCES

❧ ❧

Part I

Horace Miner, "Body Ritual Among the Nacirema," *American Anthropologist* 58 (1956): 503–507. Reprinted with the permission of the American Anthropological Association and Agnes Miner.

Kenneth L. Pike, "Etic and Emic Standpoints for the Description of Behavior," *Language in Relation to a Unified Theory of the Structure of Human Behavior.* 2nd edition. (The Hague: Mouton, 1967.) Reprinted with the permission of Mouton de Gruyter and the author.

Alasdair MacIntyre, "Is Understanding Religion Compatible With Believing?" *Faith and Philosophers.* John Hick (ed.). (London: Macmillan, 1964.) Reprinted with the permission of Macmillan.

Clifford Geertz, "'From the Native's Point of View': On the Nature of Anthropological Understanding," *Bulletin of the American Academy of Arts and Sciences* 28/1 (1974). Reprinted with the permission of the author.

Part II

Rudolf Otto, *The Idea of the Holy: An Inquiry into the Non-Rational Factor in the Idea of the Divine and Its Relation to the Rational.* Chapters I–III. John W. Harvey (trans.). 2nd edition. (London: Oxford University Press, 1950.) Reprinted with the permission of Oxford University Press.

Joachim Wach, "The Meaning and Task of the History of Religions (*Religionswissenschaft*)," *The History of Religions: Essays on the Problem of Self-Understanding.* Joseph Kitagawa (ed.). Chicago: University of Chicago Press, 1967. © 1967 by The University of Chicago. All rights reserved. Reprinted with the permission of the University of Chicago Press.

Mircea Eliade, "A New Humanism," *The Quest: History and Meaning in*

Religion. (Chicago: University of Chicago Press, 1969.) © 1969 by The University of Chicago. All rights reserved. Reprinted with the permission of the University of Chicago Press.

Rosalind Shaw, "Feminist Anthropology and the Gendering of Religious Studies," *Religion and Gender.* Ursula King (ed.). (Oxford: Blackwell, 1995). Reprinted with the permission of Blackwell Publishers.

Raymond Firth, "An Anthropological Approach to the Study of Religion," *Religion: A Humanist Interpretation.* (London and New York: Routledge, 1996). Printed with the permission of Routledge.

Part III

Immanuel Kant, "What is Enlightenment?" *Foundations of the Metaphysics of Morals & What is Enlightenment?* (Upper Saddle River, NJ: Prentice-Hall, 1989.) Reprinted with the permission of Prentice-Hall.

Robert A. Segal, "In Defense of Reductionism," *Journal of the American Academy of Religion* 51 (1983): 97–124. Reprinted with the permission of the American Academy of Religion.

Terry F. Godlove, Jr., "Religious Discourse and First Person Authority," *Method & Theory in the Study of Religion* 6 (1994): 147–161. Reprinted with the permission of Mouton de Gruyter and the author.

Daniel Pals, "Reductionism and Belief: An Appraisal of Recent Attacks on the Doctrine of Irreducible Religion," *Journal of Religion* 66 (1986): 18–36. Reprinted with the permission of the University of Chicago Press and the author.

Tony Edwards, "Religion, Explanation, and the *Askesis* of Inquiry," *Religion and Reductionism: Essays on Eliade, Segal, and the Challenge of the Social Sciences for the Study of Religion.* Thomas A. Indinopulos and Edward A. Yonan (eds.). (Leiden: E. J. Brill, 1994). Reprinted with the permission of E. J. Brill.

Part IV

Ninian Smart, "Within and Without Religion," *The Science of Religion & the Sociology of Knowledge: Some Methodological Questions.* (Princeton: Princeton University Press, 1973.) © Princeton University Press 1973. Reprinted with the permission of Princeton University Press.

Peter Donovan, "Neutrality in Religious Studies," *Religious Studies* 26 (1990): 103–116. Reprinted with the permission of Cambridge University Press and the author.

Peter Byrne, "The Study of Religion: Neutral, Scientific, or Neither?" *Method & Theory in the Study of Religion* 9/4 (1997): 339–351. Reprinted with the permission of Mouton de Gruyter and the author.

Donald Wiebe, "Does Understanding Religion Require Religious Understanding?" *Current Progress in the Methodology of the Science of Religions.* Witold Tyloch (ed.). (Warsaw: Polish Scientific Publishers, 1985.) Reprinted with the permission of Polish Scientific Publishers.

Martin S. Jaffee, "Fessing up in Theory: On *Professing* and *Confessing* in the Religious Studies Classroom," *Method & Theory in the Study of Religion* 9/4 (1997): 325–337. Reprinted with the permission of Mouton de Gruyter and the author.

Part V

David J. Hufford, "The Scholarly Voice and the Personal Voice: Reflexivity in Belief Studies," *Western Folklore* 54 (1995): 57–76. Reprinted with the permission of the editors of *Western Folklore.*

Michael Jackson, "The Witch as a Category and as a Person," *Paths Toward a Clearing: Radical Empiricism and Ethnographic Inquiry.* (Bloomington: Indiana University Press, 1989.) Reprinted with the permission of Indiana University Press.

Wendy Doniger O'Flaherty, "The Uses and Misuses of Other People's Myths," *Journal of the American Academy of Religion* 54 (1986): 219–239. Reprinted with the permission of the American Academy of Religion; "Fire and Ice" in *The Complete Poems of Robert Frost*, edited by Edward Connery Latham (Jonathan Cape.) Reprinted with the permission of the Estate of Robert Frost.

Karen McCarthy Brown, "Writing About 'the Other'," *Chronicle of Higher Education* (April 15, 1992): A56. Reprinted with the permission of the author.

Margery Wolf, "Writing Ethnography: The Poetics and Politics of Culture," *A Thrice-Told Tale: Feminism, Postmodernism, and Ethnographic Responsibility.* (Stanford: Stanford University Press, 1992.) © by the Board of Trustees of the Leland Stanford Junior University. Reprinted with the permission of Stanford University Press.

Part VI

Jonathan Z. Smith, "The Devil in Mr. Jones," *Imagining Religion: From Jonestown to Babylon*, 102–129. (Chicago: University of Chicago Press, 1982.) © 1982 by the University of Chicago. All rights reserved. Reprinted with the permission of the University of Chicago Press and the author.

Mark W. Muesse, "Religious Studies and 'Heaven's Gate': Making the Strange Familiar and the Familiar Strange," *Chronicle of Higher Education* 43/33 (April 25, 1997): B6–B7. Reprinted with the permission of the author.

Bruce Lincoln, "Theses on Method," *Method & Theory in the Study of Religion* 8/3 (1996): 225–227. Reprinted with the permission of Mouton de Gruyter and the author.

INDEX

જ્જ